TEMPUS

VERBAL ARTS: STUDIES IN POETICS

Lazar Fleishman and Haun Saussy, series editors

Tempus

The World of Discussion
and the World of Narration

HARALD WEINRICH

Translated by
JANE K. BROWN AND MARSHALL BROWN

Fordham University Press
NEW YORK   2023

Copyright © 2023 Fordham University Press

All rights reserved. No part of this publication may be reproduced, stored in a retrieval system, or transmitted in any form or by any means—electronic, mechanical, photocopy, recording, or any other—except for brief quotations in printed reviews, without the prior permission of the publisher.

This translation is based on the sixth German edition of the work, published as Harald Weinrich, *Tempus: Besprochene und erzählte Welt*, Copyright © Verlag C. H. Beck oHG. München 2001.

Fordham University Press has no responsibility for the persistence or accuracy of URLs for external or third-party Internet websites referred to in this publication and does not guarantee that any content on such websites is, or will remain, accurate or appropriate.

Fordham University Press also publishes its books in a variety of electronic formats. Some content that appears in print may not be available in electronic books.

Visit us online at www.fordhampress.com.

Library of Congress Cataloging-in-Publication Data available online at https://catalog.loc.gov.

Printed in the United States of America

25 24 23   5 4 3 2 1

First edition

To my teacher Heinrich Lausberg, in grateful memory

Contents

Translators' Note ... ix

Introduction ... 1
Jane K. Brown and Marshall Brown

1 Tense in Texts ... 9

Tense and Time, 9 • Text Linguistics, 11 • A Preliminary Reflection: Obstinate Signs, 14 • Tense Distribution, 17 • Two Tense Groups: Discussing and Narrating, 22 • On the Freedom of the Narrator, 25

2 Discussing–Narrating ... 32

Syntax and Communication, 32 • Register, 36 • Tense in Different Genres, 42 • The World of Discussion, 45 • The World of Narrating, 50 • Tense in the Language of Children, 55

3 Perspective ... 60

Time in Texts, 60 • The Future (using French as an example), 64 • The Perfekt in German, 69 • The Perfect in English, 75 • Thornton Wilder: *The Ides of March*, 78 • The Passé composé in French, 83 • The Passato prossimo in Italian, 87 • The Perfecto compuesto in Spanish, 91 • Narration, Past, Truth, 96

4 Highlighting ... 101

Narrative Highlighting, 101 • Narrative Tempo in the Novel, 106 • Baudelaire: "Le vieux saltimbanque" (The Old Mountebank), 111 • Of the Tense of Death, 117

| 5 | Tense in Novellas and Short Stories: Highlighting vs. Aspect | 121 |

Maupassant, 121 • Pirandello, 126 • Unamuno, Darío, Echegaray, 129 • Hemingway, 135 • Frame Narrative (Boccaccio), 142 • Narration in the Middle Ages, 147 • Frame and Highlighting in Modern Stories, 150

| 6 | Tense Transitions | 153 |

Tense in Dialogue, 153 • Descartes, Rousseau, and the Sequence of Tenses, 164

| 7 | Tense Metaphors | 171 |

Tense Metaphors in Texts, 171 • Condition and Consequence, Reality and Unreality, 180

| 8 | Tense Combinations | 186 |

Tense and Person, 186 • Tense and Adverbs, 190 • Combined Transitions, 197 • Semi-finite Verbs, 205

| 9 | A Crisis in Narration? | 211 |

Tense in Old French, 211 • Evidence of Language Consciousness in French Classicism, 217 • The Time of Newspapers, 224 • Albert Camus: *L'étranger*, 227 • Oral Narration in French, 236 • A Parallel: Tense in South-German Dialects, 244

| 10 | Other Languages—Other Tenses? | 252 |

Tense in Ancient Greek, 252 • Tense in Latin, 256 • Whorf, Spengler, and the Hopi Indians, 264 • Toward a New Method of Description, 270

Index   275

Translators' Note

Harald Weinrich has revised the text of *Tempus* several times. Our translation derives from the definitive sixth edition. The translation was begun over a decade ago, in consultation with Prof. Weinrich. He had hesitated about an English translation of a book concerned predominantly with Romance languages, and he undertook to revise it yet again, with more English materials and an English-language readership in view. That task was never completed, though some elements of the revision remain in the current translation. We are deeply grateful to a Semitic linguist, Vasile Condrea, for reviving the project.

Our translation tries to respect Prof. Weinrich's preferences. They include simplifying where possible. While we have not undertaken any substantial revisions, we have frequently lightened up the formulations and sometimes adapted them to the needs of Anglophone readers. We have also tried to validate and regularize the citations and references. Not all the sources were available to us (especially during Covid), but where we could, we have confirmed the texts and the citations, and we have cited published English translations when feasible. As a result, quite a few of the references postdate the original publication. Translations have been modified on occasion, typically where the tense was at issue. Using the English progressive to represent the Romance imperfect was often natural, often not possible, often more or less awkward. We apologize to the original translators whose work we have sometimes deformed, as a pointer to the original tense usage.

We have followed Prof. Weinrich's practice of quoting sources in the original, followed by translations. Where we have used a published translation, identified in the notes, that page number follows the translation. Where only one page number is given, before the translation, the translation is ours.

It remains only to thank Tom Lay and the Fordham University Press editors for supporting and improving our work and, above all, though too late, to record our deep appreciation for thirty years of Harald Weinrich's friendship and unfailing kindness.

Tempus

Introduction

Jane K. Brown and Marshall Brown

Harald Weinrich (1927–2022) was a humanist in the broadest sense of the word. Given the pressures on the humanistic disciplines in American higher education currently, this is important, because his career, and this book in particular, model how to be a humanist in the contemporary university. He held chairs in Romance languages and literatures and in linguistics, was the founding chair for the Center for Interdisciplinary Research at Bielefeld, founded and ran the first department in Germany for German as a Second Language (at the University of Munich), and ended his career as the first foreigner to hold the chair for Romance Languages and Literatures at the Collège de France. His work draws with genuine expertise on the literature, history, and linguistics of ancient and modern Western European languages (including, like Shakespeare, some Latin and a little Greek), on rhetoric, on linguistic and literary theory, philosophy, sociology, and socio-linguistics. He applied this armory not only to broad historical topics (for example, longitudinal histories of the perception of time and of forgetting), but also to significant moral questions in the culture of the twentieth century with topics like the linguistics of lying, and especially to welcoming immigrants and visitors into German culture with the Institute for German as a Foreign Language and with the Adelbert von Chamisso Prize he founded for writing in German by non-native speakers. In the turbulent politicization of culture in post–World War II Germany, Weinrich established himself as a moderate voice that embraced the inclusion of the social sciences in the literary disciplines, confronted political and social questions as a humanist, and at the same time staunchly defended the importance of precision, close reading, and history as continuing necessary intellectual equipment for the educated citizen.

Tempus, first published in 1964, is at the center of his reputation. It has been translated into many languages, but not into English, although he taught and lectured around the world, including in the U.S. It is, at its center, an argument about verb tense, grounded principally in the Romance languages, then extending further to German and to English and then to Latin and Greek, and concluding with a chapter inviting analysis of verb tense in the book's terms in languages all over the world. But why should such a book be of interest to American humanists? Because it argues for and embodies how to answer cultural questions using the central tools of the humanities: reading and analyzing language. Put more narrowly, the book returns philology (as the study of languages and discursive culture) to its roots in linguistic and stylistic analysis. Weinrich argues that verb tense is a category of syntax rather than grammar, and that syntactic analysis cannot be practiced exclusively at the level of the sentence, as has been the norm in studying languages since antiquity; instead, it must be analyzed at the level of text (whether oral or written), and text always includes context. The book thus cites work on all the major European languages, both literary and linguistic sources, narrative theory, sociology, rhetoric, and oral as well as literary texts from Greek, Latin, French, German, Italian, Spanish, Portuguese, English, various German dialects, and Hopi. At the same time this astonishing work of literary criticism combines close reading, etymology, patterns and structures in texts and within words, and stylistics with a sharp sensibility for the use of language in all different contexts—for the use of themes, tropes, irony, syntax, and grammar. Every aspect of language is fair play here.

As sketched in Chapter 1, the argument is actually very simple, and at the same time very original. Tense, according to Weinrich, has nothing to do with chronological time, despite the traditional, misleading nomenclature of verb tense in the West since antiquity. Verb tense is better understood not as grammar, but as an element of syntax and style, thus only in the fusion of stylistics and linguistics. Or, verb tense can only be understood in real texts, not in model sentences constructed for linguistic pedagogy, and rarely in units as small as a sentence. The fundamental categories of verb tense are not time and aspect—in other words, whether or not an action is completed and, if so, when. The book argues consistently against both categories—against chronology throughout, against aspect particularly in Chapters 4 and 5. The book shows consistently how categorizing tense in terms of time and aspect blocks close, sensitive understanding of language—and of the people who use language.

For Weinrich's underlying gesture is the replacement of objects with subjects. Verb tenses express primarily the speaker's orientation toward the subject matter. Consequently, as Weinrich shows in detail, tenses are much more supple and complex than traditional grammar allows. In place of chronology and aspect, he introduces three new categories. The fundamental one is register (Chapter 2), the distinction between narration and discussion. Register—in German *Sprechhaltung*, literally, speech stance—basically rests on awareness of the situation of the speaking, that is, on the context rather than the content of the utterance. Is this an interactive situation, where an argument is being presented (whether orally or in writing), where back and forth is expected? Or is it a story-telling situation, with one speaker and largely quiescent listeners. The social and psychological orientation is communicated, it turns out, by the choice of verb tense. The second category is perspective (Chapter 3), that is, the distinction between the speaker looking ahead or looking back in the text. This has to do not with when something happened or whether it is completed, but with the need to look back in the text for already-presented information or to look ahead to information not yet presented. The third category is *Reliefgebung* (Chapter 4), explicitly based on the notion of sculptural relief and here translated as "highlighting"; it concerns primarily how to focus attention in narrative—whether what is told is the point (foreground) or is ancillary (background). This distinction is particularly evident in the Romance languages, which have two parallel narrative tenses (e.g., imparfait and passé simple in French), one used for foregrounding, one for backgrounding; it is especially prominent in the poetics of novella and short-story writing, but then, in Weinrich's analysis, encompasses all kinds of expression.

The result is a tour de force of what happens to close reading when you read for tense. It also turns out that narrative acquires a special status. Weinrich points out, virtually in passing, that ancient and medieval wisdom literature is narrative. It seems to belong, as in Romantic theories of language, to an earlier stage of human language and culture than does discursive language, which opens the mind to abstraction. Furthermore, in its incredible breadth of languages and culture this book is a paradigm of the Europeanism sought especially by German intellectuals as part of the European Union.

Linguistics scholars will find in *Tempus* influential challenges to dominant structural understandings of grammar. Language here is not a tool but a vehicle, to be driven many ways on many kinds of roads. Above all, the psychological and affective dimensions that Weinrich shows to be inseparable from expression enrich and complicate any attempt at abstract formulations of linguistic rules and principles. The emphasis on ordinary language terms for analysis, beginning in Chapter 1, sets a limit on formalization that simultaneously opens avenues for more open understanding of the multi-level richness of linguistic expression, such as Weinrich later extended into his roughly one-thousand-page text grammars of French (1982) and of German (1993). Language teachers—foreign and native language teachers alike—can learn much from the subtleties of expression that Weinrich calls to awareness and from the intercultural understandings and misunderstandings that follow from them. (Weinrich subsequently wrote a great deal directly about both elementary and advanced language pedagogy that we hope some readers may be inspired and enabled to investigate.) Literary critics will be enriched by the subtleties of Weinrich's readings, especially by his insights into the psychology of narration. With or without an identifiable "speaker," narratives inevitably color their information with implicit yet essential prioritizations. You cannot report anything without making crucial judgments about the relative importance and situation of the elements. The framework for those judgments, the distinction between the narrative and discursive registers, is the core of this book.[1]

We cannot escape the trammels of language. Such is the substance of a critique of Claude Lévi-Strauss's structuralism that Weinrich published in the inaugural issue of *Poétique*, the leading French journal of literary theory since 1970. Passing with characteristic deftness and textual specificity through Plato, Ovid, Montaigne, the medieval *Roman de la rose*, Winckelmann, Lessing, and Nietzsche, his essay traces a brief history of the retreat of myth, that is to say, of respect for narrative, in contrast to the analytic spirit that prompted Lévi-Strauss to fragment myths into mythemes. Weinrich expresses full and surely sincere respect for Lévi-Strauss (and for Roland Barthes), but, at the same time, he issues a plea to complement the paradigmatic method with a syntagmatic method. Only then can scientific knowledge (*connaissance*) be joined by narrative

---

1. The German language allows Weinrich to keep the two faces of language in perfect balance; he calls them *erzählend* and *besprechend*. In English the present participles don't work. "Narrating tenses" and "discussing tenses" would be stilted at best, an awkwardness that also troubled Weinrich's French translator. Heeding Weinrich's preference for ordinary language, we have sacrificed his lexical symmetry by using a more colloquial term, "narrative tenses," for the former, but a more learned term, "discursive tenses," for the latter.

wisdom (*sagesse*).² This unmistakable echo of the celebration of folk narrative in Walter Benjamin's essay, "The Storyteller," is confirmed by the brief discussion of Benjamin's work in Chapter 9 of *Tempus*. So it is that the close reading technique of the philological linguist blossoms into profound questions about human society. As Weinrich writes eloquently in the brief preface to his collection of essays in French, "Language and literature are but two faces of a single medal, struck to serve us and polished to please us" (*Conscience linguistique*, 7).

The principles are familiar, though by no means universal. They have appeared frequently in literary criticism at least since the New Critics. But they pop up as incidental reflections. We will cite a few examples here, to illustrate the kind of stance that no book pursues in greater depth or with more clarity than *Tempus*. First, from Reuben Arthur Brower's *The Fields of Light*, a classic of American New Criticism: "In one of the briefer lyrics of 'In Memoriam,' Tennyson uses the adjective 'calm' no less than eleven times; but to learn this curious fact apart from seeing the text is to understand nothing."³ In Brower's book you will find luminous examples of seeing the text. From *Tempus* you will garner terms and methods as well as models. Here, next, from a leading Germanist, Roy Pascal, taking aim at the work of Käte Hamburger: "The meanings of the tenses cannot be equated with the temporal functions they have in normal discourse. But she has not recognized that their function in fiction cannot be judged out of context, and that they take their meanings from the context."⁴ In this case, as one of Hamburger's most systematic as well as among her most generous critics, Weinrich cites Pascal's essay and develops his insight. Third, here is a dictum from a recent theory of lyric, with specific reference to Wordsworth's Lucy poems: "For the generic device of shifting from a past to a present tense to be of anything other than categorising interest it needs to be thematically customised to serve the purposes of the specific poem."⁵ Such dicta identify the well-known concerns for which *Tempus* provides the tools for understanding, with nuanced treatments of the eight European languages that are its principal terrain. And, lastly, here, from an essay on Charles Baudelaire's sonnet "À une passante," is an example of the kind of judgment that needs Weinrich's book to correct: "The woman

---

2. Weinrich, "Structures narratives du mythe," reprinted in *Conscience linguistique et lectures littéraires* (Paris: Éditions de la Maison des Sciences de l'Homme, 1989), 9–23.

3. Reuben Arthur Brower, *The Fields of Light: An Experiment in Critical Reading* (New York: Oxford UP, 1962), 33.

4. Roy Pascal, "Tense and the Novel," *The Modern Language Review* 57, no. 1 (Jan. 1962), 11.

5. Peter Robinson, *The Sound Sense of Poetry* (Cambridge: Cambridge UP, 2018), 74.

designated in the title of the poem is a figure trapped in the eternity of the present progressive."[6] This sonnet in fact has six different tenses in its fourteen lines. Indeed, Weinrich noted tense change as part of a brief, trenchant reading of this very poem.[7] From whatever angle you approach *Tempus*—as a national literature specialist or from a general interest in poetics, narratology, linguistics, cultural studies, or even intellectual history—you will find a powerful stream of both illuminations and surprises.

And you will find a master of expository style. As a devoted pedagogue, Weinrich proceeds carefully, step by step, beginning with a "hypothesis," that he calls "preliminary," concerning a distinction that he recognizes as too simple. Chapter 1 warns against the illusion that meaningful insight can result from "simply counting forms"; the first sentence of Chapter 2 looks forward to "more precise terms," and in their occasional subsequent occurrences, "simple" and "simply" are mostly negated. Typically, a narrative will be introduced, whether by way of paraphrase of a fictional text, description of a poem, or report of a critical position, followed by discussion that complicates or nuances the presentation. While Weinrich did not shy away from respectful disagreement or criticism, his most characteristic stance, as with Hamburger, takes the form of supplementation or clarification. Politeness is a crucial element in Weinrich's pedagogy. The brief discussion of politeness in the first section of Chapter 7 is one of many clues a careful reader will find to the book's highest aspirations.

For Weinrich was not what one might think of as an "ordinary" scholar. He was, it could well be argued, the last representative of the great tradition of Romance philology in Germany. His work stands in importance right up with that of Ernst Robert Curtius (1886–1956), Leo Spitzer (1887–1960), Erich Auerbach (1892–1957), Hugo Friedrich (1904–78), and Hans-Robert Jauss (1921–97). His output bulks larger than that of any of these predecessors, his concerns range more widely, in particular in their pedagogical and cultural dimensions, and his public presence exceeded theirs.

But Weinrich's cultural formation and his character differed radically from any of the predecessors. He was born a mere six years after Jauss. But what a difference that makes! The older scholars include Jewish emigrants (Spitzer and Auerbach), an "inner emigrant" (Curtius), and a reportedly

---

6. Catherine Witt, "Passages through Baudelaire: From Poetry to Thought and Back," in *Thinking Poetry: Philosophical Approaches to Nineteenth-Century French Poetry*, ed. Joseph Acquisto (New York: Palgrave Macmillan, 2013), 31.

7. "Baudelaire-Lektüre," *Literatur für Leser* (Munich: Deutscher Taschenbuch Verlag, 1986), 115–17; in Weinrich's French, "Lecture de Baudelaire," *Conscience linguistique*, 133–36.

non-political tolerator (Friedrich). Jauss, in his early maturity, came from a nationalist family and had a very successful career in the Nazi army. Weinrich, on the other hand, born in 1927, was only seventeen at the end of the war. He experienced combat, but not commitment. Here is what he wrote, in introducing a thoughtful appraisal of Curtius's inner emigration:

> My youth was Hitler's; at the age of fifteen I learned how to man an anti-aircraft gun, at the age of seventeen I learned how to handle a bazooka, at the age of nineteen I came home from a prisoner-of-war camp. In 1948 I became a freshman and read [Curtius's just-published] *Europäische Literatur und lateinisches Mittelalter*. . . . I reacted in that 1948 post-war situation . . . as a young German who saw in this beautiful tradition and fantastic continuity between Western Literature and the Latin Middle Ages the unsuspected chance to be all at once reintegrated, together with my nation, into the good old family of civilized and cultivated mankind.[8]

What Weinrich does not say even here is that the prisoner-of-war camp is where he mastered French. He emerged from the war hardened and matured, but untainted, and with the mission of bringing the world together that he pursued for his entire career. That impelled his major and, at the time, almost unique outreach to immigrants; his devotion to cultural differences and the ensuing need for intercultural understanding; and his focus on social virtues like politeness, forgiving and forgetting, living with constraints, possession and dispossession, truth and lying, and good and evil. (Relevant essay and book titles—translated—include "Literature and Hospitality," "Politeness, an Affair of Honor," "The Right to Forget: Peace through Forgetting," *On Borrowed Time: The Art and Economy of Living with Deadlines*, *The Linguistics of Lying*, and *How Civilized Is the Devil? Brief Visits with Good and Evil*.) When reading *Tempus*, in whole or in part, it is invaluable to keep in mind the underlying drive toward the recognition and reconciliation of differences, not just between narration and discussion, or between French and German, but between culture and civilization,[9] tact and deceit, and politeness and insincerity.

---

8. "Thirty Years after Ernst Robert Curtius' Book *Europäische Literatur und lateinisches Mittelalter* (1948)," *Romanic Review* 69 (1978), 261–62. This passage appears only in the English-language publication, not the simultaneous German essay. We have not come across any other comparable reminiscences in Weinrich's writing.

9. "Wie zivilisiert ist der Teufel?", in *Wie zivilisiert ist der Teufel? Kurze Besuche bei Gut und Böse* (Munich: Beck, 2007), 131. On this topic Weinrich harks back to Norbert Elias.

And good and evil. The mark of World War II lies behind Weinrich's lifelong drive for accommodation and understanding. His generation's perilous passage to maturity scarred many of his contemporaries; so, for instance, both the great musicologist Carl Dahlhaus (1928–89) and the part-Jewish philosopher Hans Blumenberg (1920–96) raced through notoriously hectic careers. Weinrich's work confronts time in a different way. Recognizing the present as a tight passageway between past and future, he devoted himself to confronting and alleviating all the perils of the passage. Curtius was primarily a modernist, writing books on Joyce and Proust, but of course far better known as a medievalist; Friedrich is best known for his compact *Structure of Modern Poetry*, but his most ambitious studies are of early modern Italian poets and of Montaigne and antiquity; Auerbach's critique of modernity at the end of *Mimesis* is well known and resonant. Weinrich separates from all of them in his thorough commitment to the contemporary world. His work has enormous historical depth but is directed toward living in the late-twentieth and (in his latest books) the early-twenty-first centuries, as is reflected by the strong presence of modern and contemporary writers in *Tempus* and throughout his output. Modest in stature (he must have been a spindly teenager behind the anti-aircraft gun) and moderate in temperament, he wrote one of his most virtuosic essays on the middle condition of humanity, squeezed between subjection to leviathan and tyranny over small victims.[10] A rarity among his generation, or any, he even wrote repeatedly and with a steady gaze, though not at length, about Hitler.[11] Time is tight, as the title of another of his marvelous collections of tiny, packed essays has it; his mission was to loosen up the joints.[12] The study of verbs is constitutive of his visionary mission, and *Tempus* is full of marvelously illuminating details. But to read it with the fullest appreciation, it is necessary to appreciate the moral impulse underlying the book along with Weinrich's remarkable public career.

10. "Jonah's Sign: On the Very Large and the Very Small in Literature," in *The Linguistics of Lying and Other Essays*, trans. Jane K. Brown and Marshall Brown (Seattle: U of Washington P, 2005), 81–99.

11. *The Linguistics of Lying*, 54–56; "Hitler als Habenichts; Hitler am Ende," in *Über das Haben: 33 Ansichten* (Munich: Beck, 2012), 171–74; and three essays in *Wie Zivilisiert ist der Teufel*: "Als Hitler noch der Kutzner war: Über Lion Feuchtwangers Roman 'Erfolg'" (159–65), "Carl Zuckmayer zu loben" (166–73), and "Viktor Klemperer: Gedächtnismann gegen Hitler" (174–78).

12. *Knappe Zeit: Kunst und Ökonomie des befristeten Lebens* (Munich: Beck, 2004). In the excellent English translation by Steven Rendall the book is called *On Borrowed Time: The Art and Economy of Living with Deadlines* (Chicago: U of Chicago P, 2008), an imaginative substitute for German expressions that cannot be translated verbatim.

1 / Tense in Texts

Tense and Time

In the beginning was the word *chronos* (χρόνος). In ancient Greek it meant time and also certain linguistic forms—"time-words" or verbs.[1] Similarly, in Latin the word *tempus* could signify the phenomenon of time apart from language and also the linguistic forms—tenses—still identified in German with the Latinism *Tempus-Formen*. This equivalence persists in contemporary usage in many European languages: the French *temps*, the Italian *tempo*, and the Spanish *tiempo*, together with their related adjectives, mean both time and tense. Other languages, however, distinguish the terms—German, for example, with *Zeit* and *Tempus* and English with *time* and *tense*. While German maintains the distinction with the adjectives *zeitlich* and *temporal*, English allows the two categories to collapse into one another again in the adjective *temporal*.

The names of the individual tenses confirm the apparent identity of time and tense. Tense nomenclature in the various languages points with

---

1. Aristotle defines the verb as a word with a *chronos*-designation: *rhēma de phonē synthetē sēmantikē meta chronou*. The noun is defined in opposition to it: *aneu chronou* (*Poetics*, Chapter 20, 1457a 10–14). It is not possible to determine whether *chronos* is to be translated here with time or with tense. The term *Zeitwort* used for verbs in German grammars since the seventeenth century is based on this Aristotelian definition and implies, of course, both tense and time simultaneously; that is to say, the verb is the word that indicates time by means of tense-signs. (See Jacob Wackernagel, *Vorlesungen über Syntax*, vol. 1 [Basel: Birkhäuser, 1926], 149.)

suggestive persistence either directly to past, present, or future (in French, passé, présent, and futur; in German, Vergangenheit, Präsens, and Futur) or at least indirectly to such "temporal stages," as, for example, in Latin, perfectum "completed," the English preterit "gone past," the French plus-que-parfait "more than completed," the German Exakt-Futur "future led to its end," etc. And everyone who learns an additional European language finds confirmed in its grammar all the explanations learned early on in the grammar of the first.

There may well be an element of truth in all this. But for a linguistic investigation of the grammatical class "tense" it is unwise to begin with the massive presupposition that tense and time are congruent. To be sure, the present investigation is not entirely without presuppositions; without certain a priori linguistic parameters—we might call them axioms, principles, or elements—no one would ever think about investigating tense.[2] In particular, I want to allow an approximate preliminary idea of which linguistic forms count as tenses. In French, for example, these are forms like the following morphemes that determine the lexeme *chant-* in specific fashion in each case: *chantait, chanta, chantera, chanterait,* but also *chante* /ʃãt/ as a connection of the lexeme to a null morpheme (or stem). We are accustomed to calling these verb forms the imparfait, passé-simple, futur, conditionnel, and présent. But for the moment let the list serve only as an example and model. For the present it is also of no interest to distinguish the tense forms as a group from other more or less related verb forms. However, with regard to all tense forms in their subsequent in-depth functional descriptions in this book, the methodological rule shall apply, that no argument *a nomine*, i.e., from the mere name of the verb form, shall be permitted. The same applies to the generic term "tense," which I will also, if I may formulate it this way, regard as a word of unknown etymology. This convention will enable me to manage without inventing new terminology.

To be sure, a few new terms will be unavoidable; but they refer exclusively to groupings and combinations of tenses as the expression of a new theory of tense. The individual tenses, however, will still be identified by the terminology most commonly used in the grammars of the particular

---

2. On basic principles: Karl Bühler, *Die Axiomatik der Sprachwissenschaften*, ed. Elisabeth Ströker (Frankfurt/Main: Klostermann, 1969); Karl Bühler, *Sprachtheorie: Die Darstellungsfunktion der Sprache* (Frankfurt/Main: Fischer, 1965); Eberhard Zwirner, "Sprache und Sprachen: Ein Beitrag zur Theorie der Linguistik," in *To Honor Roman Jakobson* (The Hague: Mouton, 1967), 3:2453–63; Harald Weinrich, "Erlernbarkeit, Übersetzbarkeit, Formalisierbarkeit," in *Theorie und Empirie in der Sprachforschung*, ed. Eberhard Zwirner, et al. (Basel: S. Karger, 1970), 76–80.

language under discussion. Thus in German I will speak of Imperfekt, in French of imparfait, in Italian of imperfetto. This arrangement is intended to obstruct the notion that there is an imperfect tense that is identical in all languages. As a matter of principle, every tense function for each language must be determined anew. When a nomenclature offers a choice among terms, I will always prefer the one that lends itself least to an argument based on its name. Thus I will prefer the term preterit to past tense, perfecto simple to pretérito perfecto, and comparably with the other tenses.

Text Linguistics

A description of tense forms and their functions is part of the grammar of a language, more precisely of its syntax (which in my usage also includes morphology). However, syntax is only an appropriate location for the theory of tenses if it allows the necessary leeway to the investigation. That is not the case if syntax is restricted without reflection to studying sentences. The sentence was held as the highest linguistic unit until just a few years ago, as indicated by John Lyons's observation, "The sentence is the largest unit of grammatical description."[3] But what justifies that assumption? I can find no incontestable arguments for the privileged status of the sentence (what is a sentence actually?) in linguistic investigation. The sentence is obviously neither the largest nor the smallest unit of a linguistic utterance, but at best a unit of moderate length somewhere between a text and its phonemes or features. The linguist must therefore reach a definition of sentence in the course of investigation, either by constructing it from the smallest units or by segmenting it from the largest ones. In order to isolate the sentence unit, both processes must be interrupted before reaching their natural conclusion. Linguists can construct larger units than a sentence by beginning with phonemes and distinctive features, and, conversely, they can, beginning with the entire text, segment it beyond the level of the sentence and reach even smaller units. So why should they stop right at the level of sentence?

In the investigation below, the boundaries of the sentence will be denied any special respect. Instead, questions will begin at the level of text and the method to be used may be categorized as text linguistics. Text linguistics is a further development of structural linguistics,

---

3. John Lyons, *Introduction to Theoretical Linguistics* (Cambridge: Cambridge UP, 1969), 172, paraphrasing Leonard Bloomfield, *Language* (Chicago: U of Chicago P, 1984), 170.

understood here as the scholarly term for a linguistics based on Ferdinand de Saussure's *Course in General Linguistics*. It is not concerned with linguistic signs in isolation or in a merely historical ("diachronic") perspective, but investigates the significance of a linguistic sign in the larger structural context of a linguistic code or one of its subsystems. At the same time, the paradigmatic and syntactic dimensions must be distinguished from one another. Every linguistic sign—such as a tense form—is part of a paradigmatic structure, insofar as this tense constitutes together with other tenses a syntactic subsystem or "paradigm." A competent speaker of a language knows this paradigm; it is a structure preserved in long-term memory. Equally important, however, is that every linguistic sign belongs to a syntagmatic structure. A tense form does not occur in isolation, except as a grammatical example, but instead forms a sign in a longer or shorter chain of signs that then travels from speaker to hearer (or from writer to reader) in the process of communication. A sign stands in specific relations to other signs in the chain, whether they precede or follow it, and these relations can also be considered a structure. If the relations are to previous information, they are of a memorial nature (short-term memory); to the extent that they engage information to follow, they are structures of anticipation or expectation. The paradigmatic and syntagmatic dimensions of language must, as a matter of principle, be considered of equal importance. At least there is no way to see what arguments would allow one to be preferred to the other.

Historically, however, it is remarkable that linguists past and present have attended most to paradigms. Their goal was to create a grammar, perhaps, or a dictionary. In both cases the linguistic signs otherwise scattered among various texts appear sorted and systematized in the paradigms of formal series or classes of meanings. In other words, grammars and dictionaries arise from the dissolution of texts. In the process, the textual structures are not infrequently lost. Text linguistics attempts to rectify this situation. It does not, of course, claim that there should no longer be grammars, dictionaries, or other paradigmatically oriented descriptions of languages. They are necessary parts of the intellectual economy, and without them linguistics would be of no value. To study the problem of tense, for example, it is surely an indispensable goal that it be describable as a segment of a grammar. But it must not be forgotten in this bit of grammar that any investigator of tense forms encounters them first and foremost in texts, where, together with other forms—including other tense forms—they form a texture of determination. These textual values cannot be cast aside in the process of constructing a grammar of tense; they must rather become part of the paradigm of tense, perhaps in the form of index values in the text.

In the sense sketched above, the term "text linguistics" is not, for the time being, an exhaustive program for all of linguistics, but rather a reminder of the need for, and the possible fruitfulness of, this book's agenda. Its goal is to burst the framework of the syllable in phonology, that of the word in semantics, and above all that of the sentence in syntax. Instead, the basis for all questions will be the framework of the text, i.e., the phoneme in the text, the moneme (morpheme, lexeme) in the text, and the syntagm in the text.

It is occasionally claimed that text cannot be defined as a category. Whether this observation is true or false depends on what one expects from a definition (especially at the beginning of an investigation). Obviously, it is unfair to expect from an introductory definition all the information that a thorough investigation could achieve in the best-case scenario. It could, for example, turn out that tense forms are essential for the constitution of a text and have to appear in a descriptive definition (*definitio per proprietates*). But one is hardly equipped to give such a definition before the investigation. At this point it can only be a matter of a framing definition of this sort: A text is a meaningful, i.e., coherent and consistent, sequence of linguistic signs between two conspicuous interruptions of communication. For example, in oral communication, pauses longer than those necessary to catch one's breath or find a word are conspicuous, and in written communication it means perhaps the front and back covers of a book. Even arbitrarily arranged breaks create, in this sense (quasi-metalinguistic), interruptions of communication. Thus, very short texts are possible, even without the determinants of a speaking situation: the minimum is two linguistic signs (=smallest units of meaning). No maximum can be established.[4]

---

4. A few important works on text linguistics are Hennig Brinkmann, "Die Syntax der Rede," in *Satz und Wort im heutigen Deutsch: Probleme und Ergebnisse neuerer Forschung*, ed. Hugo Moser (Düsseldorf: Schwann, 1967), 74–94; František Daneš, "Zur linguistischen Analyse der Textstruktur," *Folia Linguistica* 4, no. 1–2 (1970): 72–78; Wolfgang Dressler, "Modelle und Methoden der Textsyntax," *Folia Linguistica* 4, no. 1–2 (1970): 64–71; Zellig S. Harris, "Discourse Analysis," *Language* 28, no. 1 (1952): 1–30; Jose Pedro Rona, "Für eine dialektische Analyse der Syntax," *Poetica* 2, no. 2 (1968): 141–49; Harald Weinrich, *The Linguistics of Lying and Other Essays*, trans. Jane K. Brown and Marshall Brown (Seattle: U of Washington P, 2005); Harald Weinrich et al, "Syntax als Dialektik (Bochumer Diskussion)," *Poetica* 1 (1967): 109–26.

A Preliminary Reflection: Obstinate Signs

A letter writer normally begins with the place and date. Only then is the pen let loose. The letter might remain unfinished on that first day. Or some extra comment may be added later, as in this letter from Schiller to Goethe.

Weimar, 5. September 1800
Der Humboldtische Aufsatz, den ich Ihnen hier zurückschicke, wird recht gut zu brauchen sein. Der Inhalt muß interessieren, denn er betrifft einen abgeschlossenen menschlichen Zustand, der wie der Berg, auf dem er seinen Sitz hat, vereinzelt und inselförmig ist, und mithin auch den Leser aus der Welt heraus und in sich selbst hineinführt. Die Beschreibung könnte ein wenig lebhafter und unterhaltender sein, doch ist sie nicht trocken, und zuweilen läßt sich vielleicht mit einem Worte oder einem Strich nachhelfen. Es wäre zu wünschen, daß unmittelbar neben diesem Gemälde ein entgegengesetztes von dem bewegtesten Weltleben hätte angebracht werden können, so würden beide eine doppelte Wirkung tun . . . .
Der arme Eschen, Voßens Schüler, den Sie als Übersetzer des Horaz kennen, ist im Chamonixtal verunglückt. Er glitschte im Steigen aus und fiel in einen Abgrund, wo er unter Schneelawinen begraben wurde und nimmer zum Vorschein kam. Es tut mir sehr leid um den armen Schelmen, daß er auf eine so jämmerliche Art von der Welt gehen mußte.

Den 6. September
Mir ist noch kein Brief von Ihnen gebracht worden. Ich will hoffen, daß recht großer Fleiß Sie abgehalten, mir zu schreiben. Leben Sie recht wohl und lassen mich bald von Ihnen hören.[5]

Weimar, September 5, 1800
Humboldt's essay, which I return herewith, will work very well. The content will certainly attract interest, since it treats a self-contained human situation that is isolated and insular, like the mountain on which it is located, and consequently draws the reader out of the world and into himself. The description could be a little livelier and more entertaining, but it isn't dry, and could perhaps occasionally be improved with a word or a dash. It would be nice if this tableau

---

5. Johann Wolfgang Goethe, *Der Briefwechsel zwischen Goethe und Schiller*, ed. Ernst Beutler (Zurich: Artemis, 1964), 812–13.

could have been paired with a contrasting one of very lively worldly life, so that the two would make a double impact....

Poor Eschen, Voss's student, whom you know as the translator of Horace, had an accident at Chamonix. He slipped while climbing and fell into a gorge, where he was buried in an avalanche and was never found. I am very sorry for the poor fellow, that he had to depart this world in such wretched fashion.

September 6
I still have no letter from you. I will only hope that you are too busy to write to me. Be well and let me hear from you soon.

The place name, "Weimar," once given, remains valid until the end of the letter. The entire letter was written in Weimar. The place name stands "once and for all." The date, "September 5, 1800," by contrast, does not apply to the entire letter, but only until the next date, "September 6," which invalidates the first date. It applies, therefore, only until revoked, "until further notice." Nevertheless, it does not apply, as could be imagined, only to the following group of words or to the next paragraph. It would be a nuisance and inefficient if the writer chose to begin each new sentence or each new paragraph with place and date. Composers similarly avoid such inefficient fussiness by not indicating the tempo at every line of the score, or worse, at every measure. They mark it at the beginning, and it applies until it is revoked by a new tempo marking.

The question is how long linguistic signs, once placed in a text, continue to apply. They can even apply in reverse, to previous text, but for the moment I will not consider this possibility. Still, they certainly apply not only to the moment in which they are expressed by the speaker or received by the listener. In principle, the answer to the question is that a linguistic sign in a text remains valid either until the text ends or until it is revoked by another sign from the same category. A personal pronoun, "I," for example, applies in the text until is it revoked by a different personal pronoun in the nominative, such as "he." One should note that this second personal pronoun can be semantically filled out ("expanded"), so that its place is occupied by a nominal phrase like "the neighbor."[6] Similarly, a specific article in a text, say, an indefinite article or even a demonstrative, possessive, or numeric article, remains in force until it is countermanded. In the expression, "the neighbor and friend," for example, the definite article continues, but in "the neighbor and a friend" it does not.

6. On the concept of expansion see André Martinet, *Elements of General Linguistics*, trans. Elizabeth Palmer (Chicago: U of Chicago P, 1964), sect. 4.30.

The example also makes clear that the rule can only apply sensibly if the conditions under which two signs can be identified as belonging to the same category can be precisely defined. In the example of the article it must first be established that morphemes, like demonstrative pronouns, possessive pronouns, and numbers, should not be assigned to some specific category of pronouns, as is usual, but to the class of articles. They revoke the application of a preceding definite article just as an indefinite article does.

Furthermore, it is necessary to specify what is meant by the continuing validity of a sign in a text. One must bear in mind here the basic principle of text linguistics, more precisely of text semantics, that individual linguistic signs in a text do not exist isolated from one another. A text cannot be defined as a simple line-up of signs one after the other. It is rather the nature of text that all these signs determine one another. By the validity of a sign in the text I mean exactly this capacity to determine other signs in its neighboring context. As a matter of principle, that is, without knowing a particular sign in its particular text, the limits of that sign's power to determine cannot be specified. It is entirely possible to argue that the first word of a longer text, such as a novel, can still determine the last one. Yet if we always had to begin with the unlimited determining power of every sign in the text, text-linguistic analysis would become very difficult, if not impossible. For this reason it is important to consider that, for at least some signs in language, in particular for grammatical morphemes, an established procedure exists to revoke the determining power and validity of a sign. Such is always the case when one sign is replaced by another that can be assigned more or less clearly to the same class or category as the first.

From this perspective great differences readily appear. Signs like the indication of place and date come back fairly infrequently. We say, then, these signs have low recurrence values. Tense forms, by contrast, have high recurrence values. The letter segment above has, for example, one indication of location, two dates, but twenty-four tense forms—the verbs: *zurückschicke, wird sein, muß, betrifft, hat, ist, hineinführt, könnte sein, ist, läßt, wäre, hätte angebracht werden können, würden tun, kennen, ist verunglückt, glitschte, fiel, begraben wurde, kam, tut, mußte, ist gebracht worden, will, abgehalten (hat)*. Of course, the tense forms do not always have identical recurrence values in every text. This letter of Schiller's, as printed here, has 211 words. Twenty-four tense forms in twenty-two lines is fairly high and is fairly typical of the brisk, verbal style of a letter. In other texts—it is easy to confirm this by random sampling—the recurrence values of the tense forms are lower. In the average text a safe rule of thumb is more or less one tense form per printed line.

High recurrence values like this one, say one sign per printed line, I shall characterize in what follows with the term "obstinacy," modeled on the musical term *ostinato*. I count tense forms, therefore, among the obstinate signs. Other signs, such as indications of place or date, but also macro-syntactic signals like "one day," "and now," and "finally," which will be discussed later, are normally not obstinate signs. However, no special claims should be attached to this new concept. Whoever doesn't like it may ignore it and use the less efficient terminology of higher and lower, or, better, very high and very low, recurrence values.

Tense Distribution

A text-linguistic investigation of tense cannot skimp on texts. So I request the reader's attention to a text by Thomas Mann, the beginning of his essay, "Goethes Laufbahn als Schriftsteller" (Goethe's Career as Writer):

Der 22. März 1832 war gekommen. In seinem Lehnstuhl, ein Oberbett über den Knien, den grünen Arbeitsschirm über den Augen, starb Goethe. Die Qualen und Ängste, die dem Tode oft in einigem Abstand vorangehen, waren vorüber, er litt nicht mehr, er hatte schon ausgelitten, und da man ihm auf seine Frage nach dem Datum den 22. genannt hatte, erwiderte er, so habe denn der Frühling begonnen und um so eher könne man sich erholen. Danach hob er die Hand und schrieb Zeichen in die Luft. Die Hand rückte seitwärts dabei und sank tiefer, er schrieb wirklich, zeilenweise untereinander, und sein Arm ging nieder, gewiß nicht nur, weil oben kein Platz mehr für diese Geisterschrift gewesen wäre, sondern aus Schwäche. Er lag auf dem Deckbett schließlich, und dort schrieb er weiter. Wie es schien, war es zu wiederholten Malen dasselbe, was der Sterbende unsichtbar aufzeichnete, man sah, daß er genaue Interpunktionszeichen setzte, und glaubte einen und den anderen Buchstaben zu erkennen. Dann fingen die Finger an, blau zu werden, sie kamen zum Stillstand, und als man ihm den Schirm von den Augen nahm, waren sie schon gebrochen.

Goethe starb schreibend. Er tat in letzten, verschwimmenden Träumen seines Bewußtseins, was er mit eigener Hand, in seiner schönen, klaren, reinlichen Schrift, oder diktierend sein Leben lang getan hatte: er schrieb auf, er übte diese Tätigkeit, die das Feste zu Geist zerrinnen läßt und das Geisterzeugte fest bewahrt; er bannte letztes Gedanken- und Erfahrungsleben, das ihm vielleicht als endgültige und höchst mitteilenswerte Erkenntnis erschien, obgleich es wohl nur das Produkt hinüberträumender Schwäche war, in die Runen der Schrift; er suchte bis zum Ende den Gehalt seines Busens in die formende Sphäre seines Geistes zu erheben. Er war ein Schriftsteller, noch jetzt, wie er es in dem frühen Augenblick gewesen war, als er brieflich, im Gefühl behaglicher Ergriffenheit von seinem stärksten Trieb, seiner innersten Anlage, ausgerufen hatte: "Eigentlich bin ich zum Schriftsteller geboren. Es gewährt mir eine reinere Freude als jemals, wenn ich etwas nach meinen Gedanken gut geschrieben habe." So wie er es gewesen war, in den abendlichen Morgenstunden, da er der heiligen Anämie seines Hauptes nach kurzem Greisenschlaf die letzten Sphärenklänge des "Faust" abgewonnen— eine Handbreit Schriftsatz täglich und manchmal weniger—und mit dem "Neige, neige, du Ohnegleiche" das Ende seines Lebens an den Anfang geknüpft hatte.

Ein Schriftsteller. Es ist, meine Damen und Herren, eine recht unfruchtbare kritische Manie, zwischen Dichtertum und Schriftstellertum lehrhaft zu unterscheiden—unfruchtbar und selbst undurchführbar, weil die Grenze zwischen beidem nicht außen, zwischen den Erscheinungen, sondern im Innern der Persönlichkeit selbst verläuft und auch hier noch bis zur Unbestimmbarkeit fließend ist. Dichterische Einschläge ins Schriftstellerische, schriftstellerische ins Dichterische gibt es so viele, daß die Sonderung zum wirklichkeitswidrigen Eigensinn wird, nur aus dem Wunsche geboren, dem Unbewußten, Vorgeistigen, dem, was man als das eigentlich Geniale empfindet, auf Kosten des Verstandesmäßigen zu huldigen und diesem unter der Hand Geringschätzung zu erweisen. Der ungeheure Verstand Goethes, den Emerson in seiner Besprechung der Helena-Episode aus dem zweiten Teil des "Faust" bestaunt, ist recht darnach angetan, solche Bestrebungen zu beschämen. "Das Wunderbare," sagt er, "ist die gewaltige Intelligenz darin. Der Verstand dieses Mannes ist ein so mächtiges Lösungsmittel, daß die vergangenen und das jetzige Zeitalter, ihre Religionen, Politiken und Denkungsarten, sich darin zu Urtypen und Ideen auflösen."

Der durchaus unintelligente Dichter ist der Traum einer gewissen romantischen Naturvergötzung, er existiert nicht, der Begriff des

Dichters selbst, der Natur und Geist in sich vereinigt, widerspricht seinem Dasein; und nie könnte verstandloses Schöpfertum sich in ein Lebensalter hinüberretten, wo die Natur nicht mehr oder nicht in dem Grade mehr wie in vermögender Jugendzeit der Hervorbringung zu Hilfe kommt und, um mit Goethe zu reden, Vorsatz und Charakter für sie eintreten müssen. Etwas ganz anderes ist es mit der Naivität, der Unmittelbarkeit, dieser unentbehrlichen Bedingung allen Schöpfertums. Aber man braucht nicht zu sagen, und Goethe ist ein wundervolles Beispiel dafür, daß reinste Naivität und mächtigster Verstand Hand in Hand gehen können.

Emerson hat Shakespeare den größten Dichter und Goethe, in dem doch aller dichterische Ruhm unseres Volkes gipfelt, dagegen den größten Schriftsteller genannt. "Wer die Geschichte recht erkannt hat," schreibt Goethe mit sechsundzwanzig Jahren, "dem wird aus tausend Beispielen klar sein, daß das Vergeistigen des Körperlichen, wie das Verkörpern des Geistigen nicht einen Augenblick geruht, sondern immer unter Propheten, Religiösen, Dichtern, Rednern, Künstlern und Kunstgenossen hin und her pulsiert hat; vor- und nachzeitig immer, gleichzeitig oft." Gleichzeitig oft. Das ist die Bekräftigung des Schriftstellerischen und dichterischen Seins auf einmal, dieses Ineinanders von Geist und Form, von Kritik und Plastik.[7]

March 22, 1832 had arrived. In his armchair, a quilt over his knees, a green eye-shade over his eyes, Goethe died. The torments and fears that often precede death by a certain distance, had passed, he suffered no more, he had already finished suffering, and after his question about the date had been answered with the twenty-second, he replied, then spring had begun and it would be easier to recover. Then he raised his hand and wrote letters in the air. His hand swayed to the side as he did so and sank deeper, he actually was writing, one line after another, and his arm went down, surely not only because there was no more room above for this ghostly writing, but from weakness. Finally it lay on the quilt, and there he kept writing. It seemed as if the dying man invisibly wrote the same thing over and over, he set precise punctuation marks and it even seemed as though one could recognize this or that particular letter. Then his fingers began to turn

---

7. Thomas Mann, "Goethes Laufbahn als Schriftsteller," in *Leiden und Größe der Meister* (Berlin: Fischer, 1935), 53–56.

blue, they ceased to move, and when the eye-shade was removed, his eyes had already glazed over.

Goethe died writing. In the last, blurring dreams of his consciousness he did what he had done his whole life long in his lovely, clear, neat hand or in dictation: he wrote, he exercised the activity that lets concretions melt into mind and preserves the product of the mind forever; he captured forever in the runes of writing the last drop of intellectual and experiential life that appeared to him perhaps as the ultimate and most important insight, even though it was probably only the product of weakness dreaming into death; to the very end he tried to elevate the contents of his heart into the forming sphere of his mind. He was a writer, even now, just as he had been in the early moment when he had declared in a letter, in a moment of joyous possession by his strongest drive: "I am actually born to be a writer. Nothing gives me purer joy than when I have put my thoughts into good writing." Just as he had been in the twilight morning hours, when, after the brief sleep of old age, he had won from the holy anemia of his head the last music of the spheres of "Faust"—a few lines a day and often less—and with the line "Look down, look down, thou peerless one" had tied the end of his life to its beginning.

A writer. Ladies and gentlemen, pedantically distinguishing between being a poet and being a writer is an utterly fruitless critical mania—fruitless and indeed impossible because the boundary between the two does not run externally between appearances, but inside the personality and even here is so fluid as to foil distinction. Poetic incursions into ordinary writing, writerly incursions into poetry are so frequent that distinguishing them becomes resistance to reality, born only of the wish to honor the unconscious and premental, what feels like true brilliance, at the cost of what can be rationally understood, which is then devalued sub rosa. Goethe's immense rational capacity, which Emerson so admires in his discussion of the Helena episode in "Faust II," is exactly what renders such attempts embarrassing. "The wonder of the book is its superior intelligence. In the menstruum of this man's wit, the past and the present ages, and their religions, politics and modes of thinking, are dissolved into archetypes and ideas."

The thoroughly unintelligent poet is the dream of a certain romantic nature idolatry, it does not exist, even the concept of the poet who unites nature and mind within himself contradicts its existence; and unreasoning creativity could never survive into a time of life when nature no longer aids production as it does—or to the extent that it does—in fertile youth and when, to speak with Goethe, resolution and character must take its place. The naiveté, immediacy, that is the indispensable condition of all creativity is an entirely different matter. But it is unnecessary to say, and Goethe is a marvelous example, that the purest naiveté and most powerful intelligence can go hand in hand.

Emerson has called Shakespeare the greatest poet and Goethe, the acme of the poetic fame of our people, by contrast, the greatest writer. "Anyone who has properly learned history," Goethe wrote at age twenty-six, "will know from thousands of examples, that the intellectualization of the body and the embodiment of intellect has never paused, but has always pulsed here and there among prophets, the religious, poets, orators, artist and art-lovers; always one and then the other, often simultaneously." Often simultaneously. That is the affirmation of writerly and poetic existence together, this interpenetration of mind and form, of thinking and making.

Mann's essay confirms, first of all, what we saw in Schiller's letter, namely the obstinacy of the tense forms. The text quoted here has 656 words and seventy-six tense forms. This number does not include subjunctives, infinitives, participles, and imperatives. It would be possible to count these forms as well, but it would not change the situation significantly. I have sorted the total number of tense forms by individual tenses. In decreasing order the frequencies are: Präteritum (preterit) 32, Präsens (present) 28, Plusquamperfekt (pluperfect) 9, Perfekt (perfect) 6, Futur (future) 1. The various tenses show quite different frequency values in this excerpt.

Consider now the distribution of the tense forms in the text. It would be conceivable for the varying tense frequencies to appear randomly mixed. They could be scattered according to the laws of probability. That is, however, not the case in this text, and not the rule in other texts. The sequence of tenses in a text is evidently organized in some fashion. Especially common are agglomerations of a single tense—regular clusters—in the immediate context. In this text, for example, there are clusters of Präteritum and Plusquamperfekt in the first half and clusters of Präsens in the second half. That is the most striking difference in the distribution.

If on the basis of this result we divide the text almost at the middle, between the second and third paragraphs, and count the tenses separately for each half, then the first half has the following result. In thirty-eight lines there are forty-six tense forms. Ordered again by decreasing frequency, they are: Präteritum 31, Plusquamperfekt 9, Präsens 5, Perfekt 1. The two most common tenses, Präteritum and Plusquamperfekt, constitute with their forty forms the entire total of tense forms almost by themselves.

The result for the second part of the text is very different. First of all, in forty-three lines it has only twenty-nine tense forms. This is a much lower rate of recurrence than in the first part of the text. The frequencies of the individual tenses, again in decreasing order, are: Präsens 23, Perfekt 4, Futur 1, Präteritum 1. Here, too, the two most frequent tenses, Präsens and Perfekt, constitute with twenty-seven forms almost the entire total of all occurring tense forms. But they are not the same tenses as in the first half of the text.

What has just been demonstrated? The reader can draw the conclusion that in almost all texts, from whatever different situations or literary genres they originate, a specific tense or group of tenses will predominate and provide the great majority of all occurring tense forms. Within the general phenomenon of tense obstinacy there is also the more particular phenomenon of tense dominance.

Further investigation of various texts of different types in German from this point of view reveals that this lead-tense—to use the musical model of leitmotif—is either Präsens or Präteritum. There is no more to be said on the basis of simply counting forms. At best it might evoke some surprise that language so routinely settles into a particular tense. Evidently the category of tense must be very important for language.

Two Tense Groups: Discussing and Narrating

Thomas Mann's text can accompany us for another stage of our journey. Thus far I have considered the text to be a more or less organized sequence of linguistic signs with high recurrence numbers of some signs, and I have counted up these numbers. Now the question is how to go beyond the general observation that tense is of evident importance in order to interpret the numbers. Until now the investigation has generated no clear results not already identified above. If the argument is to proceed nevertheless, then certain ideas must be anticipated. Anticipating an argument is a legitimate scientific procedure. The scientist proposes a hypothesis as the anticipation of an explanation for a specific set of circumstances; in a series of methodological steps the hypothesis is then tested for its truth or falsity. On the basis of the methodology no hypothesis can be considered impossible in principle; only the result determines its value or lack thereof. A successful result is therefore the decisive criterion for accepting a hypothesis, and this criterion is only available at the end of an experiment. Nevertheless, in the interests of efficiency it makes sense not to invent hypotheses out of the blue. Some measure of probable verification or unlikely falsification should be evident in a hypothesis from the start, or accessible through sampling. The initial observations of Mann's text, however provisional and unverified their results may be, can perhaps serve precisely this purpose. The observed predominance of tenses suggests a hypothesis that will form the basis for the rest of the argument.

Here is the hypothesis: There is a perspective from which the tenses of a language, namely German, the only language discussed so far, can be distinguished into two groups. I will call them, provisionally, tense group I and tense group II. In German, tense group I contains such tenses as Präsens, Perfekt, Futur, and Futur II (future perfect). Tense group II contains other tenses of the German language, such as Präteritum, Plusquamperfekt, Konditional, and Konditional II (past conditional). At the moment I do not intend either list to be complete. It may be useful to distinguish more tenses in German, but if so, it would in any case involve tenses of lower frequency. They do not have to appear in a preliminary hypothesis.

In the framework of this hypothesis it must also be said that in the great majority of spoken or written texts in the German language either tense group I or tense group II predominates unambiguously. There are surely texts to be found in which such dominance cannot be established. Then explaining this divergence from the postulated regularity becomes one of the conditions for verifying the hypothesis.

Our text by Thomas Mann offers a basis for the proposed hypothesis. As already suggested, in its entirety an unambiguous predominance of one or the other tense groups cannot be identified. Of its seventy-six tense forms, thirty-four can be assigned to tense group I; the remaining forty-two forms can be assigned to tense group II. But the ratio 34:42 does not demonstrate unambiguous predominance. Here our hypothesis allows and demands more detailed consideration. When the text is divided in two, then each half does reveal a predominance, and indeed reciprocally. In the first half, tense group II predominates. Of its forty-six tense forms, forty belong to this group. In the second half of the text, tense group I predominates. Of its twenty-nine tense forms, twenty-eight can be assigned to this group.

It would, however, be poor method to keep dividing the body of a text until clear patterns of predominance emerge. A division is only justifiable when the frequency values of the tense forms are also consistent with changes in content. At this point, therefore, I deliberately abandon a strictly formal approach and take content into account for the text in question. Namely, Mann talks about Goethe in the first and second parts of this passage in completely different ways. The first section reports on Goethe's death. To use our literary understanding of genre, it is a narrative. It is located, by means of non-obstinate signs, in time (March 22, 1832, spring) and space (armchair, quilt), and it narrates Goethe's death according to the rules of a secular narrative tradition first as a singular experience, second as the (typical) end of a poet's life. Right where the tenses shift, Mann's style changes. He addresses his public directly ("Ladies and gentlemen"), and he generalizes his reflection on the question of the "interpenetration of mind and form" in an author. Goethe is still the subject, but his life and death are no longer narrated. Instead, the individuality of his writing is characterized and elaborated. I shall say that now, once the narrative has been discontinued, Goethe's nature as writer and the conditions of a writer's existence in general are discussed.

So the difference in the two parts of the text lies not only in the tenses, but in other syntactic signals as well; these will be examined at length below (Chapter 8). We can also identify clear differences in the semantic vocabulary. A word group with words like armchair, quilt, eye-shade, letters, or anemia is recognizably different from one with words like personality, creativity, naiveté, critique, being, etc. But these differences, like all differences in semantics, are relatively difficult to specify. There is no completely consistent correlation between concreteness and what can be narrated on the one hand, nor one between abstraction and what can be discussed on the other. Concrete things can be discussed and abstractions can be narrated; we shall encounter some interesting examples of this. Thus the differences in tense usage are much better understood and defined as syntactic rather than as semantic.

I shall henceforth interpret my hypothesis of the distinction between two tense groups by understanding tense group I as the tenses of discussing and tense group II as the tenses of narrating. Texts in which the tenses of discussing clearly predominate will be called discursive texts. Narrative texts are those in which the narrating tenses predominate. This conclusion can apply not only to the entirety of a text, but also to greater or lesser segments of a passage. We must, however, note that grammar consists not only of tenses. The comprehensive and in each case specific constitution of a text is the result of competing signs and groups of signs. So the text types discussing and narrating are not constructed exclusively by tenses and their distribution. There are also macro-syntactic, non-obstinate signals, which will be considered below (Chapters 9 and 10). In concert with the tenses they either strengthen or weaken the discursive or narrative character of a text. Since it will not be possible to take account of the competing effect of the macro-syntactic signals at each of the early steps in this investigation, the presentation will necessarily have, at first, a certain idealizing character. The distortions in understanding the text will simply have to be accepted for the time being. They will, I trust, be compensated for by finer distinctions to be introduced later.

Insofar, now, as both the discursive and narrative tenses relate not only to the specific subjects of this essay by Thomas Mann, but to almost anything, I introduce the term "world" for this semantic open space of all possible objects of communication. This designation has no ontological significance. It simply identifies the embodiment of everything that could become the object of a communication. In this sense I call the tenses of discussing also the tenses of the discursive world, and the narrative tenses also tenses of the narrated world.

On the Freedom of the Narrator

A variety of sources stimulated my attempt to understand the categories of discussion and narration as structures of the tense system. The stimuli can no longer be precisely reconstructed, but it began from reading many grammars and linguistic monographs about tense from antiquity to the present. Here I will point to only a few discussions that are particularly relevant to my theory, prioritizing observations from outside or at least from the edges of linguistic scholarship, since these can stimulate linguistics most fruitfully.

I begin with no lesser authors than Goethe and Schiller. In a letter of April 19, 1797, Goethe imparts to Schiller as a technical poetic observation the predominant characteristic of epic poetry, namely that it constantly moves forward and backward. He calls it the law of retardation. On April 21, 1797, Schiller expresses his agreement with Goethe's idea—the epic poet does not rush impatiently to a goal, but lingers lovingly at every step. "Er erhält uns die höchste Freiheit des Gemütes" (334; He preserves for us the greatest freedom of mind). Goethe tries in his turn to broaden the context of these observations. On April 22, he asserts the principle for an epic poem, "daß man . . . den Ausgang wissen könne, ja wissen müsse, und daß eigentlich das *Wie* bloß das Interesse machen dürfe" (that one always can know, indeed must know, the ending, and only the *how* of it could be interesting [335]). Suspense should have no role in the work. Months later, on December 26, 1797, Schiller returns to the topic and writes the now famous sentences:

> Die dramatische Handlung bewegt sich vor mir, um die epische bewege ich mich selbst und sie scheint gleichsam stille zu stehn. Nach meinem Bedünken liegt viel in diesem Unterschied. Bewegt sich die Begebenheit vor mir, so bin ich streng an die sinnliche Gegenwart gefesselt, meine Phantasie verliert alle Freiheit, es entsteht und erhält sich eine fortwährende Unruhe in mir, ich muß immer beim Objekte bleiben, alles Zurücksehen, alles Nachdenken ist mir versagt, weil ich einer fremden Gewalt folge. Beweg' ich mich um die Begebenheit, die mir nicht entlaufen kann, so kann ich einen ungleichen Schritt halten, ich kann nach meinem subjektiven Bedürfnis mich länger oder kürzer verweilen, kann Rückschritte machen oder Vorgriffe tun und so fort. Es stimmt dieses auch sehr gut mit dem Begriff des *Vergangenseins*, welches als stillstehend gedacht werden kann, und mit dem Begriff des *Erzählens*, denn der Erzähler weiß schon am Anfang und in der Mitte das Ende, und ihm ist folglich jeder Moment der Handlung gleichgeltend, und so behält er durchaus eine ruhige Freiheit. (475–76)

> Dramatic action moves before me, [whereas] I move myself around epic action while it seems to stand still. In my opinion, much rides on this difference. If the action moves before me, then I am strictly bound to the experiential present, my fantasy loses all its freedom, an enduring restlessness arises and continues in me, I have to remain always with the object; all looking back, all reflection is denied me, because I am obeying an external power. If I move around the epic action, which cannot escape from me, then I can vary my pace, I can linger longer or shorter according to my subjective need, go back or jump ahead, etc. This agrees well with the concept of pastness, which can be thought of as standing still, and with the concept of narration, for the narrator knows already at the beginning and in the middle how it will end, and hence for him every moment of the action has equal worth, and so he maintains serene freedom throughout.

August Wilhelm Schlegel continues this line of argument in his aesthetics and offers Homer as an example of the fully realized "serene deliberation of the narrator." According to Schlegel, calm distinguishes the epic world from our hectic everyday world. Hence epic has its own time, whose order can run contrary to our time, "as it takes the opportunity from each detail to touch on something earlier."[8]

The aesthetics of epic have now become canonized according to the comments of Goethe, Schiller, and Schlegel, so that Wolfgang Kayser can speak of a "law of epic."[9] The law here, or better, principle of narrative perspective, describes the point of view of the omniscient narrator hovering well above the situation. Retrospection (such as flashbacks to the prehistory) and prospection (such as prophecies of the story's end) manifest the superior knowledge and also the freedom of the narrator.

This leads me to another great German writer, Thomas Mann. Mann calls his novel *The Magic Mountain* a "Zeitroman," a "novel of time."[10] The meaning is double in that a particular time—the epoch before World War I—is the topic of narration, but also that "time itself is its topic" (xi). Mann then twice poses Augustine's question, "What is time?" (61 and 316). But he answers differently from Augustine in that he tells the story of Hans Castorp, who is driven by tuberculosis from the North German plain into the isolated, mountain world of the fresh-air resort Davos. Originally intending to stay only three weeks as a visitor, Castorp remains for seven years, "the seven years of his fairytale enchantment" (vi). For here in the mountains is a different world, and here a different time obtains. This more generous economy of time, whose smallest unit is a month, comes close to "trifling with eternity" (500), yet by contrast condenses or stretches to extremes the seconds of the daily temperature measurements. Familiar objects for measuring time fail here, so that Castorp does not have his watch repaired and stops tearing off the leaves of his calendar. What counts is the value on the "Gaffky-scale" (316–17), which expresses the chance of recovery, and also the reading on the thermometer, especially on the "silent nurse," the thermometer without markings—a subtle symbol of a human time no longer based on measurement. In contrast to a supposedly normal time, this one is not simply stretched or shortened, but is paradoxically at the same time "auf eine langweilige Weise kurzweilig oder auf eine kurzweilige Weise langweilig" (entertaining in boring fashion or boring in entertaining fashion). It is qualitatively rather than quantitatively

---

8. August Wilhelm Schlegel, *Kritische Schriften und Briefe*, vol. 2, ed. Edgar Lohner (Stuttgart: Kohlhammer, 1963), 311–12.

9. Wolfgang Kayser, *Das sprachliche Kunstwerk* (Bern: Francke, 1959), 349.

10. Thomas Mann, *Der Zauberberg* (Frankfurt/Main: Fischer, 1964), xi. Further information may be found in my essay "Tempus, Zeit und der Zauberberg," *Vox Romanica* 26 (1967): 193–99.

different from time in the lowlands, the time of healthy, active people. The ill world of the sanatorium is a "closed world" (viii) with power to entrap, a "substitute life," sharply separated from the real, active life that otherwise prevails in the world. Castorp misses out on this life like one enchanted, like a sleeping dormouse ("Siebenschläfer," 651), until the thunderclap of the war breaking out recalls him to the active world.

So we find in this novel of time two completely different forms of time awareness: the fraught time of the lowlands and the heedless, lax time of those whose calling is above in the eternal snows. A strict dichotomy in the experience of time, strict as the boundary between health and illness, between ordinary vital life and the magically heightened life of the magic mountain. What has that to do with tense? At first, nothing. We have to read *The Magic Mountain* more carefully. Not only does Hans Castorp develop a new sense of time in the course of his initiation into the hermetic other world of the magic mountain, but the narrator also understands his own role differently as he accompanies his "hero" into these new experiences. As we learn in numerous digressions, the narrator has to deal with time, too. His problem with time, however, is the time he has to create: the time of the narrative. This, too, is a double time (494)—on the one hand the actual time of narrating as such, what Mann calls a musical time, and on the other the imagined and foreshortened time of the narrated plot. The narrator remarks, for example, toward the end of the story, "The time of its content rolls on so quickly that it can no longer be stopped, that even its musical time begins to ebb" (574). The initial expansion of the time of narration in relation to the time narrated (seventy pages for the first day in the sanatorium) makes sense compared to the ever-accelerating condensation toward the end. At least, that's how Mann understands it; a different novelist might work otherwise.

Mann now makes clear that the experiences of extension and condensation and the "great confusion" (497) the narrator makes as he writes are analogous to Castorp's experiences of time. Both narrator and hero live outside the demands of the normal time divisions of the working world and live in a hermetic organization of time created by an isolated world: the isolated illness-world of the magic mountain for Castorp and the isolated book-world of *The Magic Mountain* (the narrative) for the narrator of the novel. Mann leaves no doubt that the two experiences of time represent the existential intensification (xi–xii) and inspired lucidity separating the artist from the bourgeois. The patient qua "Patient" (through the "inspiring principle of illness" [559]) and the narrator qua "Narrator" (as the "murmuring evoker of the past tense") come from different worlds and live in different times.

That does have something to do with tense. Mann often expressed his conviction that the tense form Imperfekt (=Präteritum) is the correct tense for narration. In the preface to *The Magic Mountain* he asserts that he chose Imperfekt as the tense of the "deepest past" (3), appropriate to a tale from "long ago." Yet the tale covers events from 1907 to 1914, and was, in 1924, the year of publication, not really, or not primarily, temporally "deep." What makes this past deep is the great caesura of the war that changed the world. The novel's past is in truth no temporal distance, but a different quality of understanding the world, one accessible only to narrative. As a great writer, Mann knew from his daily experience of writing that narration is a special form of speech and that the connection has something to do with the tenses of speaking.

Mann's intuitions were taken up by Günther Müller in 1947 in a groundbreaking essay, "Die Bedeutung der Zeit in der Erzählkunst" (The Significance of Time in Narrative Art) and have been further developed by other scholars, in particular Hans-Robert Jauss and Eberhard Lämmert. Müller distinguishes between narrative time and narrated time. He considers narrative time to be the time in which a narrative text can be written or read. Naturally this time cannot be measured exactly; it would make no sense to measure empirically how long an author spent writing a text and at what pace one or another reader took it in. Thus the concept of narrative time has rather an illustrative value; at least a relatively short amount of time is needed to write or read a few pages—minutes or at most hours. Yet these pages can deal with events that last many years or even longer. So narration condenses time, or in Mann's words, it "leaves blanks." By contrast, even a minimal length of time can be narrated over many pages of a book. In the first case the narrated time is much longer than the narrative time, in the second much less. One could take as an example for the first type the brief biographies in the style of the *Vidas* of Provençal troubadours, in the second perhaps the minutely detailed narratives in the nouveau roman. Some novelists have made it their ambition to make narrated time and narrative time equal. Examples could be James Joyce's *Ulysses* and perhaps Michel Butor's *La modification* (Second Thoughts). In all cases, however, Müller's determination remains valid that every condensation and every extension of time represents a choice, and every choice involves interpretation. For our argument we also take Müller's correct observation that narrated time clearly cannot be identified with physical time. In the spirit of the correspondence between Goethe and Schiller, condensations and extensions by the narrator are, rather, expressions of freedom with respect to time, which takes on a different quality altogether.

About the same time as Günther Müller, Käte Hamburger drew the conclusion that the German Präteritum has a different function in narrative literature or, as she usually puts it, in epic composition, than in daily speech.[11] In her view, the "epic preterit" cannot be understood as a statement of pastness, even though outside of the circumscribed literary domain it obviously designates the past as usual. The distinction is important: Hamburger refers explicitly only to Präteritum and only when it occurs in epic or narrative writing. In her presentation certain conditions must be met before the Präteritum abdicates its actual grammatical function of marking the past and becomes the tense of fiction. In particular, the real self must withdraw and leave the scene free for the fictional characters of the narrative to act. Only then is the fiction "genuine," and only then does Präteritum take on a transformed, namely poetic function. Since that does not happen even in every single novel, there is a sharp boundary within literature, even within narrative literature. That is the *Logik der Dichtung* (Logic of Poetry, the title of her book).

Hamburger's thesis has attracted much attention, but also criticism. Some critics have especially resented her courageous withdrawal from the traditional doctrine that tenses are temporal forms. Because her thesis cannot be immediately reconciled to literary reality, they simply reject it as false and return to the familiar category of time and its linguistic expression in the supposed temporal forms of language. My conclusions from reading Hamburger were completely different. To be sure, I too had some difficulties relating my understanding of tense forms and my understanding of texts to Hamburger's theory. But the theory seemed to me nevertheless so remarkable that I never lost sight of it in all my further thinking about tense even from completely different approaches. At last I came to the conclusion that Hamburger had not gone too far, as other critics thought, but on the contrary, that she had not gone far enough. Not only does the "epic preterit," i.e., the German Präteritum as used in fiction, have the qualities described by Hamburger, but all tenses have signifying functions that cannot be adequately described as information about time. The Präteritum is especially the tense of the narrated world and in this capacity communicates information about the appropriate linguistic register for listening to it. In this sense it signals the narrative

---

11. Käte Hamburger, "Das epische Präteritum," *Deutsche Vierteljahrsschrift für Literaturwissenschaft und Geistesgeschichte* 27, no. 3 (1953): 329–57; *Die Logik der Dichtung* (Stuttgart: Klett, 1957). Further essays on this topic can be found in volumes 25 and 29 of *Deutsche Vierteljahrsschrift*. For a good summary of the topic see Roy Pascal, "Tense and Novel," *Modern Language Review* 57, no. 1 (1962): 1–11.

situation itself. No a priori distinction between oral and written expression, between literary and non-literary texts, nor, finally, between literature and poetry can be accepted as relevant. In this sense I would prefer, instead of Hamburger's "logic of poetry," a "linguistics of literature." This is not to say that all linguistics should be understood only in the service of literature, or that literary scholarship should use linguistic methods exclusively or by preference. It only means that the application of certain linguistic (not logical) methods to literary texts makes sense and that literary texts can thus yield some insights worth the attention of both linguists and literary scholars.[12]

---

12. For a continuation of my discussion with Käte Hamburger see her essay "Noch einmal: Vom Erzählen. Versuch einer Antwort und Klärung," *Euphorion* 59, no. 1 (1965): 46–71, and my response, "Tempus-Probleme eines Leitartikels," *Euphorion* 60 (1966): 263–72.

2 / Discussing–Narrating

Syntax and Communication

In more precise terms, the distinction of tense into the two groups of the discussing and narrating tenses means: Tense forms insert morphemes into the textual sequence of signs with obstinate recurrence by which the speaker gives the hearer a particular kind of signal. In the one case the signal means, "This bit of text discusses," and in the other, "This bit of text narrates." The information is evidently very important for the hearer, because it is repeated obstinately, even when the tense remains the same. So the importance of such information must be explained, and to do so, it helps to consider other syntactic signals that are similarly obstinate.

Not just tense, but also the person of verbs must be indicated in every line of a printed text, either as a morpheme, i.e., as a personal pronoun, or lexically, in the semantic expansion into a nominal group. Different languages distinguish the inventory of persons according to various markers. Many languages combine with the six (or twice three) persons certain supplementary details—about the genus and gender of individuals, about their social position (honorifics), or about the position of the speaker or hearer in the group. This last is especially noteworthy, since the plural personal forms do not represent simply an increase in number. "We" does not always mean "I" plus "you" plus "he." It can also mean "I" and "you" exclusive of "he," or "I" and "he" exclusive of "you." Many languages acknowledge these differences with the verb form by distinguishing, for example, an inclusive form that includes the second person, and an exclusive form that does not. But I know of no language that deviates substantially from the basic first-second-third-person schema. Why is this information so important in language that a speaker must unapologetically repeat it over and over? In this case the answer seems to me easier than with regard to tense. The first person "I" obviously identifies the speaker, and the second person "you" (also the politeness forms "Sie," "usted," and "lei" are of course second person, not third) identifies the addressee, the hearer. The third person, finally, whether he, she, it, or they, identifies anything in the world to the extent that it is an object of discussion. The third person is the category for leftovers.

This situation is an interesting example of syntactic functions in language. If we take the function of the syntactic person in language into account, syntax can evidently no longer be considered the study of the "position" (syn-taxis) of elements in a text or even in a sentence. The positioning of elements in a text and their mutual determination of each other also belong indubitably to semantics, insofar as semantics is understood, as is proper, not only as the semantics of lexemes, but also equally as that of morphemes, and, obviously, also as text semantics. Syntax is something different, though admittedly not completely different. The example of the category person allows the following specifically syntactic function to be identified. In this category, the world (in the previously defined sense of all possible objects of communication) is sorted according to a particular point of view, namely that of the process of communication itself. From the point of view of communication the world is roughly divided into the positions speaker (sender), hearer (receiver), and "everything else" (the category of leftovers). This is, let me emphasize, a coarse division that forces the world rather violently into one point of view. But this point of view is of fundamental importance for language: The process of communication enabled by the linguistic code itself appears in this code and is emphasized by its obstinate application. Through the obstinately recurring personal forms of a text, the contents of communication are thus anchored for the hearer in the situation of communication by memorable repetition. The hearer always knows whether the speaker is meant or whether the hearer is meant, or whether something else is meant.[1]

The coarseness of the category person appears especially in the overwhelming extension of the category third person. Every language I know

---

1. See on this topic Harald Weinrich et al., "Syntax als Dialektik (Bochumer Diskussion)," *Poetica* 1 (1967): 109–26, and Jose Pedro Rona, "Für eine dialektische Analyse der Syntax," *Poetica* 2, no. 2 (1968): 141–49.

sorts this category further, though of course still coarsely. To be sure, in this respect different languages sort differently. German, for example, sorts the leftover category into three, namely the genders masculine, feminine, and neuter. French, however, sorts into the two genders masculine and feminine and differentiates within the masculine gender a narrower definition of masculine and neuter by means of text-linguistic supplementary signals. Then there is also differentiation in terms of singular and plural. The categories singular and plural also refer to the situation of communication and not to some "objective" distinction between unity and plurality foreign to language. This category makes it possible to group the three positions in the situation of communication differently according to different points of view. I think I can stop here, having reached a conclusion that the category of person with its various sub-categories firstly articulates the communicative and secondly achieves in this manner a rough sorting of the world (from a communicative point of view). For a further sorting of the world, for all differentiation and fine shading of concepts, there are then all the other signs in the language available, especially the lexemes, whose more precise interaction can be examined with semantic methods.

Here is a second example of supplementary signals, this time of the category article. I have already stated that I include in this category, in addition to the definite and indefinite articles, also the demonstrative, possessive, and numeric adjectives. In contrast to person, articles are found not in the vicinity of the verb, but in that of the noun. Here the definite article points the hearer to information already made available, and the indefinite article, by contrast, announces further information to come.[2] In more precise terms: In a normal text a given linguistic sign x—say, a noun that can be preceded by an article—there is a context before it and another following it. This noun, like every other one, has a certain meaning generally known to the speaker and the hearer and documented, say, by a corresponding dictionary entry. But to understand precisely what this noun means in this particular text, the hearer must gather additional specifications from the context and with their help narrow the broad and vague meaning of the word in question into its specific and exact meaning in this text. This is a basic fact of semantics understood as text semantics. On what context should the hearer draw to understand this noun?

---

2. See Harald Weinrich, "Textlinguistik: Zur Syntax des Artikels in der deutschen Sprache," *Jahrbuch für internationale Germanistik* 1 (1969): 61–74, and Hans-Heinrich Baumann, "Der deutsche Artikel in grammatischer und text-grammatischer Sicht," *Jahrbuch für internationale Germanistik* 2 (1970): 145–54.

The possibly very long text that precedes it? Or the possibly equally long and not yet revealed ensuing text? It would be a real problem for quick and effective understanding between speaker and hearer if the hearer always had to review the entire preceding text and await the unrolling of the entire following text to understand a word correctly.

Here is the syntactic function of the article, which must be described as an aid in decoding. The opposition between the definite and indefinite article separates especially the information delivered by the preceding text from that expected in the following text. To be sure, the article cannot create preliminary information or posterior information, and it can also not destroy it. Articles are rather signals from the speaker to the listener to expect the specification of the meaning of a word in the text either in the preliminary information or in the ensuing information. Under some circumstances, that can still leave a long chain of signs to run through. If the nature of the text does not seem to permit such an extensive procedure, then the speaker can use a particular kind of article, namely a demonstrative or a possessive, or else a numeral. These special forms of the article offer an additional specialized direction toward one or another zone of the text's information. It is important to remember here that articles, which drew our attention by their obstinacy, also refer with their signaling function to the process of communication itself. It is not, however, as was the case with person, a matter of the communication axis speaker-hearer, but of one that crosses it: the axis between the previous and the following states of information. This axis, too, is of the highest importance for language. At the same time, however, even the forms of the article sort the world (again in the sense of a theory of information) only very roughly. At any given point in a text, *the* can mean anything at all, as long as speaker and hearer know what it is from the preliminary information. And, correspondingly, *a* can mean anything at all to the extent that it is unknown to speaker and hearer in a given communicative situation, but can become known from subsequent information.

With these considerations, I am pursuing an approach begun by Karl Bühler in his *Sprachtheorie* (1934, Theory of Language), which he had rediscovered in the writings of the great Greek grammarian Apollonios Dyskolos (second century CE). This theory focuses on deixis, that is, on the signaling function of those elements of language that refer to the I-here-now-point as the *origo* of personal, spatial, and temporal deixis. For Bühler, this *origo* is determined by the position of the speaker as "sender" in the process of communication. At the same time, as a psychologist, he identifies the thus-constituted sphere of pointing with the speaking person's sphere of perception, which can be organized through gestures of pointing. Remembering that *deiknymi*, the Greek verb for pointing, is etymologically related to *dicere*, Latin for saying, Bühler often grants pointing priority over speaking. Bühler's theory of language has been a definitive influence on the views of text syntax presented here. My further development of this theory will treat deixis not in Bühler's strictly gestural fashion, but instead more consistently as a full-blown theory of the process of communication.

These two brief examples of the morphemes of person and of the article suggest that tenses, which occur with the same obstinacy in texts as person and article do, have similar syntactic function, and hence that the significance of discussing and narrating must be understood as able to change the situation of communication in ways highly relevant for the listener. Such would not be the case if the signals of discussion or narration were understood only as information about stages of time or the like. There must be some explanation that reveals a deeper involvement in the process of communication. As for the marking of discussing or narrating inherent in the obstinately recurring tense-morphemes, I think that it enables the speaker to influence and direct the listener's reception of a text. The speaker indicates by the use of discussing tenses that the listener should receive the text attentively—listen intently. With narrative tenses, the speaker implies that the text in question should be received in relaxed fashion. I will thus call the opposition between the two tense groups, "register" (*Sprechhaltung*), by which should also be understood that the attitude of the speaker intends to evoke a particular attitude from the listener, to create congruent attitudes between speaker and listener.

Register

Tense and relaxed speaking—repeated signals to the listener to listen intently or in a relaxed manner—obviously correspond to various experiences in communication.[3] Of course, situations of communication all vary, and typologies are always to some extent arbitrary, but within the

---

3. Translator's note: *Gespannt* and *ungespannt* (tense and relaxed) cover a somewhat wider range than the English equivalents. *Gespannt* means "tense" but without the specifically negative connotation it has with regard to emotion in English. With regard to people it means more often simply eager. And *ungespannt* is not the opposite of *Spannung*, merely its absence. The image here is actually of a bow-string, either drawn or not drawn. *Spannung* also means suspense; as Weinrich points out below, the application of suspense

spectrum of possible typologies of communication, the arbitrariness can be reduced here because literature has always developed such typologies. Literary genres, namely, whatever else they might be, can be understood as types of communicative situations. I will demonstrate this with regard to the registers discussing and narrating with two examples from stories by Maupassant. They are, in a certain sense, extreme examples that can serve as ideal types to mark the issue under consideration.

The first example comes from the story "Le testament" (The Will), about the opening of a will. The whole situation is narrated. Ignoring that for the moment, let us focus on the content of the report, especially on the description of the speakers and listeners. They appear here in a typical discussion and react to a discursive text—the will. Here is the passage:

> M. de Courcils s'était levé; il cria: "C'est là le testament d'une folle!" Alors M. de Bourneval fit un pas et déclara d'une voix forte, d'une voix tranchante: "Moi, Simon de Bourneval, je déclare que cet écrit ne renferme que la stricte vérité. Je suis prêt à le soutenir devant n'importe qui, et à le prouver même par les lettres que j'ai."
>
> Alors M. de Courcils marcha vers lui. Je crus qu'ils allaient se colleter. Ils étaient là, grands tous les deux, l'un gros, l'autre maigre, frémissants. Le mari de ma mère articula en bégayant: "Vous êtes un misérable!" L'autre prononça du même ton vigoureux et sec: "Nous nous retrouverons d'autre part, Monsieur. Je vous aurais déjà souffleté et provoqué depuis longtemps si je n'avais tenu avant tout à la tranquillité, durant sa vie, de la pauvre femme que vous avez tant fait souffrir."
>
> Puis il se tourna vers moi: "Vous êtes mon fils. Voulez-vous me suivre? Je n'ai pas le droit de vous emmener, mais je le prends, si vous voulez bien m'accompagner."
>
> Je lui serrai la main sans répondre. Et nous sommes sortis ensemble. J'étais, certes, aux trois quarts fou.
>
> Deux jours plus tard M. de Bourneval tuait en duel M. de Courcils.[4]

Monsieur de Courcils had risen; he cried: "It is the will of a madwoman." Then Monsieur de Bourneval stepped forward and said in a loud, penetrating voice: "I, Simon de Bourneval, solemnly declare

---

to literary plots enters Western attitudes only in the late nineteenth century and should not influence our understanding of his terminology here—Trans.

4. Guy de Maupassant, *Contes et nouvelles*, ed. Louis Forestier (Paris: Gallimard, 1980, 1979), 1:624–25.

that this writing contains nothing but the strict truth, and I am ready to prove it by letters which I possess."

On hearing that, Monsieur de Courcils went up to him, and I thought that they were going to attack each other. There they stood, both of them tall, one stout and the other thin, both trembling. My mother's husband stammered out: "You are a worthless wretch!" And the other replied in a loud, dry voice: "We will meet elsewhere, monsieur. I should have already slapped your ugly face and challenged you long since if I had not, before everything else, thought of the peace of mind during her lifetime of that poor woman whom you caused to suffer so greatly."

Then, turning to me, he said: "You are my son; will you come with me? I have no right to take you away, but I shall assume it, if you are willing to come with me." I shook his hand without replying, and we went out together. I was certainly three quarters mad.

Two days later Monsieur de Bourneval killed Monsieur de Courcils in a duel.[5]

In our context it is important that the situation is one of considerable tension. The will involves grave interests that turn out indeed to be questions of life and death. The tension is reflected not only in the characters' gestures, but also in their manner of speaking and, since each answers the other in the same tone, in their manner of listening. Speaking is characterized with the following expressions: *crier, d'une voix forte, d'une voix tranchante, articuler en bégayant, du même ton vigoureux et sec*. The language of the characters also reflects the tension in the situation with the expressions *déclarer, stricte vérité, soutenir, prouver, provoquer*. In such a situation, it is evident that the syntactic signals exchanged in the dialogue between the characters suggest the attitude of tension on each side. And indeed we find—with the exception of a single conditional construction, the structure of which will be discussed below (Chapter 7)—exclusively discussing tenses. They are mostly forms of the présent, with one futur and one passé composé. That this whole dialogue and its tension are framed in a narrative appears only on a different page. The very removal of the dialogue from the narrative into direct speech serves to recreate as much as possible the tension of an excited argument in the generally relaxed context of the narrative.

Here now is an—again—extreme counterexample as an ideally typical

---

5. http://www.online-literature.com/maupassant/4300/

illustration of the relaxation of narrative. I have chosen the beginning of Maupassant's story "L'horrible," which, as the title says, recounts a horror story. At the beginning we are further informed that a terrible accident occurred on the previous day, and that it is now being told. The beginning of the story reads:

> La nuit tiède descendait lentement.
> Les femmes étaient restées dans le salon de la villa. Les hommes, assis ou à cheval sur les chaises du jardin, fumaient, devant la porte, en cercle autour d'une table ronde chargée de tasses et de petits verres.
> Leurs cigares brillaient comme des yeux, dans l'ombre épaissie de minute en minute. On venait de raconter un affreux accident arrivé la veille: deux hommes et trois femmes noyés sous les yeux des invités, en face, dans la rivière. Le général de G ... prononça ... (Maupassant, 2:114)

The warm night descended slowly.
The women had remained in the salon of the villa. The men, seated or astride the garden chairs, were smoking outside the door in a circle about a round table set with cups and small glasses.
Their cigars were glowing like eyes in the darkness that thickened from moment to moment. They had just been told about a dreadful accident of the day before: two men and three women drowned before the eyes of the guests, right across the river from them. General de G ... said ...

The relaxation of the situation appears clearly in the author's description. It is the evening hour, in fact, a mild one. Night falls, slowly. Dinner has been good. Now they are drinking coffee and cognac. They are smoking. They sit casually on the garden chairs. The group forms a circle. In this situation the story will be told. It is a typical circle for storytelling. It is irrelevant that the story is about a dreadful accident, or even that it happened quite recently. Despite that fact, the narrative setting itself is completely relaxed. The dreadful occurrences, though only one day old, are filtered by the narrative and substantially softened.

These are, as I have said, two extremely crafted situations of discussing or narrating, each stylized into its ideal form. Not all linguistic situations to be studied allow for such explicit polarization. Yet for each of the two kinds of situations it is possible to characterize a series of types if we accept the assistance offered by literary genres (in the extended sense mentioned above).

For the tenses of discussion, representative genres would include: dramatic dialogue, a political position paper, an editorial, a will, a scholarly presentation, a philosophical essay, legal commentary, and the forms of ritual, formalized, and performative speaking.[6] In utterances of this sort, speakers are intent (*gespannt*) and their language is purposive because it involves things that concern them directly and that the listener should therefore receive in a mode of concern. Speaker and listener are engaged; they have to act and react. The utterance is a bit of action that changes the situation of both by a bit, and thus obliges both of them by a bit. Non-narrative speech is thus categorically dangerous; Lessing's Nathan the Wise is aware of this fact when he avoids the dangerous question, "What religion, what law/Has seemed best to you?" (*Nathan der Weise* 3.5.44–45), and responds with the—categorically—undangerous little story of the ring parable (3.7.20–64). He avoids the *tua res agitur* that the discussing tenses signalize to the listener in texts of this sort.

Among the speech situations of narrative we might count: a story of one's youth, retelling a hunting adventure, a fairy tale of one's own invention, a pious legend, an artistic story, historical writing, or a novel, but also newspaper reporting about the course of a political conference, even if it is of the greatest importance. It is irrelevant whether the information is objectively important or unimportant. The issue is whether the information is intended by the speaker to evoke particular immediate reactions from the listener. Furthermore, it is immaterial to its narrative character whether the story is true or invented. It is also immaterial whether it is unassumingly domestic or artistically stylized. It makes no difference, finally, to what literary genre conventions it conforms. The general qualities of the typical narrative speech-situation rise above all these particular differences.

Narrating is evidently a fundamental human quality. We can enter into a relationship with the world by telling about it, by narrating it. When we do so, we normally use the narrative tenses. Their function in language is to communicate to the listener that the information contained is "only" a story, so that the listener can listen with a certain equanimity.

If these arguments are plausible, then it is no longer possible to consider the obstinacy we have observed with regard to tense as a contradiction to the economy of language. The principle of economy so emphasized by André Martinet is evidently a general principle that underlies language

---

6. On performative speech see J. L. Austin, "Performative Utterances," in *Philosophical Papers* (Oxford: Oxford UP, 1961), 220–39.

and all other functional systems of communication.[7] No communication system can afford to employ too many means of communication for a given purpose. It would not last long. In this respect, the obstinacy of the category of tense can be justified under the principle of economy. For it is naturally not unimportant to the economy of the intellectual faculties whether full concentration ("code red") is required for every linguistic communication or whether concentration can occasionally be relaxed ("code yellow"). It is always useful to know which is required. The obstinate use of tense forms is hence only apparently a waste of energy and in fact serves a higher-ranking economy.

But what is meant, then, by a "suspenseful story"? This seems to demand of a narration that it arouse suspense, that is, tension. Yet in our argument narrative was precisely the mode of relaxed reception. This actually makes sense and confirms rather than contradicts the argument. Let me step back a little. In ancient rhetoric, which focused on public speech, there was no conception of suspense. There isn't even a name for it among the *virtutes* of rhetoric, unless we were to understand in this sense the requirement of audience attention (*attentum facere*) for any speech. Rhetoric's demand to attend is rather only a general expression of the focus on effect, which is constitutive for all of ancient rhetoric. It is clearly obvious to teachers of rhetoric that public speech must be tense in the sense of purposive. For that element of speech that undermines the tension of language the most, *narratio* namely, they require, correspondingly, with special emphasis, brevity (*brevitas*).[8]

The official poetics of the European literary tradition remain for centuries in the paths defined by rhetoric. Up to the present the term "brevity" still plays a considerable role, while tension has only very recently, under the influence of an aesthetics of information, penetrated into poetics with concepts like "suspense."[9] There has been, however, a tendency in classical and post-classical aesthetics—it is unclear from just when—to declare tension desirable in narrations. Modern storytellers have instinctively responded to this expectation, even without pressure from an official

---

7. See Michel Butor, "Le roman comme recherche," in *Répertoire* (Paris: Minuit, 1960), 1:7–19; also Cesare Segre, *I segni e la critica* (Turin: Einaudi, 1969); Algirdas J. Greimas, *Du sens: Essais sémiotiques* (Paris: Seuil, 1970); Tzvetan Todorov, *Grammaire du Décaméron* (The Hague: Mouton, 1969); Harald Weinrich, *Literatur für Leser* (Munich: Deutscher Taschenbuch Verlag, 1986).

8. See André Martinet, *Économie des changements phonétiques* (Bern: Francke, 1955).

9. See Heinrich Lausberg, *Handbuch der literarischen Rhetorik* (Munich: Max Hueber, 1960), and Aron Kibédi Varga, *Rhétorique et littérature: Études de structures classiques* (Paris: Didier, 1970).

poetics, and have developed various techniques to generate suspense. The less they have felt committed to an official poetics, the more they have actually adopted this attitude. Tension or suspense has become a decisive criterion of quality in popular literature. The bottom line is, there are narrations that are more and less tense.

It is necessary, now, to project this literary, or sub-literary, quality onto the broader linguistic horizon sketched so far. It must be emphasized that tension is being demanded from precisely that genre whose linguistic structure requires relaxation as the mode of reception from its listener or reader. The narrator who generates tension evidently tries to counter the underlying structure. By choosing striking events and an arrangement of linguistic signals to generate tension, the narrator "fascinates" the reader and enforces an attitude of reception that secondarily undoes the primary relaxation. Apart from the choice of material, the primary tools are largely the syntactic signals of discussing, especially also the tenses of discussing (direct speech, historical present, etc.). Authors thus narrate *as if* they were discussing. This *as if* is an important constituent of suspenseful narrative literature.

Tense in Different Genres

It doesn't make sense to support my argument with my own tense counts in large quantity. I would have to choose the text and could scarcely convince my readers that the texts were chosen completely arbitrarily and would reveal the average values for the given genre. Nevertheless, I will offer at least as a hint the results of a count I have done for two texts. Both texts are by the nature of their genre recognizable as either discussion or narrative. One is the first chapter of the *Introduction à l'étude de la médecine expérimentale* (Introduction to the Study of Experimental Medicine) by Claude Bernard, the other the story "La femme adultère" (The Adulteress) by Camus.

The first chapter of Bernard's *Introduction* contains 1082 lines in the edition I used. Again, the count of tense forms does not include infinitives, participles, subjunctives, and imperatives for reasons that will be explained. On this basis, the text has altogether 865 tense forms. They distribute among the two tense groups as follows:

1. Discussing tenses: 787
    présent: 639
    passé composé: 75
    futur I: 70
    futur II: 3

2. Narrative tenses: 78
   conditionnel I: 34
   imparfait: 28
   plus-que-parfait: 5
   passé simple: 7
   conditionnel II: 4

This longer text, like the shorter German text above, reveals a similar clear predominance of discussing tenses. With 788 forms, they constitute 91% of the counted forms. I will return to this text later with other questions, and turn now to Camus.

"La femme adultère" contains 800 lines in the edition I used. Using the same exclusions as in the chapter by Bernard, the tense forms total 810. They sort as follows:

1. Discussing tenses: 39 forms
   présent: 36 forms
   passé composé: 3 forms

2. Narrating tenses: 771 forms
   imparfait: 457 forms
   passé simple: 236 forms
   plus-que-parfait: 55 forms
   conditionnel I: 16 forms
   conditionnel II: 5 forms
   passé antérieur: 2 forms

Here, in contrast to the scientific treatise, there is a clear predominance of narrative tenses. The 771 forms constitute 95.3% of the total counted in the text. This dominance is unusually high even for narrative literature. It happens here because there are so few dialogue sections. The thoughts and conversations of the characters are normally condensed into interior monologue. In texts with a high proportion of direct speech it is wise to follow Kaj B. Lindgren's example (in *Über den oberdeutschen Präteritumschwund* [Helsinki: Acta Academiae Scientiarum Fennica, 1957]) by separating the narrator's report from the dialogue sections. For Spanish, I'll offer some results from a careful set of counts conducted by William E. Bull.[10] Since Bull includes participles, infinitives, and imperatives in his statistics, his numbers can only be considered in their relative proportions

---

10. William Emerson Bull, "Modern Spanish Verb-Form Frequencies," *Hispania* 30 (1947): 451–66. Further interesting counts can be found in Manuel Criado de Val, *El verbo español* (Madrid: Sociedad Española de Traductores y Autores, 1969).

to each other. So I have selected only the tense presente from his material for the discussing tenses, and only the tenses imperfecto and perfecto simple for the narrative tenses. Using Bull's statistics, we can now observe the distribution of the two tense groups in various speech situations represented by various literary genres. The numbers are rounded-off percentages; the first number indicates the frequency of presente (tense group I), the second number the frequency of imperfecto and perfecto simple (tense group II). The other tenses of the two groups can be ignored, because they distribute similarly and have no effect on the larger picture.

Author/Title	Genre/Country	Discussion frequency	Narrative frequency
Abreu Gómez/ *Héroes mayas*	stories/ Mexico	19.8	54.5
Alfredo Cantón/ *Bravo León*	stories/ Panama	11.5	50.6
Eustasio Rivera/ *La vorágine*	novel/ Colombia	20.0	38.1
Eduardo Luquín/ *Los perros fantasmas*	novel/ Mexico	18.4	36.1
Jesualdo Sosa/ *Sinfonía de la Danzarina*	poems, Uruguay	44.3	20.0
García Lorca/ *Poeta in Nueva York*	poems/ Spain	46.4	20.0
Xavier Villarrutia/ *La hiedra*	drama/ Mexico	38.0	11.8
Jacinto Benavente/ *Una pobre mujer*	drama/ Spain	36.3	9.0
Martínez Sierra/ *Sueño de una noche de agosto*	Drama (dialogues only)/ Spain	36.3	6.3
Benjamín Jarnés/ *Cervantes*	biographical essay/ Spain	48.9	13.0
Amado Alonso/*Poesía y estilo de Pablo Neruda*	literary criticism/ Argentina	65.0	1.6
Joaquín Xirau/ *Amor y Mundo*	philosophical essay/ Spain	66.0	1.3

Despite the disparity in the number of tenses chosen to represent each tense group, the result is clear: Stories and novels have an obvious preponderance of narrative tenses, while poetry, drama, biographical, and critical essays reveal an even greater preponderance of discursive tenses.

I will return to the German language with a third set of statistics taken from Kaj B. Lindgren's impressive *Über den oberdeutschen Präteritumschwund* (p. 20). His analysis of three stories—"Viola Tricolor,"

"Immensee," and "Aquis Submersus"—by Theodor Storm is representative of his results for the tense distribution of literary German in general. Lindgren includes the subjunctive in his counts, so once again his numbers are useful only for the proportions revealed. To simplify, I will consider for tense group I only Präsens and Perfekt, and for tense group II only Präteritum and Plusquamperfekt. Lindgren separates in his analysis the reporting of the narrator from the dialogue sections. For the report of the narrator the results are:

Tense group I, 3.8%, 151 examples
Tense group II, 89%, 3932 examples

For the dialogue sections:

Tense group I, 71%, 921 examples
Tense group II, 9.8%, 128 examples

Here, too, the result is clear and thoughtfully interpreted (in the framework of a different theory). In the report of the narrator, narrative tenses prevail unequivocally, and in the dialogue sections discussion tenses dominate equally clearly. This result does not change significantly when the rest of the tenses are taken into account.

Enough statistics from literary texts. Yet because literature has been broadly defined here to include critical/philosophical texts along with the poetic genres, and because Lindgren has separated the report of the narrator from the dialogue, there is little danger of one-sided results. We may consider the literary genres as representative for certain linguistic situations.

The result confirms now in particular that tense groupings do not fluctuate randomly in genres or linguistic situations. The clear dominance of either tense group I or tense group II has been confirmed. Discussing tenses dominate in lyric poetry, drama, dialog in general, in critical essays, and in scholarly and philosophical prose. The narrative tenses dominate in story, novel, and in every kind of narration apart from included sections of dialogue. The result ought to allow simultaneously an extrapolation from literary genres to all types of language situations. At a later point it will be necessary to take account of the distinction between written and spoken language in relation to our tense distinction (Chapter 9).

The World of Discussion

In almost every grammar, the chapter on present tense resembles the chapter, "Présent," in Maurice Grevisse's grammar, *Le bon usage*, section 714–15.¹¹ The first section says that présent identifies the present time; the second, what is customary; the third, timeless facts; the fourth and following sections, finally, that présent can also refer to past and future events. Can there be a better demonstration that the present tense does not simply represent the present time? Present is a tense, the most common of the discussing tenses, and signifies a particular register of communication. The same is true of the other tenses of the world as it is discussed. For the time being I will focus on the present and on some of its uses to reveal what is special about the world of discussion and its corresponding group of tenses. Since the same relationships appear in several languages, I take the liberty of drawing examples from various ones.

As Käte Hamburger ("Das epische Präteritum," 352–53) has already pointed out, it is normal to narrate a story, perhaps a novel or a novella, in Präteritum (in German; in French in imparfait and passé simple), but we always summarize their contents in the present.¹² Her observation is confirmed with extraordinary consistency from the summaries of Plautine comedy to today's handbooks of the novel and the drama. For Hamburger, this fact corroborates her hunch that the preterit of epic poetry cannot be a statement of pastness. I add the complementary conclusion here that the present of its content summary cannot be a statement of presentness.

One might now think, the use of preterit for narrative and present for summary might depend on the fact that the preterit refers to the actual circumstances of the narrative, while the present means the circumstances in the book now before the reader. But that cannot be correct; the present will also be used if the book is not yet fully written and present before us, as in a literary sketch. André Gide notes in his diary on July 16, 1914:

> Beau sujet de roman: la jeune fille qui va se marier contre le gré de ses parents avec quelqu'un dont le passé a prêtè à redire. Peu à peu elle parvient à faire accepter son mari; mais c'est elle qui, tandis que la famille découvre à ce mari de plus en plus de qualités, comprend qu'elle s'illusionait¹³ sur con compte. Par fierté elle dévore toutes ses tristesses, ses déconvenues et se trouve d'autant plus seule, qu'à présent la famille prend le parti du mari, contre elle, et à cause de l'habilité qu'elle a eue d'abord à faire valoir son mari.¹⁴

---

11. 8th ed. Brussels: Duculot, 1964.
12. Käte Hamburger, "Das epische Präteritum," *Deutsche Vierteljahrsschrift für Literaturwissenschaft und Geistesgeschichte* 27, no. 3 (1953), 352–53.
13. On this use of imparfait, see below, Chapter 7.
14. André Gide, *Journal, 1889–1939* (Paris: Gallimard, 1982), 1:439.

Good subject for a novel: the young woman who is about to marry a man with a dubious past against the will of her parents. Gradually she gets them to accept her husband; but, while the family discovers more and more good qualities in the husband, it is she who realizes that she had misled herself about him. Out of pride she swallows all her miseries, her disappointments and finds herself accordingly more isolated, since the family now takes the husband's side against her because of the skill she showed in standing up for him.

If Gide had ever written this novel, he surely would have written it in the narrative tenses imparfait and passé simple, as he did all his other novels. Yet the tenses of the sketch are all discussing tenses: présent, passé composé, and futur proche—if the form "va se marier" may be considered a kind of future. Roy Pascal confirms that Henry James, like the French novelist, composed the sketches in his notebook in the present tense, and in fact not only the sketches for entire novels, but even the detailed sketches for individual scenes.[15]

Film scenarios, finally, should also be mentioned here. They precede the film as a sketch precedes a text. Even when later published as literary texts they remain in the tenses of group I, as for example in Sartre's scenario *Les jeux sont faits* and also in Alain Robbe-Grillet's *L'année dernière à Marienbad*. Film scenarios are related to stage directions in plays. They use the present so often that the Danish linguist Holger Sten wonders whether there should not be added the "présent scénique" as a new tense form.[16] In the same context, he points out that the literary analyses of critics and scholars favor present tense. Similarly, descriptions and captions of pictures, as well as the titles of sculptures, are in the present tense.[17] Even references to a letter being answered use the present. That is already the case in Latin, e.g., Cicero to Metellus Celer: "Scribis ad me . . ." ("you write to me . . .").[18] Here, one might want to say the picture, the sculpture, or the letter is present before the writer. But that is secondary. The Latin praesens tabulare on tables, date markers, and in chronicles stands for things being written about because they are not present.[19] Finally, there

---

15. Roy Pascal, "Tense and Novel," *Modern Language Review* 57, no. 1 (1962): 7.
16. Holger Sten, *Les temps du verbe fini (indicatif) en français moderne* (Copenhagen: Munksgaard, 1964), 21.
17. Alessandro Ronconi, *Interpretazioni grammaticali* (Padua: Liviana, 1958), 41, points to "Davide che uccide Golia" as an example.
18. Marcus Tullius Cicero, Ad fam. V,2; *Letters to Atticus. Loeb Classical Library* (Cambridge: Harvard UP, 1999). Doi: 10.4159/DLCL.marcus_tullius_cicero-letters_atticus.
19. Jacob Wackernagel, *Vorlesungen über Syntax* (Basel: Birkhäuser, 1926), 1:164–65.

are also newspaper headlines, especially in less formal papers, often in present tense, yet the articles they introduce are normally in the tenses of group II, when they deal with an occurrence.

The collection of examples should suffice to demonstrate that this question of the present—and thereby of the entire first tense group—cannot be answered with the isolated case of a summary of a novel. Summarizing a novel is but one application of the present tense, and the explanation immediately at hand—that it refers to the present time of the book that contains it—fails with most of the remaining examples. Even so, it is possible to interpret this use of the tense in terms of the structure of the tense system. One must remember not only that words belong in the context of the sentence or that sentences belong in the context of the text, but also that texts belong in the context of a linguistic situation. A text like the summary of a novel does not appear isolated in real speech. Even the alphabetical or chronological arrangement in a handbook is such a context. When it is not used for the modest purpose of refreshing one's memory, a summary of content usually serves as the basis for discussing a literary work. No one summarizes a novel out of a desire to take a story that has been written beautifully and at length to retell it briefly and badly. The goal is rather to discuss the work or to enable others to discuss it by filling in possible gaps in memory. The larger context thus reveals the summary to be part of a situation of discussion, and it is obvious that the discussing tenses also will be maintained in the process.

Here now are two examples. Thomas Mann took *Don Quixote* with him when he sailed to America and includes his diary impressions of it in his magnificent essay, *Meerfahrt mit Don Quixote* (At Sea with Don Quixote).[20] In it (35 ff.) he discusses the wedding of Camacho and summarizes it extensively—in the present. Immediately after the summary he adds the—discursive—question: "Ist so etwas erlaubt? Die Szene des Selbstmordes ist mit vollkommenem Ernst und tragischen Akzenten gegeben" (Is such a thing permissible? The scene of the suicide is presented with full seriousness and tragic accents). A few pages later he summarizes the equally curious adventures with the donkey's bray—in the present—and continues his discussion with: "Merkwürdige Geschichte! Sie hat etwas Erinnerungsvolles und Anspielhaftes, über das ich mich nicht zu irren glaube" (A remarkable story! It has something memorable and allusive, about which I think I am not mistaken).

The other example comes from Jean-Paul Sartre's philosophical-literary interpretation of Camus's novel *L'étranger*. Note the seamless transitions between discussion and summary:

---

20. Thomas Mann, *Meerfahrt mit Don Quijote* (Wiesbaden: Insel, 1956), 35 ff.

L'étranger sera donc un roman du décalage, du divorce, du dépaysement. De là sa construction habile: d'une part le flux quotidien et amorphe de la réalité vécue, d'autre part la recomposition édifiante de cette réalité par la raison humaine et le discours. Il s'agit que le lecteur, ayant été mis d'abord en présence de la réalité pure, la retrouve sans la reconnaître dans sa transposition rationnelle. De là naîtra le sentiment de l'absurde, c'est-à-dire de l'impuissance où nous sommes de *penser* avec nos concepts, avec nos mots, les événements du monde. Meursault enterre sa mère, prend une maîtresse, commet un crime. Ces différents faits seront relatés à son procès par les témoins groupés, expliqués par l'avocat général: Meursault aura l'impression qu'on parle d'un autre. Tout est construit pour amener soudain l'explosion de Marie.[21]

The Stranger will then be a novel of dislocation, of divorce, of disorientation. Hence its skillful structure: on the one hand the daily flux and formlessness of lived reality, on the other the edifying recomposition of this reality by human reason and speech. It requires the reader, having first been set into the presence of pure reality, to find it anew, now transposed into rationality, without realizing it. This will give birth to a sense of the absurd, that is to say, of our powerlessness in our position to *think* the events of the world with our concepts, with our words. Meursault buries his mother, takes a mistress, commits a crime. These different acts will be related at his trial by the assembled witnesses and explained by the prosecutor: Meursault will have the impression that they are talking about someone else. Everything is arranged to lead to Marie's sudden outburst.

As this summary reveals, it doesn't matter if the author uses présent or, occasionally, as here, futur. The agreement of parts in a unified speech situation requires only that discussing tenses are used uniformly. Only thus, even in the "narrative" of the content, can the climate of the discursive situation be reliably maintained without having to be constantly reconstructed by the author.[22]

Another example, in English, also reveals the dichotomy between

21. Jean-Paul Sartre, "Explication de *L'étranger*," in *Situations I* (Paris: Gallimard, 1947), 99–121.
22. On tense usage in fiction see also Pascal, "Tense and Novel," especially his conclusion: "the meanings of the tenses cannot be equated with the temporal functions they have in normal discourse. . . . Their function in fiction cannot be judged out of context, and . . . they take their meanings from the context" (11).

discussing and narrating tenses. George Orwell's famous novel *Nineteen Eighty-Four* begins as follows:

> It was a bright cold day in April and the clocks were striking thirteen. Winston Smith, his chin nuzzled into his breast in an effort to escape the vile wind, slipped quickly through the glass doors of Victory Mansions, though not quickly enough to prevent a swirl of gritty dust from entering along with him.[23]

The book continues for some 200 pages with a similar tense distribution, strongly favoring preterit. Yet in *Fifty British Novels*, in which Abraham Lass summarizes this novel's content for the purpose of later interpretation and critical analysis, the same material seems fundamentally different, not only in its length, but also in its tense usage. The summary is almost entirely in the present tense and begins as follows:

> One bright day in April 1984 Winston Smith takes time off from his job at the Ministry of Truth to go home and begin a secret journal. He has a lovely old notebook bought at Mr. Charrington's junk shop a few days before, a dangerous act in 1984, when secret thoughts and relics from the past are forbidden.[24]

What has happened here? Why do the same events appear in preterit in the one book and in present in the other? Has time such an effect? Such an assumption would make no sense. After all, the time of this novel is, we are told clearly enough, the year 1984. We interpret the observation, therefore, without respect to time and points in time and explain the use of the present in the summary of the contents as a generic or situation-specific signal that this text discusses.

The World of Narrating

The narrated world is evidently equally indifferent to chronological time. Whether indicated by a date in the past or by a different one in the present or future, the date has no effect on the style of the narrative nor on its actual linguistic situation. Thus, many a narrative can provocatively emphasize its indifference to time. We know, for example, how often the year in a story is replaced with three dots or a dash, as for example in Edgar Allan Poe's story "The Unparalleled Adventure of One Hans Pfaall": "It

---

23. George Orwell, *Nineteen Eighty-Four* (London: Secker & Warburg, 1949), 5.
24. Abraham Harold Lass, *A Student's Guide to Fifty British Novels* (New York: Washington Square, 1966), 343.

appears that on the—day of—(I am not positive about the date) a vast crowd of people...." And at the beginning of the story "Metzengerstein," Poe asks: "Horror and fatality have been stalking abroad in all ages. Why then give a date to the story I have to tell?" One might say these discussing sentences by Poe make explicit what is implied by the tenses of the narrative world. They indicate that it does not concern the life-world in which the speaker and listener are located and directly involved. They also indicate that the speech situation represented in the communication model is not simultaneously the stage of the events, and the speaker and listener are, for the time being, more spectators than actors in the *theatrum mundi*—even if they are observing themselves. This opening speech leaves the existence of speaker and listener out of the performance.

In fact it is possible with the preterit and the corresponding tenses in other languages to express all stages of time. As regards the past, normally first associated with the preterit, let me point without further commentary to the beginning of Thomas Mann's previously cited essay about the death of Goethe. The time is explicitly set as past by the date named at the beginning, March 22, 1832. But other times can be expressed by the preterit just as well. I have already cited the opening sentences of Orwell's utopian novel *Nineteen Eighty-Four*, written in 1949. They are all in the preterit. A few pages later, just far enough from the beginning to allow many readers to forget the date—in any case the written-out title is not automatically identifiable as a date—Orwell reminds his reader explicitly:

> He dipped the pen into the ink and then faltered for just a second. A tremor had gone through his bowels. To mark the paper was the decisive act. In small clumsy letters he wrote April 4th, 1984.– He sat back. A sense of helplessness had descended upon him. To begin with he did not know with any certainty that this was 1984. (Orwell, *Nineteen Eighty-Four*, 10)

We note the almost provocative emphasis with which Orwell sets the preterit forms *wrote* and *was* next to what was then a future date, *1984*.[25]

Italian has the same discussion/narrative dichotomy, and so, just as Orwell describes the utopian future with the past, Curzio Malaparte, in his novel *Storia di domani* (A History of Tomorrow, 1949) does the same. The narrator reports about a meeting with the politician de Gasperi, to whom he tells the story of his flight:

---

25. Compare the sentence in Aldous Huxley's futuristic novel *Brave New World* (1939), "And anyhow the question didn't arise; in this year of stability, A.F. 632, it didn't occur to you to ask it" (New York: HarperCollins, 2006, 4; A.F.=Anno Fordis).

Gli narrai brevemente le mie avventure, la mia corsa affannosa attraverso la Francia da Parigi ai Pirenei, la ressa dei fuggiaschi davanti alla frontiera spagnola sbarrata, la mia fuga in Svizzera, l'invasione della Svizzera da parte delle truppe sovietiche.[26]

I briefly narrated my adventures, my frantic dash across France from Paris to the Pyrenees, the mob of fugitives backed up at the blockaded Spanish border, my flight to Switzerland, the invasion of Switzerland by Soviet troops.

Only in the last part of the sentence, in which the narrator, with the calm of a chronicler and consistent tense use, reports the invasion of Switzerland by Soviet troops, does the reader—whom the historical name de Gasperi has misled into the false track of a documentary report—realize that this is no "true story" as claimed by the title. The passato remoto (preterit) tense of this sentence refers not to the past, but to an imaginary tomorrow in the future.

Let me remind the reader finally of Hermann Hesse's *Glasperlenspiel* (1943, The Glass Bead Game), the action of which is set some 200 years in the future. The events of Franz Werfel's *Stern der Ungeborenen* (1946, Star of the Unborn) lie a few millennia in the future. And in Jules Verne's many novels it is not possible to say specifically just how far in the future the action is set. We may unhesitatingly generalize: Novels of the future are routinely written in the preterit or in the corresponding tense of other languages. Or, more cautiously: None are written in the future tense. So it is generally true that any point in time is accessible to the narrating preterit tense.

The language of fairy tales can illustrate this argument.[27] For the world of fairy tale is a narrative world out of time. In no other narrative are we carried so far from the ordinary world as in the fairy tale. There everything is different from what children are otherwise familiar with. For this reason fairy tales mark the boundary between the worlds of narrative and of discussion more sharply than is necessary in other narrative texts by their formulaic introduction and closure.

This is so obvious that we can scarcely imagine a fairy tale that does not begin with the Brothers Grimm's formula "es war einmal," or something similar (English, "once upon a time"; French, "il était une fois"; Spanish,

---

26. Curzio Malaparte, *Storia di domani* (Rome: Aria d'Italia, 1949), 11.

27. For introductions to the literary problems of fairy tales see Max Lüthi, *Märchen* (Stuttgart: Metzler, 1962), and also André Jolles, *Simple Forms: Legend, Saga, Myth, Riddle, Saying, Case, Memorabile, Fairytale, Joke*, trans. Peter Schwarz (London, Brooklyn: Verso, 2017), Chapter 8.

"era una vez"). This "once" identifies a categorically different time, that is, a realm with its own time hardly related to the time of clocks, a time in which someone can sleep for seven years. There is an English fairy tale that clearly distinguishes our time and fairytale time. It begins: "Once upon a time, and a very good time it was, though it wasn't in my time, nor in your time, nor any one else's time. . . ."[28] Again, the "once" negates our ordinary time. Fairy tales take place "ages ago." The fairytale world actually makes fun of our ordinary world and its temporality in the Spanish fairy tale opening: "érase que se era." Here the beginning of the tale is entirely dependent on tense. And it is typical of all formulaic beginnings of fairy tales that they are in the past, that is, one of our two main tense groups. This tense in the opening formula is a signal that says: the narrated world begins here. All the tenses of a fairy tale constantly echo this initial signal to remind us that we are in a different environment from daily reality with its constant demands.[29]

After the signal, "Once upon a time," only the fairytale world exists, and anyone who has ever told children fairy tales knows how much children can lose themselves in the story. Indeed, here they are just learning, precisely through the fairy tale, that a narrated world exists at all beyond their own little world of experience. They learn that from many tales. As long as they cannot distinguish confidently between the narrated world and the "real" world, it is important to lead them back out of the narrated world with clear and dependable signs. Hence the end of a fairy tale is as formulaic as its beginning. In Germany, at least in northern Germany, there is an especially popular closing formula: "Und wenn sie nicht gestorben sind, so leben sie noch heute" (And if they haven't died, then they are still alive). If they are still alive, then we might encounter figures from the fairytale world instead of just hearing about them. So we need to look at what goes on around us and keep our eyes open. This is just what the tenses signal. In this closing formula the narrative tenses are abandoned and those of the world of discussion, mostly perfect and present, take their place. For these are the tenses in which the "real" world makes its claims. And these are the tenses with which the child must respond to its small claims.

What kind of claims? In the case of fairy tales for children it is not unusual for it to be the demand to hurry up and finish eating. Many closing formulae, especially on the Iberian peninsula, lead the fairy tale to the

---

28. Robert Petsch, *Wesen und Formen der Erzählkunst* (Halle [Saale]: Niemeyer, 1942), 165.

29. Already observed by Petsch, *Wesen*, 162; also by Tom A. Rompelman, "Form und Funktion des Präteritums im Germanischen," *Neophilologus* 37, no. 2 (1953): 82.

table. Here is a Portugese conclusion from the substantial collection of Robert Petsch: "Está a minha historia acabada, / minha bocca cheia de marmelada" (My story is over, / my mouth full of jam).[30] The motif appears in Spanish tales as well. This ending maintains the narrative tense but leads to the table with a gay nonsense rhyme:

> Y vivieron felices
> Y comieron perdices
> y a mí no dieron
> porque no quisieron.[31]

> And they lived happily
> and they ate partridges
> and didn't give me any
> because they didn't want to.

This conclusion does not belong to a particular tale but can be added to any one at will. It signals the boundary between the fairytale world and the world of discussion. For the food must now be addressed. Different countries have different closing formulae. Petsch's collection offers a good overview of the possibilities. All have in common that they mark the boundary of the narrative world very clearly. It can be completely unpretentious in a formula like, "The story's over," or, "That's all I know" or, "That's all, folks." Whatever the details, it will use the discussing tenses. The fairytale world is no longer seen from within, but from outside. The narrator steps out of his role and becomes the father who has things to do, or the uncle who is about to leave.

Petsch points out that many fairy tales are named in the conclusion or at least labeled as fairy tales. That, too, is a sign of a situation of discussion. The closing formula often takes a position on the truth value of the tale. The narrator admits to lying, or he insists on his veracity, or with a wink he leaves the question unsettled. This kind of ending also clearly marks the boundary between the narrative and the world of discussion, for the story is subjected, if I may use the expression, to a historical critique, that is, the fairy tale is discussed. The Grimm brothers love the closing formula, "Wer's nicht glaubt, zahlt einen Taler" (anyone who doesn't believe it owes me a dollar). It is a very typical boundary signal because it takes a position on the truth status, uses the discussing tenses, and makes the transition to a situation in which roast pigeons don't simply fly into our mouths, but have to be paid for.

---

30. Robert Petsch, *Formelhafte Schlüsse im Volksmärchen* (Berlin: Weidmann, 1900), 61 ff.

31. I owe this example to Manuela Manzanares Cirre.

In the correspondence of the Grimm brothers there is a report of a little girl who did not want to believe one of their stories and brought them a dollar.[32]

Tense in the Language of Children

Of course fairy tales are not just for children. But they do play a larger role in the lives of children than of those who are essentially grown. For children become acquainted with the narrated world through fairy tales. There, children see for the first time that there is another world beside the one immediately around them in which they eat, sleep, play, and learn. From fairy tales children learn to take an interest in a world beyond their own lives. In this way, fairy tales begin a course of instruction that will later be continued by the whole range of narrative literature. This is important instruction because it teaches them freedom. In fairy tales, children learn to free themselves from their immediate needs and to focus for a while on something other than themselves. For a while the prince or the poor miller's son drives the child's own surroundings from the center of interest. It is, instinctively, a good pedagogical principle to begin this instruction with fairy tales because the fairytale world is as different as possible from the everyday world. People learn more readily from extreme contrasts than from nuances. We all know how difficult it still is to accustom children to the existence of a fictional world. As with a puppet show, they mistake stories at first for the real world and try to enter into them. When Don Quixote does the same, he acts like a child (*Don Quixote*, 2.26). But that is not the point of the education about a narrative world. Children should, and eventually do, learn to take interest in a world beyond their own control. They thus learn to extend the circle of their sympathy beyond their immediate needs. The tenses have an important role to play in that process. To the extent that they consider tenses, studies of children's language acquisition have already demonstrated that the tenses are acquired in a particular order that is fairly constant over different languages, even though many psychologists consider the tenses as forms of time rather than in terms of the system presented here.

The French psychologists Decroly and Degand record that past events are expressed by the passé composé for the native French-speaking child

---

32. Wilhelm Grimm and Alexander Grimm, *Freundesbriefe*, ed. Alexander Reifferscheid (Heilbronn: Henninger, 1878), 189–90; cited by Petsch, *Formelhafte Schlüsse*, 66, note 37. On the general issues of children's language see Roman Jakobson, *Child Language, Aphasia, and Phonological Universals*, trans. Allan R. Keiler (The Hague: Mouton, 1968). The book's comprehensive bibliography extends only to 1944; for more recent research consult Hermann Helmers, ed., *Zur Sprache des Kindes* (Darmstadt: Wissenschaftliche Buchgesellschaft, 1969).

they observed at the age of two years and three months.[33] Only at two years and nine months does the imparfait appear, and then only in isolated cases. More precise and detailed observations are reported by the psychologists Clara and Wilhelm Stern of their two children learning German as their first language. According to their records, their daughter expresses the past events starting at age two with the perfect participle by itself, then by the Perfekt.[34] Only the Präteritum *war* (was) appears at this time, with others appearing at age three. Only at the age of three and a half can the Präteritum be counted among her firm linguistic skills. The boy's development is the same, though with a slight delay. He masters the perfect participle at age two and uses the Präteritum with some frequency only at age four. Both tenses—Perfekt and Präteritum—stand here as representatives of their particular tense groups, for it is obvious that the children master present before Perfekt, while the Plusquamperfekt takes even longer than the Präteritum. In summary, we may say that the acquisition of tense group I takes place in the third year of life, but that of group II only beginning in the fifth year. The isolated Präteritum form *war* (was), apparent already in the third year, can be skipped. Until the entire tense is present, the appearance of the form *war* means little for the tense system. It is only a variant of the form *gewesenist* (been), about which it would be interesting to know if it actually continues to appear next to *war*. If not, the form *war* would actually have to be interpreted, regardless of its external form, as Perfekt until we truly had both tenses of the same verb next to each other.

The fourth and fifth years, when children are discovering the narrative tenses, are now actually the times when they enjoy fairy tales the most. The two hang together; children learn the tense of the narrated world from narratives, especially from fairy tales, and also learn the differentness of the narrated world with the aid of tenses. For the transitional period when the world of discussion and the world of narrative are not clearly distinguished in a child's consciousness, they typically try to tell fairy tales with the tenses of group I. Children do that when they try to tell a story by themselves for the first time, and adults do it when they mean to speak like a child who has not yet mastered the narrative tenses. That makes the fairy tale sound very childlike. One can experiment by telling one of the Grimms' fairy tales, which are all transmitted in the narrative tenses, in the Perfekt. The begin-

33. Jean-Ovide Decroly and Julia Degand, "Observations relatives au développement de la notion du temps chez une petite fille," *Archives de psychologie* 13 (1913): 128, 155–61; see also Jean Piaget, *The Child's Conception of Time*, trans. Arnold Julius Pomerans (London: Routledge, 2007).

34. Clara and Wilhelm Stern, *Die Kindersprache* (Leipzig: Barth, 1928), see esp. 53, 65, 75, 102, 253.

ning of the tale "Der süße Brei" (Sweet Porridge, or The Magic Porridge Pot) would then read: "Es ist einmal ein armes, frommes Mädchen gewesen, das hat mit seiner Mutter allein gelebt, und sie haben nichts mehr zu essen gehabt. Da ist das Mädchen hinaus in den Wald gegangen, und ist ihm da eine alte Frau begegnet" (Once upon a time there has been a poor, pious girl, who has lived alone with her mother, and they have had nothing left to eat. So the girl has gone out into the forest and has encountered an old woman). Later I shall examine more carefully what changes when the tenses are exchanged. For the moment it suffices to note not just that one tense referring to the past has been substituted for another, but that a tense of discussion has replaced one of narrative. That has consequences for the whole story. J.M. Buffin and Jean Perrot have made similar observations for French.[35] They attempt to retell the tale of Little Red Ridinghood in the passé composé and reach the conclusion: the transformation does violence to the story. Yet it must be emphasized that however much this kind of narrating runs against the grain of normal style, it still exists under certain conditions (Chapter 9). We find it especially in the developmental phase in which a child has not yet fully achieved consciousness of the differentness of the narrated world.

Since I have no corpus of children's language of my own, I shall settle for these few suggestions and refer to various studies by Dietrich Pregel of a comprehensive corpus of oral and written text by children of various ages. Here from his corpus is the taped oral "funny story" told by a girl seven years and seven months old:

> Ich war mal im Zirkus, und da habe ich den Clown gesehen. Und da hat er mit so'n Bällen gespielt. Und der eine ist 'runtergefallen von der Hand, und da hat er sich draufgesetzt. Und da hat er geschrien, und da haben se alle gelacht. Und da hat er sich noch so'n großen Baumstamm genommen, und da hat er sich draufgesetzt. Da wollte er Handstand drauf machen. Und da ist er umgekippt. Und da ist er gleich im Purzelbaum gleich hinter den Vorhang gefallen.[36]

> Once I was at the circus, and then I have seen the clown. And then he has played with a sort of ball. And one has fallen down from his hand, and then he has sat down on it. And then he has screamed, and then everyone has laughed. And then he has taken a sort of big stick, and then he has sat on it. Then he wanted to do a handstand. And

---

35. J.-M. Buffin, *Remarques sur les moyens d'expression de la durée* (Paris: Presses Universitaires de France, 1925), 151, and Jean Perrot, "Autour des passés: Réflexions sur les systèmes verbaux du latin et du français," *Revue des langues romanes* 72 (1956): 164–65.

36. Dietrich Pregel, *Zum Sprachstil des Grundschulkindes: Studien zum Gebrauch des Adjektivs und zur Typologie der Stilalter* (Düsseldorf: Schwann, 1970), 174.

then he has fallen over. And then right in his somersault he has fallen right behind the curtain.

The syntax of this story can be analyzed from various points of view, as Pregel has demonstrated. Here I restrict myself to the simple observation that the child only has access to the Perfekt, except for the forms *war* (was) and *wollte* (wanted).

A further transcript from the same corpus reveals the penetration of isolated Präteritum forms. Here a boy seven years, ten months old tells about an accident:

> Bei meinem Vater, da arbeitet auch noch Herr Schilling. Und der wollte in die Einfahrt 'reinfahren, und hinter dem kam ein Lastwagen. Und der drin saß im Lastwagen, der war besoffen. Und der ist dem hinten 'reingefahren. Und der hat den Vorderwagen geschoben, daß Herr Schilling in den Graben 'reingefahren ist. Und den Mann da, den haben se dann mitgenommen. (Pregel, 175)

> At my father's, Mr. Schilling works there, too. And he wanted to drive into the driveway, and a truck came up behind him. And the guy who sat in the truck, he was drunk. And he has banged into him from behind. And he has shoved the car in front, so that Mr. Schilling has driven into the ditch. And that guy, they have arrested him.

In the center of the story are the four forms in Präteritum, *wollte* (wanted), *kam* (came), *saß* (sat), *war* (was); the frame is constructed from tenses of discussion.

A third story from the same corpus, finally, displays according to Pregel a form of childish narrative that is almost stylized in literary terms. The topic is "a funny story," and the narrator is a girl of nine years, nine months:

> Als mein Opa Geburtstag hatte, tranken meine Eltern Likör. Mein Vati meinte, daß ich auch einmal etwas trinken könnte, und er schenkte mir ein halbes Glas ein. Es schmeckte gar nicht so schlecht, und ich trank es ganz aus. Meine Oma hatte natürlich Angst, daß ich einen Riesenschwips bekam. Aber es war gar nicht so schlimm. Schließlich kicherte ich laut und lief in der Gegend herum und prallte gegen meine Mutter. "Um Himmels willen," sagte meine Oma, "das Kind hat ja einen Rausch." Es war schon so spät, und der Papi sagte: "Ja, jetzt fahren wir heim, da kann Gabi gleich ins Bett gehen." Dann, ich konnte schon gar nicht mehr gescheit gehen, meine Mutti mußte mich halten und ins Auto tragen. Da hinten lag ich dann und sah alles von unten nach oben. Immer wieder kicherte ich, und meine

Mutti sagte: "Die hat es stark erwischt." Als wir dann zu Hause waren, wurde ich sofort ins Bett gepackt. Doch eine ganze Weile kicherte ich und lachte. Meine Mutti meinte schon, daß ich schliefe, aber ich schlief doch noch nicht. Am andern Morgen war mein Schwipsen schon wieder weg, und ich war wieder ganz normal. (Pregel, 201–2)

When it was my grandpa's birthday my parents drank liquor. My dad thought that I could also have a drink for once, and he poured me half a glass. It didn't taste so bad at all, and I drank the whole thing. My granny was naturally afraid that I got really tipsy. But it really wasn't so bad. Finally I giggled loudly and ran around and crashed into my mother. "For heaven's sake," my granny said, "the child is drunk." It was already very late, and papa said: "Yes, now we'll go home, and then Gabi can go right to bed." Then, I couldn't walk right anymore, my mom had to hold me and carry me into the car. There I lay in the back seat then and saw everything upside down. I kept giggling, and my mom said, "It really took her hard." When we got home, I was put to bed immediately. But I giggled for a long time and laughed. My mom thought I was already asleep, but I really wasn't. The next day my tipsiness was already gone, and I was completely normal again.

In his nuanced evaluation of the results, which I render here only sketchily, Pregel concludes that the linguistic development of elementary school children can be divided into two phases. The first phase covers approximately the period between six and a half or seven to eight and a half. The second phase begins on average around the middle or end of the ninth year and lasts till the end of elementary school. In the first phase the child gradually learns to use the Präteritum in oral narratives. In the second phase Pregel notes a clearly increasing use of Präteritum in oral and written narrative, "and thereby the beginning of actual narrative." Pregel's observations are more differentiated in detail than they could be presented here, and there will be opportunity to return to these questions below (Chapter 9). For the moment it suffices that the acquisition of the narrative tenses and, in tandem with it, the acquisition of narrative as a mode of presentation as such, characterizes a significant phase in child development per se and very clearly reveals how children break out of the narrow sphere of experience of their first years and take possession of the "world."[37]

37. On the topic of children's language in Italian see Harro Stammerjohann, "Strukturen der Rede: Beobachtungen an der Umgangssprache von Florenz," *Studi di filologia italiana* 28 (1970): 295–397; for French see Janine Leclercq et al., *Enquête sur le langage de l'enfant français*, Centre de recherche et d'étude pour la diffusion du français (CREDIF), mimeograph.

3 / Perspective

Time in Texts

It is said of Protagoras the Abderite that he "was first to divide time into parts," and indeed into the three "stages of time," past, present, and future. Protagoras seems to have been following Homer, whose seer Calchas foretells "what is past, what is, and what shall come" (*Iliad* 1.70). Plato then contrasts the trinity of time to the unity of being (*Timaeus* 37d–38b). Dionysius Thrax makes the three stages of time (*chronoi*) into the basis for systematizing verb tense that became the rule also for Latin grammar. Quintilian (5.10.71) likewise makes his conception clear that the three stages of grammar represent three objective temporal stages of the order of the world: "Ut sunt autem tria tempora, ita ordo rerum tribus momentis consertus est: habent enim omnia initium, incrementum, summam" (400–3; Just as there are three divisions of time, so the order of events is made up of three stages. For everything has a beginning, a development, and a culmination). For Augustine (*Confessions* 11.17) that is now accepted doctrine: "Tria tempora, sicut pueri didicimus puerosque docuimus, praeteritum, praesens, et futurum" (three times [as we learned when we were children and then taught our children]—past, present, and future).[1] His philosophical-theological critique leaves the

---

1. Diogenes Laertius. *De clarorum philosophorum vitis, dogmatibus et apophthegmatibus libri decem* 9.8.3, ed. Anton Westermann, et al. (Paris: Firmin-Didot, 1878) 240; Dionysos Thrax *Ars grammatica*, ed. Gustav Uhlig (Leipzig: Teubner, 1883), 53; Quintilian, *Institutio Oratoria*, ed. and trans. Donald A. Russell, 4 vols (Cambridge:

tenses of language untouched, but does correct the doctrine of the three stages of time in that they exist for us only insofar as we have them present in our mind. So they ought be called: "Praesens de praeteritis, praesens de praesentibus, praesens de futuris" (*Confessions* 11.20; the presence of things past, the presence of things present, the presence of things future, 2:230–31).

With so many authorities from antiquity and post-antiquity the survival of the three stages of time into modern times was guaranteed. The stanza that opens Schiller's "Sprüche des Konfuzius" (1795, Sayings of Confucius) is a famous example:

Dreifach ist der Schritt der Zeit:
Zögernd kommt die Zukunft hergezogen,
Pfeilschnell ist das Jetzt entflogen,
Ewig still steht die Vergangenheit.[2]
(The pace of time is threefold:/ The future comes hesitantly,/ The present is gone like an arrow,/ The past stands still forever.)

The three stages appear here as a doctrine of knowledge that remains a constant in thinking about time. In Louis Aragon the three stages appear yet again as a proverb:

Le temps ce miroir à trois faces.
Avec ses volets rabattus
Futur et passé qui s'effacent
J'y vois le présent qui me tue.[3]
(Time, a mirror with three panels./ With its wings folded back/ Future and past that are effaced/ I see the present, which kills me.)

Voltaire already notes the trivialization of this doctrine when he writes in his *Dictionnaire philosophique*: "Les Lapons, les nègres, aussi bien que les Grecs, ont eu besoin d'exprimer le passé, le présent, le futur, et ils l'ont fait"

Harvard UP, 2002), 400–3; Augustine of Hippo, *Confessions*, vol. 2, ed. and trans. Carolyn J.-B. Hammond (Cambridge: Harvard UP, 2014), DOI: 10.4159/DLCL. augustine-confessions_2014.2014, 224–25. On Dionysius see Eduard Schwyzer, *Griechische Grammatik*, vol. 2: *Syntax und syntaktische Stilistik*, ed. Albert Debrunner (Munich: Beck, 1950), 248–49; on Augustine see Heinrich Lausberg, *Handbuch der literarischen Rhetorik*, 2 vols. (Munich: Max Hueber, 1960) section 151, following Quintilian 7.2.1.

2. Friedrich Schiller. *Sämtliche Werke*, ed. Gerhard Fricke and Herbert G. Göpfert, 5 vols. (Munich: Hanser, 1960–62) 1:226.

3. Louis Aragon, *Le fou d'Elsa* (Paris: Gallimard, 1959), 104.

(The Lapps, the Negroes, and even the Greeks, needed to express the past, present, and future, and they did).[4]

Obviously a linguistic theory of tense cannot derive from any kind of *Ordo rerum*, hence the three temporal stages past, present, and future also cannot be considered indubitable givens. It makes more sense to take once again the process of communication as the basis for syntactical considerations. Thus far we have examined how the tenses signal register (discussing vs. narrating) along the speaker-listener axis. These signals regulate the attitudes of both speaker and listener toward the information transmitted. It is now necessary to address a different aspect of the tense system related to an axis along which an oral or written text moves. This is naturally a movement in time, for the mass of signs in a text is arranged in a linear chain of signs (ignoring, for now, discontinuous and supra-segmental signs). That is the "stream" of information, so that every linguistic sign in a text has a textual predecessor and successor, and its meaning is determined by previous and succeeding information. In general we can speak of textual time.

Understanding, however, is not a linear process but a complex one. In order to understand a sign in the chain precisely, the listener must constantly reach back to previous information or anticipate information to come. I have already pointed out how the article morphemes assist in this process and designate either previous information, coming information, or particular segments of both. In this sense article morphemes especially refer to textual time. They indicate further, for a given sign or reference point (*origo*), how to distinguish previous from succeeding information in textual time.

We encounter the two directions of textual time in the tense system as well. In addition to the registers, discussing and narrating, that regulate the attitude of speakers and listeners, the tense system has distinctions to enable orientation with regard to textual time. Indeed, they permit relatively free control over textual time either to bring information up to date or to anticipate it. Up-dating and anticipating refer to the relationship between textual time and event-time. The event-time is the moment or moments of the content of the communication (Wunderlich 31). The textual time and event-time can be one and the same. That is especially the case in performative language, i.e., when the text is itself an action (the famous example being the act of baptism

---

4. Voltaire, *Dictionnaire philosophique* (Paris: Desour, 1817), 1334. See also Léon Vernier, *Etude sur Voltaire grammairien et la grammaire au XVIIIe siècle* (Paris, Hachette, 1888), 42.

and the ritual language that shares in constituting the act). But textual time and event-time need not be synchronized; they can lie far apart. The time of an event can lie far behind the time of the text or can just as well be far ahead of it. In either case language can express this lack of synchronicity. That is the achievement of the tense system, and the tenses remain thereby in the general grammatical framework sketched above. By signaling either the synchronicity or non-synchronicity of textual time and event-time, tenses deliver to the listener important information about the process of communication and its relation to the "world."

Each of the two tense groups consists, namely, not of a single tense, but of several tenses. Here again are the most common tenses of the two groups:

Tenses of Discussion	Narrative Tenses
Perfect	Pluperfect
Present	Preterit
Future	Conditional

The different tenses in the two groups serve to express the relation between the textual time and the event-time. Both lists are to be understood as follows: For the (relatively most common) case, when the relation between textual time and event-time is not problematic or, more precisely, when the speaker does not wish to direct the listener's attention to a possible discrepancy in the relationship between the two kinds of time, then both the discussing and narrating tenses have a neutral setting. In the discussing tenses, present tense occupies the neutral position, and in the narrating tenses the preterit. Any text with these two tense forms simply leaves the relation between textual time and event-time open, without indicating whether they coincide or not. In this case the perspective is simply not of interest. The present and preterit are the neutral or unmarked tenses within their tense groups.

The other tenses of the two groups instruct the listener to pay attention to the relation between textual time and event-time. Among the discussing tenses the perfect is the tense of retrospection, of looking back. The future, by contrast, is that of looking ahead, of prospection. Its task is to anticipate events before they happen, and hence it also indicates that textual time and event-time are not synchronous. But when an event is anticipated before it happens, the information is of necessity uncertain. It has not yet been confirmed by the event, and it is never entirely certain that it ever actually will be. The prospection of this tense is necessarily a form of expectation.

The same structure is repeated in the narrative tense group. Textual time and event-time can also be unproblematic in narratives, or at least be imagined by narrator and listener or reader to be so. The textual time and the event-time can be synchronized by the fiction, if the narrator includes himself as party to the action (first-person narrative) or as witness (third-person narrative). In that case German uses the Präteritum as the neutral setting of narration. This tense is thus by far the most frequent tense in its group. But if—and that is part of the much discussed "freedom of the narrator" (see Chapter 1)—the relation between textual time and event-time is not to remain unnoticed, then the narrator might use the pluperfect for retrospection, or conditional for looking ahead. Conditional allows a not-yet-confirmed event to be anticipated or expected.

Retrospection and prospection, or, more precisely, updated information and anticipated information, are both to be understood as parts of linguistic perspective. Also part of linguistic perspective, however, is the neutral perspective, in both tense groups. In the majority of cases the speaker takes no advantage of the possibility of calling the listener's attention to a difference between textual time and event-time. Let me point here to the word counts already adduced, which suggest it is generally true that in each tense group the neutral tenses rarely average below 80%, and often above it.

The Future (Using French as an Example)

Grammars usually distinguish between a futur 1 or futur simple (*je ferai*: I shall do) and a futur 2 or futur antérieur (*j'aurai fait*: I will have done). I will maintain, as elsewhere, the nomenclature, but change the entire focus in terms of linguistic perspective. Both the futur 1 and the futur 2 are discussing tenses. Yet narration can also have a forward-looking perspective in the sense of anticipated information. That is achieved in French by the tense normally known as conditionnel (*je ferais*: I would do). It is distinguished as conditionnel 1 or conditionnel présent from conditionnel 2 or conditionnel passé (*j'aurais fait*: I would have done). Here is an obvious parallelism in the forms of language. The conditionnel (and all notions of conditionality should be suppressed here) achieves for narrating language the same thing that future does for discussing.

For a further analysis of future tense I have chosen two passages from the pen of General de Gaulle, from the first volume of his war memoirs. The first text is part of a speech delivered by de Gaulle in England in 1942.

Ah! certes, nous ne croyons pas que l'épreuve soit à son terme.
Nous savons tout ce qui reste de force et d'astuce à l'ennemi. Nous

n'ignorons pas quels délais sont encore nécessaires au parti de la liberté pour déployer toute sa puissance. Mais, puisque la France a fait entendre sa volonté de triompher, il n'y *aura* jamais pour nous ni doute, ni lassitude, ni renoncement. Unis pour combattre, nous *irons* jusqu'au bout de la libération nationale. Alors, notre tâche finie, notre rôle effacé, après tous ceux qui l'ont servie depuis l'aurore de son Histoire, avant tous ceux qui la *serviront* dans son éternel avenir, nous *dirons* à la France, simplement, comme Péguy: "Mère, voici vos fils, qui se sont tant battus!"[5]

Ah! certainly we do not believe that the ordeal is at an end. We know how powerful and how shrewd the enemy remains. We are well aware of the time that the party of freedom still needs to deploy its full powers. But, since France has declared its will to triumph, there will never be any doubt for us, nor weariness, nor renunciation. United in the fight, we will achieve the goal of national liberation. Then, with our task over, our role forgotten, after all those who have served since the dawn of history, before all those who will serve in its eternal future, we will say to France, simply, like Péguy: "Mother, here are your sons, who have fought so hard!"

The first sentences of the passage refer to the situation of France in 1942. There follows then a look back to the declaration of resistance of 1940. Of course, the declaration is familiar to his listeners ("the French of Great Britain"). Even so, in the mouth of de Gaulle it is an up-dating in the sense of an obvious ("puisque") confirmation and reaffirmation. There follow then sentences in futur until the Péguy quotation. These sentences contain a prospective look at a still-open future. We understand them as anticipated information, since the news of the *Libération* of the year 1944 has not yet been delivered in 1942.

The next text is also from de Gaulle's war memoirs and refers to the year 1940:

Poursuivre la guerre? Oui, certes! Mais pour quel but et dans quelles limites? Beaucoup, lors même qu'ils approuvaient l'entreprise, ne voulaient pas quelle fût autre chose qu'un concours donné, par une poignée de Français, à l'Empire brittanique démeuré debout et en ligne. Pas un instant, je n'envisageai la tentative sur ce plan-là. Pour moi ce qu'il s'agissait de servir et de sauver, c'était la nation et l'Etat.

5. Charles de Gaulle, *Mémoires de guerre*, vol. 1: *L'Appel* (Paris: Edito-Service, 1971), 300.

66 / PERSPECTIVE

> Je pensais en effet que c'en *serait fini* de l'honneur, de l'unité, de l'indépendance, s'il devait être entendu que, dans cette guerre mondiale, seule la France *aurait capitulé* et qu'elle en *serait restée* là. Car, dans ce cas, quelle que dût être l'issue du conflit, que le pays, decidément vaincu, fût un jour débarrassé de l'envahisseur par les armes étrangères ou qu'il demeurât asservi, le dégoût qu'il *aurait* de lui-même et celui qu'il *inspirerait* aux autres *empoisonnerait* son âme et sa vie pour de longues générations. (71)

Pursue the war? Yes, of course! But to what end and in what limits? Many, even when they approved the enterprise, did not want to it be more than aid given by a handful of French to the British Empire that remained standing and on duty. Not for an instant did I envisage the attempt on that basis. For me, what we were there to serve and to save was the nation and the State.

I thought indeed that honor, unity, independence would all be at an end if it were to be understood that in this world war only France would have capitulated and that would have been that. For, in this case, whatever the outcome of the conflict might be, whether the country, definitely beaten, might one day have been liberated from the invader by foreign arms or whether it remained enslaved, the disgust that it would feel for itself and that it would inspire in others would poison its soul and its life for many generations.

In this text, the opening of the chapter "La France libre," de Gaulle recounts the thinking that moved him to continue the war. The introductory sentences are in imparfait and passé simple. In the following sentences, which continue de Gaulle's thoughts on the topic, the general looks ahead into the future to take account of the possible consequences of his decisions for the national consciousness of the post-war generation. Here is now the conditionnel, both conditionnel 1 and 2. I understand these two tenses as forms of the narrating future. Within tense group 2 they have the function of signalizing the linguistic perspective of anticipated information. I have chosen the two passages to eliminate any possible doubt of the temporal relationships. The first text, cited literally in the version of the year 1942, reaches ahead, as we now know, to the year 1944, and the second text, narrating thoughts of 1940, looks ahead to the years after 1944 as de Gaulle would like to imagine them. So should we characterize the future, both discursive and narrative forms, as tense forms of future time? Are tenses really "time-forms"?

But what happens to time in fictional texts? To answer this question I will consider a third text, La Fontaine's fable, "Les deux aventuriers et le talisman" (10.14; The Two Adventurers and the Talisman).[6] This fable is a fiction. It deals with two travelers. They encounter a shield by the side of the road upon which a prophecy is written that the traveler who carries a stone elephant in his arms to the top of a high mountain will experience "what no other knight errant has ever seen." The inscription turns back, within the fictional space of the fable, to information about the knights ("ce que n'a vu nul chevalier errant") and at the same time anticipates information about the course of the adventure (that he will cross a river, find a stone elephant, etc.). Thus far, concepts of time like past and future—fictional of course—can fit our understanding of the text.

The fable proceeds, however, with both wanderers thinking about the meaning of the inscription and the chances for success. One of the two (the "raisonneur" [rationalist]) has considerable doubts and he argues:

> Quelle ridicule entreprise!
> Le sage l'*aura fait* par tel art et de guise,
> Qu'on le *pourra* porter peut-être quatre pas;
> Mais jusqu'en haut du mont! d'une haleine! il n'est pas
> Au pouvoir d'un mortel; à moins que la figure
> Ne soit d'un éléphant nain, pygmée et avorton,
>   Propre à mettre au bout d'un bâton:
> Auquel cas, où l'honneur d'une telle aventure?
> On nous veut attraper dedans cette écriture:
> Ce *sera* quelque énigme à tromper un enfant.
> C'est pourquoi je vous laisse avec votre éléphant.

> What a foolish enterprise! The sage will have made it in such a manner that it can perhaps be carried four steps; but to the top of the mountain! at one stroke! that is not in mortal power, unless the image be of a miniature elephant, a pygmy and a runt, good for putting at the tip of a staff: in which case, where is the honor of such an adventure? Someone is out to trap us with this scripture: it will be some sort of enigma to fool a child. That is why I leave you with your elephant.

Thus speaks the hesitant knight. Yet the other wanderer, the adventurer, picks up the elephant without much thought and, having arrived at the summit, learns that the prophecy was in fact no deception and that he has won a kingdom.

6. Jean de La Fontaine, *Fables*, ed. É. Geruzez (Paris: Hachette, 1893), 326.

Now for the tenses. In this context, the interest lies in the futur 1 (*pourra porter, sera*) and futur 2 (*aura fait*) in the passage quoted. This speech consists entirely of conjectures about the intentions of the unknown author of the inscription toward its possible errant readers. Only one of the future forms (*qu'on le pourra porter peut-être quatre pas*) actually refers to a future that seems possible to the hesitant knight, and even that does not come to pass. The other two forms refer explicitly to the present of the shield (*ce sera quelque énigme*) or to the past (*le sage l'aura fait*).

How simple is the triad past-present-future, and how complicated does it all become when one tries to make it agree with the tense structure of a given language! All sorts of work-arounds suddenly become necessary, such as distinguishing between a real and an only possible future, or—in technical language—between a pure and a "modal" future. I will avoid these distinctions in tense theory and describe the communicative value of future forms without an absolute concept of future in the temporal sense. "Anticipated information" means only that the information is delivered prematurely in relation to the time of the event. It may be that this prematurity is to be explained by the fact that the event has not yet taken place, or because the event has already taken place but is not yet known, or is only just now occurring; until the case is confirmed we are dealing with anticipated information that remains to some extent uncertain, even if additional information provided later should reveal the correctness of the report.[7]

Languages vary in their use of the inherent capacity of the tense system to signal anticipated information. It is said that German scarcely uses the Futur any more, at most only as a "modal": Das *wird* auch wohl so sein—that will probably be so (i.e.= that is probably so).[8] Though, of course, in the theory of tense I argue for, there is no longer a distinction between a future-time future and a modal future, so that even in German Futur 1 and Futur 2 are completely valid tenses, as are likewise Konditional 1 and 2. The fact that German speakers use temporal adverbs with the present tense to indicate future time more frequently

---

7. Hermann Gelhaus describes the function of the future in modern German similarly as "a foretelling in the broadest sense that can refer to both present and future events": "Das Futur der deutschen Gegenwartssprache," *Forschungsberichte des Instituts für deutsche Sprache* 1 (1968): 19.

8. According to Gelhaus's counts (19) Futur 1 and Futur 2 account together for less than one percent of finite verbs in contemporary spoken German. In newspapers, however, he finds that the frequency can rise as high as five percent.

than speakers of other languages is irrelevant here. So far as the tense system is concerned, the future tense by itself achieves only a coarse preliminary sorting of the world, namely, in that the event reported is connected to the process of reporting. But tenses are not the only linguistic signs. Other signs are available for further, more precise information for the finer sorting of the world when desired. There are many ways to express time, including future time. There are numbers and dates in endless series, and no prophet or futurologist has ever complained of being unable to represent future events in language with all possible precision.

The Perfekt in German

Most of the European languages have a tense for catching up on information from the past. In many languages this tense is called the perfect. That is the most inappropriate name imaginable for it. After all, when a past event is discussed rather than narrated, then it is hardly finished (*per-fectum*). It is, rather, something that belongs to my world as much as things present or lying in the future that I discuss, because I have to deal with it. It is a past which I shape, because I form it with the same words with which I make things happen. And as I shape the past in discussion, I change my present and my future at the same time—an important activity and far removed from the relaxed serenity of narrators who let their worlds be.

Even if the term "perfect" is inappropriate for the backward-looking tense of the world of discussion, I shall still use it. It is not dangerous, as long as we follow the rule never to explain a tense from its common name. Otherwise we suffer the fate of Otto Behaghel, who defines the German Perfekt twice in his book on German syntax, once as the tense for a completed occurrence, and once as the tense for an uncompleted occurrence that continues into the present.[9] It would be equally possible to say that it is completely irrelevant where and when an occurrence ends. The characteristic "continuing into the future" is commonly encountered but entirely inappropriate as a description of the fact that we discuss past events with the perfect—that is, that we open them up for their application to our conduct rather than narrating them and thereby closing them off from our consideration.

9. Otto Behaghel, *Deutsche Syntax: Eine geschichtliche Darstellung*, vol. 2 (Heidelberg: Winter, 1924), 291, 294.

Other scholars have had less Latin in their ears and therefore looked more carefully. Wunderlich and Reis associate an "interior possession" with the German Perfekt. Hans Weber writes:

> Die Perfekt-Schau ist nicht rein passiv; denn das Subjekt zieht die Vergangenheit an sich heran; sie ist somit Ausdruck einer wertenden, urteilenden Stellungnahme zum vergangenen Geschehnis, das Perfekt ist das Tempus der subjektiven Feststellung oder Meinungsäußerung.

(The perfect view is not purely passive; the subject draws the past up to itself so that the perfect becomes the expression of an evaluative, judging stance toward past events, the perfect is the tense of subjective determination or expression of opinion.)

He observes further that the perfect is often found in conversation and that it "positively attracts" certain adverbs like *schon* (already) and *noch* (still). Kaj B. Lindgren, finally, identifies a certain "Ich-Bezogenheit" (subjective focus) in the German perfect and confirms that with the opinions of German native speakers.[10] All these observations are accurate and point to the fact that the past is not narrated but is discussed with this tense. We could also say that the past in the perfect tense appears not as perfectum, but as imperfectum. (In the Imperfekt [another name for German Präteritum] the past appears as perfect.) That does not make it absolutely necessary that the action expressed in the verb itself continue into the present. It can be completely over as an action, so long as I open it up in discussion.

The function of the Perfekt in German is best understood in comparison to the function of the Präteritum. I will consider the Präteritum in a "true story" and not in a fiction, so that the event lies in the past in both cases. I request the reader's attention for a passage of historical writing about past reality. Historians have, now, the same ambiguous relation to the past that all of us share, but more so if they are conscious of their

---

10. Hermann Wunderlich and Hans Reis, *Der deutsche Satzbau* (Stuttgart: Cotta, 1924) 1:263; Hans Weber, *Das Tempussystem des Deutschen und des Französischen* (Bern: Francke, 1954), 98, 100, 165. Kaj B. Lindgren. *Über den oberdeutschen Präteritumschwund* (Helsinki: Acta Academiae Scientiarum Fennica, 1957), 40. Lindgren sees correctly that the German Präteritum is a narrative tense and that Perfekt is not. See also the nice observations in Jost Trier, "Stilistische Fragen der deutschen Gebrauchsprosa—Perfekt und Imperfekt," in *Germanistik in Forschung und Lehre: Vorträge und Diskussionen des Germanistentages in Essen vom 21.–25. Oktober 1964*, ed. Rudolf Henss and Hugo Moser (Berlin: Schmidt, 1964), 195–208, as well as Sigbert Latzel, "Zur Tempus-Theorie von Harald Weinrich," *Literaturwissenschaftliches Jahrbuch* n.F. 10 (1969): 377 ff.

role. On the one hand, they are narrators of the past, indeed storytellers. A poor storyteller is a poor historian. But historians are also scholars. They do not stop at retelling the past, but they also seek to understand, explain, interpret, teach it, or whatever. In a word, they want to discuss the past. All historical writing has this doubleness, that it simultaneously narrates and discusses. And so it uses the tenses of both tense groups, and the better the historian's historical consciousness, the more consistently it does so.

The tenses of the text reveal the historian's consciousness. I shall demonstrate it in a passage by the historian Golo Mann from his essay "Staat und Heer" (State and Army, 1956). The passage is a small historical sketch about the German Reichswehr after 1933. It is set off by paragraphing in the original publication. I emphasize the tenses of discussion with italics:

Nach dem Umsturz von 1933 *hat* General von Blomberg sich *gerühmt*, das sei es nun, worauf die Reichswehr immer hinausgewollt und, in aller Verschwiegenheit, planmäßig hingearbeitet habe. Man *hat* es ihm damals wohl *geglaubt*, auch außerhalb Deutschlands. Es war aber hauptsächlich Prahlerei. Der Minister machte die Reichswehr viel böser, viel konsequenter und voraussehender, als sie gewesen war. . . . Wäre der Weimarer Staat an sich etwas Rechtes gewesen, dann hätte die Armee ihm keinen Schaden getan. Nicht sie *hat* zu den zentralen Kräften—mangelnden Kräften, Nicht-Kräften—*gehört*, welche ihn *ruiniert haben*. Ein Fremdkörper war sie. Aber die Republik bestand ja nur aus Fremdkörpern. Sie hatte keine Identität mit sich selber. Fast niemand glaubte an sie; von den großen Parteien nur die Sozialdemokraten, und so ganz fest auch die nicht, denn sie hatten sie ja ursprünglich nicht gewollt, waren widerwillig in das revolutionäre Abenteuer gerissen worden und mehr darauf bedacht, sich dafür zu entschuldigen, als es schöpferisch zu gestalten. Die anderen hatten weder Glauben noch Willen zur Sache. Sie schielten, auch wenn sie im Sattel saßen, immer nach besseren Pferden herum, sie wußten selbst nicht genau, welchen. Sie regierten ein Provisorium, eine Verlegenheit; ein, das nur hielt, weil es nicht wußte, nach welcher Seite es umfallen sollte. *Kann* man sich wundern, daß im Staat, der die rechte Haltung zu sich selber niemals fand, auch die mit der schwersten Aufgabe einer neuen Traditionsbildung belastete Armee die rechte Haltung zum Staat nicht fand? Wäre sie gutwilliger gewesen, als sie war—und zeitweise in Männern wie Reinhardt, Groener, Heye war sie ja gutwillig—, hätte sie die rechte Haltung doch nicht finden können. In das, was selber niemals integriert war, konnte sich die Armee beim besten Willen nicht integrieren.[11]

After the coup of 1933, General von Blomberg boasted that that was the result always desired by the army and always pursued in secret. He was probably taken seriously, even outside of Germany. But it was mostly showing off. The minister made the army much more malicious, more consistent and far-sighted than it had been. . . . Had the Weimar Republic been well-built, then the army would have done it no damage. It was no part of the central powers—inadequate powers, non-powers—that ruined the republic. It was an alien body. But the republic consisted only of alien bodies. It had no identity of its own. Scarcely anyone had faith in it; of the large parties only the Social Democrats, and even they hadn't much; for they had originally been opposed, were drawn into the revolutionary adventure against their will, and were more eager to apologize than to shape it creatively. The others all had neither faith nor will for the project. Even when they were in the saddle they were constantly looking around for better horses, without themselves knowing just which. They ruled a makeshift, an embarrassment, a house that stood only because it had no idea in which direction to collapse. Can it surprise anyone that, in a state that never achieved a proper relation to itself, the army, which bore the heaviest burden of developing new traditions, likewise was unable to connect to the state? Had it been more well-meaning than it was—and at times with men like Reinhardt, Groener, Heye it was well-meaning—it still could never have found the right relation. With the best will in the world the army could not integrate into an entity that itself was never integrated.

The next paragraph begins again with a present tense to judge the behavior of General von Seeckt, that is, to discuss it. This new start in a discursive tense is also the concluding sentence for the brief paragraph that is inserted here. Thus we can read it as a historical narration introduced and concluded and occasionally interrupted with discussion of what has been narrated. *Geschichte und Geschichten* (1961, History and Histories), the title of Golo Mann's collection of historical essays, characterizes with precision the double face of history as a discipline that tells histories and also discusses them.

---

11. Golo Mann, *Geschichte und Geschichten* (Frankfurt/Main: Fischer, 1962), 249–50.

More or less regular alternation between discussing and narrating segments is not always to be found in historical presentations. There is plenty of room left for the historian's personal style. In general, however, historical writing reveals a basic structure of narration embedded in discussion. Literary scholarship also has a name for this phenomenon, namely, frame-narrative. A frame of discussion surrounds the narrative. It depends on the temperament of the historian, whether the framework of scholarly questioning and problematizing is filled up with an entire book of narrative, or whether the frame is repeatedly invoked, so that discussion accompanies the narrative step by step. Historians can also structure their work as representations of an epoch. These are variations, not mutations of the basic structure.

The structure of frame-narrative does not occur only in historical writing. As we know, it is characteristic of older narrative literatures, especially in the smaller genres (see Chapter 5), but it is also found outside of literature wherever narratives are set into a general situation of discussion, even—indeed especially—in oral communication. To the extent that a past event is narrated, the retrospective tense—perfect—forms an especially appropriate introduction. It belongs to the tenses of discussion and can, as a retrospective tense, refer to things past. Kaj B. Lindgren has investigated this experimentally by having several German speakers tell him a story of their choice. (I assume he meant true stories.) In the process, he observed that most of the subjects begin in the Perfekt and then switch over to the Präteritum with the actual story (*Über den oberdeutschen Präteritumschwund*, 40). That is a frame-narrative *in nuce*. Lindgren does not report on the return to a discussion situation.

We can find "more natural" situations in literature. The beginning and end of Goethe's *Werther* (The Sorrows of Young Werther), which at least in its epilogue is narration, have often been noticed.[12] The opening frame reads: "Was ich von der Geschichte des armen Werther nur habe auffinden können, habe ich mit Fleiß gesammelt und lege es euch hier vor" (7; I have diligently collected everything I have been able to find of the story of poor Werther and offer it to you here). The famous last sentences read: "Der Alte folgte der Leiche und die Söhne. Albert vermocht's nicht. Man fürchtete für Lottens Leben. Handwerker trugen ihn. Kein Geistlicher hat ihn begleitet" (124; The old man followed the corpse, along with his sons. Albert couldn't face it. Lotte's life seemed in danger. Workers

---

12. *Werther* is a short epistolary novel, framed at the beginning as quoted here and ended with a substantial narrative of Werther's suicide. —Trans.

carried him. No clergyman accompanied him).[13] The last sentence (in the Perfekt in German) is no longer narrative. It takes a position toward suicide and toward the attitude of the clergy to suicide. The sentence discusses. And just for that reason it closes the narrative.

Let us return to the introductory frame of *Werther*, which is in the voice of the author, not that of the narrator. The words "story," "collect," and "offer to you" are technical literary terms. In the presence of such words, we are outside of a story, in the realm in which literary techniques are weighed and discussed. Frames like this are always a favorite of authors who wish to lend documentary value to a narrative. They assert truthfulness. This reveals the relationship of literary frame-narrative to that of historiography. By using frame-narrative the literary author tries to claim historiography's prestige for truth. Hence asserting truthfulness and framing go hand in hand in the literature of every period.

A final example for the different functions of Präteritum and Perfekt will come here from Franz Kafka's *Der Prozeß* (The Trial). In the second chapter, encouraged by listeners who appear to agree with him, Josef K. dares to offer a pleading to the invisible court. It takes the form of complaint about his arrest and chastisement by the court. The main part of his plea is a narration (the *narratio* of judicial rhetoric) of the process of his arrest. This narration is conducted in narrative tenses. But it is enclosed by an introductory and concluding frame. The introduction reads: "Hören Sie: Ich bin vor etwa zehn Tagen verhaftet worden, über die Tatsache der Verhaftung selbst lache ich, aber das gehört jetzt nicht hierher. Ich wurde früh im Bett überfallen" (36; Listen, I was arrested about ten days ago; I find the fact of the arrest laughable, but that is not the issue now. I was attacked in bed early in the morning). With this Präteritum the narrative begins, and it remains in this tense until he concludes, "Ich wiederhole, mir hat das Ganze nur Unannehmlichkeiten und vorübergehenden Ärger bereitet, hätte es aber nicht auch schlimmere Folgen haben können?" (37; I repeat, the whole business caused me unpleasantness and passing annoyance, but might it not also have had worse consequences?).

The two parts of the frame are related to each other. Both summarize the event elaborated in the narrative. They state and thereby transport the entire event into the situation of discussion, for the arrest is not only to be narrated, but should become the object of the court's deliberations. Furthermore, occasional uses of the Präsens and Perfekt turn up in Josef

---

13. Johann Wolfgang Goethe, *Die Leiden des jungen Werther*, ed. Erich Trunz, *Goethes Werke* (Hamburg: Wegner, 1965), 6:7, 124. Jacob Wackernagel points to this conclusion: *Vorlesungen über Syntax*, vol. 1 (Basel: Birkhäuser, 1926), 91.

K.'s narrative. One sentence reads (he is talking about the various attacks on him): "Nun ist nichts davon, auch nicht im geringsten, gelungen" (36; Now, none of that has succeeded in the least.) This too is a summarizing sentence that draws the conclusion. Not the narrative as narrative, but only the conclusion is of juridical significance as an element of the court's deliberations or judgment. In order that the narrative of the arrest can enter into any relation to the situation of judgment, it must be transformed into something that is not itself a narrative. That something is the conclusion.

The example from Kafka is so instructive because the narration and the discussion are simultaneously so close to each other and so distant. They are close to the extent that both relate to the judgment of the court. And they are at the same time so distant, because the deliberations of the court are eminently a situation of discussion and totally different from a narrating situation. Hence the tension between the narration and the discussion, and hence also the precise marking in the speech to the court of the borders between reporting and judging language. And hence, too, surely, the early attention of rhetoric for those parts of legal rhetoric in which *narratio* is sharply distinguished from the discussing sections *propositio, argumentatio*, etc.[14] Historiography and court proceedings are thus related in that they apply both narration and discussion to past events.

The Perfect in English

The English perfect is not to be equated to the German Perfekt, as in general principal no tense of one language can be equated with that of another language. Each tense is first of all part of the tense system of a given language, and only tense systems are comparable. Since German and English, however, have in common a structural division of their tense systems according to the worlds of discussing and narrating, the German and English perfect tenses have in common that they are both retrospective discussing tenses. However different their range of application may be in detail, the two qualities "discussion" and "retrospection" inhere in both. (The differences in the two tenses lie in how they combine with other elements of the text.)

The function of the English perfect has been much discussed by linguists. Otto Jespersen describes the difference between the preterit and perfect as follows:

---

14. Lausberg provides more detail.

The preterit refers to some time in the past without telling anything about the connexion with the present moment, while the perfect is a retrospective present, which connects a past occurrence with the present time, either as continued up to the present moment (inconclusive time) or as having results or consequences bearing on the present moment.

All sorts of objections have been advanced against Jespersen's description of the function. Archibald Hill rejects especially the first aspect, saying it is by no means characteristic of the perfect (or "present perfect," as it is often called) for there to be a temporal connection to the present. One of his counterexamples is this: "I have read that book twenty times, but I'm not reading it now." William Diver takes the same position. Against Jespersen's example, "I have lived about ten years in Chelsea (and I still live there)," Diver offers the counterexample: "I have lived in Chelsea, but since 1914 I have lived in London."[15]

This rejection of a temporal effect into the present as a definite sign of the English perfect shows the importance of the second part of Jespersen's description more clearly: not the action itself but its results or consequences extend into the present. That is evidently something different. It is odd that the focus on time still persists, for the influence of results and consequences cannot be comprehended as temporal extension. Jespersen then tries to narrow his general description and offers his well-known example of Newton (247). One says in the preterit, "Newton believed in an omnipotent god." In the perfect, by contrast, "Newton has explained the movements of the moon." Whether or not Newton believed in an omnipotent god, according to Jespersen, is irrelevant to our present time; however, that he has explained the movements of the moon is, as astronomical doctrine, just as relevant now as formerly. William Freeman Twaddell takes Jespersen's thinking further and writes, "*Have* + Participle explicitly links an earlier event or state with the current situation. It signals a significant persistence of results, a continued truth value, a valid present relevance of the effects of earlier events, the continued reliability of conclusions based on earlier behavior."[16] I note with satisfac-

---

15. Archibald A. Hill, *Introduction to Linguistic Structures* (New York: Harcourt, Brace, 1958), 212. Otto Jespersen, *Essentials of English Grammar* (London: Allen and Unwin, 1933), 243; William Diver, "The Chronological System of the English Verb," *Word* 19, no. 2 (1963): 93.

16. William Freeman Twaddell, *The English Verb Auxiliaries* (Providence: Brown UP, 1965), 8.

tion that this is already far from a plain temporal understanding. But it does not seem yet the correct description of the function of the perfect. Diver points out the possibility of saying things that are false or irrelevant for the present in the perfect tense, such as, "Many people have believed that the world is flat, but they were wrong" (143). And it is also possible to say something correct and relevant to the present in the preterit, such as "Newton explained the movements of the moon in a way that is still thought to be correct" (147).

Instead of examples invented ad hoc, I prefer sentences from witnesses who are less suspicious because they are less aware of the problem under discussion. So I have checked the entries for Newton in a few encyclopedias and find the following sentences: "Newton showed that white light is a mixture of light of all colours" (*Encyclopedia Britannica*). "Later he developed a corpuscular theory of light in which the largest corpuscles excite the sensation of red, the smallest of violet" (*Chambers's Encyclopaedia*). "Newton's theory has many likenesses to present-day theory—the coexisting waves and particles of light, the super-velocity of the phase wave, the phenomena of interference; and he even measured the quantity that is now called a wave-length" (*The Encyclopedia Americana*). I have intentionally chosen sentences in which the correctness is evident or the relevance explicitly acknowledged. And yet there is no perfect here.

So it is necessary to conclude that the function of tenses is not to make statements about truth and untruth, about correctness and incorrectness. That is true for all tenses, even for the English perfect. The three examples from encyclopedias demonstrate rather how the authors of the Newton articles communicate the correctness or relevance of Newton's discoveries. Either they say it explicitly ("has many likenesses to present-day theory"), they hint at it with a nuance of style ("he even measured"), or they imply it through a gap in the sequence of tenses (present following preterit with "he measured . . . is now called"; see Chapter 6).

Diver (156–58), who correctly criticizes the older descriptions of the English perfect, is himself conservative in his own description. He returns to the old schema of aspects and describes the perfect in terms of the two characteristics, past time and indefiniteness, and is convinced there exist no counterexamples. As far as indefiniteness is concerned, Diver begins, as so often in structural analyses, with the way the perfect combines with adverbs of time. He observes, correctly, that the perfect is in fact mainly combined with indefinite adverbs (*ever, wherever, always*, etc.) and can scarcely fit with definite adverbs, especially not with dates.

But there are, of course, counterexamples. Here, for example, from a linguistics book by Charles E. Bennett: "The imperfect indicative formation of Indo-European *has disappeared* in Latin." In this sentence we find a definite article, we find an implicit determination of time in the expression "in Latin," and the whole sentence is every bit as definite as a sentence in a scholarly book ought to be. The perfect is used not because Bennett speaks indefinitely, but because a linguistic situation is to be discussed very definitely. The topic is the Latin language. He looks back for a moment at the prehistory and then continues the discussion of Latin, "In Latin, accordingly, we find. . . ."[17] The tenses here are those of discussion (despite the past time), and they are entirely definite. Naturally they are not always temporally definite, because the discussion is not always, and in general fairly seldom, concerned with time. We normally discuss things that directly concern the speaker and listener, that are therefore already present to them or familiar. A temporal determination is not really necessary under the circumstances.

If we are narrating, then we remove ourselves from the linguistic situation into a different world, one past or fictional. If it is past, then indicating its time is appropriate, and so there are often precise indications of time in connection with the narrating tenses. The combination of narrating tenses and precise temporal indicators is more firmly established in English than in other languages.[18] The field of narration is hence broader than, say, in German, and many a German Perfekt must be translated with a preterit in English. These are variations in combinatorics within a structure that is in principle similar in the two languages.

Thornton Wilder: *The Ides of March*

Thornton Wilder's epistolary historical novel, *The Ides of March* (1948), is a superb work for examining the English perfect. It is often said that a letter is a dialogue cut in half, so we find the same tenses in letters as in dialogue. That is, mainly, the discursive tenses, although it is also possible to narrate in a letter, just as there can be narrative segments in a conversation. Indeed, there are epistolary novels that narrate, but not as a

17. Charles E. Bennett, *Syntax of Early Latin*, vol. 1 (Boston: Allyn and Bacon, 1910), 26. On adverbs of this type see Renate Steinitz, *Adverbial-Syntax* (Berlin: Akademie-Verlag, 1969).

18. Differences in tense usage between the individual languages do not necessarily result from differences in the tense systems in the narrower sense, but can follow exclusively from the combinatorics of the tenses with one another and with other syntactic signals. See in this regard especially Chapter 8 below.

rule. And so the letters exchanged among the elite of the Roman Empire in Wilder's novel are mostly of the sort that discuss current events. They lend the novel the charm of immediacy, for which reason Wilder doubtless chose the form. Even so, many of the letters do narrate, and they are naturally in the narrating tenses. One such is in letter V written by Sempronia Metella. The narration is clearly set off from the rest of the letter and is introduced specifically as a story, "But let us change the subject. I received a great honor yesterday which I must *tell* you about. *He* [Caesar, Wilder's italics] singled me out to talk to me."[19]

But by no means are all past occurrences (past, of course, within the fictional space defined by the novel) narrated. Mostly, past events are discussed, and the tense used is perfect. Here is an example from the beginning of letter II, written by Clodia Pulcher to her steward:

> My brother and I are giving a dinner on the last day of the month. If any mistakes occur this time I shall replace you and offer you for sale. Invitations *have been sent* to the Dictator, and to his wife and aunt; to Cicero; to Asinius Pollio; and to Gaius Valerius Catullus. The entire dinner will be conducted in the old mode. (9)

It is necessary to know that Clodia Pulcher, although a lady of the first circles in Rome, had ruined her reputation. Whether Caesar accepts her invitation or not will determine her social status as well as some other things. The letter is intended to discuss the protocol of the meal with the responsible steward. This is therefore not the time to narrate the invitation as a past event. It is the basis of all the concerns to be discussed by Clodia Pulcher and her steward and is therefore transmitted in a tense of discussion.

Caesar decides to decline her invitation, as we learn from letter VII from Clodia to Caesar's wife: "Your husband is a very great man, but he is a very rude man, too. He *has sent* me a very short word that he cannot come to my dinner" (48). This, too, is not a narration, but a discussion, since the purpose of the letter is to get the Dictator to reverse his decision through the influence of his wife. Caesar then does decide to accept the invitation, less because of his wife's pleading than because of other considerations. In letter X-A he writes to Clodia, "My wife, my aunt, and I are coming to your dinner" (45). With that, the discussion of the invitation has reached its end. The special dinner takes place. There, it turns out, under dramatic circumstances, that the invitation was properly an object of discussion—there is an attempt to assassinate Caesar.

---

19. Thornton Wilder, *The Ides of March* (New York: HarperCollins, 2003), 23.

We have two versions of the dinner and of the attack. I begin with the second version, letter XXI from Asinius Pollio to Vergil and Horace, fifteen years after the event. In this letter, Asinius Pollio reports his eyewitness account to the addressees. It is a narrative, and the letter-writer speaks of "my narration" and "the story." This narration, apart from one introductory sentence and one generalizing sentence, is in the tenses of group II. The narrator is deeply moved by the events of that memorable day and the events are told in the liveliest manner; even so, the world of this story is a closed one. Caesar is dead, Catullus is dead, the Republic exists no longer, different political problems have come to the fore, and Rome is a different society. The attempt on Caesar's life does not need to be discussed any more.

The other version of the assassination attempt in the Pulchers' home is the police report, XX-B, written at various times right after the event. This report is also a narration and correspondingly written in narrative tenses—but only to the extent that it deals with events that are no longer objects of continuing measures taken by the police. These latter are reported in discussing tenses, especially the perfect. These are truly actions "that continue into the present." But they are not in the perfect because they extend into the present. Rather, these actions are discussed because they extend into the present, and they are in a tense of group I because they are discussed.

The same applies to the previous examples from Wilder's novel. The invitation to the dinner is not in the perfect because it has "results and consequences" for the present. Instead, the invitation is discussed because it will probably have consequences; and because it is discussed, we have the perfect tense. There may well be sentences in which these differences could seem insignificant because discussions do naturally often have a temporal relationship to the present situation or allow a relationship to be constructed. If there were no connection to the present situation, no discussion would be necessary. But one cannot simply ignore the discursive register. Don't even the narrated events of the past, regarded simply as events, have some relation to the present? An assassination attempt always has consequences for the police. If that were the issue, the whole report could be written in the perfect.

And if Pascal is right that even Cleopatra's nose is partly responsible for the history of the world and hence for the present, then the perfect could be the universal tense for everything past. But not everything past is under discussion: that is the difference. It is possible to tell stories about Cleopatra. In Wilder's novel, Cornelius Nepos does so (letter XXXIII):

"The Queen *was received* at the Capitoline today. The magnificence of her train *exceeded* anything ever seen in the City. To me at a distance she *seemed* very beautiful" (139). Her appearance can also be discussed. Caesar himself does that in letter LXXI, where he unburdens himself again to his friend Lucius Mamilius Turrinus with, "she is that figure which all countries *have elevated* to the highest honor and awe: she is the mother as goddess" (243).

So, the perfect is also used frequently in Wilder's novel when there is a temporal relation to the present. It is often used where results persist into the present. But above and beyond this, it also appears where this is neither a temporal connection to the present nor even striking after-effects extending into the present, beyond the after-effect that must always be assumed when the past is to be discussed. Here is Clodia Pulcher again, writing a rather impudent letter to the poet Catullus, who loves her more than she does him (Letter XXVI). It begins,

> My sister tells me I should write you a letter. A number of other persons *have appointed* themselves to be your advocate and *have told* me I should write you a letter.
>
> Here, then is a letter. You and I long since agreed that letters are nothing. Yours tell me what I knew already or could well imagine, and they frequently depart from the rule which we laid down that a letter should consist principally of facts.
>
> Here are my facts:
>
> The weather *has been* incomparable. There *have been* many parties on sea and on land. I leave all reunions which *have been* abandoned to conversation only and for which the host *has made* no plans for entertainment. (99)

The reader attentive to tenses will note the strikingly many perfect forms in the opening sentences. Why so? "The weather *has been* incomparable"? Is it still incomparable? Does the incomparable weather have consequences? Perhaps on the mood of the letter-writer? And why? "There *have been* many parties on sea and on land"? Are these parties still going on at the time the letter is written? Or do they still continue to affect her? No, of all that we learn nothing. We don't know what the weather is like at the time of writing, nor does the letter writer intend to share with her annoying lover if the party is still going on as the letter is being written. She does not want to communicate any continuation or after-effects, but only facts. "Here are my facts," she says. Continuation and after-effects have no interest. Hence they have no influence on the choice of tense. Clodia and Catullus have previously agreed to communicate only facts in their letters to one another. This very letter, in which Clodia shares nothing but facts, proves that their agreement has strong effects into the present time of the writing. But the sentence that refers to the agreement is in the preterit—"You and I long since agreed that letters are nothing." Or else in other tenses of group II—"the rule which we laid down that a letter should consist principally of facts." None of this can be understood from the idea of "connection to the present," no matter how far we try to stretch it. Only the point of view of "discussion" can assist us. The agreement only to report facts in letters is not discussed here. Clodia does not talk about it, but rather assumes it and bases her entire letter unquestioningly on it. Only with this assumption can she reproach Catullus for not following the rules of the game. Therefore, Clodia reminds him of the agreement in a narration. Only the facts are discussed.

This only becomes completely clear from the whole letter Clodia writes to Catullus. It is truly a nasty letter. And Clodia does not write about the beautiful weather for the sake of the beautiful weather. She writes her facts because Catullus has not written his facts. Clodia has, however, found out what they are and now recounts them:

> These are the facts concerning my life this summer and those are the answers to the questions contained in your extremely monotonous letters. On rereading them I find that you *have given* me very few facts. You *have not been writing* to me but to that image of me lodged in your head whom I have no wish to confront. The facts about you I *have learned* from my sister and your other advocates. You *have paid* visits to my sister and to Manilius and Livia [Torquatus]. You *have taught* their children how to swim and how to sail. You *have taught* their children how to train dogs. You *have written* reams of verses for children, and another poem for a wedding. I tell you again you will lose your poetic gift if you abuse it. (101)

It has nothing to do with an exchange of facts. Clodia has reported her facts to justify her scolding list of Catullus's facts. This listing of facts is a statement of accounts. Clodia calls Catullus to account because Catullus has not made his own statement of accounts. So the facts are not narrated but are discussed. Making accounts is discussion. Thus we find the perfect tense often in situations in which justification is made. Such situations are related to judicial procedures and hence can sometimes include narrations of events. But the actual justification is not narration but discussion.

Yet another letter in the novel is a justification. It is letter LXIX, written by Caesar to Lucius Mamilius Turrinus. Caesar defends himself against the charge that he is an enemy of freedom:

> In the eyes of my enemies I sit clothed in the liberties which I *have stolen* from others. I am a tyrant and they liken me to the potentates and satraps of the East. They cannot say I *have robbed* any man of money, of land, or of occupation. I *have robbed* them of liberty. I *have not robbed* them of their voice and their opinion. I am not oriental and *have not kept* the people in ignorance of what they should know, nor *have I lied* to them. The wits of Rome declare that the people are weary of the information with which I flood the country. Cicero calls me the Schoolmaster, but he *has not charged* me with distorting my lessons. They are not in the slavery of ignorance nor under the tyranny of deception. *I have robbed* them of their liberty.
>
> But there is no liberty save in responsibility. That I cannot rob them of because they *have not got* it. I *have never ceased* from placing before them the opportunity to assume it, but as my predecessors learned before me, they know not where to grasp it. I rejoice at the extent to which the outposts of Gaul *have shouldered* the burdensome freedom which I *have accorded* them. It is Rome which *has been* corrupted. The Romans *have become* skilled in the subtle resources for avoiding the commitment and the price of political freedom. They *have become* parasites upon the freedom which I gladly exercise—my willingness to arrive at a decision and to sustain it—and which I am willing to share with every man who will assume his burden. (237-8)

The words of justification in the perfect are simultaneously an accusation against the civic laziness of the Roman people. In this letter, Wilder would have us sense all the political tension of the age. We are far indeed from narration.

The Passé composé in French

The passé composé in French (*il a chanté*) raises a series of questions in relation to the disappearance of the passé simple (*il chanta*) from the spoken language. These will be put aside for the time being and saved for a more extensive presentation in Chapter 9. Here, I will consider only written French, where both tenses—passé composé and passé simple—still maintain their ground.

The passé composé is the retrospective tense of discussion in the French system of tenses. It shares this function with the German Perfekt and to a degree with the English perfect. So when Jean-Paul Sartre begins his book *L'être et le néant* (Being and Nothingness) with a passé composé form, the reader is fairly sure that something will be discussed here. The first sentence reads, "La pensée moderne *a réalisé* un progrès considérable en réduisant l'existant à la série des apparitions qui le manifestent" (Modern thought has realized considerable progress by reducing the existent to the series of appearances which manifest it).[20] We do not yet know, however, whether this book should be taken as scholarship or as literature. This distinction is the same as that between discussing or narrating.

Even a work of literature can begin in the discussing tenses, as, for example, can be seen at the beginning of Paul Valéry's *La soirée avec Monsieur Teste* (Evening with Monsieur Teste): "La bêtise n'est pas mon fort. J'*ai vu* beaucoup d'individus; j'*ai visité* quelques nations; j'*ai pris* ma part d'entreprises diverses sans les aimer; j'*ai mangé* presque tous les jours; j'*ai touché* à des femmes" (I cannot abide stupidity. I have met many people. I have visited several nations. I have undertaken different enterprises without liking them. I have eaten nearly every day. I have frequented women).[21] Robert Champigny points to this passage and interprets the passé composé in these sentences as a tense of indifference. That is only partly true. The passage does sound tiredly indifferent. This derives, however, not from the tense, but from the style—from the disconnected listing of unrelated experiences. The tense contributes something different. It lends the presentation the character of a justification. And such accounting is a favored form of modern literature. An example is the prose-poem "Nuits partagées" (Shared Nights) by Paul Éluard:

> Je m'obstine à mêler des fictions aux redoutables réalités. Maisons inhabitées, je vous ai peuplées de femmes exceptionnelles, ni grasses, ni maigres, ni blondes, ni brunes, ni folles, ni sages, peu importe, de femmes plus séduisantes que possibles, par un détail. Objets inutiles, même la sottise qui procéda à votre fabrication me fut une source d'enchantements. Etres indifférents, je vous ai souvent écoutés, comme on écoute le bruit des vagues et le bruit des machines d'un bateau, en attendant délicieusement le mal de mer. J'ai pris l'habitude des images les plus inhabituelles. Je les ai vues

---

20. Jean-Paul Sartre, *L'être et le néant: Essai d'ontologie phénoménologique* (Paris: Gallimard, 1976), 11; *Being and Nothingness: An Essay on Phenomenological Ontology*, trans. Hazel Barnes (New York: Pocket Books, 1993), 3.

21. Cited in Robert Champigny, "Notes sur les temps passés en français," *The French Review* 28, no. 6 (1955): 523; Paul Valéry, *An Evening with Mr. Teste*, trans. Ronald Davis (Paris: R. Davis, 1925), 13.

où elles n'étaient pas. Je les ai mécanisées comme mes levers et mes couchers.... Pour me trouver des raisons de vivre, j'ai tenté de détruire mes raisons de t'aimer. Pour me trouver des raisons de t'aimer, j'ai mal vécu.²²

I persist in mingling fictions with fearful realities. Untenanted houses, I have peopled you with exceptional women, not fat, not thin, not blond, not dark, not silly, not wise, it doesn't much matter, impossibly seductive women more seductive than can be imagined, through one detail. Useless objects, even the folly that led to your fabrication was a source of enchantment for me. Uninteresting things, I have often listened to you, the way we listen to the sound of the waves and the sound of a ship's engines, deliciously waiting for seasickness. I have become accustomed to the most unaccustomed images. I have seen them where they were not. I have made them as mechanical as my rising and my going to bed.... To find reasons for living, I have tried to destroy my reasons for loving you. To find reasons for loving you, I have lived badly.²³

It is impossible to conceive of this prose-poem being written in the French narrative tenses. It would seem translated from serious to more frivolous language. It would be a different poem. There are occasional narrative tenses inserted into the text (in the English: "that led to" and "was"). They stand at the points where fantasy escapes the spirit of justification and momentarily forgets the strictly discursive stance.

Yet stricter discussion is to be found in the courtroom. Remember the pleading of Josef K. in Kafka's *Prozeß*. A similar situation in French literature occurs in Maupassant's story "Un parricide" (A Parricide). The title already indicates that it is about the murder of parents. The accused is convicted and confesses. Now is the time to discuss the motivation for the deed, "Pourquoi les avez-vous tués?" (Why did you kill them?).²⁴ The accused answers, "Je les ai tués parce que j'ai voulu les tuer" (I killed them because I wanted to kill them). The interrogator's question and the answer are both in the passé composé. Interrogation and testimony are forms of

---

22. Paul Éluard, *Choix de poèmes* (Paris: Gallimard, 1954), 129–30. Another justificatory poem is "Je ne suis pas de ceux qui trichent avec l'univers" (Aragon, *Le fou d'Elsa*, 54).

23. "Éluard: Shared Nights," trans. Lydia Davis, *Paris Review* 25, no. 88 (Summer 1983), 238.

24. Guy de Maupassant, *Contes et nouvelles*, ed. Louis Forestier, 2 vols. (Paris: Gallimard, 1980, 1979) 1:553; www.online-literature.com/maupassant/268/.

discussion. There follows the plea of the defense attorney, who attempts to figure out the motive and to justify it: "Ces tristes doctrines, acclamées maintenant dans les réunions publiques, ont perdu cet homme. Il a entendu des républicains, des femmes même, oui, des femmes! demander le sang de M. Gambetta!" (1:554; These gloomy doctrines, now applauded in public meetings, have ruined this man. He has heard republicans—even women, yes, women!—ask for the blood of M. Gambetta!) The defense attorney has no idea whether the accused has heard the seductive republican speeches; he is conjecturing and inventing a justification. He cannot narrate it, but must introduce it as part of the discussion. Hence the passé composé.

But now the novella takes an unexpected turn. The accused, who has been listening for a while to his lawyer's speech, interrupts the flood of words and makes a new statement that sweeps away all the lawyer's inventions: "Je me suis vengé, j'ai tué" (1:556; I have taken revenge, I have killed). And now the invented plea is replaced by the narrative of the accused. It is in the narrative tenses (imparfait and passé simple). It extends up to just before the murder, and continues,

> Alors, mon président, il [mon père] leva la main sur moi, je vous le jure sur l'honneur, sur la loi, sur la République. Il me frappa, et comme je le saisissais au collet, il tira de sa poche un revolver.
>
> J'ai vu rouge, je ne sais plus, j'avais mon compas dans ma poche; je l'ai frappé, frappé tant que j'ai pu.
>
> Alors elle [ma mère] s'est mise à crier: "Au secours! à l'assassin!" en m'arrachant la barbe. Il parait que je l'ai tuée aussi. Est-ce que je sais, moi, ce que j'ai fait, à ce moment-là?
>
> Puis, quand je les ai vus tous deux par terre, je les ai jetés à la Seine, sans réfléchir.
>
> Voilà.—Maintenant, jugez-moi.
>
> L'accusé se rassit. Devant cette révélation, l'affaire a été reportée à la session suivante. Elle passera bientôt. Si nous étions jurés, que ferions-nous de ce parricide? (1:558-9)

> "Then, your honor, he [my father] struck me. I swear it on my honor, before the law and my country. He struck me, and when I seized him by the collar, he drew a revolver from his pocket.
>
> The blood rushed to my head, I no longer knew what I was doing, I had my compass in my pocket; I struck him with it as often as I could.

Then she [my mother] began to cry: "Help! murder!" and to pull my beard. It seems that I killed her also. How do I know what I did then?

Then, when I saw them both lying on the ground, I threw them into the Seine without thinking.

That's all. Now sentence me."

The prisoner sat down. After this revelation the case was carried over to the following session. It comes up very soon. If we were jurymen, what would we do with this parricide?

This is the end of the story. The tenses demand interpretation. The narrative, recognizable by the narrative tenses, extends until just before the murderous act. The father's threat is still narrated. But the reaction of the threatened son and the murder itself are in the passé composé—because this murder is the object of consideration before the jury, which has to decide between life or death for the accused. Here, at this decisive moment, the narrative of the accused returns to declaration, and the judgment can now be pronounced: "Maintenant, jugez-moi."[25]

The Passato prossimo in Italian

The passato prossimo is once again the retrospective tense of discussion. So I can be brief and illustrate rather than argue in this section.

I shall begin by contrasting the Maupassant story just discussed with two Italian stories. First, Luigi Pirandello's "Difesa del Mèola" (In Defense of Meola). Here is the plot: A young man named Meola steals money from the pocket of the bishop of his diocese by all sorts of dirty tricks, but with the best of intentions. And all this happened some time ago. In what tense should it be reported?

---

25. Gerold Hilty, "Tempus, Aspekt, Modus," Review of *Tempus*, *Vox Romanica* 24 (1965): 278, points to the mixing of tenses in the second section while interpreting this section. I share his view that the imparfait "j'avais" cannot be explained as a tense metaphor. Yet I cannot follow him in the interpretation that the passé composé in the language of the accused should be understood as a narrative tense. Earlier the same accused used passé simple as his narrative tense. The solution is probably that the boundary in this text between the narrating part (*narratio*) and the discussing part (*argumentatio*) based on the evidence is not drawn sharply. The second section is transitional; it does have a narrative tense with its imparfait, but is already more focused on the criminally relevant act of murder with the majority of its tenses.

Pirandello's story is especially illuminating because the same action is told twice. The first version is in the frame of the story. It reads:

> *Ho tanto raccomandato* ai miei concittadini di Montelusa di non condannare cosí a occhi chiusi il Mèola, se non vogliono macchiarsi della píù nera ingratitudine. Il Mèola *ha rubato*. Il Mèola *s'è arricchito*. Il Mèola probabilmente domani si metterà a far l'usuraio. Sí. Ma pensiamo, signori miei, a chi e perché *ha rubato* il Mèola. Pensiamo che è niente il bene che il Mèola *ha fatto* a se stesso rubando, se lo confrontiamo col bene che da quel suo furto *è derivato* alla nostra amatissima Montelusa.[26]

> I have urged my fellow citizens of Montelusa not to condemn Meola with their eyes closed, or they will besmirch themselves with the blackest ingratitude. Meola has stolen. Meola has enriched himself. Tomorrow Meola will probably set out to practice usury. Yes. But let us consider, gentlemen, whom Meola has robbed and why. Let us consider that the good that Meola has done for himself by his robbery is nothing in comparison to the good that his robbery has led to for our beloved Montelusa.

This idea is taken up again at the end of the story in almost the same words and is thus clearly framed by it.

Within the frame is the actual narrative, we might say the narrative body of the story. Here are the tenses of narrative, imperfetto and passato remoto. The narrative body begins, "Un incubo orrendo *gravava su* tutti noi Montelusani, da undici anni: dal giorno nefasto che Monsignor Vitangelo Partanna, per istanze e mali uffizii di potente prelati a Roma, *ottenne* il nostro vescovado" (150; A horrible nightmare [had] weighed on all of us Montelusans for eleven years: since the ill-omened day when Monsignor Vitangelo Partanna, by petitions and evil offices of powerful prelates in Rome, obtained our bishopric). Meola's deceit will now be told.

In the frame, Meola's deceit is not narrated, but discussed. Readers are informed about the facts and called on to correct their negative opinion of Meola. It is Meola's fellow citizens who sit in judgment on him, not legally but morally. One of them therefore tells the story in this novella to prepare the citizens of Montelusa and all right-thinking and well-

---

26. Pirandello, Luigi, *Novelle per un anno*, 150, https://www.liberliber.it/mediateca/libri/p/pirandello/novelle_per_un_anno/pdf/pirandello_novelle_per_un_anno.pdf.

meaning minds in Italy to make a judgment. This is the main point of the delicate irony of the novella. The narrative itself is presented as secondary; it is more or less only a document in the dossier "Meola." We know, however, that for Pirandello that narrative was in reality, of course, more important. But we enjoy the game with the discursive frame. Story writers have always loved it.

Now I'll change authors. Dino Buzzati wrote a story, "Il crollo della Baliverna" (The Collapse of the Baliverna), which is also about right and wrong.[27] The similarity in the juridical theme makes them more comparable. The Baliverna, an old building outside the city, inhabited by many impoverished families, collapsed two years ago. There were many lives lost in the disaster. In one week the trial will take place. We learn all this from the first-person narrator, a tailor, whose name we never learn. He tells us, the readers, how the disaster took place. We are given to understand that he simultaneously tells the course of events to himself, in order to clear his own conscience. For the narrator is in some incomprehensible way involved in the disaster himself. He had taken a walk to Baliverna on that day two years earlier. Out of curiosity and a bit recklessly he clambers around in the building. In the process an iron bar is displaced. Nothing happens to him, the "mountaineer." But the minor damage to the building causes additional damage, that in a chain reaction has further impact and ultimately triggers the great disaster.

Or was there a different cause? The tailor repeatedly ponders whether he caused the catastrophe or whether his small mishap only coincided with the great disaster by chance. In any case, he sees no reason to accuse himself during the judicial investigations. But the actual trial is still to come. Perhaps in fact someone has seen that he is guilty of the whole thing. With all this in mind he tells us the story.

Formally, this is a frame story. The beginning and end of the story point toward the impending trial. "Ho paura," the narrator confesses at the beginning, and "I am afraid" is also his last word. In between is the narration of the disaster. This narration is dominated by the imperfetto and passato remoto tenses. I will not consider how the two are distributed for the time being, in order to concentrate entirely on the distribution of the passato prossimo forms, of which there are exactly eight. They refer to various moments of the action, namely: the preliminary investigation,

---

27. Dino Buzzati, "Il crollo della baliverna," in *Sessanta racconti* (Milan: Mondadori, 1958), 215–21.

the beginning of the narration, the time between the disaster and the narration, the time since the disaster, a random moment in this period, the moment of the disaster (twice), and the very day of the narration. Evidently, the passato prossimo cannot be understood as the expression of a particular moment in time or period of time.

If one begins instead from the literary stylistic structure of the story, it requires little effort to explain the distribution of passato prossimo forms. All the forms of the passato prossimo, with one exception, refer to the juridical problem of right and wrong. The exception is an example from the middle of the narrative of the disaster, right at the point where the narrator moves from the descriptive background narration to the presentation of the actual disaster. The sentence reads: "Giunti alla Baliverna, si prese a costeggiare la parete posteriore che ho descritta" (When we reached the Baliverna, we began to walk along the back wall that I have described). This sentence is obviously summary in character; it pulls the first—descriptive—part of the narration together.

Here are the other sentences in the passato prossimo:

Della mia responsabilità il giudice istruttore non ha avuto neanche il minimo sospetto.

Ho inconsciamente manovrato per vederlo il meno possibile.

Da allora egli si è ordinata nella mia sartoria una decina di vestiti.

Forse ha capito tutto.

Io soltanto so chi ha provocato il crollo.

L'ho visto coi miei occhi.

Anche oggi è venuto per provarsi un completo di flanella.

Se ne è andato.

(The examining magistrate had not the slightest suspicion of my responsibility.

I unconsciously maneuvered to see him as little as possible.

Since then he has ordered about ten suits in my shop.

Maybe he understood everything.

I alone know who provoked the collapse.

I saw him with my own eyes.

This very day he came to try on a flannel outfit.

He left.)

Some of the sentences are obviously to be understood as hints about the trial situation. Others depend on awareness of a secondary circumstance. The narrator fears in this situation namely nothing more than eyewitnesses to his possible guilt. Especially that Professor Scavezzi might have seen with his own eyes how he caused the disaster. Just this very professor visits him strikingly often in his shop and looks at him—at least the tailor thinks he notices this—with strange and knowing glances. The same thing has just happened today. After he has left with an emphatically ceremonial greeting, the tailor remains alone with his fear.

In summary, the event in question lies two years in the past, and thus belongs to the past. But the narrator is related to this past event in radically different ways, depending on whether he tells the story of it, or whether he evaluates it in terms of right and wrong. In the first case he routinely uses narrative tenses, especially imperfect and preterit, while in the second case he uses, with other tenses of discussion, the perfect, the passato prossimo. The tenses draw a structural boundary right through the past and organize it according to viewpoints that are not temporal, but imply taking a position about the past.

The Perfecto compuesto in Spanish

There are numerous word-counts of the perfecto compuesto (*ha cantado*) in Spanish, too.[28] Manuel Paiva Boléo compares it with the narrative tense perfecto simple (simple past) in a novel by Benito Pérez Galdós and a play by the Nobel Prize winner Jacinto Benavente. The ratios of perfecto simple to perfecto compuesto for Galdós's novel *Doña Perfecta* are 131:22 (Chapters 1 and 2), 77:28 (Chapter 19), 110:25 (Chapter 21)—an unambiguous surplus of simple pasts. Benavente's popular play *De muy buena familia* (Of a Very Good Family) is the reverse—20:62

---

28. I adopt here the terms "perfecto compuesto" and "perfecto simple" from Emilio Alarcos Llorach, "Perfecto simple y compuesto en español," *Revista de Filología Española* 31 (1947): 108–39. Spanish grammars otherwise use the names "pretérito perfecto" (*ha cantado*) and "pretérito indefinado" (*cantó*).

(Act 1), 14:77 (Act 2), 37:34 (Act 3). The first two acts have a surplus of perfecto compuesto, while the two tenses are about equal in Act 3. Paiva Boléo notes, however, that Act 3 contains a longish narration, which by itself contains twelve forms of the perfecto simple. From these numbers he draws the conclusion that elevated language favors perfecto simple, and colloquial language perfecto compuesto.[29]

Correct statistics do not prevent an incorrect interpretation here. The distribution of perfecto simple and perfecto compuesto has nothing to do with the stylistic level of the language. There are more perfecto simple forms in Galdós's novel because the novel is narrated, while in Benavente's comedy narration is the exception. Most of the dialogue sections are discussion and hence often contain the tenses of group I, among them the perfecto compuesto.

This conclusion is supported by the counts done in Emilio Alarcos Llorach's study of Benavente's equally popular comedy *Señora Ama* (The Lady of the House). In contrast to 185 forms of perfecto simple there are 372 forms of perfecto compuesto, a ratio of 1:2. However, in scenes dominated by narration perfecto simple dominates: 1.4; 2.3; 3.10. Newspapers reveal a similar pattern. In general, as Paiva Boléo already noticed, perfecto compuesto dominates, but Alarcos Llorach readily finds newspaper articles with a majority of perfecto simple forms. There simply are also narrative articles in newspapers. Alarcos Llorach recognizes perfecto simple as the tense of narration, without, however, renouncing the notion of its reference to an "absolute past." He regards the perfecto compuesto simply as recent past. He rejects Samuel Gili y Gaya's view that the perfecto compuesto is subjective in contrast to the objective perfecto simple.[30] But this view is not as false as Alarcos Llorach thinks, so long as subjectivity is understood as the engagement characteristic for the situation of discussion.

The most comprehensive set of counts comes from William E. Bull ("Modern," 458), whose statistics were already adduced in a different context above (Chapter 2).[31] In the accompanying table, I consider from his rich material only the ratios of perfecto simple to perfecto compuesto.

---

29. Manuel de Paiva Boléo, "O perfeito e o pretérito em português em confronto com as outras línguas românicas: Estudio de carácter sintático-estilístico" (PhD dissertation Universidade de Coimbra, 1936), 52–53. Paiva Boléo finds similar ratios in Italian as well (66).

30. Samuel Gili y Gaya, *Curso superior de sintaxis española* (Mexico: Minerva, 1943), 138–39.

31. William Emerson Bull, "Modern Spanish Verb-Form Frequencies," *Hispania* 30 (1947): 451–66.

Author	Title	Genre	% perfecto simple	% perfecto compuesto
Abreu Gómez	*Héroes mayas*	novellas	30.8	1.2
Alfredo Cantón	*Bravo León*	novella	26.0	1.1
Eustasio Rivera	*La vorágine*	novel	22.4	2.2
Eduardo Luquín	*Los perros fantasmas*	novel	20.5	1.7
Benjamín Jarnés	*Cervantes*	biogr. essay	8.1	2.7
Jesualdo Sosa	*Sinfonia de la danzarina*	poems	5.9	0.7
García Lorca	*Poeta en Nueva York*	poems	5.8	2.2
Xavier Villaurrutia	*La hiedra*	play	6.1	6.9
Jacinto Benavente	*Una pobre mujer*	play	2.5	8.2
Amado Alonso	*Poesía y estilo de Pablo Neruda*	criticism	0.8	3.4
Joaquín Xirau	*Amor y mundo*	essay	0.8	1.4

These counts confirm the earlier ones. Once again, narrative literature has a striking surplus of perfecto simple—maximally 25:1, minimally 6:1. The variation in the ratios reflects the greater or lesser amount of dialogue in the narratives. The statistics demonstrate that the biographical essay is to be counted as narrative literature. It narrates here the life of Cervantes. The surplus of narrative tenses is, however, smaller than in the literary narratives. The volumes of poems also have more forms of the perfecto simple than of the perfecto compuesto. In this case one should note that the normally shorter forms of the perfecto simple (*cantó*, two syllables) are easier in prosodic terms to handle than the less mobile forms of the perfecto compuesto (*ha cantado*, four syllables). Drama, criticism, and essays, by contrast, have a clear surplus of perfecto compuesto. It is most obvious in literary criticism with its ratio of 4:1.

William Bull's numbers confirm that the perfecto simple is a narrative tense, and the perfecto compuesto is one of discussion. It is incomprehensible to me how Bull could say in a later book, *cantó* and *ha cantado* are "potential free variants," and that many Spaniards see no significant difference between the two forms.³² There is a very significant difference, just not in the temporal stage or temporal ordering, but certainly in the speaker's attitude toward the concrete linguistic situation.

Let us leave these abstract considerations and return to a text—to a concrete bit of language. If one opens the second volume of José Ortega y Gasset's *Obras completas* and looks just at the beginnings of the fifty-eight more or less essayistic pieces in the volume, one finds among them forty-three first sentences in the presente and six in the perfecto compuesto.³³ The other nine have various other tenses. That is a relatively high number for the perfecto compuesto in comparison to the present. It is attractive to look back at what has passed and what is to come. Here are the six beginning sentences in perfecto compuesto:

> El prospecto de *El Espectador* me ha valido numerosas cartas llenas de afecto, de interés, de curiosidad (15).

> Un azar ha traído a mis manos el *Adolfo*, de Benjamin Constant (25).

> Por tierras de Sigüenza y Berlanga de Duero, en días de agosto alanceados por el sol, he hecho yo–Rubín de Cendoya, místico español–un viaje sentimental sobre una mula torda de altas orejas inquietas (43).

> Me ha complacido mucho su carta, amigo mío (347).

> En un libro mío–*España invertebrada*–he insinuado una doctrina sobre el origen de las sociedades que discrepa sobremanera de las usadas (355).

> Con su máquina fotográfica Ortiz Echagüe ha conseguido algo épico (695).

> (The prospectus for *El Espectador* has earned me numerous letters full of feeling, of interest, of curiosity.

> By chance Benjamin Constant's *Adolphe* has come into my hands.

> Through the regions of Sigüenza and Berlanga de Duero, under a piercing August sun, I, Rubín de Cendoya, Spanish mystic, have taken a sentimental voyage on a dapple-gray mule with erect, restless ears.

> My friend, your letter has pleased me greatly.

32. William Emerson Bull, *Time, Tense and the Verb* (Berkeley: U of California P, 1968), 65.
33. José Ortega y Gasset, *Obras Completas*, vol. 2: *El Espectador* (Madrid : Revista de Occidente, 1963).

> In one of my books, *Invertebrate Spain*, I have slipped in a doctrine about the origin of societies that deviates greatly from the customary views.
>
> With his photographic machine Ortiz Echangüe has achieved something epic.)

The small, chance assemblage in the second volume of the *Complete Works* shows clearly that these sentences do not intend to narrate. They draw a connection—to a prospect, a book, a journey, a collection of photos. The reference looks back and forms the basis for the discussion of the topic to follow.

It might be of interest as a counterexample, to collect the beginning sentences in the perfecto simple. There are three of them:

> En aquel tiempo–podrá decirse del nuestro hacia el siglo XXIII o XXIV–comenzó el predominio de un nuevo clima moral, áspero y extraño, que produjo rápidamente la muerte de todas las "frases" (481).
>
> En abril último apareció en algunos periódicos la noticia (510).
>
> Los discípulos preguntaron una vez al sabio maestro de la India cuál era el gran brahmán; es decir la mayor sabiduría (625).
>
> (In that era—say, from our century until the twenty-third or twenty-fourth—there began to prevail a new moral climate, harsh and strange, that rapidly produced the death of all "slogans."
>
> Last April the notice appeared in several periodicals.
>
> The disciples once asked the wise Indian master what the great Brahma was; that is to say, the greater wisdom.)

These three pieces are also essays. They treat the moral problem of honesty, an archeological excavation, and silence. But Ortega y Gasset is a master of the art of writing, and he awakens the expectation of his readers by distancing his essays with a narrative introduction. In none of the examples is the narrated world simply a past that could be equally well expressed by the perfecto compuesto. In the first example it is a utopian future lying between our present and the twenty-third or twenty-fourth century. In the second sentence it is only apparently that past identified as "last April." In fact, it has to do with a strange past. The sentence seems mysterious. A mystery novel might begin like this. Ortega intends this mysterious atmosphere at the beginning of his essay because he is going to write about the sphinx. The third example, finally, is a real little story. It is told as all stories are told. With its twist ("the greatest wisdom is silence") Ortega shifts to the topic of his discussion.

Among the sentences in perfecto compuesto with which Ortega opens his essays, one stands out as different. It begins the essay, "Tierras de Castilla" (The Lands of Castile). The beginning is unusual for an essay; Ortega speaks not in his own name, as is typical for the genre, but slips into the guise of the Spanish mystic Rubín de Cendoya, who is riding a mule through the Castilian landscape. Right in the first section of the essay there appear a few comments especially relevant to the problem of the past. In the mask of this mystic, Ortega y Gasset writes,

> Soy un hombre que ama verdaderamente el pasado. Los tradicionalistas, en cambio, no le aman: quieren que no sea pasado, sino presente. Amar el pasado es congratularse de que efectivamente haya pasado, y de que las cosas, perdiendo esa rudeza con que al hallarse presente arañan nuestros ojos, nuestros oídos y nuestras manos, asciendan a la vida más pura y esencial que llevan en la reminiscencia.

> I am a man who truly loves the past. Traditionalists, however, do not: they want the past not to be past, but to be present. Loving the past means rejoicing that it is actually past and things lose the rawness with which they scratch our eyes, ears, and hands when they are present, and instead of that enter into the purer and more essential life that they lead in memory.

These sentences are meant as a critique of the ideology of Spanish traditionalism. Apart from that, the passage implies there are evidently two possible attitudes toward the past. One lets the past be past, is glad that past things are stripped of their rawness, and seeks to give them a more essential form in memory. The other attempts to make the past present again. If these two possibilities solidify into ideologies, then we understand that Ortega is making a choice. But it is unnecessary to take them as ideologies; we can understand them instead in the wider sense suggested by language itself. Without being traditionalists, we can take the past into the present of our concerns by discussing it. Or we can let the past be past by narrating it. What is lost in immediacy is gained, if Ortega is right, in beauty and essential meaning.

Narration, Past, Truth

In opposition to tense group I (including the retrospective perfect), the preterit and the other tenses of group II are signals that narration is the matter at hand. Their task is not to signal that the past is the matter at hand. It would not be justifiable to equate what is narrated with what is past. The two concepts are not congruent. We can make the past present without narrating it, and we can narrate without talking about the past.

Our relationship to the past is after all not simple. Jean-Paul Sartre (*L'être* 152–56; *Being*, 114–20) has already pointed out that the controversy about the being or non-being of the past does not exhaust the problem.[34] Whether the past, according to Bergson and Husserl *is*, or according to Descartes, *is no more* comes to the same thing if the bridges between past and present are destroyed. The only difference is that between a dead and a "retired" being ("être mis à la retraite") and does not explain why the past can haunt us, revive, exist *for us*. Sartre answers, the past as my past belongs to my life and to my present existence: "I am my past."

I think Sartre has built his bridge between past and future too broadly. There is not only my past, but I also have an inconsequential past. Not all of my past, nor that of all humanity, weighs on my existence. Sartre at one point attributes approvingly to Heidegger the sentence, "I am what I speak." Why doesn't he connect this sentence to his own formulation, "I am my past," to say, "I am, as I speak my past"? After all, I can narrate the past, and that is also a way to free myself from the past and to *suspend it* (*aufheben*) in my narrative. But I can also discuss the past. Many languages have a special tense reserved for discussing the past—the perfect (or its equivalents in other languages). The past that I discuss is a part of me. I discuss it precisely because it still affects me. Even though it is past, it may mean more to me than present things that I do not discuss or future things that I tell about. The structural boundary between the world of discussion and that of narration runs right through the middle of the past. Under these circumstances the question is whether it makes any sense at all to speak of "the" past. Language, at least, does not dictate any such thing. Language knows two kinds of past—one that belongs to me and that I discuss just like the things I physically encounter in my linguistic situation, and another that is distanced from me by the filter of narration.

If the past is thus not always narrated, it is also true that not all narrations are about the past. We have already pointed to novels whose plots lead into the present or that take place entirely in the future, without

---

34. Compare the dialog between Paola and Lionardo in Arthur Schnitzler's one-act play *Die Frau mit dem Dolche* (The Woman with a Dagger). Paola: "Es ist nicht mehr und also war es nie!"/Lionardo: "Paola, nein! Es war und darum ist es!" (Paola: "It exists no longer and so it never was!"/Lionardo: "Paola, no! It was and therefore it is!"). Schnitzler, *Die Frau mit dem Dolche*, in *Lebendige Stunden: Vier Einakter* (Berlin: Fischer, 1922), 60.

needing to use other than the narrative tenses. What is generally true for all fictional literature is especially obvious for novels of the future. The fictional space of fictional narrative is not only the past. Even if a date from the Middle Ages appears, the reader still does not really know if it is not, in the words of Paul Claudel, a "Moyen-Âge de convention" (a conventionalized Medieval Era). As a basic principle, so long as the opposite is not made obvious, it is a simulated Middle Ages, because it is a narrated Middle Ages. Of course, it can also be a historical novel encouraging identification of the narrated Middle Ages, by use of sources, congruence with known historical facts, and other stylistic means, with the "real" Middle Ages that belongs directly to the reader's own world because, as a historian for example, it can be discussed. But the historian Golo Mann reminds us, "daß Erzählen selbst dessen, was sich wirklich begeben, immer auch Dichtung ist" ("Schiller" 84; that narration even of what has actually taken place is always also literature).

We see then, the narrative tenses in themselves tell the hearer or listener nothing about the truth or fictionality of a narrative. That must be determined from supplementary information. If the narrative is really truth and not fiction, then it relates itself to past events. It must be documented as a "true history" and there must therefore have been time for it to have been experienced, observed, or heard from a different mouth. Most narrations of everyday life are of this sort. When I narrate a minor experience or a long journey, I am rarely posing some big riddle to my listeners as to whether the story is true (i.e., past) or invented (i.e., temporally indifferent). Probably the story is true. But the listener knows that not from the tenses, but from supporting indications and from the general knowledge that fictional (may I say "lying"?) narration is recognizable from the particular arrangement of the linguistic situation: from a smirk, an exaggeration, the speaker's tone of voice—or through the publication in connection to the genre markers of acknowledged fictional genres. Should this arrangement be lacking, when, for example, a writer of romances pretends to be a chronicler, the truth or fiction of the narrative remains unclear. That is known to all novelists, who have always loved to play with the truth. Fictional literature teems with claims of truth-telling. For older fiction it is generally the rule that the more fictional the story, the more claims there are of its truthfulness. Fixing the narrative chronologically by giving a date became one of the best-loved ways of asserting truth until narrators under the sign of realism noticed that the attestation of pastness can also narrow the range of the genre and that it is better to try to narrate the present and indeed narrate as if one were discussing it. The untiring play with truth found in narrative literature of the most varied epochs and countries is the surest indication that truth is not so simple that it can be read from verb tense. Tenses are indifferent to truth. Hence even as narrative tenses they do not tell whether the narrated world is a past one or an invented one. To learn that, it is necessary to listen to other signs. If doubt still remains, then the narrative needs to be—discussed. That is called historical criticism.

Historical criticism is appropriate not only for historical sources, but also for literary texts and their tenses. What should be said about Franz Werfel having written his novel *Das Lied von Bernadette* (*The Song of Bernadette*) entirely in the tenses of discussion, but his forward, in which he describes his flight to Lourdes, in the narrative tenses? Käte Hamburger tries to explain it with literary criticism: the present is intolerable as a narrative tense and betrays poor taste on the part of the writer.[35] To be sure, the novel is not one of the best. But let us move from literary criticism to historical criticism, a criticism that cares only about the question of truth or untruth. There can be no doubt that Werfel intentionally avoided narrative tenses in order to accredit the novel as truth and to characterize it thereby as a personal confession. In his "personal forward" he writes,

> *Das Lied von Bernadette* ist ein Roman, aber keine Fiktion. Der mißtrauische Leser wird angesichts der hier dargestellten Ereignisse mit größerem Recht als sonst bei geschichtlichen Epen die Frage stellen: Was ist wahr? Was ist erfunden? Ich gebe zur Antwort: All jene denkwürdigen Begebenheiten, die den Inhalt dieses Buches bilden, haben sich in Wirklichkeit ereignet ... Meine Erzählung verändert nichts an dieser Wahrheit.[36]

---

35. Käte Hamburger, "Das epische Präteritum," *Deutsche Vierteljahrsschrift für Literaturwissenschaft und Geistesgeschichte* 27, no. 3 (1953): 352. It is possible to consider a novel written entirely in present tense an extension of "historical present," a stylistic figure taught in rhetoric since Antiquity and recommended to "enliven" narration. But then the framing narration that normally surrounds the historical present disappears (as, for example, in Voltaire's *Candide*, Chapter 5, and in the messenger's speeches at the end of French classical plays). Robert Petsch cogently remarks in this regard, "A story written entirely in the present resembles a letter in which every word is underlined": *Wesen und Formen der Erzählkunst* (Halle: Niemeyer, 1942), 365–66. It is striking that the American translator of Franz Werfel's *Das Lied von Bernadette* follows the German text in translating first with the discursive tenses, but then from Chapter 11 on jumps abruptly into the narrative tenses.

36. Franz Werfel, *Das Lied von Bernadette: Historischer Roman*, ed. Karl-Maria Guth (Berlin: Contumax, 2016), 6.

> *The Song of Bernadette* is a novel, but not a fiction. A mistrustful reader confronted by the events portrayed here will have more reason than elsewhere in historical epics to pose the question: What is true? What is invented? I answer: All those memorable events that make up the contents of this book really took place . . . My narration changes nothing of this truth.

For the sake of the story's truth, Werfel fears to use the narrative tenses. We may understand the constant use of the tenses of discussion thus as an especially difficult form of confirming the truth. That leads to a problematic leveling of the narrative profiling, and indeed is contradicted by Werfel's own practice; in his personal forward, where he certainly tells his own truth, he uses narrative tenses without casting the least shadow of doubt on its historical truth. Tenses are of no use as truth-signals.

A second example of this sort is the screenplay for the film *L'année dernière à Marienbad* (1961, Last Year at Marienbad) by Alain Robbe-Grillet, already mentioned above as written entirely in tenses of discussion. That is obvious, since the screenplay is the basis for the film. It is written for work, for the working day in the studio and not for reading by the fire in the evening. Even as a printed book it is documentation, not for reading. This screenplay also has a forward, in which Robbe-Grillet tells about his cooperation with the director, Alain Resnais. It is partly narration, and we find passé simple next to other narrative tenses. And yet this narrative is evidently true. We know the film that arose from it. Even though it is written in tenses of discussion, no one considers the plot of the screenplay truer than the events reported in the forward, even though narrative tenses are used here. Once again, the same result: Tenses have nothing to do with truth and do not determine whether a narrative is true and past or invented and not past. The boundary between poetry or invention and truth is not the same as that between the worlds of narration and discussion.[37] The world of discussion has its truth (whose opposite is error and lie), and the narrative world has its truth (whose opposite is fiction). Thus the world of discussion has its poetry (lyric and dramatic) and the narrative world has its poetry (epic). I have intentionally invoked here the names of the three major genres—lyric, dramatic, epic—even if they are only approximately accurate, because I want to make clear that my discussion addresses questions that have always drawn the attention of critics.

[37]. A continuation of these considerations may be found in my *Linguistics of Lying and Other Essays*, translated by Jane K. Brown and Marshall Brown (Seattle: U of Washington P, 2005).

4 / Highlighting

Narrative Highlighting

In describing the function of the French tense pair imparfait and passé simple, it is impossible to overlook the simple fact that this language—like the other Romance languages and various additional languages—has two tenses where other languages like German or English have (or seem to have) only one. *Er sang* or *he sang* is sometimes to be translated with *il chantait*, at others with *il chanta*. From the point of view of perspective neither of these tenses can be considered retrospectively recovered information or prospective information. They evidently have in common the neutral setting of perspective. With regard to register, both belong to the narrative tense group. It makes sense, therefore, to gear all description exclusively to the function of these tenses in the context of narratives.[1]

---

1. The scholarly context of this chapter is the doctrine of aspects and classes of actions. Relevant studies are Jens Holt, *Études d'aspect* (Aarhus: Universitetsforlaget i Aarhus, 1943); Hans Helmut Christmann, "Zum Aspekt im Romanischen: Bemerkungen zu einigen neueren Arbeiten," *Romanische Forschungen* 71, no. 1/2 (1959): 1–16; and (with extensive bibliography) Lars Johanson, *Aspekt im Türkischen: Vorstudien zu einer Beschreibung des türkischen Aspektsystems* (Stockholm: Almqvist och Wiksell, 1971). My critique of this theory of aspect based exclusively on sentences may be found in "Zur Textlinguistik der Tempus-Übergänge," *Linguistik und Didaktik* 1, no. 3 (1970): 222–27. Occasional divergences in counts between the book and my essay arise from differing evaluations of borderline-cases (such as forms like *je vais faire*); they do not affect the heart of the theory.

I begin with a small legend to be found in the fourth act of Albert Camus's *Les justes* (1949, The Just). Before giving the text, I will note the tense structure of the legend. Here are the tenses in order of occurrence: imparfait, imparfait, passé simple, imparfait, passé simple, imparfait, passé simple, passé antérieur, passé simple, imparfait. From this simple scaffold of tenses it is already possible to make certain generalizations about the functions of the various narrative tenses. I have already stated that tenses can occur mixed, and later I will deduce more consequences. There are no narratives that employ exclusively imparfait forms or exclusively passé simple forms. The ratios in the mixture can vary, but it is uncommon to find texts with a striking preponderance of the one tense or the other. In order to arrive at this realization result it is necessary to consider the text as a whole. Within a single text, tenses are by no means so evenly mixed that any single passage would reveal the same ratio as in the text overall.

In this regard our little legend is typical. For the sake of clarity it is necessary to note that the passé antérieur is now a strictly literary variant of the plus-que-parfait in French, using the passé simple of the auxiliary verb instead of the imparfait. So passé antérieur goes with the passé simple, whereas the plus-que-parfait uses the imparfait. Our text then appears as follows: imparfait forms dominate the beginning and end of the legend. Passé simple forms (including the functionally related passé antérieur) prevail in the middle section:

> Il *avait* rendez-vous dans la steppe avec Dieu lui-même, et il se *hâtait* lorsqu'il *rencontra* un paysan dont la voiture *était* embourbée. Alors saint Dmitri l'*aida*. La boue *était* épaisse, la fondrière profonde. Il *fallut* batailler pendant une heure. Et quand ce *fut fini*, saint Dmitri *courut* au rendez-vous. Mais Dieu n'*était* plus là.[2]

> He had an appointment on the plains with God himself, and he was hurrying there until he encountered a peasant whose cart was stuck in the mud. Then Saint Dimitri helped him. The mud was thick, the rut was deep. They had to struggle for an hour. And when it was over, Saint Dimitri ran to his appointment. But God was no longer there.

---

2. Albert Camus, *Théâtre, récits, nouvelles*, ed. Roger Quilliot (Paris: Bibliothèque de la Pléiade, 1962), 362. I ignore here the moral of the story, that is naturally in discursive tenses: "Il y a ceux qui arriveront toujours en retard au rendez-vous parce qu'il y a trop de charrettes embourbées et trop de frères à secourir" (There are those who will always arrive too late for the meeting because there are too many carts stuck in the mud and too many monks to rescue).

On the basis of the text we may now understand the two shifts between passé simple and imparfait. The legend is a religious story; it is not really about a cart stuck in the mud, but about the missed meeting with God. The saint could have been delayed by any kind of good deed, not just by a cart that was stuck. The issue for the legend is that he met someone and helped him. This is only moral. It is relatively unimportant in comparison that the cart was all muddy and that the mud was thick. So the secondary details are in the imparfait. That is emphasized by the sentence structure, since the imparfait is in a relative clause (*dont la voiture était embourbée*). The heart of the story is in the passé simple from the third verb (*rencontra*) until the second-to-the-last one (*courut*). Within this heart two minor details are in the imparfait.

Around this heart there is a frame, consisting of an introduction and conclusion, both in the imparfait. These are not secondary details for the legend. The whole story would be incomprehensible if the reader did not know that St. Dimitri had an appointment with God, and the theological or humanistic point would be lost if the final sentence were not there. But the introduction and conclusion are not simply the first and last sentences of the narrative; rather, they are parts of it with their own technical functions. The introduction is the exposition; it identifies the world to be narrated and invites the reader or listener to enter this strange world. The conclusion closes off the mysterious narrative world in which a mortal can have an appointment with God and separates it from the moral of the legend, which belongs to the world of discussion. These two functions are qualitatively different from plain narration because they mark the border between the worlds of discussion and narration. They encircle the body of the story in which the narration proceeds.

First, a methodological note: the concern is no longer with "aspect," "kind of action," or the like. These linguistic concepts, whatever they might mean, refer to sentences. Here the question is rather what these tenses contribute to texts. And since the imparfait and passé simple are narrative tenses in French, the question is what they do in texts. They highlight the narrative by organizing it into foreground and background. In narrative the imparfait is the *tense of the background*; the passé simple is the *tense of the foreground*.

What is background and what is foreground in a narrative cannot be identified a priori if one has not yet accepted that background is in the imparfait, foreground in the passé simple. There are no fixed rules about the distribution of imparfait and passé simple in narrative except that they always come mixed. The individual distribution is up to the narrator. The narrator's freedom is, however, limited by several basic structures of narrative. A certain amount of exposition is necessary at the beginning of a story. Hence a narrative normally has an introduction. An introduction is usually in the background tense. Many narratives mark the end with an explicit conclusion. A conclusion, too, prefers the background tense. It is not required and is not always the case, but we do encounter relatively frequently a clustering of background tenses at the beginnings and endings of narratives, as seen in the legend of St. Dimitri. In the actual heart of the story we find background tenses (imparfait and plus-que-parfait) for secondary detail, description, reflection, and all other things the narrator wants to place in the background.

On the other hand, it can't be determined a priori what should be foregrounded in a narrative and hence should be in passé simple. The foreground is what the narrator wants to have understood as foreground. Here, too, the narrator's latitude is limited by some basic conditions of narration. According to the basic laws of narration, foreground is usually the reason the story is told; what the table of contents identifies; what the title summarizes or could summarize; whatever it is that makes people stop working and listen to a story whose world is not their everyday world; in a word, the "unerhörte Begebenheit" (extraordinary event; an expression used by Goethe and by subsequent literary critics over the centuries to characterize the novella genre). From this it becomes possible, conversely, to decide what the background of the story is. Background is, in the most general sense, what is not extraordinary, what in and of itself would cause no one to listen, but which aids the listener in listening and facilitates orientation in the narrated world.[3]

This explains why French has more narrative tenses than discussion tenses. Many languages offer more narrative tenses because it is more difficult to find one's way in the narrative world than in the world of discussion, our everyday world. When we discuss something, we normally have a variety of guides to understanding from the situation itself. Usually it is not difficult to figure out if the situation of the speaker and listener

---

3. Harro Stammerjohann takes a more extreme position, despite many agreements in principle; he considers only the French passé simple and the Italian passato remoto to be narrative, that is, tenses that drive the story forward. He considers neither the French imparfait nor the Italian imperfetto to be narrative tenses because they constitute the background, which he considers a generally past (completed) background. This view has some plausibility in regard to the short stories he uses as his corpus. I do not see, however, how this theory can describe larger and more complicated forms of narrative, such as long passages of free indirect discourse in modern novels. "Strukturen der Rede: Beobachtungen an der Umgangssprache von Florenz," *Studi di filologia italiana* 28 (1970): 295–397.

constitutes the topic of discussion. All sorts of gestures and the deictic elements of language make that clear, in which case the language of discussion mostly concerns the foreground. In the absence of all deictic pointers and the aids to understanding offered by the situation, the object of discussion withdraws of its own accord into the background, i.e., out of the immediate situation into something abstract or distant. Such language usually requires no tenses to make that clear. The situation itself speaks a clear language.

So non-linguistic means of communication do play a role even within the tense system, but they aid in determining meaning only in situations of discussion. The situation is of no help in the narrated world; this world can be communicated only with linguistic means. In particular, the communicative situation does not tell what is to be considered foreground and what background in the narrated world. Yet more linguistic means can be deployed in narration to compensate for the missing non-linguistic aids to communication, so that the same clarity of language can be achieved, namely the tense pairs imparfait—passé simple and pluperfect—passé antérieur. They perform for narrative what the situation does for discussion, in that both profile the meaning into foreground and background. Thus, beneath the observed asymmetry of the tense systems in French and the other Romance languages there lies at a more fundamental level a "beautiful" symmetry of the two tense groups. The narrative world has more tenses, and the world of discussion more situations (pragmatics).

The equivalence of situation and context is a constant in language. As a matter of principle, context and situation work together to determine the meanings of words and the opinion of the speaker and so to establish the sense of a speech act. This is a basic fact of semantics. The less determination there is available from the situation, the more must come from the context, and conversely. In comprehensible language, the sum of determination is constant, and the tenses participate in this system.

The function of highlighting has been noticed occasionally by linguists, but usually only as a secondary function of the imparfait and passé simple tenses, which continued to be seen primarily as temporal forms. In this context, for example, Larochette looks at the beginning of the messenger speech of Théramène (5.6) in Racine's *Phèdre* and notes the cluster of imparfait forms. For as long as the imparfait is used, Larochette writes, we understand that Racine is presenting the situation, the climate, the atmosphere. He characterizes imparfait as the tense of description, passé simple as the tense of narration. I agree with him, with the addition that the imparfait of course only serves as a tense of description within a narrative, that is, as narrated description. Sten also sees these functions. He writes it is often justified to speak of imparfait as a tense of description and of background which is then interrupted by some action. But he limits it by adding, "everything is subjective."[4] And in any case he regards that as only one function among many. All these reservations should be ignored. Highlighting with background and foreground is the one and only function of the opposition of imparfait and passé simple in narration.

Narrative Tempo in the Novel

It is possible, then, to predict only in general, but not in detail, how an author will distribute foreground and background. The details depend on the kind of narrative and also on the temperament of the author. Some dwell longer on the background; others prefer to spend their time on the foreground. The differences give narratives different tempos. It is possible to generate a historical typology of narrative literature on this basis, but that is not my intention here. I will only sketch briefly what such a typology might look like, illustrating it with the two extreme types, the first with more foreground tenses and the second with more background tenses.

Robert Champigny has called the passé simple "the preeminent Voltairian tense."[5] It is a lovely insight. Voltaire writes his novels in a terse and swift style that spends little time in the background. The imparfait occurs correspondingly seldom. Here is an example from the first chapter of his philosophical tale, *Candide*:

> Elle [Cunégonde] *rencontra* Candide en revenant au château, et *rougit*; Candide *rougit* aussi; elle lui *dit* bonjour d'une voix entrecoupée, et Candide lui *parla* sans savoir ce qu'il disait. Le lendemain après le diner, comme on sortait de table, Cunégonde et Candide se *trouvèrent* derrière un paravent; Cunégonde *laissa* tomber son mouchoir, Candide le *ramassa*, elle lui *prit* innocemment la main, le jeune homme *baisa* innocemment la main de la jeune demoiselle avec une vivacitè, une sensibilité, une grâce toute particulière, leurs bouches se *rencontrèrent*, leurs yeux *s'enflammèrent*, leur genoux *tremblèrent*, leurs mains *s'égarèrent*. Monsieur le baron de Thunder-ten-tronckh

---

4. Joe Larochette, "L'imparfait et le passé simple," *Les études classiques* 13, no. 1–2 (1945): 63–67; Holger Sten, *Les temps du verbe fini (indicatif) en français moderne* (Copenhagen: Munksgaard, 1964), 129. The expression *fond du décor* appears already in Jacques Damourette and Édouard Pichon, *Des mots à la pensée: Essai de grammaire de la langue française*, vol. 5 (Paris: d'Artrey, 1936), section 1731.

5. Robert Champigny, "Notes sur les temps passés en français," *The French Review* 28, no. 6 (1955): 522.

passa auprès du paravent, et, voyant cette cause et cet effet, *chassa* Candide du château à grands coups de pied dans le derrière; Cunégonde *s'évanouit*: elle *fut souffletée* de madame la baronne dès qu'elle *fut revenue* à elle-même; et tout *fut consterné* dans le plus beau et le plus agréable des châteaux possibles.⁶

Cunégonde met Candide on the way back to the castle, and blushed; Candide blushed too; she said good morning to him in a faltering voice; and Candide spoke to her without knowing what he was saying. The next day after dinner, as everyone was leaving the table, Cunégonde and Candide found themselves behind a screen; Cunégonde dropped her handkerchief, Candide picked it up, she innocently took his hand, the young man innocently kissed the maiden's hand with a very special vivacity, sensibility, and grace; their lips met, their eyes glowed, their knees trembled, their hands wandered. My Lord the Baron of Thunder-ten-tronckh passed near the screen and, seeing this cause and this effect, expelled Candide from the castle with great kicks in the behind; Cunégonde swooned; she was slapped in the face by My Lady the Baroness as soon as she had come to herself; and all was in consternation in the finest and most agreeable of all possible castles.⁷

This text, too, mixes forms of the imparfait (underlined) and of the passé simple (italics). But the ratio is so unusually tilted toward the passé simple as to create a particular stylistic effect. Against the nineteen forms of the passé simple (plus a passé antérieur) there are only two of the imparfait (disait, sortait). This is a very unusual disproportion. The narrative stays almost entirely in the foreground. The reader notices how the story remains on the one hand all on the surface (the anti-Voltairean might say superficial), on the other hand fleetfooted (the Voltaire enthusiast might say, winged). This is the terse style of "Veni, vidi, vici" (I came, I saw, I conquered), which also cannot be translated into other tenses.⁸ It, too, derives its vehemence precisely from the way it leaps beyond all circumstances and conditions. The events are compressed and reduced to their essence, which then emerges with particular clarity. When this narrative technique is elevated to a consistent stylistic pattern, the impression is

---

6. Voltaire, *Romans et contes*, ed. Henri Bénac (Paris: Garnier, 1965). 139.

7. Voltaire, *Candide, Zadig and Selected Stories*, tr. Daniel M. Frame (New York: Signet, 2009), 3.

8. See William Emerson Bull's discussion, *Time, Tense and the Verb* (Berkeley: U of California P, 1968), 53.

strengthened. In its most extreme compression ("their lips met, their eyes glowed, their knees trembled, their hands wandered") it reaches the expressiveness of caricature and enters the service of irony. Ironic caricatures are drawn mostly without background. Just for that reason they seem enigmatic, to be hiding something behind the foreground.

What serves Voltaire for caricature can also be made to serve other stylistic ends. As a comparison here is a passage from Flaubert's novel *L'éducation sentimentale* (1869, A Sentimental Education). It comes toward the end of the novel, at the beginning of the next-to-last chapter (3.6). It is about the protagonist, Frédéric Moreau.

> Il *voyagea*.
>
> Il *connut* la mélancolie des paquebots, les froids réveils sous la tente, l'étourdissement des paysages et des ruines, les amertumes des sympathies interrompues.
>
> Il *revint*.
>
> Il *fréquenta* le monde, et il *eut* d'autres amours encore.
>
> Mais le souvenir continuel du premier les lui rendait insipides.[9]
>
> (He traveled.
>
> He came to know the melancholy of the steamboats, the cold awakenings in a tent, the whirl of landscapes and ruins, the bitterness of interrupted friendships.
>
> He returned.
>
> He went into society, and he had still other loves.
>
> But the ever-present memory of the first made them insipid.)

In this passage, five forms of the passé simple follow one another in quick succession. Only then is there an imparfait (*rendait*, with others to follow). To understand this tense distribution correctly it helps to realize that the author is bridging over a period of some twenty years of experienced time with these five verbs in passé simple. The passage condenses the time and offers only a scanty summary of the events. What disappears first is of course the background, and the impression of condensed time increases to the degree that the background falls away.

---

9. Gustave Flaubert, *L'éducation sentimentale: Histoire d'un jeune homme*, ed. Édouard Maynial (Paris: Garnier, 1964), 419.

I have moved from Voltaire to Flaubert. Yet the passage cited from Flaubert is atypical. Flaubert's novels, like all the narrative literature of realism and naturalism, are characterized by a striking preponderance of imparfait forms. In this group Balzac, Flaubert, Zola, and even Proust stand at the contrary pole to the brisk passé-simple style of Voltaire. If we associate the prose of the eighteenth century with passé simple, then that of the nineteenth can be assigned to the imparfait. Examples are unnecessary here. The frequency of the imparfait can be confirmed by opening any random page of a realistic or naturalistic novel. One can see in *L'éducation sentimentale* how slowly and sparsely any kind of foreground action emerges from the broad description of conditions and then always falls back into it.

The phenomenon has often been observed since it was first noted by Ferdinand Brunetière.[10] His correct observation has attracted many problematic explanations in its wake. Antoine Meillet explains the preference of realistic and naturalistic novels for imparfait with the dislike of novelists for passé simple because it was disappearing from the spoken language and therefore "unrealistic."[11] That is not a good argument; in the twentieth century passé simple is even rarer than in the nineteenth century, yet it is used more frequently in the modern novel than it was in realist and naturalist novels.[12] Thus the profiling functions of passé simple and imparfait continue undiminished into the most recent French. Eugen Lerch also ties his impressionistic doctrine of "an imparfait of lively imagination" to Brunetière's observation and believes he has found it already in medieval French.[13] According to Lerch, the author imagines the material in lively fashion and dallies over it with loving elaboration. The realists, however, are interested less in lively imagination than with cool observation, and they do not elaborate their objects lovingly, but describe them with precision. That is something different.

The tense usage of the realist and naturalist writers in the nineteenth century is not a foible. To understand it the gates of grammar must be opened at least a crack in the direction of literature and literary history. From the

---

10. Ferdinand Brunetière, *Le roman naturaliste* (Paris: Calmann-Lévy, 1883), 84; see also Gustave Lanson, *L'art de la prose* (Paris: Librairie des Annales politiques et littéraires, 1909), 266.

11. Antoine Meillet, *Linguistique historique et linguistique générale* (Paris: E. Champion, 1921), 151.

12. Lewis Charles Harmer, *The French Language Today: Its Characteristics and Tendencies* (London: Hutchinson's University Library, 1954), 302 ff.

13. Antoine Meillet, *Linguistique historique et linguistique générale* (Paris: E. Champion, 1921), 151.

nineteenth century on, beginning with Balzac, the novel becomes realistic, and that means sociological. It no longer settles for telling a more or less beautiful and stimulating story, but increasingly develops the ambition to offer dependable—with the naturalists, even scholarly—information about the social relations of their time. To this end the main plot, which continues as earlier to involve few characters, is embedded in a broad—and, as time passes, ever broader—representation of the social background. The high point comes in *L'éducation sentimentale*, where Flaubert, with complete artistic and scholarly awareness, allows the main plot to suffocate in its own banality. The relationship between foreground and background in the narrative is reversed, in a sense, in that the background now becomes more important, the foreground less important. Even so, the foreground remains tied to passé simple and the background to imparfait. To the extent that the description of the (sociological) background takes over significance from the (only anecdotal) foreground, imparfait becomes not only more frequent, but also takes on more weight in the economy of the novel. The labels "realism" and "naturalism" together with their accompanying aesthetic theories refer to what stands in imparfait and take less and less interest in what appears in passé simple: any old incident will do. The essence of realist fiction and its particular relevance for literary study lies in the background.

Balzac's *Père Goriot* is a good example. The novel begins in three tense waves.[14] A first passage is in présent. Then comes one in imparfait. And only in the third wave does passé simple appear. The first passage describes the Pension Vauquer, which is not only the setting of the novel but also a typical pension. The description is a discussion of the social entity "Paris pension." Hence the present tense. In the second passage Balzac presents the situation of this pension at the time of the novel and describes its inhabitants. That too is not the picturesque description of some particular group of people, but a representative selection of Parisian society at a particular epoch. At the same time this description, in which the characters do not yet move, is the background for the main plot about to begin, when everyone will come alive and start to encounter their fates. That this second passage is in imparfait is motivated by the theory of narrative and by the theory of the novel. With the final passage the novel reaches the action to be narrated. In the course of the novel, however, Balzac constantly returns to sociological observation of what is typical.

The preference of a modern writer for the imparfait can also have other motivations. As Marcel Proust observed,

---

14. Roy Pascal, "Tense and Novel," *Modern Language Review* 57, no. 1 (1962): 10–11.

J'avoue que certain emploi de l'imparfait de l'indicatif—de ce temps cruel qui nous présente la vie comme quelque chose d'éphémère à la fois et de passif, qui, au moment même où il retrace nos actions, les frappe d'illusion, les anéant dans le passé sans nous laisser, comme le parfait, la consolation de l'activité—est resté pour moi une source inépuisable de mystérieuses tristesses.[15]

I confess that a certain use of the indicative imparfait—this cruel tense which presents life to us as something at once ephemeral and passive, which in the very moment that it relates our actions brands them as illusions, annihilates them in the past without consoling us, as the parfait does, with activity—has remained for me an inexhaustible source of mysterious sadness.

Furthermore, at least since Flaubert, novelists increasingly avoid drawing the attention of readers to themselves. They prefer to present the events from the perspective of the characters, that is, as their observations and reflections. The forms of this presentation are interior monologue and free indirect discourse. Both appear in imparfait. I shall return to this topic in another context (Chapter 8). This narrative technique, too, contributes to the frequency of imparfait in the novel since Balzac.

Baudelaire: "Le vieux saltimbanque"

The metaphor underlying the prose-poem, "Le vieux saltimbanque" (1861, The Old Mountebank), comes from some distance. We are dealing with the image of the world as a fair, which is related to the world as a game and the world as a theater. Baroque poetry loved these metaphors, and modern literature has not forgotten them. First, the text:

Partout s'étalait, se répandait, s'ébaudissait le peuple en vacances. C'était une de ces solennités sur lesquelles, pendant un long temps, comptent les saltimbanques, les faiseurs de tours, les montreurs d'animaux et les boutiquiers ambulants, pour compenser les mauvais temps de l'année.
    En ces jours-là il me semble que le peuple oublie tout, la douceur et le travail; il devient pareil aux enfants. Pour les petits c'est un jour de congé, c'est l'horreur de l'école renvoyée à vingt-quatre heures.

---

15. Marcel Proust, "Journées de lecture," in *Pastiches et mélanges* (Paris: Nouvelle Revue Française, 1919), 239, n. 1.

Pour les grands c'est un armistice conclu avec les puissances malfaisantes de la vie, un répit dans la contention et la lutte universelles.

L'homme du monde lui-même et l'homme occupé de travaux spirituels échappent difficilement à l'influence de ce jubilé populaire. Ils absorbent, sans le vouloir, leur part de cette atmosphère d'insouciance. Pour moi, je ne manque jamais, en vrai Parisien, de passer la revue de toutes les baraques qui se pavanent à ces époques solennelles.

Elles se faisaient, en vérité, une concurrence formidable: elles piaillaient, beuglaient, hurlaient. C'était un mélange de cris, de détonations de cuivre et d'explosions de fusées. Les queues-rouges et les jocrisses convulsaient les traits de leurs visages basanés, racornis par le vent, la pluie et le soleil; ils lançaient, avec l'aplomb des comédiens sûrs de leurs effets, des bons mots et des plaisanteries d'un comique solide et lourd comme celui de Molière. Les Hercules, fiers de l'énormité de leurs membres, sans front et sans crâne, comme les orangs-outangs, se prélassaient majestueusement sous les maillots lavés la veille pour la circonstance. Les danseuses, belles comme des fées ou des princesses, sautaient et cabriolaient sous le feu des lanternes qui remplissaient leurs jupes d'étincelles.

Tout n'était que lumière, poussière, cris, joie, tumulte; les uns dépensaient, les autres gagnaient, les uns et les autres également joyeux. Les enfants se suspendaient aux jupons de leurs mères pour obtenir quelque bâton de sucre, ou montaient sur les épaules de leurs pères pour mieux voir un escamoteur éblouissant comme un dieu. Et partout circulait, dominant tous les parfums, une odeur de friture qui était comme l'encens de cette fête.

Au bout, à l'extrême bout de la rangée de baraques, comme si, honteux, il s'était exilé lui-même de toutes ces splendeurs, je vis un pauvre saltimbanque, voûté, caduc, décrépit, une ruine d'homme, adossé contre un des poteaux de sa cahute; une cahute plus misérable que celle du sauvage le plus abruti, et dont deux bouts de chandelles, coulants et fumants, éclairaient trop bien encore la détresse.

Partout la joie, le gain, la débauche; partout la certitude du pain pour les lendemains; partout l'explosion frénétique de la vitalité. Ici la misère absolue, la misère affublée, pour comble d'horreur, de haillons comiques, où la nécessité, bien plus que l'art, avait introduit le contraste. Il ne riait pas, le misérable! Il ne pleurait pas, il ne dansait pas, il ne gesticulait pas, il ne criait pas; il ne chantait aucune chanson, ni gaie ni lamentable, il n'implorait pas. Il était muet et immobile. Il avait renoncé, il avait abdiqué. Sa destinée était faite.

Mais quel regard profond, inoubliable, il promenait sur la foule et les lumières, dont le flot mouvant s'arrêtait à quelques pas de sa répulsive misère! Je sentis ma gorge serrée par la main terrible de l'hystérie, et il me sembla que mes regards étaient offusqués par ces larmes rebelles qui ne veulent pas tomber.

Que faire? A quoi bon demander à l'infortuné quelle curiosité, quelle merveille il avait à montrer dans ces ténèbres puantes, derrière son rideau déchiqueté? En vérité, je n'osais; et, dût la raison de ma timidité vous faire rire, j'avouerai que je craignais de l'humilier. Enfin, je venais de me résoudre à déposer en passant quelque argent sur une de ses planches, espérant qu'il devinerait mon intention, quand un grand reflux de peuple, causé par je ne sais quel trouble, m'entraîna loin de lui.

Et, m'en retournant, obsédé par cette vision, je cherchai à analyser ma soudaine douleur, et je me dis: Je viens de voir l'image du vieil homme de lettres qui a survécu à la génération dont il fut le brillant amuseur; du vieux poète sans amis, sans famille, sans enfants, dégradé par sa misère et par l'ingratitude publique, et dans la baraque de qui le monde oublieux ne veut plus entrer![16]

Everywhere the holiday crowd was parading, spread out, merrymaking. It was one of those festivals on which mountebanks, tricksters, animal trainers and itinerant merchants had long been relying, to compensate for the dull seasons of the year.

On such days it seems to me the people forget all, sadness and work; they become children. For the little ones, it is a day of leave, the horror of school put off twenty-four hours. For the grown-ups, it is an armistice concluded with the malevolent forces of life, a respite in the universal contention and struggle.

The man of the world himself, and even those occupied with spiritual tasks, hardly escape the influence of this popular jubilee. They absorb willy-nilly their share of the atmosphere of devil-may-care. As for me, I never fail, like a true Parisian, to inspect all the booths that flaunt themselves in these solemn epochæ.

They made, in truth, a formidable gathering: they bawled, bellowed, howled. It was a mingling of cries, of blaring of brass and bursting of rockets. The clowns and the simpletons convulsed the

---

16. Charles Baudelaire, *Oeuvres complètes*, ed. Marcel Ruff (Paris: Seuil, 1968), 165–66.

features of their swarthy faces, hardened by wind, rain, and sun; they hurled forth, with the assurance of comedians certain of their wares, witticisms and pleasantries of a humor solid and heavy as that of Molière. The Hercules, proud of the enormousness of their limbs, without forehead, without cranium, like orang-outangs, stalked majestically about under vests fresh washed for the occasion. The dancers, pretty as fairies or as princesses, leapt and cavorted under the flare of lanterns which filled their skirts with sparkles.

All was light, dust, shouting, joy, tumult; some spent, others earned, both equally joyful. Children clung to their mothers' skirts to obtain a sugar-stick, or climbed upon their fathers' shoulders the better to see a conjurer dazzling as a god. And spread over all, dominating every aroma, was an odor of frying, which was the incense of the festival.

At the end, at the extreme end of the row of booths, as if, ashamed, he had exiled himself from all these splendors, I saw an old mountebank, stooped, decrepit, emaciated, a ruin of a man, leaning against one of the pillars of his hut, more wretched than that of the most besotted barbarian, the distress of which two candle ends, guttering and smoking, lighted up only too well.

Everywhere joy, gain, revelry; everywhere certainty of the morrow's bread; everywhere frenetic outbursts of vitality. Here, absolute misery, misery bedecked, to crown the horror, in comic tatters, where necessity, rather than art, produced the contrast. He was not laughing, the wretched one! He was not weeping, he was not dancing, he was not gesticulating, he was not crying. He was singing no song, gay or grievous, he was imploring no one. He was mute and immobile. He had renounced, he had withdrawn. His destiny was accomplished.

But what a deep, unforgettable look he cast over the crowd and the lights, the moving stream of which paused a few steps from his repulsive wretchedness! I felt my throat clutched by the terrible hand of hysteria, and it seemed as though glances were clouded by rebellious tears that would not fall.

What was to be done? What good was there in asking the unfortunate what curiosity, what marvel he had to show within those reeking shadows, behind his threadbare curtain? In truth, I dared not; and, although the reason for my timidity will make you laugh, I confess that I was afraid of humiliating him. At length, I had resolved to drop a coin while passing his boards, in the hope that he would divine my purpose, when a great backwash of people, produced by I know not what disturbance, carried me far away.

And leaving, obsessed by the sight, I sought to analyze my sudden sadness, and I said to myself: "I have just seen the image of the aged man of letters, who has survived the generation of which he was the brilliant entertainer; of the old poet, friendless, without family, without child, degraded by his misery and by public ingratitude, into whose booth a forgetful world no longer wants to go!"[17]

There would be much to discuss in an interpretation of this prose-poem, but here only the tense distribution will be considered. But this already reveals significant structural elements. In this text the narrative tenses dominate. The narrator reports a memorable incident: the meeting with an old mountebank at the fair. From the beginning he makes clear, however, that the meeting interests him not for its uniqueness. "C'était une de ces solennités" (It was one of those festivals), he says, with one of those famous formulas from Balzac that sets a unique occurrence into the horizon of a known context. The context is made explicit immediately after the exposition. After this first paragraph in imparfait as the tense of narrative exposition, he shifts into présent, with which he discusses the general phenomenon of the fair in the second and third paragraphs. The fair, as a particular event that can be narrated, has thus now become the fair as a typical popular festival that can be discussed.

Once the reader has been prepared in this way to understand the individual as implying the general, the narrator continues his tale. At the end he returns once again, and now definitively, to the world of discussion. Now he reflects on the event and interprets it. The interpretation is explicit, it uses technical terms of interpretation like "vision," "image," and "analyze." With corresponding clarity the final lines set the mountebank equal to the man of letters who has outlived his generation and with the elderly poet who lives out the rest of his life abandoned by the world. In contrast to the broader image of the world as fair, this interpretation of the world has narrowed to the literary world. The favorite theme of modern poetry is poetry.

The shift from the narrated to the discussed (that is, interpreted) encounter with the mountebank at the end of the prose-poem is of course at the same time another shift of tenses. After the tenses of the narrated world come now again the tenses of discussion—présent and passé composé. The shift is marked formally, in addition to the tense change, through two verbs of communication: "je cherchai à analyser," "je me dis"

---

17. Charles Baudelaire, *Baudelaire: His Prose and Poetry*, ed. T. R. Smith, tr. Joseph T, Shipley (New York: Boni and Liveright, 1919), 67–68, translation modified.

(I sought to analyze, I said to myself). In the midst of these markers of discussion stands yet another narrative tense, "dont il fut le brillant amuseur" (of which he was the brilliant entertainer).

In the narrative segment of the prose-poem the persona reports about a visit to the Paris fair. As a genuine Parisian, we learn, the narrator routinely visits entertainments of this sort. Apparently he likes anonymously disappearing into the tumult and observing the crowd at its most crowded. First described by Baudelaire himself and after him by Walter Benjamin, he is the flaneur who makes his observations in passing. This flaneur is assigned—apart from the tense shift just mentioned—all the forms of the passé simple contained in this text: "je vis," "je sentis," "il me sembla," "m'entraîna," "je cherchai," "je me dis" (I saw, I felt, it seemed, carried me away, I sought, I said). If the argument of this book is correct, that passé simple is the foreground tense in narrative, then we must imagine the flaneur in the foreground of the scene. The gay figures of the performers together with their booths as well as the tumultuous crowd of visitors to the fair observed by the flaneur constitute the background of the scene. There, in the background, the old acrobat also has his place. The extraordinary event signalized by the first passé simple, "je vis," happens only to the observer, not to the man he has observed. Henceforth he is narrated in imparfait, just like the other curiosities of the fair. He remains a bit of this background. We may understand this to mean that he does not even recognize what meaning his fate suddenly takes on in the reflection of the flaneur.

The flaneur is without companion. He moves as an individual through the crowd. The reader, too, is an individual, and addressed once directly by the narrator ("although the reason for my timidity will make you laugh"), as if sharing a confidence. From various signs in the text it can be concluded that the narrator tells this occurrence to someone he considers his equal. Both are well read, both intellectuals. So the experience of reversal between the flaneur in the foreground and the crowd in the background is an experience the reader is to share. To read the poem adequately the reader must join the flaneur and share his views. Not by chance almost all passé simple forms in this text are verbs of communication—saw, felt, seemed, sought, said. They force upon the reader the view of the fair from the perspective of the flaneur. The single passé simple that is not a verb of communication characterizes the narrator as flaneur: "quand un grand reflux de peuple, causé par je ne sais quel trouble, m'entraîna loin de lui" (when a great backwash of people, produced by I know not what disturbance, carried me far away). This form stands on the boundary between the narrative and the interpretive discussion.

These few observations by no means exhaust Baudelaire's prose-poem. Yet they perhaps suffice to make clear how linguistic textual structures can be the basis for suggestive literary interpretation. Among these, tense structures carry substantial weight. If the distribution of tenses in this text in connection with other grammatical signals renders visible a narrative structure that causes the reader to identify with the narrator and to share his experience, then this prose-poem is not told just to entertain. The reader should read from this poem that the mountebank is personally relevant. The prose-poem is told in a mood of dismay. For that effect one can also use a term much loved of the baroque and connected to the world-as-fair motif ever since. This prose-poem is invested in "desengaño," dis-illusioning.[18]

Of the Tense of Death

What difference does it make to say "il mourait" (he died, imparfait) vs. "il mourut" (passé simple), or "il se noyait" (drowned, imparfait) vs. "il se noya" (passé simple)? Grammars adore this example, and not only Romance grammars, but also Greek and Russian grammars.[19]

Expressions of dying seem to be especially suitable for illuminating the essence of verb aspect. Anyone of whom it is said "il mourait" or "il se noyait" can live on happily. But anyone of whom they say "il mourut" or "il se noya" is really dead. This is the substance of the grammatical rule abstracted from the two tenses. Imparfait is often characterized in this context as "imperfectum de conatu," as imparfait of a mere attempt, and compared to the corresponding imperfect in Latin. The example in a whole series of grammars is a sentence from Victor Hugo's play *Marie Tudor* (1.2), "Moi je me noyais un beau jour dans la Tamise, tu m'as tiré de l'eau" (As for me, I was drowning one fine day in the Thames, you pulled me from the water).[20] Examples can be inherited, and the explanations

---

18. I have analyzed additional Baudelaire poems in "Baudelaire-Lektüre," *Literatur für Leser* (Munich: Deutscher Taschenbuch Verlag, 1986), 101–31.

19. Harry Thornton and Agathe Thornton, *Time and Style: A Psycho-Linguistic Essay in Classical Literature* (London: Methuen, 1962), 97; Wolfgang Pollak, *Studien zum "Verbalaspekt" im Französischen* (Vienna: Rudolf M. Rohrer, 1960), 42.

20. The example sentence from Hugo's *Marie Tudor* is found in Bernhard Schmitz, *Französische Grammatik* (Berlin: Reimer, 1867), in Eduard Mätzner, *Französische Grammatik mit besonderer Berücksichtigung des Lateinischen* (Berlin: Weidmann, 1885), in Philipp Plattner, *Ausführliche Grammatik der französische Sprache* (Freiburg im Breisgau: Bielefeld, 1920), and, with the word "mourir" instead of "se noyer," in Henri Bonnard, *Grammaire française des lycées et collèges* (Paris: Sudel, 1960).

resemble one another closely. They describe this use of the imparfait as an "imperfect of an action begun only but not completed" (Plattner 273). Similarly in Bonnard's French grammar, "L'action de mourir n'a pas été accomplie, d'où l'imparfait" (the action of dying is not completed, hence the imparfait). This explanation is so popular because it seems to justify so convincingly the term imperfect, imparfait, for the tense and the aspect of incomplete action. Spanish grammar has also adopted the example. In the syntax of Samuel Gili y Gaya it appears in the form, "Le dió un dolor tan fuerte que se moría; hoy está mejor" (He had such pain that he was dying; today he is better). The patient who was said to be dying is still alive. Gili y Gaya also calls the tense "imperfecto de conatu." Knud Togeby says the same and attributes to the expression "se moría" the possible nuance "to be about to die."[21]

How does imperfect come to take on the nuance of being about to—of trying? Sten (25 ff.) turns to semantics to explain the example of "il se noyait." The meaning of the word "drown" has been met, even if help arrives at the last minute and the drowning does not end in death. Howard B. Garey opposes this view.[22] He posed this question to a series of French speakers, "Figurez-vous un homme qui se noyait, mais qu'on a tiré du fleuve avant qu'il n'ait pu mourir: s'est-il noyé?" (Imagine that someone is drowning, but that he is pulled from the river before he has died: did he drown?). All the French speakers unhesitatingly answered, "No, of course he didn't drown." Garey then offers his own solution by combining the concepts of aspect and kind of action. The French language has a number of verbs whose kind of action implies completion. He calls these "telic verbs" (from Greek *telos*, goal). "Mourir" and "se noyer" belong to this group. Whenever such words appear as imparfait—and Garey understands imparfait to be a past tense with the aspect of incompletion—then the incomplete aspect defeats the point of the telic verb and causes "il mourait" to mean "he lay dying," and "il se noyait" to mean "he almost drowned."

I will argue against all positions in this discussion and cannot agree with even a single argument here because the whole way of posing the question is distorted. If it is reformulated, then the problem disappears. The verbs of dying relate to tenses no differently from other verbs. The death of a person, like any other occurrence, can be discussed or narrated.

---

21. Samuel Gili y Gaya, *Curso superior de sintaxis española* (Mexico: Minerva, 1943), 140; Knud Togeby, *Mode, aspect et temps en espagnol* (Copenhagen: Munksgaard, 1953), 125.

22. Howeard B. Garey, "Verbal Aspect in French," *Language* 33, no. 2 (1957): 91–110.

Hence the verbs of dying can obviously appear in all tenses. Assume the death (drowning) took place some time ago. Then, in a retrospective discussion, one can say, "Il est mort" (he died). Someone who has to report a death—certainly no situation for relaxed narration—would say it this way. But it is possible to narrate a person's death. Histories and novels often have to do that. They use a narrative tense. Which one? That is impossible to predict and depends, like all determination of tenses in narrative, on the structure of the narrative and on the place of this bit of text in the whole of the narrative. One must not forget in the grammatical analysis that a person's death is not one occurrence in an arbitrary series of other events. Death is the most important event in a person's life. That is also reflected in language, as long as it is not separated from every real situation. So when a person's death is narrated, the narrator of course sets this important event in the tense of the narrative foreground, and we find passé simple, "Il mourut" ("Il se noya"). What events could be put in the foreground if the death of a character in the story is left in the background? Death is by definition an extraordinary event.

But under certain circumstances death can also retreat to the background of a narrative. No one but the narrator decides on the distribution of foreground and background. There are now some conditions under which a narrator is impelled to place even a human death in the background. One of these conditions is the special status of the introduction and conclusion in a narrative. These tend to surround the main plot as background. Thus Victor Hugo begins his narrative poem "L'expiation" (Atonement) with a large introductory tableau of the defeat of Napoleon's army before Moscow. This tableau is background description vis-à-vis the main narrative. It is told in imparfait. Only in line 60 does the main narrative begin with a passé simple. Georges and Robert Le Bidois criticize this use of tense (1:432–3); they have misunderstood its art. They could have learned from Stendhal's *Chartreuse de Parme* (The Charterhouse of Parma) and Tolstoy's *War and Peace* how effectively a battle tableau from the background perspective can highlight a literary narrative.

In the introductory battle tableau of Hugo's poem, the following lines appear: "Chefs, soldats, tous mouraient. / Chacun avait son tour" (Leaders, soldiers, all died. / Each had his turn). Napoleon's soldiers are really dying. The verb form "mouraient" cannot possibly mean here "they lay dying," certainly not with the implication "but they escaped." No, they did not escape death. The supposedly imperfective aspect of the imparfait does not defeat the purpose of the "telic" verb "mourir." This sentence is in the background tense imparfait exclusively for the sake of the narrative economy of the poem and for no other reason. If this battle description were the main topic of the poem—the title, "L'expiation," already shows that it is really about something else—then Hugo might, possibly but not necessarily, have used passé simple. The thing narrated would not have changed, but only the status of the narration, that which I have been calling its "highlighting."

The same observation can be made about Spanish. In Spanish, too, a verb of dying in imperfecto by no means implies that the death might not have taken place. Here are two examples from the ends of stories by Miguel de Unamuno.[23] In both, someone's dying is in imperfecto, even though death is not avoided, and even though the action is punctual:

> Y la Virgen de la Fresnada, Madre de Compasiones, oyendo los ruegos de Matilde, a los tres meses de la fiesta se la *llevaba* a que la retozasen los ángeles. ("El espejo de la muerte," 221; And the Virgin of Fresneda, compassionate mother, hearing Matilda's prayers, carried her off three months after the fiesta so the angels could frolic with her).

> Dias después Pérez se *pegaba* un tiro, después de escribir a Ibarrondo una carta en que le decía que le había puesto ante los ojos un espejo en que vio su inutilidad ("Una tragedia," 383; Days later Pérez shot himself after writing a letter to Ibarrondo in which he said that he had placed before him a mirror in which he saw his uselessness).

As a counterexample, in the middle of the main plot of another story, a foreground tense seems obvious: "A los cuatro dias Enrique se *quitó* la vida de un tiro dejando escrita una carta para Antonio" ("El padrino Antonio," 311; Four days later Enrique shot himself after writing a card to Antonio). In order to understand this tense it is necessary to know that Enrique is not the hero of this story. The hero is, as the title indicates, Antonio, whose story begins only with the death of his young rival Enrique, who has seduced his fiancée. What we thought was foreground was really only background, and to our surprise comes only now the real extraordinary event. This reversal shows that the choice of foreground tense or background tense is determined only by its position in the narrative and nothing else, even in narrating a person's death.

---

23. Miguel de Unamuno, *Cuentos completos*, ed. Óscar Carrascosa Tinoco (Madrid: Páginas de Espuma, 2011).

5 / Tense in Novellas and Short Stories: Highlighting vs. Aspect

Maupassant

Around 1850, as Charles Bruneau observes in his revision of a classic grammar, there appears in French, first and foremost in Maupassant, a new imparfait that irritatingly deviates from the traditional markers of time and aspect. At issue are sentences like this: "Le lendemain, vers une heure de l'après-midi, Marius Paumelle . . . rendait le portefeuille" (The next day, about one in the afternoon, Marius Paumelle . . . returned the pocketbook). Bruneau calls this new tense "imparfait de rupture."[1] It has attracted so much attention because it appears exactly in those sentences that, according to the old doctrine of aspect, identify a punctual occurrence. In the sentence above the occurrence is specified by an exact time, indeed by the eminently punctual one o'clock bell so beloved of the doctrine of aspect; it is also specified by the meaning of the sentence, since the return of a wallet is a singular and punctual event. So, why imparfait?

All sorts of explanations for this imparfait de rupture have been advanced, but they cannot gloss over the failure of aspect, as traditionally understood, to explain it. Here, too, we are better served by a text-linguistic interpretation of tense in relation to narrative considerations,

---

1. Guy de Maupassant, *Contes et nouvelles*, ed. Louis Forestier, 2 vols. (Paris: Gallimard, 1980, 1979) 1:1085; Ferdinand Brunot and Charles Bruneau, *Précis de grammaire historique de la langue française*, 3rd ed. (Paris: Masson, 1949), 377. Online translations from Maupassant are used where available; here, online-literature.com/maupassant/270/. Where no online source is given for a story, the translation is ours.

specifically highlighting. Why does the imparfait de rupture emerge only around 1850, and just in short stories? Why has it been observed only in French even though the narrative tense group is identically structured in the other Romance languages? With these questions let us turn to Romance language stories, naturally without limiting the investigation to the imparfait de rupture but taking account of the full distribution of narrative tenses.

In its entirety, the first example reads as follows: "Le lendemain, vers une heure de l'après-midi, Marius Paumelle, valet de ferme de maître Breton, cultivateur à Ymauville, rendait le portefeuille et son contenu à maître Houlbrèque, de Manneville" (The next day, about one in the afternoon, Marius Paumelle, a farmhand of Maître Breton, the market gardener at Ymauville, returned the pocketbook and its contents to Maître Houlbreque, of Manneville). It comes from the story, "La Ficelle" (The Piece of String). It is impossible to understand either the sentence or the tense without knowing the story. Only after an interpretation of the story, and then with some effort, can the imparfait de rupture be explained. It is necessary to know that Maître Hauchecorne, as a thrifty man, has picked up a piece of string at the market and stuck it in his pocket. Chance will have it that another visitor to the market has lost his wallet. Maître Hauchecorne comes under suspicion of having found the lost wallet and kept it. Then the wallet is found by another market visitor and turned in. The suspicion is dispelled, and the story is at an end. At least that's what the reader assumes, but Maupassant has lured him down the wrong track. In reality, the suspicion sticks to the unfortunate finder, and he is destroyed by it.

The narrative cleverness of the wrong track is precisely that the return of the wallet seems to lead to a happy ending, to which the actual tragic ending contrasts all the more blatantly. At this point comes the imparfait de rupture. It should mark the denouement, the solution of the tale's complication and its retreat into the background tense. It is a misleading signal of conclusion, and it could not mislead the reader if the imparfait were not unambiguously established as a signal of closing in a narrative. The tense depends exclusively on the narrative value of the position of the sentence in the story. In the same story, there is the sentence: "Ils s'injurièrent une heure durant" (1:1084; They railed at one another for an hour). The verb is just as durative as one could desire. Yet it is passé simple. The sentence belongs, namely, to the foreground of the story.

In the story, "La main d'écorché" (The Flayed Hand), Maupassant narrates the process of a progressive mental illness that ends in death. The illness spreads slowly and persistently. We thus find sentences like this:

Pendant sept mois, j'*allai* le voir tous les jours à l'hospice (1:6; For seven months I went to see him daily at the hospice).

Pendant deux heures, il *resta* fort calme (1:7; For two hours he remained very calm).

Il *fit* deux fois le tour de la chambre en hurlant (1:7; He circled the room twice screaming).

In terms of the aspect of the action, these sentences are clearly durative or iterative. But from a different point of view, we note simply that these sentences belong to the main plot of the story, which deals exactly with the progressive, and indeed slowly progressive mental illness. Anyone summarizing the story has to mention it, otherwise it would not be possible to identify the summary with the actual story. For this reason, therefore, and for no other reason, we have passé simple, and not for anything to do with aspects or kinds of action. Passé simple is found similarly in the following sentence: "Le lendemain, comme je passais devant sa porte, j'*entrai* chez lui" (1:4; The next day, as I was passing his door, I went in to him). Despite the indication of a later time ("le lendemain") as in the story *La Ficelle*, we do not find here imparfait de rupture. It is not caused simply by a particular adverb of time, nor an adverb of later time, but is a function of the larger narrative structure. This sentence comes in the middle of the story, and the progression of the disease continues to be the topic. "As I was passing his door" is the background for the decision to enter. Then we are in the main plot, for which passé simple is the obvious tense. At the end of the story Maupassant brings the narrative back out of the foreground into the background and thereby closes the story. There again we really have imparfait de rupture: "Le lendemain tout *était* fini et je *reprenais* la route de Paris après avoir laissé cinquante francs au vieux curé pour dire des messes pour le repos de l'âme de celui dont nous *avions* ainsi troublé la sépulture" (1:8; The next day it was all over and I resumed my journey to Paris after having left fifty francs with the old curé to say some masses for the soul of the one whose grave we had disturbed). This is the final sentence of the story. If one did not know it, it could have been predicted from the tense, that the narration, or at least a segment of it, was ending. The indication of time, "le lendemain," however, allows no such prediction.

The story, "Le lit 29" (Bed 29), is similarly told as if Maupassant wanted to show off the whole range of possible highlighting by means of tenses. It tells of the love affair between Captain Épivent and Irma, a lady of easy virtue. The story begins with a leisurely broad introduction in imparfait": "Quand le capitaine Épivent *passait* dans la rue, toutes les femmes se *retournaient*. Il *présentait* vraiment le type du bel officier de hussards (2:174; Whenever Captain Épivent passed along the street, all the women turned to look. He represented truly the epitome of a handsome officer of the hussards). After the broadly painted introduction the main plot emerges with sharp shifts to passé simple: "Or, en 1868, son régiment, le 102ᵉ hussards, *vint* tenir garnison à Rouen" "Or, un soir, la belle Irma, la maîtresse, disait-on, de M. Templier-Papon, le riche manufacturier, *fit* arrêter sa voiture en face de la Comédie" (2:176, 177; Now, in 1868, his regiment, the 102ⁿᵈ hussars, took up quarters in Rouen.... Now, one evening, the lovely Irma, the mistress, it was said, of M. Templier-Papon, the rich manufacturer, halted her carriage in front of the Comédie). Sentences beginning with "or" and an indication of time are typical for the beginning of main plots in Maupassant. Normally then he uses passé simple. Again Maupassant sets his readers on the wrong track. It looks as though the handsome captain immediately displaces his rival and wins Irma's favor in the twinkling of an eye: "Elle le *vit*, se *montra*, *sourit*. Le soir même, il *était* son amant" (2:177; She saw him, showed herself, smiled. That very evening he was her lover). If the text were defective at this point, so that we had only the sequence of tenses (passé simple, passé simple, passé simple, imparfait) as a cluster, perhaps in conjunction with an indication of time having passed, we would be able to determine the importance of this point in the narrative economy of the story with considerable precision. The veni-vidi-vici model with imparfait de rupture following indicates clearly victory and triumph.

But the story would not be by Maupassant if it remained so idyllic. War destroys the swiftly won happiness: "Mais voilà que la guerre *éclata* et que le régiment du capitaine *fut* envoyé à la frontière un des premiers. Les adieux *furent* lamentables. Ils *durèrent* toute une nuit" (2:178; But then war broke out and the captain's regiment was one of the first sent to the frontier. The farewells were pitiful. They lasted an entire night). Nothing could be more durative than their night-long embrace. But the tense here is passé simple because these sentences are the turning point of the story and so are eminently part of the main plot. Just as the captain's love affair began with the assignment of his regiment to Rouen (the sentence was cited above, and naturally in passé simple), the destruction of the affair begins with the departure of the regiment and the farewells of the lovers. The choice of tense in these sentences depends only on their position in the whole story and on nothing else.

The story, "Le parapluie" (The Umbrella), begins similarly with a broad background narrative. Then the foreground narrative begins. How can we tell? Maupassant piles into the first sentence of his foreground plot no less than four signals. The sentence begins with "Or," it has a time indication, it uses the title-word, umbrella, for the first time in the story, and it is the first sentence in passé simple: "Or, pendant deux ans, il *vint* au bureau avec le même parapluie rapiécé qui donnait à rire à ses collègues" (1:1184; Now, for two years he came to the office with the same old patched umbrella, to the great amusement of his fellow clerks [online-literature.com/maupassant/4296/]). The action is certainly iterative, or whatever term one prefers to use, but that is not the issue. The everyday tragedy of the story depends on the umbrella: that alone is of concern to Maupassant and only for that reason is the verb passé simple. It would seem that these examples show clearly enough that foreground and background as narrative highlighting cannot be defined a priori. Anyone reading a narrative will notice immediately and usually so clearly that no doubt is possible, where the foreground plot begins, where it is interrupted, and where it ends. Should doubt ever arise, one ought to try to summarize the plot. The summary will order the events by itself into foreground and background—by dropping the background.

This general observation will have to be nuanced for realistic and naturalistic novels, in which the social background is especially important, but it need not be retracted. In Flaubert's *L'éducation sentimentale*, to return to an example already discussed, imparfait is used even in the inner parts of the novel with greater frequency and is found much more often in coherent descriptions. But at bottom, even a novel like this is built on the same principles of narration as a story by Maupassant. In the novel, too, we find the introductory imparfait: "Le 15 septembre 1840, vers six heures du matin, *la Ville-de-Montereau*, près de partir, *fumait* à gros tourbillons devant le quai Saint-Bernard" (On September 15, 1840, around six in the morning, the "City of Monterau," about to depart, was sending up great whirls of smoke at the Saint-Bernard pier).[2] And there is a representative imparfait de rupture in the last chapter: "Quant à Frédéric, ayant mangé les deux tiers de sa fortune, il *vivait* en petit bourgeois" (424; As for Frédéric, having consumed two-thirds of his fortune, he was living a modest bourgeois existence). The big difference from Maupassant, however, lies in the fact that this sentence does not simply add a final gratuitous nuance, but delivers the quintessence of the novel. To be sure, it is not the last sentence in the novel (the novel ends with dialogue), but it is surely Flaubert's "last word." Frédéric Moreau's various attempts to

---

2. Gustave Flaubert, *L'éducation sentimentale: Histoire d'un jeune homme*, ed. Édouard Maynial (Paris: Garnier, 1964), 1.

elevate himself above the dull average of his social milieu and to lead the existence of a literary hero have failed definitively. He will never again be in the foreground of a novel or in the floodlights of the public interest, but will return for the rest of his days to the background of his petit-bourgeois everyday life. The background is important, to be sure, but only as background. It becomes an object of sociological interest, but not the foreground of the narrative.

Pirandello

Why don't the other Romance languages have an imparfait de rupture, since they use the same structure of tenses for narrative highlighting? An answer to this question is hardly necessary: They do use the narrative tenses in the same way as French. Italian stories strongly resemble French ones in their use of tenses and do indeed use, if I may construct a term in analogy to French, an imperfetto di rottura. It never became as fashionable in Italy as in France. But it appears in Pirandello's stories with considerable frequency.

In "La casa del Granella" (The Haunted House), the house has a ghost. Granella laughs about it and undertakes to spend a night alone in the haunted house. It does not agree with him. The supposed ghost attacks him so viciously that he doesn't last the night and runs off. Pirandello narrates the phases of Granella's consciousness, from the courageous entry to the ignominious exit. That is the topic of the story, at least in its last section. It is told, appropriately, in the tense of the narrative foreground, passato remoto: "I capelli gli si *drizzarono* su la fronte . . . E *rise* Granella della paura . . . Granella non *potè* più reggere (412–13; His hair stood on end . . . And Granella laughed from fear . . . Granella could not take any more). The final sentence of the story reads, however: "Ma il povero Granella, tutto tremante, *piangeva*, e non *poteva* parlare" (415; But poor Granella, trembling all over, was crying and unable to speak).[3] It is imperfetto di rottura, since the narrative breaks off here. The last sentence does not mean that Granella cries continuously, repeatedly, or especially pitifully. It is preceded by the spiteful question of Lawyer Zummo whether he believes in spirits, and his crying is the answer to the question. It belongs exclusively to this particular linguistic situation. It ends the story and dismisses the reader into the real world.

---

3. Pirandello, Luigi, *Novelle per un anno*, https://www.academia.edu/9730466/Pirandello_novelle_per_un_anno, 412–13, 415.

Especially suggestive for the art of tense usage in Pirandello is "L'uomo solo" (The Lonely Man). It is the story of four men who all have no wife and suffer from loneliness. And they all wait for a woman who will redeem them from loneliness. They wait in vain. One of the men, the father Groa, finally takes his own life. The tense usage of the story is unusual, in that it is written almost entirely in imperfetto. Only the dramatic climax to suicide is in passato remoto. The tense usage artfully emphasizes the narrated situation. The imperfetto is the linguistic equivalent of waiting. Nothing exceptional happens in the lonely lives of the four men; they feel like they have been pushed into the background. The story is in three parts, but the introductory and concluding sections—the first more than the last—are much expanded, while the middle foreground action is tightly squeezed between them.

Narrative highlighting becomes especially evident when the same event is told several times. In this story it happens twice. Right at the beginning, the meeting of the four characters in a café is described and the story begins with the imperfetto: "Si *riunivano* all'aperto, ora che la stagione lo *permetteva*, attorno a un tavolinetto del caffè sotto gli alberi di via Veneto. *Venivano* prima i Groa, padre e figlio. . . . *Venivano* alla fine insieme gli altri due: Filippo Romelli e Carlo Spina" (776; They met outdoors, now that the season allowed it, around a small cafe table beneath the trees in the via Veneto. First came the Groas, father and son. . . . At last the other two arrived together: Filippo Romalli and Carlo Spina). Is that supposed to mean that they met there customarily? They presumably did, but Pirandello by no means uses his tenses to indicate whether they met once or repeatedly. Certain hints about the season and the order of arrival, which can scarcely always be identical, suggest rather that this meeting should be understood as a single occurrence. Most accurate would be to say, the narrator is indifferent at this point as to whether or not they meet regularly. He does not write minutes for a meeting, but for the sake of a story. And the story demands that somewhere at the beginning the situation and characters be explained. These sentences are the exposition. The reader wants to know the names of the characters and their problem. And exactly that is presented, as the additional context, not cited here, reveals.

Then, however, after five pages of introductory narrative in imperfetto, Pirandello returns to the entire scene. Once again the four friends come to the meeting place, or, more precisely, Pirandello narrates their meeting once again. He sets us in the moment where the Groas, father and son, have already arrived at the café but still await Romelli and Spina: "I due amici Spina e Romelli tardavano ancora a venire.... Alla fine, quegli altri due *arrivarono*" (783–84; Their two friends Spina and Romelli were again late in coming.... At last the other two arrived). Here is now the story's first passato remoto. We have reached the main action and are now in the foreground of the narrative. The same event, therefore—the arrival of the friends Spina and Romelli—is told once in the imperfetto (*venivano*), then in the passato remoto (*arrivarono*). The narrator's choice of tense is determined by the basic laws of narration.

Another event is also told twice. Groa, who is divorced from his wife, sends his son to her several times to persuade her to return. The mission fails every time, and Groa is disappointed and embittered. The event is narrated first in the long introductory section that is characterized as a unit by the monotony of the imperfetto. Groa receives the bad news thus: "Ah, niente, è vero? E si *mordeva* le mani dalla rabbia; poi *prorompeva*" (781; Ah, nothing, right? And he bit his hands in rage; then he burst out). Here, too, is the imperfetto, even though old Groa's reaction is intense and passionate. Then, once the foreground plot has begun, he has to hear the same evil news, and his reaction is narrated thus (now in passato remoto): "Il Groa *guardò* il figlio con occhi atroci.—No?—*fremette*.—No? E lo *respinse* da sé, piano, senza aggiungere altro" (785; Groa regarded his son with horrid eyes. No? He trembled. No? And he pushed him away, quietly, without adding anything else). This scene lacks the earlier scene's outburst of feeling; the lonely man's pain has reached a point where it can no longer express itself in a loud lament, but only in a quiet one. But the tense usage in these two scenes is driven not by that, but only by the location of the scene in the narrative. In the second scene it is the last time Groa sends the youth to his former wife. After this answer he knows there is no longer any hope for his loneliness. He decides to depart from life. This is the climax of the action.

The execution of his decision is, by contrast, a falling away from the height of narrative tension, and Pirandello ends the story in a scene of extended imperfetto di rottura:

> Lo Spina *voleva* ora convincere il padre del torto del Romelli, che *seguitava* ad asciugarsi il volto in disparte. Il padre *stava* a guardar lo Spina con occhi sbarrati, feroci; all'improvviso lo *afferrava* per il bavero della giacca, gli *dava* un poderoso scrollone e lo *mandava* a schizzar lontano; poi balzando sul parapetto dell'argine, *gridava* con le braccia levate, enorme:
>
> Ecco, si fa cosí!

E *giú*, nel fiume. Un tonfo. Due gridi, e un terzo grido, da lontano, piú acuto, del figlio che non *poteva* accorrere, con le gambe quasi stroncate dal terrore. (786-7)

Spina wanted to convince the father of the injustice of Romelli, who kept aside, wiping his face. The father stood glaring fiercely at Spina; unexpectedly he grabbed him by the collar of his jacket, shook him violently, and told him to high-tail it; then leaping onto the parapet he shouted, towering, with his arms raised:

"Look, this is how to do it!"

And down, into the ravine. A thump. Two cries, and a third cry, from afar, shriller, from the son, who was unable to run up, with his legs nearly crippled from terror.

The imperfetto form "afferrava" (grabbed) at this point clearly designates an action that is punctual, closed, and sudden. So what? The sentence stands in the conclusion of the story, and therefore in imperfetto.

Unamuno, Darío, Echegaray

For Spanish, we have the excellent observations of Knud Togeby, who has noted the more or less regular alternation of imperfecto and perfecto simple in Spanish narratives, such that the sentences in imperfecto form the background, those in perfecto simple the foreground.[4] He does not speak explicitly about introductory and concluding imperfecto, but in the example sentences adduced in Samuel Gili y Gaya's study of syntax it is possible to find "imperfecto de ruptura" (again I imitate the French term).[5] But in order to make anything of such an example, it is necessary to imagine an entire story around it. It is better to examine some real stories. Then it will be seen that we are not dealing with "secondary functions" of tenses, but that imperfecto and perfecto simple in Spanish too have *only* the main function of dividing the story into background and foreground.

Consider first a few story endings in Unamono. Unamuno likes to close his narratives with a general observation, let us say, a moral. That

---

4. Knud Togeby, *Mode, aspect et temps en espagnol* (Copenhagen: Munksgaard, 1953), 122–23.
5. "Al amanecer salió el ejército, atravesó la montaña, y poco después establecía contacto con el enemigo" (At dawn the army went out, crossed the mountain, and shortly afterward was making contact with the enemy): Samuel Gili y Gaya, *Curso superior de sintaxis española* (Mexico: Minerva, 1943), 140.

is not the point at the moment, but only those conclusions that relegate the narrated action into the background. Thus the story "La sangre de Aitor" (Aitor's Blood) ends with an apostrophe from the narrator. Already, however, Unamuno has calmed the narrative down by turning from foreground to background:

> Más tarde, en época de elecciones, *hizo* Lope de muñidor electoral. Cuando *llegaban* éstas el santo fuego le *inflamaba, evocaba* a Aitor, a Lecobide, a los héroes del Irnio y se *despepitaba* para sacar triunfante con apoyo del primero que *llegara* a ser candidato unido a un blanco, negro, rojo o azul, y aquí paz y después gloria.[6]
>
> Later, during the campaign season, Lope became an electoral colluder. When the elections came, a holy fire inflamed him; he invoked Aitor, Lekobide, the heroes of Irnio and pulled every string to come out ahead with the support of the first that might emerge as a triumphant candidate with either a white, black, red, or blue vote, since this made for peace then, and glory later.

The turn away from the main plot is also clear from the content, which leaps into a later time. The story ends with a view forward. Those who think of tenses as expressions of time will need to say here that imperfecto identifies a "future in the past." But that has nothing to do with tenses. Imperfecto is used because the story comes to an end, and the reader must realize that. To use a somewhat drastic image, imperfecto puts on the brakes.

Other Unamuno stories end with views forward. So, for example, "Redondo, el contertulio" (Redondo and His Coffeehouse Circle), which ends with the death of the hero and his coffeehouse companions:

> Su fortuna se la legó a la tertulia, repartiéndola entre los contertulios todos, con la obligación de celebrar un cierto número de banquetes al año y rogando se dedicara un recuerdo a los gloriosos fundadores de la patria. En el testamento ológrafo, curiosísimo documento, *acababa diciendo*: . . .[7]

---

6. Miguel de Unamuno, "La sangre de Aitor," https://www.euskadi.eus/contenidos/informacion/euskara_mintzagai/eu_mintzaga/adjuntos/sangre_aitor.pdf. This story is not included in the "complete" edition consulted for the remaining stories. Our thanks to Donald Gilbert-Santamaria and Travis Landry for help with the Unamuno translations.

7. Miguel de Unamuno, *Cuentos completos*, ed. Óscar Carrascosa Tinoco (Madrid: Páginas de Espuma, 2011), 246.

He left his fortune to the group, dividing it among all the members with the stipulation that they hold a certain number of banquets each year and imploring them to commemorate the glorious founders of the fatherland. In his handwritten will—a most curious document—he concluded saying: . . .

There follows a quote from the Bible in direct speech. Here, too, imperfecto (*acababa*) is the tense of closure. In the story "El padrino Antonio" (Godfather Antonio) the tripartite structure of narration is especially evident in its leitmotif and also in its tense structure. The leitmotif is a visit to a chapel and reciting an Ave Maria before the altarpiece. It appears three times. The first is in the introduction to the story. Antonio makes pilgrimages by himself to the holy place: "Antonio *solía* irse solo, de tiempo en tiempo, a una iglesiuca perdida en los arrabales a pasarse largos ratos delante del altar de una Piedad, bebiendo con los ojos las lágrimas de aquella cara macilenta y lustrosa" (310; From time to time Antonio went alone to a miserable little chapel lost in the outskirts to pass hours before the Pietà on the altar, drinking in with his eyes the tears of the sorrowing, shining face). Is this imperfecto because Antonio (habitually) was accustomed to visit the chapel? Whether once or customarily is irrelevant for the choice of tense. The verb is imperfecto here because the main action, namely the marriage of the hero under unpleasant circumstances, has not yet emerged from the background.

But the promise of marriage exchanged by the lovers in this very chapel does belong to the main action: "Al día siguiente *llevó* a su ahijada y ya novia a aquella iglesiuca perdida en los arrabales e *hizo* que allí, delante de la Piedad de cara macilenta y lustrosa, mezclase con él un avemaría" (312; The next day he took his goddaughter and now fiancée to that little chapel lost in the outskirts and arranged it so that she joined him in an Ave Maria before the Pietà with the sorrowing, shining face). Is the verb perfecto simple because the action is unique and "punctual"? The aspect of the action is irrelevant. The foreground tense is here because this sentence is the center of the main action.

The pair appear yet a third time in the small chapel, now in the last sentence of the story: "De tiempo en tiempo visitaban marido y mujer a la macilenta y lustrosa Piedad de la iglesiuca del arrabal y allí *mezclaban*, con sus almas, sus avemarías" (314; From time to time the husband and wife visited the sorrowing and shining Pietà in the chapel in the outskirts and there they would join both their souls and their Ave Marias).

The three quoted sentences, which contain in essence the whole story and which Unamuno has marked with the weight of his central motif, are interesting not only because they display the function of tense in the tripartite structure of narrative so clearly; they also serve to clarify the misunderstanding of aspects. When does one actually tell a story? When Cervantes wants to call the reader's attention to a story, he calls it a "jamás vista ni oída aventura" (*Don Quijote*, Part 1, Chapter 20, title; an adventure never heard of nor seen). And Goethe defines the story as the narration "einer unerhörten Begebenheit" (of an extraordinary event).[8] I shall weaken this wonderful formulation slightly and say: People tell stories when they know something unusual. What is worth telling are less the everyday, repetitive, consistent occurrences, but rather those that break the monotony of the ordinary to seem unusual. The same is true for Maupassant and his successors, who have discovered what is unusual about a piece of string or an umbrella. Stories are told *for the sake of what is unusual*. This develops naturally into the foreground action, and the ordinary events from which it emerges remain in the background of the tale. That is the basic structure of all narrative, which the individual narrator may occasionally ignore, but which normally prevails. In the background, ordinary and commonplace things appear, in the foreground uncommon, exceptional things. For this reason the doctrine of aspect, even though it is blind to narrative structure, can occasionally chance to be correct that what is durative, imperfective stands in the background tense, while what is perfective, punctual stands in the foreground tense.

In principle, the narrator remains free to set the highlighting. In the story "El semejante" (Another Fool), Unamuno tells about the fool Celestino being teased by a crowd of boys in the street: "Al salir le *rodeó* una tropa de chicuelos: uno le *tiraba* de la chaqueta, otro le *derribó* el sombrero, alguno le *escupió*, y le *preguntaban*, '¿Y el otro tonto?'" (115; As he left, a horde of little boys surrounded him: one was pulling at his jacket, another knocked off his hat, a third spat at him, and they were all asking him, "and the other fool?"). There is no good reason why tugging at his jacket should be imperfecto but tearing off his hat perfecto simple. The choice of tense is at the discretion of the narrator, who uses the tenses in this little scene to achieve his highlighting. The boy who tugs at the jacket is pushed into the background (he probably pulls from behind); the one who knocks off his hat stays in the foreground. The teasing question we must again read as "accompaniment" to the naughty actions.

As the final story by Unamuno, let us consider "¡Cosas de Franceses!" (The Ways of the French!). The famous toreador Don Señorito delivers

---

8. Johann Peter Eckermann, *Gespräche mit Goethe in den letzten Jahren seines Lebens*, ed. Ernst Beutler (Zurich: Artemis, 1948), 225 (Jan. 29, 1827).

a speech at a political rally in support of Don Pérez, who is standing for parliament. The speech is narrated with bullfighting metaphors:

> Después de brindar por la patria *desplegó* don Señorito el trapo, *dió* un pase a España con honra, otro de pecho a Gibraltar y sus ingleses, uno de mérito a don Pérez, *sostuvo* una lucidísima brega, aunque algo *bailada*, acerca de la importancia y carácter de la química, y, por fin, *remató* la suerte dando al Gobierno una estocada hasta los gavilanes.
> El público *gritaba* ¡olé tu salero!, y *pedía* que dieran al tribuno la oreja del bicho, uniendo en sus vítores los nombres de don Pérez y don Señorito....
> El buen don Pérez se *dejaba* hacer, traído y llevado por sus admiradores, sin saber en que había de acabar todo aquello.

> After toasting the fatherland don Señorito unfurled his cape, took one pass to honor Spain, another *pase de pecho* for Gibraltar and its English, and a *pase de mérito* for Don Pérez, carried on a brilliant fight, even if a bit showy in terms of the importance and character of the chemistry he performed, and, finally, finished off the fight by giving a fatal stroke to the government. The public shouted "*olé*, you wit!" and asked them to award the speaker the ear of the beast, joining in their rejoicing the names of Don Pérez and Don Señorito.... Good Don Pérez allowed it to happen, lifted and carried by his admirers, without knowing how this all would end.

It is necessary to imagine the physical reality of the scene in order to understand the tense usage here. The dais on which Don Señorito performs stands in the foreground. The rows of spectators, among whom the candidate is included, form the background. This is the arrangement of the story, and the tenses are distributed accordingly. The foreground is in perfecto simple, the background in imperfecto. The tenses here have an almost spatial value. But only because the foreground and background of the narrative are also represented spatially. Normally foreground and background are only to be understood as metaphors and identify two different intensities of the narrative technique.

I turn now to Rubén Darío for a few further observations about tense and narrative technique in Spanish stories. In "Las tres Reinas Magas" (The Three Wise Queens) Darío tells an allegorical story of three queens who journey from the East to the Child in the manger. They are the Queens of Jerusalem, Ecbatana, and Amatunte. They are also the Queens of Purity, Glory, and Love. The Child, the Soul, thanks them for their gifts and promises the three Queens, corresponding to their gifts, the paradises of gold, of incense, or of myrrh. Asked which of the three paradises he would prefer for himself, Child Soul turns to the Queen of Love, "I shall be with you in the paradise of myrrh!"[9]

All through the story the three Queens appear to be similar and of the same rank. The language emphasizes this: "La primera le *ofreció* incienso. La segunda, oro. La tercera, mirra. *Hablaron* las tres: –Yo soy la reina de Jerusalén. –Yo soy la reina de Ecbatana. –Yo soy la reina de Amatunte" (383; The first offered him incense. The second, gold. The third, myrrh. The three said: –I am the Queen of Jerusalem. –I am the Queen of Ecbatana. –I am the Queen of Amatunte). Their equivalence, so emphasized by the narrator, is broken down in the moment that the Child Soul distinguishes the Queen of Amatunte before the other two: "La reina de Jerusalén *suspiraba*. La reina de Ecbatana *sonreía*. La reina de Amatunte *dijo* . . . (385; The Queen of Jerusalem was sighing. The Queen of Ecbatana was smiling. The Queen of Amatunte said . . .). We can imagine it again almost in spatial terms. The Queen of Amatunte steps forward to speak and also takes precedence with her gift. That is the twist of the tale. The twist is highlighted also by the tenses, as the jump from background tense to foreground tense ("dijó") emphasizes.

Distantly connected to this tale is "El pacto" by the 1904 Nobel Prize winner José Echegaray. In an introduction (in imperfecto) we learn that Don Benigno does justice to his name. He is truly a good man. One day he goes off and makes a pact with the devil. He sells his soul in return for power and wealth in this world. But then he turns all his gains solely to doing good. Then he dies. As an angel is about to carry him to Heaven, the devil presents his pact. There is an argument over Don Benigno's soul. God himself interferes and brings Don Benigno to Heaven. The devil is left empty-handed and flounces off. The story ends as follows:

> Y don Benigno, apoyando blandamente en el ángel, *subió* la gradería del pórtico. A todo esto el diablo, a cuyo rabo se *había* enredado sin saber cómo el pergamino del pacto, *corría* todo corrido hacia el infierno como perro con maza, murmurando con acento rencoroso: "Eso es, está bien; hágase el milagro y hágalo el diablo."[10]

And Don Benigno, leaning gently on the angel, ascended the staircase of the gateway. At all this the devil, whose tail had become tangled in

---

9. Rubén Darío, *Cuentos completos*, ed. Ernesto Mejía Sánchez (Mexico: Fondo de Cultura Económica, 1950), 385.

10. José Echegaray, "El Pacto," in *Florilegio de cuentos españoles*, ed. Paul Rogers and Charles W. Butler (New York: Macmillan, 1961), 10.

the parchment without his knowing how, was running lickety-split to Hell like a dog with a noisemaker, muttering bitterly, "So be it; let the miracle take place, and let it be the work of the devil."

(Such had been the words of God, now echoed by the devil.) To judge these sentences correctly one must know what happened in the story and its twist, and know that the devil has lost out. While Don Benigno, "leaning gently on the angel," goes to Heaven, the devil is left behind and disappears into the distance. Here the narrator goes to Heaven with Don Benigno (and with the reader) and pushes the devil and everything about him into the background. And so *imperfecto* and *perfecto simple* become in effect attributes of the characters in a particular phase of the story and emphasize the thematic highlighting of good and evil.[11]

Hemingway

In Hemingway we can find the "progressive" tense, *he was singing* (I use the paradigm rather than a tense name), serving a narrative function similar to that of the Romance imperfect. It forms the background of his narratives. It appears, for example, when a story begins with nature description, as in "Banal Story": "So he ate an orange, slowly spitting out the seeds. Outside, the snow was turning to rain."[12] Or with nature in a conclusion, as in "Ten Indians": "In the morning there was a big wind blowing and the waves were running high up on the beach and he was awake a long time before he remembered that his heart was broken."

Let me clarify to avoid misunderstanding. If we compare the English *he was singing* with the Romance imperfect, it is immediately obvious that it occurs much more rarely than the imperfect. Yet this impression arises only if the comparison is made to a particular phase of Romance narrative literature. We have already seen that Voltaire's narrative style strikingly favors *passé simple* over *imparfait*. To go further back in the history of narrative, *imparfait* is even rarer in medieval narrative. In many older texts it is restricted almost entirely to narrations of dreams and visions. In general, the distribution of the tense *he was singing* in contemporary English and of *imparfait* in medieval French is quite similar. It would,

---

11. In the Spanish translation of the 1964 version of *Tempus* I analyzed Emilia Pardo Bazán's story "El pañuelo" in terms of foreground and background, as here with Maupassant's tales (*Estructura*, 238–42).

12. Hemingway quotes (unpaginated) from Ernest Hemingway, *The Complete Short Stories*, (New York: Scribner, 1987), www.antilogicalism.com/wp-content/uploads/2018/04/hemingway.pdf.

however, be bold to predict a possible spread of the tense *he was singing* in the English of the future on the basis of this observation.

If the tense *he was singing* is rarer than imparfait in contemporary Romance languages, then background and foreground are distributed differently in English. There is indeed a difference. But it exists within the fundamental similarity that both English and the Romance languages can distinguish background and foreground in narrative with the formal means of tense selection. And this function, characterizing the background of a narrative, is the *only* function of the tense *he was singing*. It is not a secondary function alongside a function of aspect or anything of the sort. There is no aspect with regard to the form *he was singing*, and especially no durative or "progressive" aspect. This form is entirely indifferent vis-à-vis the course of the action and can equally well characterize a punctual or a durative event, as long as it takes place in the background of the narrative. If we want to give it a name that completely describes its function, we must call it the English background tense of narration.

There is a further comment to be added to the two sentences cited above from Hemingway's stories. The texts no longer allow us to maintain the initial methodological principle of separating tenses from the other verb forms. It is not possible to talk about the tenses with *-ing* in English without considering the present participle, *singing*, at the same time. Where does the participle stop and the tense begin? Grammar authorizes us to say there is a participle in the expression "there was a big wind blowing," but a tense in the continuation "the waves were running." The distinction makes a certain amount of sense in terms of grammar, but does not do justice to the function of narrative highlighting. The present participle that completes a verb and the tense in *-ing* share the same role with respect to highlighting. Both the sentences and the parts of sentences with a present participle form the background of a narrative. Also, anyone who seeks to explain the tenses with *-ing* on a historical basis (though I will not go further into this controversial question here) must take account of the commonality of function of participle and tense.

Now consider a Hemingway story as a whole. "Indian Camp" narrates the following: An Indian woman suffers severe labor pains. The white doctor is called. His young son Nick and Uncle George accompany him. The woman's husband is present at the birth; he lies in the upper bunk because he has injured himself in the foot with an ax a few days earlier. The birth turns out to be very difficult. The doctor must perform a Cesarean section without anesthesia. But the operation is successful. A son is born. Everyone rejoices at the happy outcome. As they turn to congratulate the father, they find him covered in blood: during his wife's labor he has slit his own throat.

As many have pointed out, the story is built on the principle of leading the reader astray. It divides the story clearly into two parts. The first part contains the gynecological operation, whose successful course seems to promise a happy end. The second part brings the discovery of the suicide and transforms the euphoria into tragedy. The two parts are separated by a narrow narrative valley. They are both enclosed in an introduction describing the journey and arrival of the doctor and a conclusion, in which the doctor and his young son talk about death.

It is necessary to have this structure in mind in order to understand why the forms in *-ing* (the tense "he was singing" and the participle "singing") are not evenly distributed, but concentrate in particular phases of the text. They occur in the introduction: "At the lake shore there was another rowboat drawn up. The two Indians stood waiting." It is unnecessary to worry whether the form "stood waiting" should be understood as a sequence of verb-participle or as a variant of the tense *he was singing*. It doesn't matter, since the participle following a preterit and the tense *he was singing* in any case share the function of creating background. This is the reason I didn't bother to detail all the tenses in setting up the tense system in the first place. It doesn't matter how many verb forms are acknowledged as tenses that fit into either tense-group I or tense-group II. With the form "stood waiting" there can be no doubt. A participle that completes a preterit verb belongs to the same tense-group as the preterit tense.

The background tense also occurs in the conclusion of Hemingway's story, indeed twice. Hemingway first returns the narrative into the background after the husband's suicide is discovered. There is nothing left for the doctor to do. The sentence takes the form of a natural outcome: "It was just beginning to be daylight." Then follows the conversation between father and son about dying, and after the conversation Hemingway closes the story again. This definitive conclusion contains yet again elements of a natural outcome, but it turns meditative because of the preceding conversation:

> They were seated in the boat, Nick in the stern, his father rowing. The sun was coming up over the hills. A bass jumped, making a circle in the water. Nick trailed his hand in the water. It felt warm in the sharp chill of the morning.
>
> In the early morning on the lake sitting in the stern of the boat with his father rowing, he felt quite sure that he would never die.

It is an impressive close to a story. When we pause at this point for a moment to admire it, we must also include in our admiration the narrative highlighting between foreground and background.

I have already pointed to how the story misleads the reader as to what is special in it. The story has two central actions that actually run simultaneously, because the husband's suicide takes place at the high point of his wife's labor (as is learned from a hint that is only understood in retrospect). But these two simultaneous occurrences are slightly displaced from one another, in that the suicide is discovered only after the successfully concluded operation. Thus it happens that the first action, the operation, already has a conclusion. It reads (about the doctor): "He was feeling exalted and talkative as football players are in the dressing room after a game." As far as the meaning of the verb is concerned, Hemingway could just as well have written "he felt." But not from the narrative structure and not from the principle of the wrong track. For the sake of the artistic economy of the narrative Hemingway requires the sharp contrast between the euphoria of the doctor and the tragedy that interrupts it. So he has to suggest for a moment that the story ends with the success of the operation and that everything is working out. He does that in two ways. First in terms of content with the frivolous and bumptious simile "like football players." This simile erases all the pain and worries of the operation. He also uses the tense "he was feeling" to bring the story back into the background. This tense suggests that the dramatic course of the story is now at an end and that the characters are returning to the ordinary world of unexceptional events. The story seems to die off quietly, but this is actually the silence before the storm.

The narrative valley before the tragic discovery is marked yet again by tense. Here again we have the most favorable conditions for observing because the same event is told twice. Uncle George has been helping during the operation and supporting the woman with her arm. In her pain she bites him in the arm. That is told first as part of the operation: "Uncle George looked at his arm. The young Indian smiled reminiscently." The verbs are preterit as the appropriate tense for the narrated foreground. We know it is foreground because the doctor immediately reacts, "I'll put some peroxide on that." That is still part of the operation and hence belongs to the narrative foreground. The reader is not yet to notice that the main point of the story is yet to come.

A few sentences later—now we are in the euphoria-filled valley between the two main plots—the same event is told again: "Uncle George was standing against the wall, looking at his arm." It would be a misunderstanding not only of this sentence, but of the entire story, if we understood here that Uncle George was standing for a long time and constantly looking at his arm. A certain duration or repetition of looking is expressed, if at all, by that fact that it is told twice. No duration is expressed in the -*ing* forms. Their function is exclusively to highlight the narrative. Uncle George praises the doctor in this moment, "Oh, you're a great man, all right." And then they look at the child's father and learn that in fact not everything is all right. Here is a double contrast, in content through the "all right" and the dreadful discovery, formally through the background tense in -*ing* and the foreground preterit tense in which the discovery is reported.

There is only one -*ing* tense blended into the foreground narration of the operation. It reads: "'See, it's a boy, Nick,' he said. 'How do you like being an interne?' Nick said, 'All right.' He was looking away so as not to see what his father was doing." This "was looking" is not motivated by the verb or the verbal aspect. Once again the same thing is immediately told again, this time in preterit: "Nick didn't look at it." And, "Nick did not watch." No justification is necessary for the use of preterit in these two sentences. This is the main plot and its narrative tense is preterit. But the background tense "was looking" deviates from the rule and must be explained. Here again the explanation is the artistic sharpening of the contrast. The boy says, "All right," but he doesn't feel that way, and he looks away. Looking away undercuts his brave words. To be sure, he remains by the bed of the laboring woman, but his eyes, at least, wander furtively into a background that is less anxious.

Hemingway's story, "The Old Man at the Bridge," narrates an event from the Spanish Civil War. The narrator reports in the first person. He is a soldier and is on sentry duty. At a bridge over the Ebro he encounters a seventy-six-year-old refugee who stops in exhaustion. As he watches for the advancing enemy, he questions the refugee about his fate. In the old man's report are formulaic stereotypical forms in -*ing*: "'I was taking care of animals,' he explained . . . . 'Yes,' he said, 'I stayed, you see, taking care of animals.'" And again: "'I was taking care of animals,' he said dully, but no longer to me. 'I was only taking care of animals.'" The last sentence sounds like an ending. The old man leaves, his words drift away. Beyond that, the fate of this man in a war he does not understand is condensed into this stereotypical formula. His limited, peaceful life forms the background of the war. Hemingway emphasizes the contrast between the fate of the man and the events of the war also in terms of content: the herd of animals the old man was caring for consisted of two goats, a cat, and four pairs of pigeons.

The narrative is divided into foreground and background in yet another sense. The narrator's assignment is to report enemy contact at the bridge over the Ebro. While he speaks with the old man, his assignment remains in his consciousness. Unlike the old man's formulaic lament, the conversation with him is narrated in preterit. It is the foreground. In the background, referring mentally to the divided attention of the narrator and spatially to the far side of the bridge, several reminders of the sentry assignment appear, again stereotypically in the *-ing* form:

> I was watching the bridge and the African looking country of the Ebro Delta and wondering how long now it would be before we would see the enemy, and listening all the while for the first noises.
>
> "And you have no family?" I asked, watching the far end of the bridge where a few last carts were hurrying down the slope of the bank.
>
> "Why not," I said, watching the far bank where now there were no carts.
>
> There was nothing to do about him. It was Easter Sunday and the Fascists were advancing toward the Ebro.

There is no use operating with concepts like simultaneity in discussing this use of tenses. Of course the conversation with the old man and the observation of the bridge take place at the same time. But simultaneity is not the issue, but rather that the narrator chooses a perspective when he narrates simultaneous events one after the other. He puts one of the simultaneous events into the foreground, the other into the background. He does so with the aid of tenses because he knows that his readers prefer a story with narrative highlighting to one without.

In conclusion I insert a self-contained text by Hemingway. It is the sketch entitled "Chapter XII" (it could almost be called a prose-poem):

> If it happened right down close in front of you, you could see Villalta snarl at the bull and curse him, and when the bull charged he swung back firmly like an oak when the wind hits it, his legs tight together, the muleta trailing and the sword following the curve behind. Then he cursed the bull, flopped the muleta at him, and swung back from the charge, his feet firm, the muleta curving and at each swing the crowd roaring.
>
> When he started to kill it was all in the same rush. The bull looking at him straight in front, hating. He drew out the sword from the folds of the muleta and sighted with the same movement and called to the bull, Toro! Toro! and the bull charged and Villalta charged and

just for a moment they became one. Villalta became one with the bull and then it was over. Villalta standing straight and the red hilt of the sword sticking out dully between the bull's shoulders. Villalta, his hand up at the crowd and the bull roaring blood, looking straight at Villalta and his legs caving.

The text takes its character from the numerous participles. There is no tense of the sort *he was singing* among them. Even so the text is divided into foreground and background just as if a tense of this sort were present in place of each participle. And beyond this, the distribution of verb forms is reminiscent of Unamuno's story "¡Cosas de Franceses!" discussed above. The tenses and verb forms are almost attributes of the characters and things. The toreador, as actor and attacker, has the attribute of preterit tense. He stands in the foreground. Participles, as verb forms of the background narrative, are the attribute of everything that surrounds the toreador: of the public, the muleta, and the sword in their elegant movements.

This principle of division is violated at two points and these violations are significant for the artistic intention: As the bull attacks he too has the preterit attribute, and as Villalta freezes for a moment after he has delivered the death-blow, he receives the participial attribute. The whole text is arranged so that the verbs are the carriers of a specific idea to be expressed; the preterit here means attack and the participle everything that suffers or accompanies the attack. After the death-blow that closes the attack, there are no more preterit verbs. It makes little sense to ask if the numerous participles of the story should be considered tenses or counted as such. In the context of the entire story they have the function of finite verbs and to that extent stand "absolutely." They serve as verbs. However the question is judged, they have the function of background vis-à-vis the preterit forms, and thus of highlighting. Just because the background is so emphatically characterized, it creates the impression of a *scene*, in which epic approaches lyric.

Since this text hovers between epic and prose-poem, it could be imagined in the tenses of group I, but with the same participles. In that case the participles would serve the same purpose of highlighting. Thus we can say the same of the tenses in *-ing* that belong to group I (he is singing, he has been singing, he will be singing). An indication may be sufficient here. The *-ing* tenses of group I serve to highlight, even though the text is not narrative. They also identify in discussion the background, as opposed to the foreground in which what is actually worthy of discussion takes place. They stand back in the face of what is more important. That has nothing to do with aspects and is independent of the order of events. The -*ing* tenses are also less significant than other tenses in their degree of commitment. "England expects every man will do his duty" demands more obligation than "is expecting... will be doing," and the lover says, "I love you," not "I am loving you."[13] He says it namely with the engagement of his person and places it completely in the foreground of his speaking. That is the real "durative form."

In contrast to the Romance languages, then, highlighting of foreground and background is found not only in the narrative world, but also in the world of discussion. In the entire language, therefore. In discussion, foreground and background appear as differing grades of commitment. The -*ing* tenses oblige to less and demand less than the "simple tenses."

Frame Narrative (Boccaccio)

Thus far, all our examples of narrative highlighting have come from relatively modern narrative literature. The observations and conclusions in this form apply only to narrative literature from the eighteenth century onward. In earlier European literature the narrative technique is different, and the tenses are distributed differently.

I begin with the first classic of the novella tradition, Giovanni Boccaccio.[14] If we compare the tense usage in Boccaccio's tales with those of Pirandello or of other modern writers, it is immediately evident that in the older stories imperfetto (*cantava*) is rarer, passato remoto (*cantò*) is more common. Especially absent is the introduction in the background tense. Only occasionally does a story begin like 4.5: "*Erano* adunque in Messina tre giovani fratelli" (288; In Messina there were three young brothers, 279). Much more frequent and actually stereotypical is the beginning in passato remoto, as in 1.6: "*Fu* adunque, o care giovani, non è ancora gran tempo, nella nostra città un frate minore inquisitore dell'eretica pravità" (69; Not long ago, my dear young ladies, there lived in our city a minor friar, an

---

13. It can, of course, occur under particular stylistic conditions, as for example in Esther Matthews's poem "Song," the second strophe of which reads: "But that's not sayin' that I'm not lovin'. Still water, you know, runs deep, An' I do be lovin' so deep, dear, I be lovin' you in my sleep" (Esther Matthews, "Song." https://www.poetryfoundation.org/poetrymagazine/browse?contentId=22179).

14. See Hans-Jörg Neuschäfer, *Boccaccio und der Beginn der Novelle* (Munich: Fink, 1969), and Tzvetan Todorov, *Grammaire du Décaméron* (The Hague: Mouton, 1969). Boccaccio is quoted from Giovanni Boccaccio, *Decameron*, ed. Cesare Segre (Milan: Mursia, 1966), and (modified) from *The Decameron*, trans. Mark Musa and Peter Bondanella (London: Penguin, 1982).

official inquirer into all kinds of depraved heresies, 45). Similarly, coming from the modern story we miss imperfetto in the conclusion. There is no imperfetto di rottura or its like to be found in Boccaccio's entire collection of stories. The formulaic conclusions are also in passato remoto. Here is one example (5.2) that can stand for many: "Quivi Martuccio la *sposò*, e grandi e belle nozze *fece;* e poi appresso con lei insieme in pace ed in riposo lungamente *goderono* del loro amore" (335; And there, Martuccio married her and gave a grand and beautiful wedding feast; and thereafter they enjoyed each other's love in peace and quiet for a long time to come, 329).

This does not mean, however, that there is no highlighting through foreground and background. Imperfetto is present in the text and it alternates more or less regularly with the passato remoto. It clearly has a backgrounding function. Indeed, it appears with striking frequency in the opening sentences of the tales, just not in the first sentence. While the opening sentences are in passato remoto with a certain formulaic regularity, they are followed almost as routinely with forms in imperfetto, mostly in relative clauses. These sentences in imperfetto contain the actual exposition. Novella 1.8 begins as follows:

> *Fu* adunque in Genova, buon tempo è passato, un gentile uomo chiamato messere Ermino de' Grimaldi, il quale, per quello che da tutti era creduto, di grandissime possessioni e di denari di gran lunga *trapassava* la richezza d'ogni altro ricchissimo cittadino che allora si sapesse in Italia. E sí come egli di ricchezza ogni altro *avanzava* che italico fosse, cosí d'avarizia e di miseria ogni altro misero e avaro che al mondo fosse *soperchiava* oltre misura. (75)
>
> Now, some time ago there lived in Genoa a nobleman named Messer Ermino de' Grimaldi, whose rich estates and enormous wealth far surpassed that of every other rich citizen then known in Italy. And just as he outdid every other Italian in his wealth, so did he surpass beyond all measure in avarice and stinginess every miser or greedy person in the world. (52)

More sentences in imperfetto follow to complete the exposition by characterizing the miser.

The beginning action of the story cuts into this background with a sharply highlighted passato remoto form, and this too is a typical narrative technique for Boccaccio: "*Avenne* che in questi tempi che costui, non spendendo il suo *multiplicava*, *arrivò* a Genova un valente uomo di corte e costumato e ben parlante, il quale fu chiamato Guiglielmo Borsiere" (76; Now, while he was increasing his wealth by not spending a thing, it happened that at that time a worthy, cultivated, and witty courtier named Guiglielmo Borsiere, came to Genoa, 52). Especially the beginning with *Avenne che* (It so happened that) is typical for the opening of the main action and appears in many other of Boccaccio's stories. This beginning requires passato remoto tense almost automatically.

The imperfetto is not the only verb form used for highlighting. The same purpose is served—not unlike in Hemingway—by present and perfect participles, which Boccaccio likes to use for backgrounding. Here is an example from 1.3 (the tale with the parable of the three rings):

> Il Saladino, il valore del quale fu tanto che non solamente di piccolo uomo il fe' di Babilonia soldano, ma ancora molte vittorie sopra li re saracini e cristiani gli fece avere, *avendo* in diverse guerre e in grandissime sue magnificenze speso tutto il suo tesoro, e per alcuno accidente *sopravenutogli bisognandogli* una buona quantità di denari, né *veggendo* donde cosí prestamente come gli bisognavano avergli potesse, gli venne a memoria un ricco giudeo, il cui nome era Melchisedech. (61)

> Saladin, whose worth was such that from humble beginnings he became Sultan of Babylon and won many victories over Christian and Saracen kings, one day discovered on an occasion in which he needed a large amount of money that he had consumed all his wealth fighting many wars and displaying his grandiose magnificence. Not being able to envision a means of obtaining what he needed in a short time, he happened to recall a rich Jew, whose name was Melchisedech. (37)

Certainly this is also Ciceronian periodic style, but the one explanation does not exclude the other.

So the most striking deviation from modern novella style lies in the treatment of beginning and end. At the beginning the action does not emerge from a background, and at the end it does not recede back into a background. This difference is evidently related to the structure of the frame of the hundred novellas, in which ten ladies and gentlemen of the city of Florence have withdrawn to a country house during the great plague of 1348 and pass the time telling tales to each other. Not counting Sundays there are ten days of storytelling, and each day ten stories are told. The narrators take turns. After each tale Boccaccio returns to the frame. The merry listeners discuss the motif of the tale. From this conversation there emerges the transition to the next story, whose narrator usually picks up on the previous one or on its moral. Thus no story stands alone, each is embedded in the ten-day-long frame action.

The frame also explains the differences in the beginnings and endings in the *Decameron*. It makes a substantial difference for the tale if its beginning rises from silence or if it emerges from a sociable conversation. Boccaccio's tales emerge from the chatting of a sociable group. They begin at the height of the conversation and the introduction is tightly connected to the frame. Many thus begin: "Dovete adunque sapere che ne' tempi passati furono" (6.9, p. 401; You must remember, then, that in past times there were, 400). In many stories the connection to the frame is expressed with the particular adverb *adunque*. Here are some additional examples: "Fu adunque" (Now, some time ago); "Dico adunque che . . . avvenne" (Let me say, then, that . . . it happened); "Non è adunque . . . gran tempo passato" (Not long ago); "Dico adunque che . . . abitarono" (Let me say, then, that . . . there once lived; 1.8, 1.9, 5.4, 5.5; 75, 78, 342 347; 52, 54, 336, 341). *Adunque*, which could be translated with "therefore" or—weaker—"now," expresses that the following tale illustrates something that has just been *discussed* by the company. For most of the tales that is the moral of the preceding one, and for those that begin each day, it is the theme set for the day. Through this connection to the frame all the tales take on the traditional character of exempla—they exemplify something that has already been the subject of discussion and that will become so again after the narrative. Having been assigned the topic of love with an unhappy result by the king for the fourth day, Fiammetta begins her story with the significant expression: "Fiera materia di ragionare n'ha oggi il nostro re data" (4.1, p. 261; Today our king has given us a sad topic for discussion). The ten tales of the fourth day will be ten *narrative* variations on a theme set for *discussion*.

Thus we find in older tales and in older fiction altogether a clear awareness of the opposition between the worlds of narrating and discussing. Older tales are told so that the hearer or reader knows the connection between the contexts of narrating and discussing. The frame, without which we can hardly imagine older fiction, is not a pretty flourish around the "actual" narratives, but it signifies the substance of narrative generally. Anyone who had the unfortunate idea of removing Boccaccio's stories from their frame and putting them in an unconnected sequence would corrupt his whole art of telling stories. It would be immediately obvious from the tenses. The passato remoto tense at the beginning ("Fu . . ." or "Fu adunque . . . ") would literally be left hanging in the air. The same is true for the ends of the stories. Boccaccio does not return his stories to a narrative background because they do not end in silence. The frame narrative is there waiting at the end of each story to catch the novella up and continue it in a discussion. The closing sentences of the story don't damp down the narrative, as in modern stories, at whose ends everything is over; instead, they give the signal for the discussion to begin immediately. Instead of putting on the brakes, they shift gears.

I shall elaborate what I mean with novella 1.8 again. It is titled "With a witty saying, Guiglielmo Borsiere rebukes the avarice of Messer Ermino de' Grimaldi." There is no need to discuss or interpret this story. The listeners in the frame take care of that. Lauretta, the narrator, introduces her tale as follows: "La precedente novella, care compagne, m'induce a voler dire come un valente uomo di corte similmente, e non senza frutto, pugnesse d'un ricchissimo mercatante la cupidigia" (75; Dear companions, the previous tale moves me to tell you how a worthy courtier, in like fashion and not without results, attacked the covetous ways of a very rich merchant, 52). This is the language of discussion, in which two stories are compared—what otherwise interpreters do. Hence there is not a narrative tense here, but a tense of relevance, in this case the present.

After Lauretta has told her story, the right to tell a story passes to another lady in the gallant circle. Before she tells her own story, she returns briefly to Lauretta's story, and comments:

> Giovani donne, spesse volte già addivenne che quello che varie riprensioni e molte pene date ad alcuno non hanno potuto in lui adoperare, una parola molte volte per accidente, non che *ex proposito*, detta l'ha operato. Il che assai bene appare nella novella raccontata dalla Lauretta, ed io ancora con un'altra assai brieve ve l'intendo dimostrare. (77)

> Young ladies, it often happened that a remark uttered more by accident than *ex proposito* has succeeded where various reproaches and much pain have proved to be ineffectual. And this appears to be quite clear from the story told by Lauretta, and I intend to demonstrate this to you again with another much shorter tale. (54)

The tenses here are predominantly those of discussion, passato prossimo and presente. The story itself is of course told in the narrative tenses. But the content of the story is so arranged that it leads back into the frame of discussion. Lauretta turns the end toward a moral that already points toward the commentary of the next storyteller: "E da questo dí innanzi, di tanta virtú fu la parola da Guiglielmo detta, fu il piú liberale ed il piú grazioso gentile uomo e quello che piú ed i forestieri ed i cittadini onorò che altro che in Genova fosse a' tempi suoi" (77; So powerful was the word pronounced by Guiglielmo, that from that day on [Grimaldi] became the most generous and affable of gentleman, a man who entertained more splendidly both foreign visitors and fellow citizens than any other in Genoa during his lifetime, 54). This is all in a narrative tense, passato remoto, to signify the foreground. The narrator does not want to let the story die out in order to prepare for the silence that follows narration. Instead she brings her story to an end so that the talkative company can start in without the least pause for reflection or emotion. She leads the story to its moral and thereby gives a prompt for the discussion that will, in its turn, lead to the next story. She provides, to use a modern expression, an agenda for the discussion.

Narration in the Middle Ages

Other older collections of tales confirm what we have seen in Boccaccio. As a comparison, consider the Latin version of a collection very popular in the Middle Ages, *Historia septem sapientium* (Story of the Seven Wise Men). Here too the tales are embedded in a frame with the following plot: A king (*quidam rex*) has entrusted the education of his son to seven wise men. After the agreed-on term, the king desires to test whether his son has really become a paragon of learning. The son, however, has just consulted the stars and learned that he will die if he speaks a single word during the next seven days. To the great distress of the king, his son answers none of his questions and does not even defend himself against the most extreme slanders. The king commands that his worthless son be executed. The seven wise men now try to delay the execution for seven days. So day after day they tell stories with morals intended to persuade the king to withdraw his command. After each story told by a wise man, the king countermands his order. But the evil queen also tells stories—intended to influence the king against his son. And after each of the queen's tales the king reinstates his command. Only on the seventh day is the tension resolved. The son opens his mouth and tells a story himself; it is full of wisdom.

I have described the frame in such detail because it reveals something important, namely, that the moral of a story, i.e., that content of the story that can be translated into discursive speech, is not just an appendage added at will. Frames are arranged so that stories are told for the sake of their morals. Here the life of the prince depends on them. The same arrangement is familiar from the *Arabian Nights* and many other framed collections of tales. We may surely read this as a hint about the function of narrative in older cultures. For them, narrative is the form in which wisdom matures to decision. Discussion and narration are not separate categories; instead, discussion takes place through narration. Wisdom is not the product of a discursive thought process. It is the blossom and fruit of narration.

We can identify a further point from the frame of the *Historia septem sapientum* (as also from the frame of the tales in the *Arabian Nights*). The frame itself is narration. How, then, is it possible to give the tension and drama otherwise typical of discussion to the frame if it is narrated? Through the thematic motif of constant risk of death, whether for seven days or even for a thousand and one nights. The threat of death is a motif of content in the service of suspense. It compensates for the lack of tension in the frame as simply narrated frame and creates the illusion that the individual stories are embedded in the real world with all its tensions and decision-making.

The tenses of the story are tied to this frame. Just as in Boccaccio, they stand in immediate relation to the frame with no narrative background intervening. In the *Historia septem sapientum* it is even clearer because the transition is more formulaic. The king asks in the dialogue situation, say, "Dic quomodo fuit" (Tell how that was).[15] And then the third story begins: "Fuit quidam vir lavator" (Once there was a washerman). The fifth story echoes the *fuit* and begins: "Fuit quidam mercator" (Once there was a merchant). Or: "Quomodo fuit?" (How was it that?) And in response the seventh story: "Fuit quidam comes Imperatoris" (Once there was a follower of the Emperor). After this beginning with *fuit* there follows the exposition, still necessary in at least brief terms. With formulaic regularity it takes the form of a relative clause in imperfectum (*sedebat/ habebat/ iacebat/ erat*), from which the beginning action stands out sharply in perfectum (*misit/ vocavit*). In the seventh story it looks like this: "Fuit quidam comes Imperatoris qui sedebat in domo sua et habebat quendam parvulum natum, et iacebat coram eo et non erat in domo alius praeter eum. Misit autem Caesar et vocavit eum" (Once there was a follower of the emperor who was staying at home and had a small boy, and lay near him and there was no one else at home besides him. The emperor, however, sent and summoned him).

Here is another example that illustrates the connections especially clearly. The eighth tale begins with the tense sequence perfectum/ imperfectum/ perfectum: "Quidam iuvenis *adamavit* quandam feminam maritatam et *cupiebat* nimis concumbere cum ea. Tunc *dedit* praemia cuidam vetule" (A youth fell in love with a married woman and was yearning to lie with her. Then he gave a bribe to an old woman). Why the tense change from perfectum to imperfectum and then back to perfectum? The choice of tense is determined by the position of the verbs in the story and the frame. The verb *adamare* is in perfectum because this is the beginning

---

15. *Historia Septem Sapientium*, https://www.thelatinlibrary.com/septsap.html.

of the story. It responds to the preceding question of the king, who has given the signal for the storytelling to begin from out of the discursive context: "Dic quomodo fuit." The perfectum *adamavit* picks up on the perfectum *fuit*. After this initial response to the frame, the narrator moves for a moment into the background and presents a brief exposition with an imperfectum verb (*cupiebat*). The very next verb is already perfectum (*dedit*) and sets the plot going. Each of the three verbs marks a different phase of narration, and each tense has a corresponding role. I conclude from this that Latin imperfectum and perfectum have similar status for narrative technique as imparfait and passé simple in French.

It is now evident that a particular use of tense often cannot be judged solely on the basis of its place within the closed text of a single story. If the story is part of a larger frame narrative, certain tenses can then only be interpreted from the narrative structure of the entire collection. I intentionally say "interpreted" and not "analyzed" because logically pursued linguistic analysis eventually reaches the point where it becomes literary interpretation. Grammar and poetics, linguistics and literary scholarship can often be combined successfully.

This view of the *Historia septem sapientum* can with some justification be generalized to the entire Middle Ages. Emidio De Felice has already noted it and recognized the *fuit*-beginning as a stylized topos and actual grammaticalized narrative introduction.[16] He follows it from Latin narrative of the republic and early imperial period through early Romance literature up to the fables of La Fontaine, and he describes the rise of a competing *erat*-beginning in Petronius and Apuleius. This is an important essay to which my presentation owes a great deal.

English literature of this early period also deserves a thorough investigation from this point of view. In Chaucer's *Canterbury Tales* I find two kinds of opening in quite similar frequency. "The Cook's Tale" begins, "A prentys whilom dwelled in oure citee."[17] "The Freres Tale," however, begins, "Whilom ther was dwellynge in my contree / An erchedeken, a man of heigh degree" (89). I think it is reasonable to compare these two types to the *fuit*-beginning and the *erat*-beginning in Latin and Romance stories. Chaucer's tales are also connected to the frame by (sometimes very long) prologues and then they are also led back into the frame. Only occasionally is an *-ing* form (tense or participle) used to lead the narrative into the background. This can also happen in the narrative itself, as

---

16. Emidio De Felice, "Problemi di aspetto nei piú antichi testi francesi," *Vox Romanica* 16 (1957): 1–51.

17. Geoffrey Chaucer, *Works*, ed. F. N. Robinson (Boston: Houghton Mifflin, 1957), 60.

the following example shows: "He slow Phitoun, the serpent, as he lay / Slepynge agayn the soone upon a day" ("The Manciple's Tale," 225). That is, in principle, if in different distribution, the function of verb forms in *-ing* that appears in modern narratives like Hemingway's. The differences derive from the frame structure.

Frame and Highlighting in Modern Stories

The connection of stories to frame gradually loosens in the early modern period. It is barely noticeable in Marguerite de Navarre (sixteenth century). Marguerite's *Heptaméron* still has a firm frame plot modeled in detail after the frame in Boccaccio's *Decameron*. Here too the tales, told by a company stranded together by a storm, are discussed before and after telling. Correspondingly, as in Boccaccio, the tales do not conclude in background tenses, and the first story ends, for example, "Et la mauvaise femme, en l'absence de son mary, continua son peché plus que jamais, et mourut miserablement" (And the poor woman, in the absence of her husband, continued her sin more than ever, and died miserably).[18] That is then immediately discussed.

But the *fuit*-beginning does not appear as a rule in Marguerite. Her stories mostly begin with exposition and from the first sentence on use imparfait, which is then interrupted by passé simple when the action begins. The beginning of the fifth story reads: "Au port de Coullon, près de Nyort, y *avoit* une basteliere qui jour et nuict ne *faisoit* que passer ung chacun. *Advint* que deux Cordeliers du dict Nyort *passerent* la riviere tous seulz avecq elle" (35; In the port of Coulon, near Niort, there was a woman who, day and night, ferried passengers. It happened that two Franciscans from Niort crossed the river alone with her). In this introduction the connection to the frame is weaker and there is a narrative gap between the frame and the plot of the tale. That is the first indication of the disappearance of the frame from narrative.

Modern stories are as a rule no longer set in an enclosing frame. To be sure, there are some famous exceptions, such as Gottfried Keller's "Sinngedicht" (Epigram). But the rule is illustrated through individual stories or collections of stories with no thematic unity. At most there is an occasional organized collection such as Pirandello's *Novelle per un anno* (Stories for a Year) or Albert Camus's *L'exil et le royaume* (Exile and the Kingdom). The turning away from the frame can be set around 1834-35, when (according to Karl Maurer) Balzac give up his plans for stories on the theme of the thirty-year-old woman and in place of this technique

---

18. Marguerite de Navarre, *L'heptaméron*, ed. M. François (Paris: Garnier, 1967), 17.

developed a new one based on returning characters who connect several novels into a single grand work of sociological relevance.[19]

The frame does not, however, disappear without a trace. It dissolves, I would like to say, into many parts and survives in many stories in the form of the single frame, which is still popular in later stories. The reader will know stories of this sort: they begin with the narrator preparing to talk, looking at the listeners one by one and then beginning to talk. And at the end of the story the narrator wipes his forehead with his hand, lights his pipe again, and transitions with a sign to a general observation about human life on the basis of the story just told. The image of the narrator that often appears in Maupassant is based on that kind of frame situation.

When a story is placed in such an individual frame, then the same conditions obtain as with the large frame of an entire story collection in older narrative literature. A story in a single frame also needs less of a feed back into the background, since the story has already been absorbed into the frame. Then it looks like, for example, Maupassant's "L'enfant." This child-murder story (one of two stories with this title) ends,

> elle tomba inanimée sur l'enfant noyé dans un flot de sang.
> Fut-elle bien coupable, madame? Le médicin se tut et attendit. La baronne ne répondit pas. (1:986)

> (She fell senseless onto the child drowned in a stream of blood. Was she really guilty, madame? The doctor waited, without speaking. The baroness did not answer).

The frame, clearly recognizable from the address to the listener is, as in the case of the larger frame of the earlier period, a narrated frame. But with the motif of narrated shock it approaches the world of discussion, in which there is real shock. Here the shock is for the woman listening, who was previously indignant at the deed because of her strict morality. Now that she has heard the story, she has become thoughtful, and the reader should become thoughtful with her. The story has, if you will, a moral. Above all, we can say more generally, it has a frame in which the events of the story are discussed. In this case, a return into a narrative background would only be disturbing. It would only make the beginning of a moral discussion more difficult. Here the narrator must intend the shift achieved by continuing the passé simple from the last sentence of the story ("tomba inanimée") to the moral question ("Fut-elle bien coupable, madame?").

---

19. Karl Maurer, "Erlebnis und Dichtung in Balzacs 'Frau von dreißig Jahren,'" *Romanistisches Jahrbuch* 10, no. 1 (1959): 147–66.

There is, in fact, in modern stories an observable relationship of exclusion between the frame and the highlighting according to foreground and background. An author is more likely to do without an introduction from and conclusion into the background if the story has a strong tie to a frame. This happens more frequently with the conclusion than with the introduction, where obviously certain expository needs will remain. This is indeed clearer than in the older stories, which are more strongly stylized. But if there is no frame, then an author rarely gives up foreground and background highlighting, especially the creation of background at the beginning and end of the narrative.

If this observation is correct, then it is reasonable to consider the modern narrative technique of background use in introductions and conclusions as the continuation of and replacement for the older frame technique. Since, apart from the difference between typical and atypical situations and characters, the needs of the exposition are the same whether there is a frame or whether there is modern highlighting, the difference between the two situations is clearest with regard to the conclusion. This explains why imperfect becomes more common as the background tense just at this time and why for example as imparfait de rupture it opens new areas of use, since narrators are mostly giving up both general frames and individual frames. They broaden the function of imperfect to provide more highlighting within their narratives in compensation for the lost frame. There is a historical connection between the dates of the appearance of imparfait de rupture in French and the period given for the increased appearance of tenses in *-ing* in English, 1800-1850, and also the date 1834-35 when Balzac decides to create a combined super-novel rather than a series of thematically connected stories in a frame. This decision leads to the great realistic art of the novel in the nineteenth century, in which the narrative background of sociological conditions as frame achieves undreamt-of importance.

So why does French develop a new tense around 1850? And why do the English tenses in *-ing* become especially common around the same time? It is now clear that we should delete this question from the single-minded history of language. Nothing changes with regard to tenses and their functions. What does change profoundly around this time is narrative technique in literature. It orients itself away from frame technique to background technique. That is simultaneously a reorientation from morality to sociology. This shift in orientation is what enabled the realistic novel and its later avatars. With the growing importance of background in narrative the background tenses of narration extend their areas of use. That is a piece of the history of modern literature. It is simultaneously history of language.

6 / Tense Transitions

Tense in Dialogue

Dialogue, considered for itself, offers no particular difficulties with regard to tense. As speaker and hearer exchange roles in the back and forth of conversation, they generally use the same tenses. And if it is correct that the tenses, in addition to other functions, also harmonize the register (discussing vs. narrating) between speaker and hearer, then it makes sense that transitions of tense generally take place in dialogue no differently than in monologue. For managing the change in role between speaker and hearer there are other syntactic signals, most notably the grammatical forms of person (I / you).

The situation changes, however, when a dialogue is embedded in a narrative as direct quotation. This is very often the case in literary narratives like stories and novels, but also in oral narration. Individual genres and different literary periods, however, exploit this grammatical (not stylistic) possibility to varying degrees. In early poetics and rhetoric, interruption of the narration by passages of direct quotation was valued as a way to enliven narrative. Modern fiction, by contrast, is more reserved in its use of direct quotation. Only popular literature, in its various genres, indulges without scruple in long passages of direct quotation.

To simplify the discussion, I shall assume in what follows that a story, a novel, or a tale, for example, is told in the third person. Such is normally the case in fiction, though not necessarily in oral narratives. When quoted dialogue is embedded into a narrative flow, the grammatical person usually changes, and the third person is replaced by a rapid exchange between first and second person. These are fairly dependable signals, and often they suffice to indicate the transition from narration to direct quotation. In the great majority of cases the participants in quoted dialogues have something to discuss with one another. We then have before us a discussion embedded in a narrative text (novel or tale). I shall illustrate its workings in French with Albert Camus's story, "La femme adultère" (1957, The Adulterous Wife). Here is a brief passage:

> Le chauffeur riait en revenant vers la portière. Posément, il prit quelques outils sous le tableau de bord, puis, minuscule dans la brume, disparut à nouveau vers l'avant, sans fermer la porte. Marcel soupirait. "Tu peux être sûr qu'il n'a jamais vu un moteur de sa vie." — "Laisse!" dit Janine.
>
> The driver laughed, coming back toward the doors. Deliberately, he took some tools from under the dashboard, then, tiny in the fog, disappeared again toward the front of the bus without closing the door. Marcel sighed. "You can be sure he's never seen an engine in his life." — "Leave it be!" Janine said.[1]

It is appropriate to ignore the punctuation marks for direct speech, namely the quotation marks, in the analysis that follows. The narrative structure of the story has to be comprehensible even in oral delivery, and it is not customary to speak the punctuation, unless it is taken as a basis for changing one's tone of voice, within the limits of what is appropriate, to imitate the voices of the speakers. But that is neither indispensable nor probably even desirable for a good presentation. In any case, the syntactic signals in this passage are strong enough to mark the narrative shift to direct discourse. There are (at a minimum) the following signals: 1) Change from third person (Marcel) to second person (*tu*); 2) Tense shift from imparfait to présent; 3) Use of a verb of communication (*soupirait* [sighed]).

This last expression requires longer explanation. There is a grammatical expression *verbum dicendi*, and in its wake often follow similar terms like *verbum sentiendi*, *verbum putandi*, etc. More thorough grammars class these verbs as verbs of speaking, thinking, and feeling and require, allow, or forbid corresponding grammatical constructions.

---

1. Albert Camus, *Théâtre, récits, nouvelles*, ed. Roger Quilliot (Paris: Bibliothèque de la Pléiade, 1962), 1561; "The Adulterous Wife," trans. Carol Cosman, *Kenyon Review*, n.s. 28, no. 2 (Spring 2006): 45–46.

In similar fashion, I will now consider verbs of communication as a general category, with, however, an important methodological caveat: Although the category is based in semantics, it is to be used exclusively for syntactic purposes. There is, therefore, no need for extended discussion of possible semantic boundaries for the word-fields "speaking," "feeling," and "thinking." The decision whether a verb should count as a verb of communication will be made on the basis of semantic and syntactic criteria taken together. That, however, assumes a concept of syntax like that defined at the beginning of this book. Syntax, let me repeat, is understood as the study of the function of morphemes that orient textual communication. The text, to the extent that it is exchanged orally or in writing between a speaker and a listener, is naturally communication in all its contributing signs. But not all signs in a text refer to communication itself. Only the syntactic signs, that is, if I can be forgiven an awkward formulation, are communication-directing signals. In a certain sense they make the process of communication self-conscious. Whether the narrator of a story uses présent or passé simple, for example, says nothing about the real world, but gives particular instructions for understanding this communication.

Although this function is usually filled by morphemes, there are also some lexemes that do so, namely the ones that are here being called verbs of communication. The verb *say* is of this sort. Whether the verbs *think* or *feel* or others of related meaning should also be called verbs of communication I will not determine definitively. As is obvious for the text-linguistic method, that has to depend on the context. The criterion is whether the verb at some particular place in the text activates the communicative situation and makes it conscious, in other words, whether it steers the process of communication between speaker and listener. The example above from Camus is an interesting illustration. Whether *sigh* is a verb of communication is not unambiguously determinable by general semantic methods. Yet in this particular quotation it definitely is one. It stands in an exposed position directly where other, syntactic signals mark the shift from narrative to direct quotation. In this combination of syntactic signals the verb *soupirer* is clearly determined as a verb of communication, independent of whatever role it may play in other texts. It is not necessary to activate communication more explicitly and to say, "Marcel sighed and said, ..."

Before leaving this example, however, let me point to another sign that marks the transition in this passage, namely the appearance of the proper names Marcel and Janine in the framework of the direct quotation. There is nothing obvious about it. As often elsewhere in the story it would be possible to use the corresponding pronouns *il* or *elle*. We often find such "renominalizing" of pronouns used to frame dialogue, where it serves an important expressive function.

Of the 811 tense shifts in "La femme adultère," twenty-eight involve shifts from narrating to discussing. Of these twenty-eight, seventeen involve embedding direct quotes into the narration. And of these seventeen transitions, fourteen are marked by verbs of communication, of which the following occur several times: *dire* (say), *demander* (ask), *soupirer* (sigh). They are distributed before and after the quotation, with a slight majority coming after. In a few cases the quotation is framed by a preceding and a following verb of communication; several times a quotation is interrupted by a verb of communication. In three cases there is no verb of communication in the neighborhood of a direct quote. In these cases, however, a change of syntactic person is clearly marked, in addition to the tense shift. Under these circumstances a verb of communication would be redundant.

While direct quotation in narration is marked by a rich combination of signals at either end, the syntactic signals in indirect discourse are sparser and must be set with greater care. A dialogue rendered indirectly rather than directly requires giving up the important signals of change in person and tense. If we continue with the model of a third-person narrative with predominantly narrating tenses, then the embedded dialogue in indirect discourse must also be rendered in third person and with narrating tenses. What signals then remain for marking the beginning and end? In this situation the verbs of communication become especially important. As an illustration, here is another passage from Camus's story:

> Mais le chauffeur revenait, toujours alerte. Seuls, ses yeux riaient, au-dessus des voiles dont il avait, lui aussi, masqué son visage. Il annonça qu'on s'en allait. Il ferma la portière, le vent se tut et l'on entendit mieux la pluie de sable sur les vitres. (*Théâtre, récits, nouvelles*, 1561)

> But the driver was coming back, ever alert. Only his eyes were laughing above the veil with which he, too, had masked his face. He announced that they were on their way. He closed the doors, the sound of the wind was silenced, and now they could hear the rain of sand on the windows. ("Adulterous Wife," 46)

The only indirect discourse in this passage is, clearly, the phrase *qu'on s'en allait*. In direct speech it would be: *on s'en va*. It is introduced with a verb of communication, *annoncer*. That would separate the direct statement clearly enough from the rest of the narrative text. In indirect discourse it also serves to make the readers recognize the shift from the narrative voice to that of the bus driver.

But indirect discourse raises here an important issue that highlights the achievements of tense. To be sure, it is true that indirect discourse dispenses with sharp shifts from narrating to discussing tenses. While the marking signal disappears here, French—like the other languages able to profile foreground against background in the narrative tenses—introduces an interesting substitute signal at this point to achieve the necessary marking with a certain cleverness, if not the same clarity. Of the two plain retrospective narrative forms, passé simple and imparfait, passé simple is not permitted in indirect discourse. This is, therefore, a negative signal. The accumulation of forms of the imparfait in a text, no matter how numerous, is not of itself a definitive indication that we are dealing with indirect discourse, but the appearance of the passé simple, even of only a single form, makes clear that there is no indirect discourse. So, in our example it is not possible to say unambiguously whether the imparfait forms *revenait, riaient,* and *s'en allait* indicate indirect discourse or not. Nevertheless, from the passé simple forms *annonça, ferma, se tut,* and *entendit* it is definite that they do not mark indirect discourse. The same is also true for passé antérieur and plus-que-parfait (here: *avait masqué*), where the passé antérieur is likewise excluded from indirect discourse.

Since the narrating tenses do not contribute positively, but only negatively, toward marking indirect speech in narrative texts, the additional lexical marking by verbs of communication is especially important. In the case of this example, the status of "qu'on s'en allait" as indirect discourse can be read unambiguously from the combination of the following signals: 1) The verb of communication *annoncer*; 2) The shift from third person to the vague indicator of person *on*, which in spoken French frequently replaces the first person plural; 3) The absence of passé simple in an environment that includes otherwise many examples of it; 4) The introduction of the indirect speech by the conjunction *que* (subordinate clause).

It is difficult to find examples of indirect discourse in Camus's narratives. They are just as rare as the examples of direct quotation. Like many modern authors, Camus prefers to render what is spoken or thought in free indirect discourse, sometimes also called interior monologue (in French *discours indirect libre,* in German *erlebte Rede*). Here again it should be noted that this is not a matter of style, but of a thoroughly regular, though not inelegant use of syntactic signals of communication. It is especially important not to misinterpret this usage hastily as "psychological." It has nothing to do with experience, as suggested by the German, or with the interiority of the English term. So, the French-derived term free indirect discourse seems to me preferable. Indeed, free indirect discourse is most simply described as indirect discourse liberated from syntactic dependence on a governing verb of communication. Verbs of communication appear just about as often in free indirect discourse as in ordinary indirect discourse. But these verbs of communication are followed by "free" clauses not subordinated to anything, either by *que* (that) or any other conjunction. The verbs of communication signal the beginning of the speech without a conjunction to connect them. Indeed, their effect on the entire passage that follows is less limited, since it is not confined by the structure of a subordinate clause. Under these circumstances a single verb of communication can turn entire passages into free indirect discourse, and the author can linger in this narrative perspective at will. In modern literature this technique is often practiced with amazing virtuosity.

Here is another scene. Janine, Camus's "adulteress," is in a hotel room with her husband. He sleeps next to her. She herself lies in bed awake:

> La chambre était glacée. Janine sentait le froid la gagner en même temps que s'accélerait la fièvre. Elle respirait mal, son sang battait sans la réchauffer; une sorte de peur grandissait en elle. Elle se retournait, le vieux lit de fer craquait sous son poids. Non, elle ne voulait pas être malade. Son mari dormait déjà, elle aussi devait dormir, il le fallait. Les bruits étouffés de la ville parvenaient jusqu'à elle par la meurtrière. Les vieux phonographes des cafés maures nasillaient des airs qu'elle reconnaissait vaguement, et qui lui arrivaient, portés par une rumeur de foule lente. — Il fallait dormir. Mais elle comptait des tentes noires; derrière ses paupières paissaient des chameaux immobiles; d'immenses solitudes tournoyaient en elle. Oui, pourquoi était-elle venue? Elle s'endormit sur cette question. (*Théâtre*, récits, nouvelles, 1569)

> The room was cold as ice. Janine felt the cold overtake her even as her fever rose. She was breathing badly, her blood pulsed without warming her; a kind of fear was growing inside her. She turned over; the old iron bed creaked beneath her weight. No, she did not want to be ill. Her husband was already asleep; she should sleep, too, it was imperative. The stifled sounds of the town reached her through the narrow window. At the Moorish cafes the old phonographs droned out their tunes, which she vaguely recognized, reaching her through the murmur of the idle crowd. She ought to sleep. But she was counting black tents; behind her eyelids motionless camels grazed; vast

solitudes wheeled within her. Yes, why had she come? She fell asleep on this question. ("Adulterous Wife," 53)

To avoid confusion, it must be understood that the linguistic status of free indirect discourse is the same, whether it is actually spoken audibly or whether it is only thought. This is not unique to free indirect discourse or interior monologue, but is always the case for indirect or direct speech. The syntactic signals are no different whether the speech is out loud or "only" thought.

These are the thoughts of a woman lying awake—but how does the reader know that? Couldn't they also be the thoughts of the narrator? And what criteria distinguish between the thoughts of the narrator and those of a particular character in the narration? There are syntactic signals. There is, for example, tense. The passage has almost exclusively imparfait forms. Only the last sentence is in passé simple (*s'endormit*). The final signal is the most definitive. This last sentence is clearly neither indirect discourse nor free indirect discourse because the foreground tense, passé simple, is not permitted in either one. All the remaining sentences in the passage are not definitely indirect or free indirect discourse just because they are in the imparfait. But they could be. There are no syntactic dependencies in the sense of a subordinate clause like *he said that* . . . So, this must be a matter of free indirect discourse if at all. Is it free indirect discourse, and if so, where does it start?

There is certainly none at the beginning of the passage. The second sentence, at least, is clearly written from the perspective of the narrator. The signal for that is the proper name, Janine. That is a negative signal, since the name of the indirect "speaker" is excluded from free indirect discourse by definition. In the remainder of the passage the suppressed name becomes a pronoun, either the personal pronoun (*elle, lui*) or possessive pronoun (*son, ses*). But the absence of the proper name is no more an unambiguous sign of free indirect discourse than the absence of the passé simple. What can we depend on? The clearest indicator is probably the verbs of communication, to which, in monologue, may be included the *verba sentiendi* and the modals (*sentait / une sorte de peur grandissait / voulait / devait / il fallait / les bruits parvenaient / reconnaissait / comptait*). At the end of the passage the verbs of communication are again summarized by closing with a noun of communication (*question*).

Since free indirect discourse lacks the definite markers of indirect or direct discourse, it uses stylistic elements that imply "oral style" as an additional signal, which, however, distinguishes free indirect discourse from the narrative context only in the aggregate. In this passage, for example, the beginning of the indirect discourse is characterized by a repeated negation typical for exaggerated oral discourse: *Non, elle ne voulait pas être malade.* Further, we find loosely organized syntax to suggest only passing thoughts, as in *son mari dormait dejà, elle aussi devait dormir, il le fallait.* Repetitions are also allowed that a narrator would never permit himself as artist (*il le fallait, il fallait dormir*). Rhetorical questions, here again with a musing *oui* leading into it, turn up fairly frequently in free indirect discourse (*Oui, pourquoi était-elle venue?*). Finally, there are a few "poetic" metaphors in the free indirect discourse that Camus otherwise avoids as a modern narrator (*derrière ses paupières paissaient des chameaux immobiles*). These are now truly stylistic and no longer syntactic signals. Each taken alone contributes only a nuance, but cumulatively they result in a clear textual function and signal that this bit of text is really not the responsibility of the narrator, but must be attributed to the spontaneous and, at this point in the text, somewhat confused thoughts of a narrated character.

In order to show that the syntactic problems sketched here are not specific to a single language but appear in similar fashion in other languages with similar tense structures, I offer an Italian example as well, from Pirandello's story "Va bene" (1905, Things are fine). Professor Vabene is described here:

> E si *domandò* perché mai egli, che non *aveva* mai fatto per volontà male ad alcuno, *doveva* esser cosí bersagliato dalla sorte; egli, che anzi s'era inteso di far sempre il bene; bene lasciando l'abito ecclesiastico, quando la sua logica non s'era piú *accordata* con quella dei dottori della chiesa, la quale *avrebbe dovuto* esser legge per lui; bene, sposando per dare il pane a un'orfana, la quale per forza *aveva voluto* accettarlo a questo patto, mentr'egli onestamente e con tutto il cuore *avrebbe voluto* offrirglielo altrimenti. E ora, dopo l'infame tradimento e la fuga di quella donna indegna che gli *aveva spezzata* l'esistenza, ora quasi certamente gli toccava a soffrire anche la pena di vedersi morire a poco a poco il figliuolo, l'unico bene, per quanto amaro, che gli fosse rimasto. Ma perché? Dio, no: Dio non *poteva* voler questo. Se Dio *esisteva*, *doveva* coi buoni esser buono. Egli lo *avrebbe offeso*, credendo in lui. E chi dunque, chi dunque *aveva* il governo del mondo, di questa sciaguratissima vita degli uomini?[2]

> And he asked himself, why exactly he, who had never intentionally done evil to any one, had to be such a butt of fate; he, who on the contrary had intended always to do good; good in giving up his

---

2. Luigi Pirandello, *Novelle per un anno*, https://www.liberliber.it/online/autori/autori-p/luigi-pirandello/novelle-per-un-anno/, 1362–63.

ecclesiastical garb when his logic no longer accorded with that of the doctors of the church, which should have been law for him; good in marrying in order to give bread to an orphan who would only accept it on those terms even though he was honestly and from the depths of his heart willing to give it to her otherwise. And now, after the infamous betrayal and flight of this vile woman, who had shattered his life, now it was also almost certainly his lot to suffer the punishment of seeing his son die slowly, the one good that remained to him, however bitter it might be. But why? God, no: God could not possibly want this. If God existed, he would have to be good to good men. He must have insulted Him by believing in Him. And so who, then, who then ruled over the world and over this cursed life of mankind?

Pirandello narrates here the unhappy thoughts of Professor Vabene, who has been mistreated by fate. The meaning of the entire text depends on the introductory verb of communication *si domandò* (passato remoto). With increasing distance from the introduction the sentences become more independent syntactically, without, however, ceasing to be the thoughts of Professor Vabene. Even if the first sentences could still be read as subordinate clauses, the later sentences no longer depend on the initial verb. They are no longer indirect discourse, but free indirect discourse. In this text, too, we find stylistic elements with the natural liveliness characteristic of oral style. This time they are certain adverbs (*ora*), demonstrative pronouns (*quella donna indegna*), coarse language (*questa sciaguratissima vita*), rhetorical questions (*ma perché?*), and repetitions (*Dio, no: Dio no / E chi dunque, chi dunque*). They lend the free indirect discourse a stylistic atmosphere, as if it were directly reproduced, oral, and direct quotation.

Free indirect discourse belongs by nature to narrative and is therefore formed from the narrating tenses. It can, however, in some cases, also appear in discussion. It happens, for example, when a narrator uses discursive tenses unexpectedly. Part of the story "Va bene" works this way. Here is such a passage for comparison (again about Professor Vabene): "Si toglie le mani dal volto e resta attonito, ad ascoltare. Un vetro si scuote, appena appena, alla finestra. Ah, il vento—ecco—il vento è cessato. E come mai?" (He takes his hands from his face and remains shocked, listening. A pane rattles, barely audible, at the window. Ah, the wind—yes—the wind has let up. And how come?)[3] The narrator speaks here not in his own name but reports the

---

3. Translators' note: This passage, which is close to a stage direction found in Pirandello's dramatization of the novella, does not appear in the text of the stories cited elsewhere in our translation. It is included, however, in www.pirandelloweb.com/va-bene.

occurrence from the perspective of the character in the story. Except for the first, these sentences are free indirect discourse. Again, how do we know? No distinction between the narrative voice and the character's voice can be drawn on the basis of tense, because the tenses of discussion in Italian, as in the other Romance languages, do not distinguish between foreground and background as the narrative tenses do. Yet the free indirect discourse can be recognized, even if it is marked less clearly. The single signal of free indirect discourse in a context of discursive tenses is the accumulation of the stylistic signals of oral style, which appear generously in this passage: repetition (*appena... appena / il vento... il vento*), exclamation (*ah! / ecco!*), and the colloquial question to oneself (*e come mai?*). They have to appear in such density precisely because the other important signal of free indirect discourse—renunciation of foreground tenses—is not available here.

These conditions must be kept in mind as we now turn to free indirect discourse in German, where free indirect discourse must always operate as the Romance languages do in the context of the discussing tenses. Since German lacks the equivalent of Romance profiling in the narrative tenses, tense shift disappears as a signal for free indirect discourse, which then depends exclusively on signals based on natural orality. Hence free indirect discourse is more difficult in German than in Romance narratives, though not more difficult than in Romance discursive speech. It is used less frequently and scarcely ever raised to the dominant form in a novel. Nevertheless, German writers use it even under these more difficult circumstances, indeed often with some virtuosity, as this passage about Friedrich Schiller from Thomas Mann's story "Schwere Stunde" (1905, Painful Hour) illustrates:

> Das war ein besonderer und unheimlicher Schnupfen, der ihn fast nie völlig verließ. Seine Augenlider waren entflammt und die Ränder seiner Nasenlöcher ganz wund davon, und in Kopf und Gliedern lag dieser Schnupfen ihm wie eine schwere, schmerzliche Trunkenheit. Oder war an all der Schlaffheit und Schwere das leidige Zimmergewahrsam schuld, das der Arzt nun schon wieder seit Wochen über ihn verhängt hielt? Gott wußte, ob er wohl daran tat. Der ewige Katarrh und die Krämpfe in Brust und Unterleib mochten es nötig machen, und schlechtes Wetter war über Jena, seit Wochen, seit Wochen, das war richtig, ein miserables und hassenswertes Wetter, das man in allen Nerven spürte, wüst, finster und kalt, und der Dezemberwind heulte im Ofenrohr, verwahrlost und gottverlassen, daß es klang nach nächtiger Heide im Sturm und Irrsal und heillosem Gram der Seele. Aber gut

war sie nicht, diese enge Gefangenschaft, nicht gut für die Gedanken und den Rhythmus des Blutes, aus dem die Gedanken kamen.[4]

It was an unusual and uncanny cold that never went away entirely. His eyelids were inflamed and the rims of his nostrils were all raw from it, and this cold sat in his head and limbs like a heavy, painful drunkenness. Or was all the inertia and heaviness just the result of confinement to his room, to which the doctor had condemned him again weeks ago? God knew if that was well judged. Perhaps the constant catarrh and cramps in the chest and abdomen made it necessary, and the weather in Jena had been terrible, for weeks, for weeks, it was true, miserable and hateful weather that you felt in all your nerves, wild, dark, and cold, and the December wind was howling in the chimney, desolate and godforsaken, so that it sounded like the moors at night in storm and chaos and unholy affliction of the soul. But it wasn't good, this narrow imprisonment, not good for one's thoughts or for the rhythm of the blood from which thoughts arose.

The accumulation of stylistic devices to express natural speaking is remarkable. They include especially the question to oneself (*Oder war...?*), the exclamatory idiom (*Gott wußte / das war richtig*), the colloquial expression (*der ewige Katarrh / ein miserables Wetter*), repetition (*seit Wochen, seit Wochen*), lists of strong synonyms (*wüst, finster und kalt / verwahrlost und gottverlassen*), the tacked-on clause after what should have been the end of the sentence (*daß es klang nach...*), and the prolepsis (*Aber gut war sie nicht, diese...*). Mann has to use these relatively coarse stylistic devices because he has no assistance from the structure of the German tense system for free indirect discourse. Under these difficult circumstances, his achievement of writing this entire story as free indirect discourse is a real tour de force.

Franz Werfel arrived at a unique way for dealing with this difficulty in his novel *Das Lied von Bernadette* (1941, The Song of Bernadette), which is written entirely in the tenses of discussion. He adopts for his novel the idiosyncratic arrangement of using the narrative tenses, otherwise unused, for free indirect discourse. It looks like this in a passage from the first chapter:

> Soubirous *ist* ein sonderbarer Mann. Mehr als die elende Stube *ärgern* ihn diese beiden vergitterten Fenster, eines größer, das andere kleiner, die zwei niederträchtig schielenden Augen, die auf den engen, dreckigen Hof des Cachot *hinausschaun*, wo der Misthaufen der

---

4. Thomas Mann, *Sämtliche Erzählungen* (Frankfurt/Main: Fischer, 1963), 294.

ganzen Gegend *duftet*. Man *war* schließlich kein Landstreicher, kein Lumpensammler, sondern ein freier, regelrechter Müller, ein Mühlenbesitzer, auf seine Art nichts andres, als es Monsieur de Lafite *ist* mit seinem großen Sägewerk. Die Boly-Mühle unterm Chateau Fort *hatte sich sehen lassen können* weit und breit. Auch die Escobé-Mühle in Arcizac-les-Angles *war* gar nicht übel.[5]

Soubirous is a strange fellow. Even more than by the miserable room, he is irritated by two latticed windows, one larger, the other smaller, these two maliciously squinting eyes that look out onto the cramped, filthy courtyard of the prison that is perfumed by the dungheap of the whole neighborhood. After all, one wasn't a peasant, a trash collector, but a free, proper miller, a mill owner, no different in his way than Monsieur de Lafite is with his large sawmill. The Boly Mill under the fortress could show forth far and wide. And the Escobé Mill in Arcizac-les-Angles was not at all bad.

The problem of signaling the shift into indirect discourse might also be studied in German translations of Romance narratives. There one can find many disappointments, but also many clever solutions. The stylistic art of the translator has to compensate for what is lacking in the language.

Descartes, Rousseau, and the Sequence of Tenses

The observations made here about transitions between tenses in various texts are not entirely unknown to grammar. In traditional grammars they appear in the chapter *Consecutio temporum* (sequence of tenses).[6] Especially the ancient languages are reputed to obey a more or less strict sequence of tenses in structures involving a main clause and subordinate clause, so that if one tense is used in the main clause, then it harmonizes only with certain others in the subordinate clause. There has also been lively discussion as to whether French has a *concordance des temps* or not. The argument has been especially acute since Ferdinand Brunot declared categorically, "Le chapitre de la concordance des temps se résume en une ligne: Il n'y en a pas" (The chapter on sequence of tenses can be summarized in one line: It does not exist).[7] Yet Paul Imbs has already pointed out that Brunot allowed

---

5. Franz Werfel, *Das Lied von Bernadette: Historischer Roman*, ed. Karl-Maria Guth (Berlin: Contumax Hofberg, 2016), E-book, 7–8.

6. The *consecutio temporum* was already identified and formulated by the ancient grammarians: Jakob Wackernagel, *Vorlesungen über Syntax* (Basel: Birkhäuser, 1926), 1:252.

7. Ferdinand Brunot, *La pensée et la langue: Méthode, principes et plan d'une théorie nouvelle du langage appliquée au français* (Paris: Masson, 1922), 782.

the sequence of tenses to sneak back in and admits at least that the tense of the second clause, if not determined by the first clause, still is determined by the sense of the sentence as a whole.[8] Then there is the interesting contradictory formulation about sequence of tenses in Charles Bruneau's revision of Brunot's historical grammar, "Cette règle n'a jamais été observée par les bons écrivains" (This rule has never been followed by good writers).[9] A survey of the positions on sequence of tenses in French in general reveals the commonly accepted opinion that there is a certain required sequencing of tenses within a sentence, but the requirement is not absolute.[10]

Rather than discussing here the old and new arguments for and against tense sequencing in French or another modern language, I will once again point out that the text-linguistic method, applied with reasonable strictness, does not even allow a discussion of sequence of tenses within a single sentence. Instead, I will offer a small piece of text, from Descartes's *Discours de la méthode* (Discourse on Method, 1637). Special in this philosophical text is that Descartes presents his insights mostly in narrative form. He tells how he has arrived at his philosophical ideas and how he has pursued the path of his method step by step. Hence the dominant tenses used are narrative ones. Even the sentence "Je pense, donc je suis," as a self-quotation lifted from the text, stands in a narrative context:

> Mais aussitôt après, je pris garde que, pendant que je voulais ainsi penser que tout étoit faux, il fallait nécessairement que moi, qui le pensais, fusse quelque chose. Et remarquant que cette vérité: *je pense, donc je suis*, était si ferme et si assurée, que toutes les plus extravagantes suppositions des sceptiques n'étaient pas capables de l'ébranler, je jugeai que je pouvais la recevoir sans scrupule pour le premier principe de la philosophie que je cherchais.[11]

> I resolv'd to faign, that all those things which ever entred into my Minde, were no more true, than the illusions of my dreams. But presently after I observ'd, that whilst I would think that all was false, it must necessarily follow, that I who thought it, must be something. And perceiving that this Truth, *I think*, therefore, *I am*, was so firm and certain, that all the most extravagant suppositions of the

---

8. Paul Imbs, *L'emploi des temps verbaux* (Paris: Klincksieck, 1960), 207.

9. Ferdinand Bruno and Charles Bruneau, *Précis de grammaire historique de la langue française*, 3rd edition (Paris: Masson, 1949), 387.

10. There is an extensive summary of research on this discussion in Imbs, *L'emploi*, 207 ff.

11. René Descartes, *Oeuvres philosophiques*, ed. Ferdinand Alquié (Paris: Garnier, 1963), 1:603.

Scepticks was not able to shake it, I judg'd that I might receive it without scruple for the first principle of the Philosophy I sought.[12]

As he writes these thoughts looking back, Descartes is evidently still as convinced as ever that certainty of one's existence can be derived from self-consciousness and that this grounding constitutes an "eternal" truth. He simply follows the sequencing rules of the French tense system in placing after the lead tense passé simple ("je pris garde que," "je jugeai que") imparfait as the textual transition (foreground tense ÷ background tense) to mark indirect speech or, in this case, "indirect thinking." This has no effect on the truth value of the philosophical statement. (The possibility of lifting an especially important formula like "Je pense, donc je suis" as a quotation out of this homogeneously narrative text of narrated philosophy and marking its character as quotation by a profiling tense-change from a narrative to a discursive tense, remains unaffected. The quotation can be understood as direct speech or direct thinking; the corresponding rules for tense-change in direct speech remain in force.)

I'll explain these connections with a further passage from the *Discours de la méthode*, in which Descartes tries to extend his method to learning the nature of God:

> Puis, outre cela, j'avois des idées de plusieurs choses sensibles et corporelles: car, quoique je supposasse que je rêvais, et que tout ce que je voyais ou imaginais était faux, je ne pouvais nier toutefois que les idées n'en fussent véritablement en ma pensée; mais parce que j'avais déjà connu en moi très clairement que la nature intelligente est distincte de la corporelle, considérant que toute composition témoigne de la dépendance, et que la dépendance est manifestement un défaut, je jugeais de là que ce ne pouvait être une perfection en Dieu d'être composé de ces deux natures, et que par conséquent, il ne l'était pas; mais que s'il y avait quelques corps dans le monde, ou bien quelques intelligences, ou autres natures, qui ne fussent point toutes parfaites, leur être devait dépendre de sa puissance, en telle sorte qu'elles ne pouvaient subsister sans lui un seul moment. (*Oeuvres philosophiques*, 607)

> Besides this, I had the *Ideas* of divers sensible and corporeall things; for although I supposed that I doted, and that all that I saw or imagined was false; yet could I not deny but that these *Ideas* were truly in my thoughts. But because I had most evidently known in my self, That

---

12. René Descartes, *Discourse of a Method for the Well Guiding of Reason* (London: Thomas Newcombe, 1649), 51–52, www.gutenberg.org/files/25830/25830-h/25830-h.htm.

the understanding Nature is distinct from the corporeall, considering that all composition witnesseth a dependency, and that dependency is manifestly a defect, I thence judged that it could not be a perfection in God to be composed of those two Natures; and that by consequence he was not so composed. But that if there were any Bodies in the world, or els any intelligences, or other Natures which were not wholly perfect, their being must depend from his power in such a manner, that they could not subsist one moment without him. (*Discourse*, 56–57)

In this passage also Descartes tells the story of his mind. The truths that reveal themselves stepwise to his growing knowledge are narrated in this passage, too. For an analysis of narration as a phenomenon, it should be noted that not only processes, here thought processes, can be narrated, but also connections of other sorts, as here, for example, the truth or falsity of psychic perceptions. Even when the nature of God is the topic, which according to all the laws of philosophy and theosophy must be independent of time, Descartes does not disdain narrative tenses.

The passage selected is, however, especially interesting because it shows that Descartes sometimes proceeds differently. At three points in the text he uses présent, even though the narrative perspective continues forward ("que la nature intelligente est distincte de la corporelle," "que toute composition témoigne de la dépendance," "que la dépendance est manifestement un défaut"). These three present forms stand in textual sequence between a previous verb in plus-que-parfait ("j'avais connu") and a following imparfait ("je jugeais"). Of course, it is possible to appeal once more to logic at this point and to point out that, according to Descartes's view, the *res cogitans* is actually and for all time different from the *res extensa*, that what is simple is more independent than what is compound, and that every dependency is an imperfection. All of that can be "eternal truth," at least within the consistency of Cartesian philosophy. But it is no more and no less true than the unity of God's nature, about which Descartes reports in the following sentence not in présent, but in imparfait. Evidently the tense choice depends not on the logical or ontological status of these statements, but on the sequencing rules of the French tense system.

It must be noted here that the philosophical positions in question are presented as dependent on certain introductory verbs known in an old expression as *verba putandi* (verbs of thinking). In this passage they are verbs like *avoir des idées, supposer, nier, connaître, considérer, juger*. They can be counted generally as verbs of communication. In this passage these verbs consistently drive the communicative situation so that the reader at any point knows exactly whether the narrating or the narrated

"I" of the philosopher is speaking. These verbs of communication can be interpreted as shifters. Using these shifters allows for more frequent contrasting tense shifts, in this text especially from narrating to discussing, even if not required. The special status of verbs of communication thus enables Descartes, so long as he uses them syntactically, to choose regular or irregular tense sequences essentially as he pleases, that is in traditional terminology, either to respect or not respect the *consecutio temporum*. So, the rule of text-linguistics here is that the rules of tense sequencing in a sentence or in a text cannot be discussed reasonably without taking account of the presence or absence of verbs of communication.

Looking back to the question of highlighting, we note that the two texts of Descartes cited here differ from one another in that the verbs of communication in the first passage are passé simple ("je pris garde que," "je jugeai que"), and in the second imparfait. Descartes draws a careful distinction here. He uses imparfait when he stands still in his thinking, and passé simple when he moves forward in his thought process.

It might perhaps be useful to compare and contrast Descartes's text with that of another philosopher, Jean-Jacques Rousseau in his *Discours sur l'origine et les fondements de l'inégalité parmi les hommes* (1755, A Discourse upon the Origin and the Foundation of the Inequality Among Mankind). This text, too, can be considered narrated philosophy, although in completely different fashion from Descartes. Here, to begin, a passage from Part 2 of the *Discours*:

> Dans ce nouvel état, avec une vie simple et solitaire, des besoins très bornés, et les instruments qu'ils avoient inventés pour y pourvoir, les hommes joüissant d'un fort grand loisir l'emploiérent à se procurer plusieurs sortes de commodités inconnues à leurs Peres; et ce fut là le premier joug qu'ils s'imposérent sans y songer, et la premiere source de maux qu'ils préparérent à leurs Descendans; car outre qu'ils continuérent ainsi à s'amollir le corps et l'esprit, ces commodités ayant par l'habitude perdu presque tout leur agrément, et étant en même tems dégénérées en de vrais besoins, la privation en devint beaucoup plus cruelle que la possession n'en étoit douce, et l'on étoit malheureux de les perdre, sans être heureux de les posséder.
>
> On entrevoit un peu mieux ici comment l'usage de la parole s'établit ou se perfectionne insensiblement dans le sein de chaque famille, et l'on peut conjecturer encore comment diverses causes particuliéres purent étendre le langage, et en accélérer le progrès en le rendant plus nécessaire. De grandes inondations ou des tremblemens de terre environnérent d'eaux ou de précipices des Cantons habités; Des révolutions

du globe détachérent et coupérent en Iles des portions du Continent. On conçoit qu'entre des hommes ainsi rapprochés, et forcés de vivre ensemble, il dut se former un Idiome commun plutôt qu'entre ceux qui erroient librement dans les forêts de la Terre ferme. Ainsi il est très possible qu'après leurs premiers essais de Navigation, des Insulaires aient porté parmi nous l'usage de la parole; et il est au moins très vraisemblable que la Société et les langues ont pris naissance dans les Iles, et s'y sont perfectionnées avant que d'être connües dans le Continent.[13]

In this new state of things, the simplicity and solitariness of man's life, the limitedness of his wants, and the instruments which he had invented to satisfy them, leaving him a great deal of leisure, he employed it to supply himself with several conveniences unknown to his ancestors; and this was the first yoke he inadvertently imposed upon himself, and the first source of mischief which he prepared for his children; for besides continuing in this manner to soften both body and mind, these conveniences having through use lost almost all their aptness to please, and even degenerated into real wants, the privation of them became far more intolerable than the possession of them had been agreeable; to lose them was a misfortune, to possess them no happiness.

Here we may a little better discover how the use of speech insensibly commences or improves in the bosom of every family, and may likewise from conjectures concerning the manner in which divers particular causes might have propagated language, and accelerated its progress by rendering it every day more and more necessary. Great inundations or earthquakes surrounded inhabited districts with water or precipices, portions of the continent were by revolutions of the globe torn off and split into islands. It is obvious that among men thus collected, and forced to live together, a common idiom must have started up much sooner, than among those who freely wandered through the forests of the main land. Thus it is very possible that the inhabitants of the islands formed in this manner, after their first essays in navigation, brought among us the use of speech; and it is very probable at least that society and languages commenced in islands and even acquired perfection there, before the inhabitants of the continent knew anything of either.[14]

---

13. Jean-Jacques Rousseau, *Oeuvres complètes,* ed. Bernard Gagnebin, Robert Osmont, and Marcel Raymond (Paris: Gallimard, 1964), 1:168–69.

14. Jean-Jacques Rousseau, *A Discourse upon the Origin and the Foundation of the Inequality Among Mankind,* https://www.gutenberg.org/cache/epub/11136/pg11136.html.

Differently from Descartes, this is not the history of a thinking mind. It is a history of humanity and the thinking mind of the philosopher presents this history by telling it from a stable narrative perspective. He compresses the ages ("Je parcours comme un trait des multitudes de Siécles" [176; My pen ... flies like an arrow over numberless ages]), hence the high frequency of passé simple compared to imparfait. Although this passage is relatively homogeneous narrative with regard to tense, there are still some discursive tenses mixed in, namely: "on entrevoit," "l'on peut conjecturer," "on conçoit," "il est très possible," "il est au moins très vraisemblable." There are also two examples of passé composé: "ont pris naissance," "s'y sont perfectionnées." The first five examples all involve verbs of communication combined with an indeterminate person (*on*, *il*). The philosopher narrates not what he experienced, but what he conjectures. Rousseau knows and admits as much: "J'avoue que les évenements que j'ai a décrire ayant pu arriver de plusieurs maniéres, je ne puis me déterminer sur le choix que par des conjectures" (162; I must own that, as the events I am about to describe might have happened many different ways, my choice of these I shall assign can be grounded on nothing but mere conjecture). To express this honesty about the conjectural character of his history of humanity, Rousseau blends verbs of communication into the narrative text more or less frequently to confirm its conjectural status. The verbs listed above belong to this class. I consider them verbs of communication because they inform the reader about the mode of communication on which the author has based his narrative and which he wishes to make clear. While Rousseau tells the history of humanity, he still discusses its limited historicity with his readers. In this case, too, the specific rule of sequencing for verbs of communication applies, that contrasting tense changes between narrative and discursive tenses are readily permitted, even within a sentence between main clause and subordinate clause. Under these circumstances it is possible to find in the passage an accumulation of the abrupt change présent to passé simple. At the same time, however—and here the two forms of passé composé at the end of the passage come in—the end of the passage is marked by the absence after the last verb of communication of an abrupt shift from discussion to narration. Instead, we find only the softer tense shift présent to passé composé, which remains inside the world of discussion. That is also a closing signal for the passage.[15]

15. My further thoughts on tense structures in Descartes and Rousseau are in the essay "Erzählte Philosophie oder Geschichte des Geistes," in *Literatur für Leser* (Munich: Deutscher Taschenbuch Verlag, 1986), 184–202.

7 / Tense Metaphors

Tense Metaphors in Texts

We normally speak of metaphors in semantics, not in syntax. However, since grammar as presented here is not independent of meaning, even the study of tenses can take metaphors into account. This presupposes continuing with a strict text-linguistic methodology. In terms of text linguistics, a metaphor is to be defined as a linguistic sign in a heterogeneous context which generates an unexpected, counter-determining effect. Hence a linguistic sign can never be a metaphor all by itself. A metaphor is always a structure of determinations, that is, a bit of text.[1] This is true not only for lexical metaphors (e.g., *the stream of words*), but also for a grammatical metaphor, as, for example, a particular tense in a heterogeneous tense context, which similarly generates a counter-determining effect.

The category "tense metaphor" has a long tradition, as Lausberg demonstrated.[2] Quintilian already translates the Greek concept of *metástasis* with *translatio temporum*. He does not, however, apply the term within a consistent theory, but means with it above all the so-called "historical present." He writes: "Transferuntur et tempora . . ., praesens enim pro praeterito positum est" (tenses are also changed around . . ., for the

---

1. For more on metaphor in general see my *Sprache in Texten* (Stuttgart: Klett, 1976), 276–341.
2. Heinrich Lausberg, *Handbuch der literarischen Rhetorik* (Munich: Max Hueber, 1960).

present is put in for the past).³ Lausberg emphasizes in his commentary that the way ancient rhetoricians treat tense metaphor is reminiscent of their treatment of lexical metaphor.⁴ Following the ancestors in ancient rhetoric we find individual views of tense metaphor also among modern linguists.⁵ I welcome this agreement, but must point out that tense metaphor can be seen in very different ways, depending on the systematic framework within which it is examined.

Metaphor is a realm of nuance. The same is true, though with some restriction, to morphemic metaphor, here of tense morphemes. I shall explain with an example from Bainville's *Histoire de France* (History of France). Bainville tells about the plebiscite of December 10, 1851, when Louis-Napoléon was elected president:

> Ce fut une situation bien extraordinaire que celle de ce prince-président qui n'était rien la veille, qui n'avait qu'une poignée de partisans et qui devenait chef d'Etat. Le premier mouvement des députés fut de considérer son élection comme un accident (le président n'était pas rééligible) et de le traiter lui-même comme une quantité négligeable. En effet, n'étant pas initié aux affaires, il montrait de l'embarras et même de la timidité. Pourtant, il avait déjà une politique. Il choisit ses ministres parmi les conservateurs, et, mesurant l'importance de l'opinion catholique, lui donna une satisfaction en décidant l'expédition de Rome pour rétablir le Pape dans ses Etats d'où une Révolution l'avait chassé. Jusqu'à la fin, Napoléon III sera conservateur à l'extérieur et libéral à l'intérieur ou inversement, pour contenter toujours les deux tendances des Français.⁶

> The situation of this prince-president was very extraordinary; he was nothing the day before, he had but a handful of supporters, and he became head of state. The first reaction of the deputies was to consider

---

3. Quintilian, *Institutio oratoria*, ed. and trans. Donald A. Russell (Cambridge: Harvard UP, 2002), 9.3.11; IV:102–3.

4. Quintilian, *Institutio* 9.2.41 and 9.3.11, and Lausberg's discussion, sections 523 and 814. Lausberg notes in detail that daring tense metaphors, just like semantic metaphors, tend to be introduced with a softening formula, such as *credite vos intueri* ("trust your intuition"); *ponite ante oculos* ("just imagine"). The tense metaphor is thus "verecundior" (more modest). It also involves the use of verbs of communication to mark a transition, similar to that between direct and indirect speech.

5. Joe Larochette, "L'imparfait et le passé simple," *Les études classiques* 13, no. 1–2 (1945): 78–80; Holger Sten, *Les temps du verbe fini (indicatif) en français moderne* (Copenhagen: Munksgaard, 1964), 6; Paul Imbs, *L'emploi des temps verbaux* (Paris: Klincksieck, 1960), 17; William Emerson Bull, *Time, Tense and the Verb* (Berkeley: U of California P, 1968), 60–62.

6. Jacques Bainville, *Histoire de France* (Paris: Arthème Fayard, 1924), 483–84.

his election an accident (the president could not be reelected) and to treat him as negligible. Indeed, untrained in public affairs, he appeared to be embarrassed, even timid. However, he already had a strategy. He chose his ministers from among the conservatives and, taking account of the importance of Catholic opinion, satisfied it by deciding on the expedition to Rome to reestablish the Pope, who had been chased from his states by a revolution. Until the end Napoleon III will be externally a conservative and internally a liberal, or the other way around, in order to keep satisfying the two tendencies of the French.

Most of this passage has all the signs of a narrative. The dominant tenses are imparfait and passé simple, mixed to profile the historical narrative. At the end of the passage, however, the author suddenly switches to a discursive tense, indeed to the futur (*sera*).[7] Bainville surely does not intend to express his own future with this verb, since Napoleon III is long since dead at the time he writes these lines. The future tense expresses, therefore, a forward perspective that applies only within the narrative. This phenomenon has occasionally been called the "historiographic future." It is not a new tense in its own right, however, but an ordinary French futur whose tense character is contradicted by a narrative context. Its grammatical meaning in the system of the language has not changed, only its contextual meaning in this particular text. This is a tense metaphor.

To look in the opposite direction, there is a tense metaphor when a conditionnel is counter-determined by a discursive context. Here is an example from a work we have already looked at, Claude Bernard's *Introduction à l'étude de la médecine expérimentale* (1865, Introduction to the Study of Experimental Medicine):

> Cette définition représente une opinion assez généralement adoptée. D'après elle, l'observation serait la constatation des choses ou des phénomènes telles que la nature nous les offre ordinairement, tandis que l'expérience serait la constatation de phénomènes créés ou déterminés par l'expérimenteur. Il y aurait à établir de cette manière une sorte d'opposition entre l'observateur et l'expérimentateur; le premier étant passif dans la production des phénomènes, le second y prenant, au contraire, une part directe et active. Cuvier a exprimé cette même pensée en disant: "L'observateur écoute la nature; l'expérimentateur l'interroge et la force à se dévoiler."[8]

---

7. On the "historiographic future," see Sten, 62.
8. Claude Bernard, *Introduction à l'étude de la médecine expérimentale* (Paris: Delagrave, 1920), 13.

This definition represents a widely adopted opinion. According to it, observation would be the ascertainment of things or phenomena as nature ordinarily presents them to us, while an experiment would be the ascertainment of phenomena created or determined by the experimenter. This would establish a sort of opposition between the observer and the experimenter; the first being passive in the production of phenomena, the second, by contrast, taking a direct and active role. Cuvier expressed the same thought when he said, "The observer listens to nature; the experimenter interrogates it and forces it to unveil."

It is evident that this passage is thoroughly discursive, an observation confirmed by what precedes and follows it. The primary tense is présent, but in its wake come the narrative forms *serait* (twice) and *aurait* (as a modal: *il y aurait à établir*). Evidently the author wants to limit the validity of his assertions. The definition mentioned at the beginning of the passage is not his own opinion, but that of another writer. The result can be generalized and at the same time joined to the impression the reader gets from reading Bernard. The author always diverges from his main tense, présent, via a tense metaphor into conditionnel, especially of helping and modal verbs, at the point that he wants to take back his methodological observations to some degree. This limitation is supported by other syntactic signals. In general, one can call this function "restricted validity." I emphasize once again that this function does not belong to the conditionnel per se, but only comes into being when this tense is used under the conditions just formulated as a tense metaphor.

Now, this is not a new function that is added onto the old function ("anticipated information" in the narrative context) or that replaces it. The old ("systematic") function cannot be abrogated; it is only modified by the new one. This is actually the case with all metaphors. A word (lexeme) does not lose its "actual" meaning when it is used as a metaphor; it only acquires a new, unexpected, textual meaning from a counter-determinative context. In the case of the conditionnel as a tense metaphor, it loses its narrative character, but retains the reduced binding character typical of the narrative sphere in contrast to the discursive one. It loses the weight of the anticipated information in the strict sense, but retains the uncertainty necessarily connected to such information. From both these modified functional qualities arising from the counter-determining context there arises the new contextual meaning of restricted validity that characterizes the conditionnel as a tense metaphor.

I will offer here some examples from the work of André Gide.[9] A certain abundance of examples seems especially appropriate in this section in order to show sufficiently that with the instrument of tense metaphor language can create ever finer nuances, which are barely hinted at by the generalization "limited validity." The languages of discretion, modesty, politeness, and diplomacy all depend on such nuances. In his diary, Gide reports on a visit from Paul Claudel. He describes Claudel's appearance, using the tenses of discussion: *Paul Claudel est plus massif, plus large que jamais; on le croirait vu dans un miroir déformant; pas de cou, pas de front; il a l'air d'un marteau-pilon* . . . (1:384 [November 19, 1912]; Paul Claudel is more massive, larger than ever; one would think one was seeing him in a distorting mirror; no neck, no forehead; he looks like a jackhammer). Among the présent forms there is suddenly a conditionnel. It obviously does not have the function of introducing a new temporal perspective, and it still applies to the same situation otherwise expressed in the présent. What would be different if Gide had written: *On le croit vu dans un miroir déformant* (One thinks one is seeing him in a distorting mirror)? The components of the description would not change, but the reader would take them differently. After all, the description of Claudel as a jackhammer is of course a caricature. If Gide had introduced this caricature in the présent, his distorting mirror would have been meant seriously, and one would assume a certain hostility. But the conditionnel softens the distortion and reduces the seriousness of its impact. The validity of the expression has been reduced and should be taken not as claim or definition, but as an impression, a witty remark. That is the contribution of the conditionnel used metaphorically.

Here is a further example from Gide's diary in which the tense metaphor is especially obvious, since it depends on the sentence structure:

> Pour moi je crains toujours (un peu mystiquement encore, je l'avoue) de renforcer la position de l'adversaire en mettant l'injustice de mon côté. Et puis de toute manière, et lorsqu'elle amènerait ma victoire, l'iniquité m'est intolérable; j'aime encore mieux en être victime. (1:1071 [September 1, 1931])

> Me, I always fear (again a bit mystically, I admit) reinforcing the position of my adversary by attributing injustice to myself. And so in every way, and even if it brought me victory, iniquity is intolerable to me; I prefer to be the victim.

---

9. André Gide, *Journal, 1889–1939* (Paris: Gallimard, 1982).

176 / TENSE METAPHORS

The nuance of the metaphoric conditionnel might be translated with a "perhaps" or, as here, with an English temporal metaphor ("brought"). This, only as a brief hint that many other languages, English among them, can deploy metaphors of tense and can express similar nuances with them.

Tense metaphors appear in journalistic style in striking and especially schematic form. Georges and Robert Le Bidois call it the "statement conditionnel," Paul Imbs the "conditionnel of hypothetical information."[10] It has the value of *dicitur* (it is said that): *le ministre préparerait une conférence de presse* (the minister is supposed to be preparing a press conference). Here, too, it is necessary to say first that the implication "unconfirmed report" does not inhere in the tense itself, but only in the metaphor. It requires the appearance of this conditionnel in a counter-determining context. A further example, from a very old newspaper, is the report of the London correspondent:

> Il est triste d'entendre nos ministres et leurs adhérens parler même en ce moment de leur espoir d'influencer la cour de Vienne, et de leur confiance dans la mission de lord Walpole. Est-il rien de plus puéril qu'un tel langage? Ils n'ont pas honte d'émettre l'opinion qu'un jeune homme sortant de l'école doit effectuer un changement dans les conseils de l'empereur d'Autriche. Si nous pouvons même en juger d'après le ton élevé que prennent les journaux à la solde des ministres, ceux-ci espéreraient que François ira jusqu'à déshériter son petit-fils.[11]

> It is sad to hear our ministers and their followers speaking in this very moment about their hope to influence the court of Vienna, and about their confidence in the mission of Lord Walpole. Is there anything more childish than such language? They are not ashamed to express the opinion that a young man leaving school can effect a change in the councils of the Emperor of Austria. If we are able even to judge from the elevated tone taken by the papers in the pay of the ministers, these latter would hope that Franz will go so far as to disinherit his grandson.

The context is homogeneous: the political mission of Lord Walpole is the topic. The tenses are présent and futur. One conditionnel is mixed in. It implies a conjecture based on certain indications (*Si nous pouvons même en juger d'après le ton élevé*) and thereby restricts the truth value of the

---

10. Georges and Robert Le Bidois, *Syntaxe du français moderne*, vol. 1 (Paris: Picard, 1935), 462–63; Imbs, *L'emploi*, 71.

11. *Journal de Paris*, January 1, 1813.

report. This is again the effect of the conditionnel as a tense metaphor. It loses its position as prospective narrative tense and is redefined by its context. The nuance of the tense metaphor arises precisely from the tension between the prospective narrative character of this tense and the determination by its discursive context. The truth value is not so restricted that the report is declared invalid, but its validity is questioned. At least, the speaker refuses to take responsibility for its correctness.

The restriction of validity is common not only in cautious language, but also in polite language. Anyone who wants to be polite does not say, "I want to ask you," but more likely, "I would like to ask a favor." One also does not say, "You must tell me," but, "Would you tell me." One does not say, "I don't know," but, "I couldn't say." One doesn't say, "Do you have any money?" but, "Would you have any money?" The nuance of politeness arises from the restricted validity that is simultaneously a restriction of obligation. The hearer is not to be required to comply if he does not want to. The conditional of politeness is so widespread that it is especially easy to overlook the tense metaphor. In analogy to semantic metaphors, we may speak here of the conditionnel of politeness, especially when it has become a formula, as a faded tense metaphor, a dead metaphor.

The conditional of politeness turns up in various languages. We may translate freely "I'd like to know, J'aimerais savoir, Me gustaría saber, Gostaría de saber, Ich möchte gern wissen." The formulaic character of this tense usage also explains why the contextual conditions are so relaxed. It doesn't have to be embedded in a context that contains a lot of discursive forms. Just a hint, or even the non-linguistic context suffices. The same phenomenon obtains with semantic metaphors. They fade to the same degree that they become independent of their context.

Apart from the future and conditional, the preterit and imperfect, can also be used metaphorically, and in a text they express the same grammatical nuance of restricted validity. This is especially the case when these tenses are used with a modal verb, which in its own lexical terms already lags behind the full meaning of a verb. That leads to a special nuance within the framework of restricted validity, modest speech. One often says in discussion or in an equivalent situation, "I would like to ask you." (In German one can also use a modal particle, that itself also restricts, "Ich wollte Sie *mal* fragen"). This nuance of modesty appears just as clearly in the Romance languages, even without the modal particle, since in these languages the background narrative tense is used: "Je voulais vous demander, quería preguntarle, volevo chiedere, vinhamos fazer un pedido" (I would like to ask you), or, as already in Plautus, one can respond to the question "quid quaeritas?" (what are you looking for?) with "Demaenetum volebam" (I wanted to see Demaenetus).[12]

It needn't always be a combination of modal verb and infinitive. Philippe Martinon offers an example that reads, "Je pensais que vous feriez peut-être bien de" (I thought that you might do well to). He recommends such expressions with a sensitive interlocutor whom one "does not want to shock."[13] Of course, one restricts the validity of a statement carefully when an unfriendly reaction of the interlocutor is to be expected and one wants to avoid it. That is precisely the modesty or the discretion or the politeness. The nuance arises here because the abrupt change from present to imperfect in an oral context produces a tense metaphor that means "just an idea." The example also shows clearly that the different narrative tenses, here imparfait and conditionnel, can work together to characterize the nuances of restricted validity.

The imparfait as a tense-metaphor can, however, produce a much stronger restriction than in polite or modest speech. It can extend to invalidating. I shall explain with a literary example, a longer passage that includes just a single metaphor. The context is necessary so that the imparfait will be clearly recognizable as a tense-metaphor. Pyrrhus's speech in act 3, scene 7, of Racine's *Andromaque* is the example. Pyrrhus woos Andromache. His courtship is simultaneously a threat. Andromache's fate and that of her son are at stake. We can say that this fate is the subject of discussion. The dominant tense of the passage is the présent. Only one narrative tense, the imparfait, disturbs the homogeneity of the series of verbs:

> Madame, demeurez.
> On peut vous rendre encor ce fils que vous pleurez.
> Oui, je sens à regret qu'en excitant vos larmes
> Je ne fais contre moi que vous donner des armes.
> Je *croyais* apporter plus de haine en ces lieux.
> Mais, Madame, du moins tournez vers moi les yeux:
>
> Voyez si mes regards sont d'un juge sévère,
> S'ils sont d'un ennemi qui cherche à vous déplaire.

---

12. Alessandro Ronconi, *Interpretazioni grammaticali* (Padua: Liviana, 1958), 148 (the Plautus phrase is *Asinaria* 392). See also 146 ff. and 179. On this topic see also Martin Raether, "Untersuchungen über die Konstruktion 'Verb + Infinitiv' im Französischen" (PhD diss. University of Cologne, 1968).

13. Philippe Martinon, *Comment on parle en français* (Paris: Larousse, 1927), 345.

> Madam, wait.
> It is possible to save the son whom you mourn.
> Yes, I regret that in arousing your tears
> I only succeed in providing you weapons against me:
> I was thinking I would bring more hate into this place.
> But, madam, at least turn your eyes toward me:
> See whether my looks are of a severe judge,
> If they are those of an enemy who wants to displease you.

Here again is a double restriction of validity, first lexically through the verb "was thinking" (*only* thinking!). And then grammatically through the tense metaphor of an imparfait in an otherwise coherently discursive text.

Tense metaphors for invalid opinions are to be found in various languages. Here is a Spanish example from a travelogue by Camilo José Cela in which he reports only the progress of the journey. The context is in the discursive tenses. The example reads, "Al llegar al cruce, el vagabundo, que pensaba irse en derechura a Peñafiel, siente que sus ánimos han cambiado" (on arriving at the crossroad, the wanderer, who was thinking of going right on to Peñafiel, feels that his mind has changed).[14] Here, too, we find a combination. Hence, we note once again a nuance of restricted validity that extends to the borders of invalidation. It would not be possible to replace this imperfecto "pensaba" with another random past form, such as a perfecto compuesto. A pluscuamperfecto form, on the other hand, would be possible; it would even increase the gap from presente as the lead tense of the context.

The examples reveal a double restriction, lexically with the verb *pensar* (think) and grammatically with the tense metaphor, where the conditions of tense metaphors even allow a shift in the middle of the sentence. In fact, we find the most variations from the normal sequence of tenses in complex sentences with tense metaphors of this type, and this once again, in very different languages. "He is younger than I thought"—this sentence together with its tense metaphor can be translated without difficulty: "Er ist jünger, als ich dachte, È più giovane di quanto io pensavo, Es más joven que yo pensaba, È mais novo do que eu pensaba, Il est plus jeune que je (ne) pensais." With regard to the final, French, example I shall only add that the so-called *ne explétif* of the French language in combination with tense metaphors, as well as in connection with the subjunctive, can be

---

14. Camilo José Cela, *Judíos, Moros y Cristianos: Notas de un vagabundaje por Ávila, Segovia y sus tierras* (Barcelona: Destino, 1956), 73.

effortlessly analyzed as a signal of restricted validity. But it is interesting that the *ne explétif* can drop out in less polished speech. The tense metaphor has its effect already with the tense shift in combination with the restriction of the verb "penser" in the sense of "just an idea." The *ne explétif* is simply a supplement.[15]

Condition and Consequence, Reality and Unreality

Language also offers syntactic means to identify conditions and consequences. One can connect a condition and its consequence with the conjunction *if* (or some other conjunction with a similar function) to form a conditional sentence. The special sentence category required here is relatively easy to define: A conditional sentence is a sentence structure in which two clauses are related by a conditional conjunction in such fashion that the first clause identifies the condition and the second the consequence of a set of circumstances. The border between temporal and conditional clauses, however, cannot always be drawn precisely. That has, for the time being, nothing to do with tense. In both the first and second clause of a conditional sentence (almost) any tense is possible. But the rules of tense usage in conditional sentences are especially interesting with respect to metaphoric tenses. Generally, we can say that in conditional sentences tense shifts between discursive and narrative tenses tend not to be allowed, while tense shifts between perspectives (looking back / neutral / looking forward) are actually preferred.

Marcel Proust's *À la recherche du temps perdu* (1913–27, In Search of Lost Time) is to be sure a novel by genre, therefore narrative in nature. But the novel contains discursive sections here and there, mostly in direct quotation. Some of these are found, for instance, in the section of *Le temps retrouvé* (Time Regained) where Monsieur de Charlus discusses the causes of World War I. Here are some examples:[16]

> Eh bien, si vous êtes de bonne foi, vous ne pouvez pas excepter la guerre de cette théorie (3:796; If you are serious, you can't exclude the war from this theory).

---

15. On *ne explétif* see Wolfgang Rothe, *Strukturen des Konjunktivs im Französischen* (Berlin: De Gruyter, 1967), 221 ff.

16. Marcel Proust, *À la recherche du temps perdu*, ed. Pierre Clarac and André Ferré, 3 vols. (Paris: Gallimard, 1954).

Si l'Aimée actuelle existe, ses espérances se réaliseront-elles? (3:797; If a present-day Beloved exists, will her hopes come true?).

Et si c'est lui, qu'a-t-il fait autre chose que Napoléon par exemple? (3:797; And if he is the one, what has he done differently from Napoleon, for example?)

All three sentences are conditional, but they use different tenses. All have présent in the first clause, but in the second clause there is présent, futur, or passé composé. The tense shifts thus all remain within the tenses of discussion. These are to serve as a brief illustration of the simple fact that conditional sentences can certainly be constructed in the discursive world (even though the conditional tenses are all narrative). Nevertheless, French usage does not permit the future tense in the first clause (which identifies the condition). This tense, if used at all, is restricted to the second clause. Once again, as we have often seen already, it is a negative signal for expressing the consequence of a previous given condition.

It is, of course, also possible to narrate the connection of condition and consequence. Hence conditional sentences can also be constructed with the narrative tenses. Here is a second series of examples, all from the first two volumes of the *Recherche*:

> Maintenant si nous rencontrions l'un ou l'autre des camarades, fille ou garçon, de Gilberte, qui nous saluait de loin, j'étais à mon tour regardé par eux comme un de ces êtres que j'avais tant enviés (1:541; Now, if we met a girl or a boy from the circle of Gilberte, who greeted us from a distance, I was regarded by them in my turn as one of the beings whom I had so greatly envied).

> Si je ne compris pas la Sonate, je fus ravi d'entendre jouer Mme Swann (1:532; If I didn't understand the Sonata, I was thrilled to hear Mme Swann playing it).

> Et même si elle ne lui avait pas écrit la première, si elle répondait seulement, en y acquiesçant, à sa demande d'une courte séparation, cela suffisait pour qu'il ne pût rester sans la voir (1:305; And even if she wasn't the first to write, if she only answered, acquiescing to his request for a short separation, that sufficed to make him unable to resist seeing her).

> Ou bien, si elle n'avait pas eu le temps de lui écrire, quand il arriverait chez les Verdurin, elle irait vivement à lui et lui dirait... (1:225–26;

Or, if she hadn't had the time to write to him, when he would arrive at the Verdurins', she would run up to him and would tell him . . .).

Et en effet si, à cette époque, il lui arriva souvent, sans se l'avouer, de désirer la mort, c'était pour échapper moins à l'acuité de ses souffrances qu'à la monotonie de son effort (1:317; And indeed if, at this time, it often happened that, without admitting it to himself, he desired to die, it was less to escape from the keenness of his suffering than from the monotony of his effort).

This series of examples should suffice. Each is a conditional construction. All the tenses belong to the narrative group. The tense combinations are: imparfait, imparfait ; passé simple, passé simple ; plus-que-parfait, imparfait, imparfait ; plus-que-parfait, conditionnel ; passé simple, imparfait. As we saw above with conditional constructions in the discursive world, all the major tenses occur, except for the conditionnel, which, like the futur, can occur only in the second clause, if at all. It, too, is simply a negative sign to mark the consequence of a given condition. All this still has nothing to do with counterfactuals. If conditional sentences in which discursive tenses are combined are understood as real sentences (whatever that may mean), then, for better or for worse, the last group of examples, in which narrative tenses are combined, must also be included among the real conditionals. To be sure, they are "only" narrated, but their content is not explicitly unreal, as counterfactual conditionals are said to be. The topic of condition and consequence is not yet exhausted because there is still the familiar grammatical distinction of real and counterfactual conditionals. One trivial example sentence reads, "If it rains, he will stay at home." That is called a real conditional sentence, because the reality of the condition and consequence, if not explicitly claimed, is nevertheless not explicitly called into question. Maurice Grevisse speaks of a plain hypothesis.[17] Counterfactual conditional sentences are to be sharply distinguished from these. Example sentence: "If it were raining, he would stay at home." Grevisse (sec. 1037) explains the irreality as follows: "La proposition conditionnelle exprime un fait présent ou passé que l'on regarde comme contraire à la réalité" (The conditional clause expresses a present or past fact that we regard as contrary to reality). With this sentence the reader must add the idea, "But it isn't raining." The reality of the condition is denied, and the consequence is thereby also excluded from the realm of reality. Many grammarians, like Grevisse, following the

17. Maurice Grevisse, *Le bon usage*, 8th ed. (Brussels: Duculot, 1964).

Latin model, also mention, in addition to the real and counterfactual conditional sentences, a potential conditional sentence. In our example it would be, perhaps, "If it were raining, he would stay at home." It does not explicitly question the reality of the statement, but dismisses the situation into the realm of what might happen or what might be imagined.

This description of conditional sentences is inadequate. The problem has remained unnoticed because of the now often criticized method of arguing with isolated and invented examples of sentences taken from an unknown context, if they ever had a context at all. Without the context of a conditional sentence it is impossible to make any assertion about the reality, potentiality, or irreality of the circumstances. It is entirely hopeless if one depends in this case on the fact that one of the French tenses is called "conditionnel" (*il chanterait, il aurait chanté*). That is a most unfortunate term. The conditionnel is a tense like all others and has nothing more to do with conditional sentences than any other tense. There is no tense that could, by its nature, express irreality. I have continued to use the term here, because a misleading term that everyone understands is better than a good one that would require constant explanation. But that works only if the rule that nothing is to be explained on the basis of its name is strictly observed.

Indeed, a conditional sentence, if it uses imparfait in the first clause, can also be a counterfactual, that is, its condition and its result can argue against the facts of reality. In order to grasp the irreal meaning of the sentence, I need the context of the conditional sentence. Here is a longer passage, also from the second novel of Proust's *Recherche*:

> Depuis que j'ai vu ce tableau, c'est peut-être ce que je désire le plus connaître avec la Pointe du Raz, qui *serait*, d'ailleurs, d'ici, tout un voyage. — Et puis, même si ce n'*était* pas plus près, je vous *conseillerais* peut-être tout de même davantage Carquethuit, me répondit Elstir. La Pointe du Raz est admirable, mais enfin c'est toujours la grande falaise normande ou bretonne que vous connaissez. Carquethuit, c'est tout autre chose avec ces roches sur une plage basse. Je ne connais rien en France d'analogue, cela me rappelle plutôt certains aspects de la Floride. (1:854)

"Since I saw this painting, that is perhaps what I most desire to get to know, along with Pointe-du-Raz, which from here, moreover, would be a long journey." "And then, even if it weren't closer, I would perhaps encourage Carquethuit all the same," Elstir responded. "Pointe-du-Raz is admirable, but finally it's just one more grand Norman or Breton cliff, such as you already know. Carquethuit is something altogether different, with its rocks on a low beach. I don't know anything analogous in France; it reminds me instead of certain aspects of Florida.

All of this passage is part of the narrative of the novel. But it is separated from the narration as direct speech. This quotation (Elstir is addressing the narrator) discusses the advantages of a French beach compared to other landscapes. The tenses of discussion serve this purpose. Among them there suddenly appear, in a conditional sentence, two narrative tenses—imparfait and conditionnel. The reader has to shift quickly between the two tense groups. It is easy to recognize the two narrative tenses as intruders in a context dominated by tenses of discussion. They are metaphorical tenses.

This results, then, if you will, in a perspectival illusion. Strictly speaking, language is indifferent to the reality or unreality of what is said. Yet it is not indifferent to the validity of what is said. It has created possibilities for strengthening or limiting validity, both with a great variety of nuances. If now validity is restricted by substituting tenses not expected from the context, so that our expectation is disappointed, then we interpret the restriction as contrary to fact. The issue is not tenses in themselves, but the transitions between tenses. In modern French the combination of imparfait and conditionnel in the counterfactual conditional sentence has emerged as typical. Yet it is not the tenses that limit the validity, but these tenses insofar as they are narrative tenses and diverge unexpectedly from the prevailing register of the context (or sometimes only from a situation that represents the context).

The discussion thus far has only demonstrated how to limit the validity of a conditional assertion in a discursive context, since the imperfect and conditional tenses become metaphoric only in a discursive context. But what happens when the context is narrative? Is irreality in a conditional sentence possible at all? I will illustrate this again with an example from Proust. In the episode "Un amour de Swann" (Swann in Love) the narrator reports on the strange quality that has developed in Swann's relation to Odette. From the second sentence on, the narrator shifts to a psychological perspective in which there then appears, as the narrative continues, a counterfactual conditional sentence. Here is the text:

Souvent elle avait des embarras d'argent et, pressée par une dette, le priait de lui venir en aide. Il en était heureux comme de tout ce qui pouvait donner à Odette une grande idée de l'amour qu'il avait pour elle, ou simplement une grande idée de son influence, de l'utilité dont il pouvait lui être. Sans doute si on lui *avait dit* au début: "c'est ta situation qui lui plaît," et maintenant: "c'est pour ta fortune qu'elle t'aime," il ne l'*aurais pas cru*, et n'*aurait pas été* d'ailleurs très mécontent qu'on se la figurât tenant à lui—qu'on les sentît unis l'un à l'autre—par quelque chose d'aussi fort que le snobisme ou l'argent. (1:267)

She often was short of money and, pressed by a debt, asked him to come to her aid. He was happy, as with everything that could give Odette a grand notion of his love for her, or simply a grand notion of his influence, of how useful he could be to her. Doubtless if one had said at the start, "it is your situation that she likes," and now, "she loves you for your fortune," he would not have believed it, and moreover would not have been very unhappy if she were imagined holding to him—if the two of them were felt to be united to one another — by something as strong as snobbism or money.

Until the beginning of the conditional construction the text uses only imparfait. Then there follows in its first clause the plus-que-parfait (*avait dit*). Then in the second clause—with an abrupt jump from backward- to forward-looking perspective—conditionnel II (*aurait cru, aurait été*). With this specific combination of tenses that operates exclusively in the arena of perspective, even though it continues in the narrative register of its larger context, the conditional constructions stand apart from their surroundings and, as metaphorical tenses, are able to point to irreality (counterfactual argumentation), just as we saw above with the narrative tenses imparfait/conditionnel as metaphorical tenses in the discursive context of "simple" conditional constructions. Depending on the context there are metaphorical tenses that operate either with register signals and perspective signals, or, sometimes, only with those of perspective.

8 / Tense Combinations

Tense and Person

Tense forms do not occur in isolation; that is the distinctive fact taken into account by text linguistics. Of course, a verb form found in a text can always be isolated for the purposes of analysis, but only with methodological awareness, which means that the conditions of its isolation must be analyzed at the same time.

Tense morphemes are mixed in texts with a great variety of other linguistic signs. A general theory of linguistic combination has to consider whether regular patterns can be identified according to which a given linguistic sign is strengthened by combination with certain signs, whether it is weakened by others. So far as tense morphemes are concerned, they seem to be indifferent to combinatorial issues. What noun, for example, might occur in the neighborhood of a given tense morpheme, what adjective might modify such a noun, what numerals, possessives, etc.—none of this seems subject to significant rules of combination. This is obviously quite different from other verb morphemes, especially those that indicate person, affirmation, and negation. With regard to the latter, Harro Stammerjohann has found significant frequency values in Italian narrative prose to demonstrate that verbs in passato remoto are negated much less frequently than those in imperfetto.[1] He locates the explanation in

---

1. Harro Stammerjohann, "Tempus und Negation," *Folia Linguistica* 3 (1969): 242–44.

the idea that most narratives tell what happened rather than what did not happen. At this point I will accept this suggestion and instead elaborate some combination rules for tense forms and grammatical person.

It is well known that the passé simple in contemporary French has become largely unusable, especially in the spoken language, as will be discussed at length below in Chapter 9. Yet with the disappearance of the passé simple some characteristic differences in the combination with grammatical person have appeared. In the spoken language the passé simple has become unusable with all the persons, but not in the contemporary written language. In certain spheres (essay, newspaper, etc.) third person singular and plural are still possible, while the first and second person seem strange and are avoided, even by conservative writers.[2] Manuel de Paiva Boléo notes similar connections between tense and person in Spanish, where there is a certain affinity between perfecto simple and third person, and also one between perfecto compuesto and the first and second persons.[3]

The affinity derives from the close relation between tense morphemes and person morphemes mentioned in the introduction; both characterize the speech act within the communicative situation. The first and second person of the verb identify the speaker and the hearer and are thus to be expected in higher frequency when a speaker and a hearer are in direct contact because they have things to discuss. By contrast, they are to be expected less frequently in narrative, since one narrates about an (absent) third person or object. So, if the passé simple appears more frequently joined with the third person, that only confirms that it is a narrative tense. In novels and other narrative texts, it is used primarily in combination with the third person because fiction is mostly written in the third person. Novels in the first person are less common than novels in the third person, and of novels in the second person only Michel Butor's *La modification* (1957, Second Thoughts) and Paul Zumthor's *Les puits de Babel* (1969, The Wells of Babylon) are known to me. The incidence of

---

2. Lucien Foulet, "La disparition du prétérit," *Romania* 46 no. 182/183 (1920): 310; Philippe Martinon, *Comment on parle en français* (Paris: Larousse, 1927), 347; Émile Benveniste, "The Correlations of Tense in the French Verb," in *Problems in General Linguistics*, trans. Mary Elizabeth Meek (Miami: U of Miami P, 1971), 209.

3. Manuel de Paiva Boléo, "O perfeito e o pretérito em português em confronto com as outras línguas românicas: Estudio de carácter sintático-estilístico," 53–54 (1936, PhD dissertation, Universidade de Coimbra, 1936). Emilio Alarcos Llorach adds that the affinity between tense and person depends not on grammar, but on the conditions of society and expression: "Perfecto simple y compuesto en español," *Revista de filología Española* 31 (1947): 139.

the combination passé simple—third person compared to its combination with first or second person—pretty much mirrors the incidence of third-person novels compared to those in first or second person. Indeed, I suspect that the relations between person to passé simple and the choice of person as narrator in novels correspond closely, though I have no numbers on hand to support the claim. Preliminary supporting evidence may be seen in the fact that Lucien Foulet ("La disparition du prétérit," 310), in counting the especially rare forms of passé simple used with second and third person, also counts uses of first person plural among the rare forms. That fits with my suspicion, since first-person novels have, as a rule, first-person singular narrators. It is therefore inaccurate to say in historical discussions that the passé simple is disappearing more rapidly in combinations with the first and second person than with the third person. It is more correct to say that in combination with the second and first person (the latter especially in the plural), the passé simple has always been weaker, simply because as a rule one tells one's auditors things that they don't already know.

But there is still an unanswered question. If narrative tenses prefer a combination with the third person, then all the narrative tenses in a language with several of them should reveal the same affinity. In French one would especially expect imparfait also to appear with weakened use of the first and second persons. To be sure, there are no complete statistics on the combination of tense and person in French, so there can be no definite assertions on whether imparfait tends to combine more with one person than another. Nevertheless, it is evident that the combination imparfait with the first and second persons is perfectly ordinary and is in no way disappearing from the spoken and written languages as is passé simple in this combination.[4]

Émile Benveniste came up with an ingenious theory to explain the way the simple past combines with grammatical person. He begins from a phenomenon that he initially presents as an inconsistency or weakness in the French tense system. To express the past, Benveniste argues, French has two tenses: the simple past (*il fit*) and the perfect (passé composé; *il a fait*). In order to explain this doubling, he turns to the usual distinction in Greek and Latin grammars between primary and secondary tenses, and he uses it as a basis for a theory of tenses that operates with not one, but two tense systems. He calls them *discours* and *histoire* and understands

---

4. Gabriele Beugel und Ulrike Suida, "Perfekt und Präteritum in der deutschen Sprache der Gegenwart." *Forschungsberichte des Instituts für deutsche Sprache* 1 (1968): 10.

thereby two different, but complementary, registers of expression. With regard to the phenomena, though not to the method, these two registers can be identified to a certain degree with the categories of discussion and narration used in this book.

According to Benveniste, *discours* should be understood in the broadest sense possible, namely as that kind of speech that assumes a speaker and a hearer and assumes that the speaker intends to influence the hearer in some way. This appellative manner of speech is to be found in both oral and written expression. All tenses in the French language, with the exception of the simple past (which Benveniste calls *aoriste*) are in principle allowed in a *discours*; présent, futur, and parfait (i.e., passé composé) are, however, the real tenses of this register.

Histoire, in contrast, ignoring a few marginal tenses, consists really of passé simple, imparfait, and plus-que-parfait. The register, also, has not only tenses that belong, but also those that are excluded, namely présent, futur, and parfait. For further exclusion, Benveniste looks to questions of combination, especially of tense and person. He actually admits passé simple, imparfait, and plus-que-parfait to the *histoire* register only when they are combined with the third person (singular or plural). Thus, the structural boundary between *discours* and *histoire* runs right through the individual tenses. Combination is his real criterion. Imparfait and plus-que-parfait belong only then to *discours* if they are combined with the first or second person; in the third person they belong to *histoire*. Passé simple, now, which practically never appears in the modern language with first or second person, belongs, for the same reason, exclusively to *histoire*. The register *histoire* is now restricted to the written language, but is by no means generally endangered. Whoever wants to write stories obviously uses—apart from a few exceptions—the tense system of *histoire*.

The complementary interplay of the two tense systems—I continue to summarize Benveniste—has some critical points. Anyone who wants to narrate orally or wants to narrate in the first person (as in autobiography) cannot use the passé simple, but must try to narrate in the passé composé. But that means using a tense not intended for presenting past occurrences, but, as a composite tense, for characterizing its material as completed (*accompli*). Passé composé acquires in this fashion a double status, revealed, for example, in a new composite form built upon it as if it were a simple tense which Benveniste (*Problems*, 212) calls "Parfait surcomposé" (*j'ai eu fait*). These new tense forms render a historical dynamic visible: Both tense systems exist in a labile balance whose probable changes can be predicted within certain limits.

Benveniste has observed well and analyzed shrewdly. I owe much to his theory. Benveniste's consistency in pursuing the implications of combining two categories in the text for the grammatical system is especially instructive for linguistic method. However, the following considerations in this book will demonstrate that it is not only the combination of tense and person that is relevant for the system, but also the combination with other categories in verb syntax. Especially the connections of tense and adverb play an important role. Considering this combination further will require that some of the results of Benveniste's analysis be called into question or reinterpreted.

Tense and Adverbs

The class of adverbs is a large conglomerate of miscellaneous forms that threatens to lose all contours when adverbial expressions and idioms are also taken into account. Grammarians usually try to bring some order by distinguishing various kinds of adverbs. There are, for example, adverbs of manner, of quantity, of time, of place, of affirmation, of negation, or of doubt. These distinctions all depend on meaning, and are clarified by asking how? how many? when? where? or whether? But grammarians also know that the borders between the classes cannot be drawn precisely; some adverbs must be assigned to more than one class.[5] The linguistic problems deriving from adverb classification cannot be treated comprehensively in this book. It will suffice here to point to a few text-linguistic aspects of the problem, above all to those that can be illuminated by the structural context of tense.

The question is then: Are there rules according to which the combination of specific tenses with specific adverbs or adverbial determinations are either encouraged or discouraged? I am deliberately expressing myself cautiously here in speaking only of encouragement or discouragement. There is in fact no positive rule that ties a particular tense to a particular adverb, nor is there a negative rule that would absolutely forbid the combination of a particular tense with a particular adverb. Given that this book analyzes the tense system in terms of the three categories of register, perspective, and highlighting, the question can be pursued more concretely by investigating the class of adverbs (by which are meant both adverbs and adverbial phrases) with regard to each of these categories.

---

5. Maurice Grevisse, *Le bon usage*, 8th ed. (Brussels: Duculot, 1964), sect. 832. The problems of classifying adverbs are beautifully clarified by Renate Steinitz, *Adverbial-Syntax* (Berlin: Akademie-Verlag, 1969).

So, are there, to begin with register, adverbs that by preference are used in combination with the discussing tenses, and others that are preferred with the narrative ones? It must be said, to begin with, that there are certainly some adverbial expressions for which no such combination rules can be discovered. The entire group of dates belongs to this type. The actual temporal adverbs, by contrast, show definite preferences in their tense affinities. These are temporal adverbs of the type *hier, en ce moment, demain* (yesterday, at this moment, tomorrow) on the one hand, and the temporal adverbs of the type *la veille, à ce moment-là, le lendemain* (the day before, at that very moment, the next day) on the other. Both groups can be expanded. One could add to the first group: *l'année dernière* (last year), *maintenant* (now), *la semaine prochaine* (next week), etc. And, similarly, to the second group: *la semaine précédente* (the preceding week), *ce jour-là* (that day), *l'année suivante* (the following year), etc. In both cases, however, the longer the series is extended, the less precise and explicit does the rule of combination become.

The general rule states that the temporal adverbs of the type *hier, en ce moment, demain* appear by preference in combination with discursive tenses, while the adverbs of the type *la veille, à ce moment-là, le lendemain* display a significant preference for combination with narrative tenses. This observation depends on the results of an extensive and careful collection of data by Arne Klum on French prose texts.[6] The extent of my dependence on this material will be discussed further below. The exact numbers of adverbs of both types are shown in the accompanying table.

	Discursive Tenses	Narrative Tenses
hier (with *avant-hier*)	80	33
en ce moment	37	5
demain (with *après-demain*)	81	7
la veille (with *l'avant-veille*)	0	12
à ce moment(-là)	19	48
le lendemain	16	91

The combinations of tenses and adverbs in this enumeration unmistakably reveal frequencies in almost converse relationships. They imply that the adverbs of the first group should be classified as discursive adverbs, and those of the second, narrative. As I have already said, by no

6. Arne Klum, *Verbe et adverbe* (Stockholm: Almqvist & Viksell, 1961).

means all temporal adverbs can be so clearly assigned to the one group or the other. For details see the numbers in Klum.

At this moment it is a sufficient basis for my further argument to remain with the cautious conclusion that there are evidently some adverbs that prefer to combine with discursive tenses, and others that favor combination with narrative tenses. Shifts from discussing to narrating thus demand, as a consequence, that temporal adverbs of the one type be translated into those of the other. Thus *hier* becomes *la veille*, *en ce moment* becomes *à ce moment(-la)*, *demain* becomes *le lendemain*, and vice versa. In principle it is the same phenomenon as translating a play into the form of a novel or condensing a novella into a plot summary: In the first case discursive tenses must be translated into narrative ones, and in the second, narrative tenses to discursive ones.

This conclusion should not be understood normatively. It is always possible not to make the translation and, say, to write a novel in present tense or to mix many discursive adverbs with narrative tenses. Either way results in a stylistic phenomenon that I will illustrate. Klum's statistics have made clear that it is necessary to search a long time in a corpus to find adverbs of *la veille, à ce moment-là, le lendemain* in combination with a discursive tense. There is, however, one way to find examples of this sort quickly and without much looking. All you have to do is open a lexicon like Laffont-Bompiani's *Dictionnaire des œuvres* that summarizes the contents of literary works.[7] In texts of this sort, in plot summaries, this kind of combination occurs with some frequency. Here are three examples:

> La légende veut que dans la nuit qui précède la Sainte-Agnès, les jeunes filles voient en songe leur futur époux (4:664; The legend has it that young girls see their future husbands in a dream on the night that precedes Saint Agnes' day).

> Celui-ci l'insulte, le dégrade, et le remet à la garde du palais, commandée cette nuit-là par Lefebvre (3:301; The latter insults him, degrades him, and hands him over to the palace guard, commanded that particular night by Lefebvre).

> Elle écrit une lettre qu'elle lui demande de ne lire que le lendemain, puis se met au lit (3:298; She writes a letter, which she asks him not to read until the next day, then goes to bed).

7. Robert Laffont and Valentino Bompiani, *Dictionnaire des œuvres de tous les temps et de tous les pays: Littérature, philosophie, musique, sciences* (Paris: Société d'édition de dictionnaires et encyclopédies, 1962).

The function of the abnormal combination in plot summaries makes good sense. The plot summary of a work, say of a story, is not the story itself, but the basis for a discussion. The plot summary uses therefore, as a rule, the discursive tenses (see Chapter 2). We may say that a plot summary, even of a narrative text, translates the text's narrative tenses into discursive tenses—of course only for those verbs that are retained in the course of condensation. Yet the summary is the equivalent of the entire work in the sense that the difference should only be quantitative. The narrative character of the work ought to be summarized also where necessary. That can be done by not translating the temporal adverbs when the narrative tenses are changed. This unusual combination of discursive tenses and narrative temporal adverbs generates a certain ambivalence that, together with other characteristics, constitutes the "genre" of plot summary.

With regard to the statistical method (of Klum and of everyone else) it must be noted here that very different results for the combination of tense and temporal adverbs would be expected, depending on whether or not texts like plot summaries are included in the corpus. It would take an extremely extensive corpus, far too large to be analyzed by a single individual, to even out the anomalies of choice. Klum based his work on a corpus of forty-five books with some 11,000 pages, and he mixed the genres. With that he has surely met the expectations that can be made of a single linguist. Nevertheless, as best I can tell from the bibliography, there are no plot summaries in this corpus. How should Klum ever have landed on the idea of including such absurd texts as plot summaries in his corpus! This is not intended as a criticism, but rather only to show that even a very large corpus cannot prevent particular limitations in the selection, so that the results, however dependably they have been reached, cannot be used dogmatically, but must be related to a particular theory.

The second dimension of the tense system is perspective. For this signal we can distinguish a neutral level (for which the perspective is irrelevant) different from the retrospective (information provided after the fact) and prospective (anticipated information). This dimension of the tense system can also be extended through combination into the class of adverbs, so that, in positive terms, combination preferences or, in negative terms, restrictions can be identified. It can again be explained with the series *hier, en ce moment, demain* and its structural equivalent *la veille, à ce moment(-là), le lendemain*. These adverbs also reveal a regular pattern in their combinations with perspective, as Klum's results (for which I am again grateful) clearly reveal. To begin with the discursive tenses, Klum's numbers from his corpus appear in the accompanying table.

	Retrospective (passé composé)	Neutral (présent)	Prospective (Futur)
hier	76	4	0
en ce moment	0	37	0
demain	0	20	61

The numbers again reveal the regularity of the combination, and on this basis it is again surely possible to call *hier* a retrospective adverb, and *demain* a prospective one, while *en ce moment* evidently shares with the présent tense a neutral position.

If we look for similar equivalencies with the narrative adverbs, the results are less clear. These results appear in the accompanying table.

	Retrospective (plus-que-parfait)	Neutral (imparfait, passé simple)	Prospective (conditionnel)
la veille	7	5	0
en ce moment(-la)	4	44	0
le lendemain	4	85	2

No preferred combinations with regard to perspective are discernible in this overview; instead, all the adverbs excepting *la veille* tend toward combination with the neutral position, that is, with imparfait or the passé simple. This surely has to do with the fact that looking back and looking forward only become perspectives in the narrative when the narrator jumps around in time. In most cases the pressure of the narrative flow seems to prevail and retrospection and anticipation are expressed only through temporal adverbs, not also through tense. Nevertheless, at issue here is only to demonstrate that some adverbs do reveal an extension of the tense system. That may be sufficiently supported by the group of adverbs just discussed.

To see whether there are combination preferences between tense and adverb with regard to highlighting, it is necessary to look at adverbs that do not appear in Klum's work, since he considered only a few temporal adverbs, and highlighting requires some that he did not investigate. In the absence of better statistics, I have done my own count to identify what combinations of tense and adverb appear within a smaller framework, which does not offer the same validity. I have looked instead for combinations of tense and adverbs in various narrative passages.

Here first is the result for Part 2, Chapter 10, of *Madame Bovary*. I am looking here only at indicative verbs in imparfait and passé simple, but at all adverbs that appear in the normal semantic classifications of temporal adverbs.[8] The results are as follows: temporal adverbs combined with imparfait are: *à present, à chaque minute, de temps à autre, pendant tout l'hiver trois ou quatre fois la semaine à la nuit noire, quelques fois, enfin, puis, cependant, durant les soirs d'été, de temps à autre, parfois, enfin, à l'occasion, à présent, souvent, puis, quelquefois, au bout de six mois, toujours, toujours, il y avait longtemps, quelquefois, maintenant, alors.* Temporal adverbs in combination with passé simple are: *peu à peu, un matin, tout à coup, brusquement, jusqu'au soir, sans cesse, après le diner, tout à coup, enfin, alors, le lendemain, alors, quelques minutes, puis, enfin, le soir, consécutivement, alors.*

As a check, here is an enumeration from a different novel. In Chapter 2 of André Malraux's *La voie royale* (1930, The Royal Way) the following combinations occur: Temporal adverbs in combination with imparfait are: *depuis quelques minutes, déjà, toujours, quelquefois, parfois, maintenant, déjà, toujours, maintenant, alors, de nouveau, déjà, beaucoup plus souvent, toujours, maintenant, de nouveau, à nouveau, maintenant, maintenant, toujours, toujours.* Temporal adverbs in combination with passé simple are: *à l'instant même, enfin, d'un coup, soudain, au cinquième effort, puis, de nouveau, aussitôt, de nouveau, enfin, soudain, après une sorte de moulinet de tout son corps, aussitôt, enfin, une seconde, soudain, enfin, puis, puis, puis, en quelques minutes.*

If I had listed these two groups of adverbs without saying with which tense they were combined, anyone with an active and passive knowledge of French would doubtless have been able to identify the correct tense partner for most of them, but not all. For example, the adverb *de (à) nouveau* appears in the Malraux with the imparfait and with the passé simple. This observation holds true generally. Every temporal adverb can in principle combine with every tense. Only the frequencies vary, and to some extent they vary by a lot. That cannot be observed in the context of a sentence, but a text makes it possible to observe the preference for combination between the two groups. In both texts temporal adverbs that indicate a calmer pace clearly prefer to combine with imparfait; these are adverbs like *quelquefois, parfois, de temps à autre,* and *toujours.* Conversely, adverbs that signal a more rapid narrative pace prefer passé simple. In both examples this involves such adverbs as: *enfin, tout à coup, soudain,* and *brusquement.* And yet, even these short example texts include

---

8. When tense and adverbs are combined, all kinds of other forms, including subordinate clauses, may come between verb and adverb; such insertions are ignored here. This procedure may not be necessary, but it is preferable here, since the further combining with conjunctions cannot be taken into account.

counterexamples, like the adverb *sans cesse* with passé simple (Flaubert) and the adverb *soudain* with imparfait (Malraux). It is, let me repeat, not a matter of exclusivities, but of preferences.

To give numerical expression to such preferences I have assembled a small corpus of narrative prose texts by ten French authors and counted the combinations of the most common temporal adverbs.[9] It resulted in the following list (total numbers): Combinations with imparfait and (in parentheses) with passé simple: *parfois/quelquefois* 16 (0), *souvent* 11 (0), *toujours* 22 (1), *déjà* 15 (0), *maintenant* 27 (0). Combinations with passé simple and (in parentheses) with imparfait: *enfin* 14 (5), *tout à coup* 12 (1), *soudain* 12 (2), *brusquement* 8 (1), *bientôt* 5 (0), *aussitôt* 9 (1), *puis* 41 (10), *alors* 24 (5).

These results reveal that in French the third dimension of the tense system—what I am calling highlighting—also extends its influence into the temporal adverbs. Some adverbs belong clearly to the narrative background (calmer narrative pace), and others to the narrative foreground (more rapid pace). The allegiances are often confirmed by the semantics of the words. Here, too, not all temporal adverbs display a preference for the narrative background or for the foreground; some are indifferent. It is not, therefore, possible to rely entirely on the semantics of the adverbs. Who could tell from its meaning that *maintenant* would have a strong affinity for imparfait as the background tense? That cannot be seen from the semantics, but only by counting its empirical distribution. Anyone who knows from the start for sure that *maintenant* means "now" and identifies exactly with "temporal deixis" the "I-here-now" moment, that person will not, I am afraid, pay any attention to the text.[10]

One more comment on method may be appropriate here. Thus far I have followed grammatical custom in speaking of "temporal adverbs," and thereby implicitly accepted the semantic criterion of time. That has been necessary in order to separate out from the mass of adverbs those

---

9. My sources here are passages from Francis Carco, *Brumes*; Gustave Flaubert, *Madame Bovary*; André Malraux, *La voie royale*; Guy de Maupassant, "La rempailleuse" and "Le testament"; Henri de Montherlant, *Le songe*; Marcel Proust, *La fugitive*; Alain Robbe-Grillet, *Le voyeur*; Antoine de Saint-Exupéry, *Vol de nuit*; Stendhal, *La Chartreuse de Parme*.

10. Klum, *Verbe et adverbe*, 198, has already noted the virtual exclusion of the combination of *maintenant* with passé simple. On adverbial combinations in German see Werner Winter, "Relative Häufigkeit syntaktischer Erscheinungen als Mittel zur Abgrenzung von Stilarten," *Phonetica* 7, no. 4 (1961): 193–216; for Italian, Harro Stammerjohann, "Strukturen der Rede: Beobachtungen an der Umgangssprache von Florenz," *Studi di filologia italiana* 28 (1970): 325 ff.

that can be positively said to answer the question "when" and, negatively, not to include adverbs of manner, quantity, place, opinion, etc. But these criteria have heuristic value at best. Does *déjà* answer the question "when"? Is *soudain* an indication of time? Does the series *parfois, souvent, toujours* also include adverbs like *cette fois, pour la première fois, une fois de plus,* and *l'un après l'autre* (all from Malraux)? Furthermore, if *soudain, tout à coup,* and *brusquement* are temporal adverbs, then should one also count adverbs like *précipitamment, rapidement, doucement,* and *lentement* (also Malraux)? In both cases I did not count these adverbs. But, really, why not? These words determine the pace or the tempo, in a word, the narrative highlighting, in similar fashion to those adverbs that also happen to answer the question "when" or a similar question relevant to time. If, therefore, the concept, "temporal adverb" still seems a necessary category for talking about language, it is hardly the last word in linguistic wisdom.[11]

Combined Transitions

Tense forms, we have said, can be described as grammatical signals that have the function of preliminary sorting of linguistic material, that is, of organizing all possible subjects of communication from the perspective of this particular communication process. Most situations require a further process of finer sorting, and for this, we have said, there are other, less repetitive, linguistic signs—in the case of tenses these are especially certain adverbs, conjunctions, and prepositions. The relation between tense and other forms can be described as expansion. Expansion means the semantic filling of a given syntactic framework. The meaning of the syntactic morpheme is thereby made more precise. So, for example, the syntactic framework established by the personal pronoun, "he," can be made more precise by expansion with semantic material such as a noun group like "the man" or "the young man" or "the young man from next door." The speaker determines the grade of precision appropriate in a speech situation by the choice of words. Occasionally the listener is dissatisfied with this dose of information. Perhaps the degree of precision is insufficient at some point in the text and the thread has been lost. Then

---

11. Analysis at the level of features (Ger. *Merkmal,* Fr. *trait*) has been a general tendency in linguistics for some time. The method was originally tried out in phonology by the Prague school and then, under the influence of Roman Jakobson, extended to semantics and syntax. Roman Jakobson and Morris Halle's *Fundamentals of Language* (The Hague: Mouton, 1956) is an especially good introduction to the topic.

the conversation partner interrupts the text with a question. The question is a syntactic signal that demands additional information at the given place in the text. For example, the speaker has used only the syntactic frame "he," and the listener continues the syntactic frame with the question, "who?" In response, the listener normally receives the additional information in the form of an expansion, such as, "the young man from next door."

The text-linguistic method, to be sure, normally prompts a description of the phenomenon in question from the opposite point of view. At the beginning of a communication the speaker usually provides fuller semantic material without being asked; that is the exposition. In the further development of the text this material can then be tapped as preliminary information that continues to be relevant and can hence settle for syntactic signals that sort more coarsely as references. It is thus also possible to speak of semantic reduction. Since, however, primarily tenses and only secondarily adverbs (likewise conjunctions and prepositions, but these will not be considered in detail) are under discussion, for the purposes of this investigation, it is better to focus on expansion rather than on its reverse, reduction.[12]

The temporal adverbs discussed thus far can be seen without a doubt as expansions of the tense features in their category. The features "narrative" and "retrospection" that accrue to the plus-que-parfait tense morpheme are made semantically more precise with the adverb *la veille*, with which it may appear in a particular text; after all, this adverb also contains the features "narrative" and "retrospection," but, more precisely, differentiated, for example, from *l'avant-veille*, that carries the same syntactic features. Similarly, in the case of passé simple, its features of "(narrative) foreground" are expanded, i.e., made semantically more precise, say, with the adverb "soudain," which has the same features, but again more precise, namely distinguished from "brusquement," "précipitamment" and other synonymous adverbs. It could happen in some particular situation that the named expansions would actually be elicited by a listener asking a question. In the first case, the question would probably be "quand?" and in the second case possibly also "quand?" but perhaps also "comment?" or whatever—it doesn't even need to be a grammatically recognized form of question. Many temporal adverbs do not even have an associated question form other

---

12. Both expansion and reduction are to be understood in the sense of the textual flow from earlier to later.

than saying the adverb with a questioning tone where communication is perhaps blocked: "et puis? et alors?" (and then?, and then?). Then the speaker usually resumes with this same adverb—"Et puis, on avait arreté une petite fourgonnette—Alors on est arrivé en même temps que le car" (And then they flagged down a small van. — So they arrived at the same time as the coach).[13]

As these examples show, the possible expansions of tense markers do not proceed only in a direction that can be indicated by chronological expressions. There can be no doubt that the question morpheme *when* is a universal indicator for the expansion relationships between tense and adverb. Of course, temporal adverbs tell what time. But apart from this tautology, not only can other adverbs answer the question *when*, but there are also other adverbs that answer other questions raised by tenses and that expand individual markers in order to make the various signaling values of tenses more precise and thereby help manage communication. Hence, they are also temporal adverbs. Especially significant here are the signal values I have called highlighting (or "tempo") of narrative and that are based on a general concept of narrative arrangement. *Then what?* might be taken as a general form of the question that can trigger such an expansion.[14]

Once the question of the relation of tense to adverb has been extended in this way, it is no longer sufficient to consider the simple combination of a given tense with a given temporal adverb. For tense forms and adverbs are combined not only in sentences, but also in texts more broadly, in combination with other tense forms and with other temporal adverbs. Maupassant's famous story, "La parure" (1884, The Necklace), to take an example at random, begins with a two-page exposition. Correspondingly, its dominant tense is imparfait. Then the actual story (the exceptional event) begins, and this beginning is marked doubly by the tense and by a temporal adverb. Here is the passage:

> Elle avait une amie riche, une camarade de couvent qu'elle ne voulait plus aller voir, tant elle souffrait en revenant. Et elle pleurait pendant

---

13. These example sentences are drawn from the passage quoted at length in Chapter 9.

14. On narrative sequencing in general see Günther Müller, "Die Bedeutung der Zeit in der Erzählkunst," in *Morphologische Poetik: Gesammelte Aufsätze* (Tübingen: Niemeyer, 1968), 10; Eberhard Lämmert, *Bauformen des Erzählens* (Stuttgart: Metzler, 1967), 19 ff.; Harald Weinrich, "Erzählstrukturen des Mythos," in *Literatur für Leser* (Munich: Deutscher Taschenbuch Verlag, 1986), 167–83.

des jours entiers, de chagrin, de regret, de désespoir et de détresse. — Or, un soir, son mari rentra, l'air glorieux et tenant à la main une large enveloppe.[15]

She had a wealthy friend, a comrade from the convent whom she no longer wanted to visit, she suffered so much upon returning. And she cried for whole days at a time, of embarrassment, regret, despair and distress. — Now, one evening, her husband came home, full of pride and holding a large envelope in his hand.

The adverbial signal at the beginning of the last sentence, "or, un soir" (now, one evening), which can be considered (in the terminology of Elisabeth Gülich's *Makrosyntax*) a "macro-syntactic organizing signal," marks the beginning of the main plot here together with the tense shift from imparfait to simple past (the husband brings home the invitation that causes the problem with the necklace).[16] The signal cannot be attributed to either tense as such, but to the specific shift from background to foreground. For those who continue to classify adverbs, it might be called an adverb of tense shift.

A transition combined of tense and adverb like this is strikingly common in literature. It occurs not just in the transition from exposition to main plot, but also repeatedly within a narrative wherever the narrator wants to change the tempo, such as returning to the plot after inserting background information. I will not stop here to offer statistical verification for my observations. The counting could go on forever! Macro-syntactic organizing signals do not occur "obstinately," that is, repetitively. They derive their impact precisely because they occur rarely; that's why they organize the text into larger units. Thus, they form a small proportion of the signals in a text, yet, because of their combination with other signs, they perform an important function. The two strengthen one other.[17]

---

15. Guy de Maupassant, *Contes et nouvelles*, 2 vols., ed. Louis Forestier (Paris: Gallimard, 1980, 1979), 1:1199.

16. Elisabeth Gülich, *Makrosyntax der Gliederungssignale im gesprochenen Französisch* (Munich: Fink, 1970).

17. See here also Stammerjohann's figures ("Strukturen der Rede," 322 ff.) for macro-syntactic organizing signals in Italian slang in Florence. Wolf-Dieter Stempel's *Untersuchungen zur Satzverknüpfung im Altfranzösischen* (Braunschweig: Georg Westermann, 1964) develops interesting views on this topic. Elisabeth Gülich, to whom I owe many suggestions, has examined transitions in narrative structures in "Ansätze zu einer kommunikationsorientierten Erzähltextanalyse (am Beispiel mündlicher und schriftlicher Erzähltexte)," in *Erzählforschung 1: Theorien, Modelle und Methoden der Narrativik*, ed. Wolfgang Haubrichs (Göttingen: Vandenhoeck & Ruprecht, 1976), 224–56.

While temporal adverbs of the type *or, un soir* can be understood as adverbs of tense change, there are other adverbs that tend to signal continuity in the narrative, of course always in combination with the tenses. These include especially *(et) puis* and, somewhat less definitively, *alors*, both also in combined form as *(et) puis alors*. I would like to consider *(et) puis* in more detail, on the basis, once again, of Camus's story "La femme adultère." The adverbial form *(et) puis* occurs eighteen times in the story, if we exclude one occurrence in a nominal context. It occurs sixteen times in combination with a continuation of the same tense, and only twice with a change in tense. The observations suggest that *(et) puis* is to be considered an adverb of continuing tense and, since this is a narrative text, as an adverb of continuing narrative. Similarly, in Camus's novel *La peste* (The Plague) the form *puis* occurs sixty-one times with a continuing tense and twelve times with a tense change. In comparison, the adverb *alors* occurs eighty-four times in this novel with a continuing tense form and thirty-nine times with a tense change. This material is intended to make plausible the sense in which adverbs like *(et) puis* and perhaps also *alors* and their connections with one another can function as adverbs of narrative sequencing. When they occur in substantial frequency with a continuing tense, then they evidently intensify this phenomenon, which constitutes one of the most important aspects of all in a text, its consistency or its very textuality.

Among the macro-syntactic organizing signals in Maupassant's stories, I have been particularly struck by the expression, *or, jeudi dernier* (now, last Thursday), in "Les bécasses" (The Snipes).[18] On the one hand, it functions as a macro-syntactic adverb that creates a major division of the story and correspondingly is combined with a tense shift from imparfait to passé simple. Yet on the other hand, because of the word *dernier* (last), it belongs to the class of discursive adverbs, represented above by the series *hier* (or *l'année dernière*), *en ce moment, demain*. Evidently *or, jeudi dernier* contains both a narrative and a discursive component and must be understood as a complex signal. This is indeed the case, as we can see from the story's frame-narrative. The frame, which introduces a narrator, validates the narrative as a true story. This inner narrator reports as an eyewitness. The exposition is in the discursive tenses. We may therefore interpret the element *dernier*, which together with the date establishes the connection to the discursive situation, as a validation signal. The narrator

---

18. Maupassant, *Contes et nouvelles*, 2:562–71. "Les Bécasses" is introduced in présent, then Maupassant shifts with the adverb "or depuis quinze jours" (564) into imparfait. A few lines later the main plot begins with "or, jeudi dernier."

intends to remove the story from the realm of fiction and to re-situate it as much as possible in that of truth, and that means, for fiction, in the lived past. The past, as this example makes amply clear, is not communicated linguistically through simple signs, but through complex ones, namely through the connections of signs for fiction and for truth. But the truth signals here are the syntactic signs of the discursive world.

At this point I turn to a combination of tense and temporal adverb that has attracted considerable discussion in the literature of tense. Can one actually say: "I will go to the zoo yesterday"? Or, "I found the solution to the problem tomorrow?" In Dieter Wunderlich's book on tense, conceived entirely in terms of time, these sentences are offered as a production of "calculated intuition" and immediately rejected on the same grounds.[19] Fine; my intuition would make the same judgment if I were using it to defend my own theory. But does this plausibility suffice as the basis for an entire theory of tense according to which tense morphemes refer, if not exclusively, at least primarily to time?

So, "it contradicts our intuition" to combine a Präteritum verb with the adverb for tomorrow in a German sentence. Why then does the German language, as Wunderlich cannot deny, permit the combination of the Perfekt tense with a future adverb, as for example, "Ich habe das bis morgen für dich erledigt" (I [will] have that finished for you by tomorrow)? Why can Käte Hamburger find in real texts, not just in invented sentences, many combinations like this one: "Morgen ging das Flugzeug, das ihn nach Kanada bringen sollte" (The plane that was to carry him to Canada left tomorrow)? Or: "Heute abend wollte der König Flöte spielen" (The king wanted to play the flute tonight)?[20] Wunderlich deals with the first case by "reinterpreting" the Perfekt form, and "transforming" the Präteritum in the second. It is a matter of course that a linguist can defend any theory he likes by altering his material with calculated interventions or, more simply, disallowing authentic material.

Hamburger and her followers have invested more effort in texts. This sentence, for example, "Unter ihren Lidern sah sie noch heute, nach soviel Jahren, mit erstaunlicher Deutlichkeit die Miene vor sich, die er bei dem überaus trockenen Empfang gemacht," comes from Thomas Mann's

---

19. Dieter Wunderlich, *Tempus und Zeitreferenz im Deutschen* (Munich: Max Hueber, 1970), esp. 14, 24–25, 140, 165–66, 311. Similarly, William Diver, "The Chronological System of the English Verb," *Word* 19, no. 2 (1963): 153: "Extra-verbally, such sentences as 'He walked tomorrow' do not occur."

20. Käte Hamburger, "Das epische Präteritum," *Deutsche Vierteljahrsschrift für Literaturwissenschaft und Geistesgeschichte* 27, no. 3 (1953): 333, and *Die Logik der Dichtung* (Stuttgart: Klett, 1957), 65–66, with several further examples.

Lotte in Weimar (Lying there with her eyes shut, she could see, as though it were yesterday, most vividly indeed the face he put on at his very cold reception).[21] Once Hamburger called attention to such sentences, others have collected examples from other languages: "L'enterrement avait lieu dans une heure" (the funeral took place in an hour), "A cow broke in (tomorrow morning) to my uncle Toby's fortifications, and eat up two ratios and half of dried grass."[22] From combinations like these Hamburger draws the conclusion already mentioned above, that the past tense in narrative literature cannot mean the past. Franz Stanzel takes a more restrictive position, that the combination of a past tense with a "future adverb" and similar combinations can only occur in free indirect discourse or similar narrative situations. That is doubtless correct, but the question then is how else we know that we are dealing with free indirect discourse in the individual case if not from the tenses and adverbs and the way they are combined in the text?

Let us look at the sentence from Thomas Mann in its context. Charlotte Kestner, née Buff, we have learned, registered on September 22, 1816, at the Elephant Hotel in Weimar. (Kestner, the model for the heroine of Goethe's *Sorrows of Young Werther*, expects to meet its famous author for the first time since the events of the novel some forty years earlier.) Now she is stretched out on the bed with closed eyes and muses over old memories. The omniscient narrator communicates her thoughts, primarily through free indirect discourse. The dominant tense is the Präteritum, both in the verbs of communication with which the narrator signals the indirect discourse, and in the "experienced" thoughts of the heroine. In addition to tense, the temporal adverbs help identify the free indirect discourse. Among them is the adverbial expression, "noch heute", which occurs first in a direct quote and thus as part of the discursive realm: "Noch heute sag' ich es Kestnern" (This very day I will tell Kestner). Shortly afterward this expression is taken up by the narrator as part of the narrated realm translated into its equivalent in narrative tenses: "an dem Tage noch" (on that very day). Finally, the same expression occurs for the third time, now in the free indirect discourse, the experienced language, of the heroine, whose thoughts can be recognized as having been experienced

---

21. Thomas Mann, *Lotte in Weimar* (Frankfurt/Main: Fischer, 1959), 26–27; *The Beloved Returns*, trans. H. T. Lowe-Porter (New York: Knopf, 1940), 28–29. Roy Pascal in "Tense and Novel," *Modern Language Review* 57, no. 1 (1962): 2, points to this passage.

22. Georges Simenon, *La fenêtre des Rouet*, cited by Holger Sten, *Les temps du verbe fini (indicatif) en français moderne* (Copenhagen: Munksgaard, 1964), 136; Laurence Sterne, *Tristram Shandy* 3.38, cited by Franz K. Stanzel, "Episches Präteritum, erlebte Rede, historisches Präsens," *Deutsche Vierteljahrsschrift* 33, no. 1 (1959): 6–7.

from the combination, one might almost say "contamination," of a narrative tense, a Plusquamperfekt ("hatte gemeldet"; had reported) with a discursive adverbial form ("noch heute," exactly as earlier in the quote). Here is the entire passage for an overview:

> Denn es war in aller Herzlichkeit ein wirrer und sinnloser, ein unerlaubter, unzuverlässiger und wie aus einer anderen Welt kommender Kuß gewesen, ein Prinzen- und Vagabundenkuß, für den sie zu schlecht und zu gut war; und hatte der arme Prinz aus Vagabundenland auch Tränen danach in den Augen gehabt und sie ebenfalls, so hatte sie doch in ehrlich untadligem Unwillen zu ihm gesagt: "Pfui, schäm' Er sich! Daß Er so etwas nicht noch einmal beikommen läßt, sonst sind wir geschiedene Leute! Dies bleibt nicht zwischen uns, daß Er's weiß. *Noch heute sag' ich es Kestnern.*" Und wie er auch gebeten hatte, es nicht anzusagen, *so hatte sie es doch an dem Tage noch ihrem Guten redlich gemeldet*, weil er's wissen mußte: nicht sowohl, daß jener es getan, als daß sie es hatte geschehen lassen; worauf sich denn Albert doch recht peinlich berührt gezeigt hatte und sie im Laufe des Gesprächs, auf Grund ihrer vernünftig unverbrüchlichen Zusammengehörigkeit, zu dem Beschlusse gelangt waren, den lieben Dritten nun denn doch etwas kürzer zu halten und ihm die wahre Sachlage entschieden bemerklich zu machen. *Unter ihren Lidern sah sie noch heute, nach soviel Jahren, mit erstaunlicher Deutlichkeit die Miene vor sich*, die er bei dem überaus trockenen Empfang gemacht, den ihm die Brautleute am Tage nach dem Kuß und namentlich am übernächsten Tage bereitet, als er abends um zehne, da sie miteinander vorm Haus saßen, mit Blumen gekommen war, die so unachtsam waren aufgenommen worden, daß er sie weggeworfen und sonderbaren Unsinn peroriert, in Tropen geredet hatte. (26-7)

> That kiss—it had been in all truthfulness quite mad. It came out of a different world, it was a prince-and-vagabond kiss, she was too good for it and not good enough. The poor prince of Vagabondia had had tears in his eyes, forsooth, and so had she. But she had comported herself with utmost propriety, saying: "Fie, for shame!" If such a thing happened again, they must part. She would not conceal it, he should understand that. That very day she would tell Kestner of it. And however much he had begged her not to, she had honourably confessed to her good, upright bridegroom, who had to know; not so much that He had kissed, but that she had suffered Him. Albert had been most distressed. They had talked for long, and on the ground of the inviolable bond between them, based on reason and good sense, had

decided to be a little strict with their dear friend and make it clear to him where matters really stood.

Lying there with her eyes shut, she could see, as though it were yesterday, most vividly indeed the face he put on at his very cold reception on the day after the kiss and particularly on the ensuing day, when he had arrived bearing flowers, at ten o'clock in the evening as the pair were sitting in front of the house. She received his tribute so carelessly that he flung it away and harangued them in a string of veiled, fantastic metaphors. (28-9)

I must still add that the special, "contaminating," treatment of temporal adverbs in the same chapter also returns with the locative adverbs. In the free indirect discourse, the adverb pairs "hier / dort" (here / there) and "hienieden / droben" both appear with narrative tenses. That is simply the special nature of free indirect discourse as a mixed perspective: On the one hand the narrator distances himself from his authorial perspective (with narrative tenses and narrative adverbs), and on the other hand he makes the perspective of the thinking or speaking characters present (with the adverbs and other linguistic signs of direct discursive speech).

Such disparate combinations create in the listener or reader an effect (one might also say, an illusion), to which we give the label free indirect discourse. It is, namely, a speech or thought sequence that is so narrated as if it were discursive speech.

Semi-finite Verbs

Since Quintilian, grammar has had the concept of mood. Strengthened by the logic of modality in medieval philosophy of language, this concept is still current even in modern grammar.[23] Depending on the particular language, there are the following moods: indicative, subjunctive, infinitive, imperative—and in many languages conditional, optative, and others. According to Jacob Wackernagel, "The difference among the modal forms refers to the relation of action to reality."[24] That may be understood to mean that the indicative asserts an action as real, the other moods, by contrast, only as possible, undetermined, commanded, conditional, desirable, etc. I consider the concept of moods somewhat problematic,

---

23. Quintilian, *Institutio Oratoria*, ed. and trans. Donald A. Russell (Cambridge: Harvard UP, 2002), 1.5.41.
24. Jacob Wackernagel, *Vorlesungen über Syntax* (Basel: Birkhäuser, 1926), 1:210.

because they are burdened with all kinds of ontological imaginings.[25] I prefer to speak instead of semi-finite verb forms that regularly work together with the previously discussed finite verb forms.[26]

I begin with the *infinitive*. In French it has the forms *chanter, avoir chanté, aller chanter, venir de chanter, être en train de chanter,* and *devoir chanter* (rare, future). One might remove one or another form from this list or add one or another. The issue is the series, not its length.

First, as with all verb forms, it conveys semantic information—singing. There is no information about person. There is no information about register, so that we do not know if we are in a world of discussion or one of narration. There is information about the perspective, that is, with *avoir chanté*, that the singing is understood as looked back to. And, finally, there is no information about the highlighting.

The semi-finite verb *avoir chanté* offers thus much less information than the finite verb *il chantait*. Many languages do have infinitive forms that are somewhat richer in information. Think about the so-called accusative-with-infinitive, that is, as is well known, much used in Latin and English, but is also found in many other languages. Again I respect the name, even though it emphasizes something inessential. It is not important that an accusative is used with the infinitive. In English (*I hear the boy sing, I want you to sing*) it isn't possible to make any reasonable determination of case, and in French (je *vous entends chanter; cette chanson, je la lui entends chanter* [I hear you sing; this song, I hear him sing it]), if you insisted on seeing case at any price (which it would be better not to do), you would have to speak sometimes of accusative, sometimes of dative. Even in Latin under certain conditions accusative is replaced with a nominative with the infinitive. The issue is not the case, but the person being connected with the infinitive. The accusative (or dative, or nominative) with the infinitive is a personal infinitive. It has the same structure as the Portuguese "infinitivo pessoal" (*cantarmos*) in a sentence like, "Chegamos para cantarmos" (We come in order to sing). The historical development of the personal infinitive in Portuguese has nothing at all to do with the "accusative with infinitive" of Latin or other Romance languages. Indeed, there exists in Portuguese next to the infinitivo pessoal another personal infinitive on the model of the Latin accusative with

---

25. A critique of the concept of mode may be found in Wolfgang Rothe, *Strukturen des Konjunktivs im Französischen* (Berlin: De Gruyter, 1967), 1 ff.

26. In the first edition of this book (1964) I termed these semi-finite forms "semi-tenses." I have dropped that expression because the term "semi-finite" seems to me less pretentious.

infinitive. They have different distributions, hence do not interfere with, but rather supplement, one another. Both are personal infinitives, i.e. infinitives that carry additional information about person along with their infinitive information.

Under the term *participle* I will gather various semi-finite verb forms in French. The traditional terminology is again sorely at odds with the present argument. The so-called participe présent (*chantant*), for example, is distinguished from the participe passé (*ayant chanté* and *chanté*), even though it forms a series with other active participles, namely *ayant chanté*, and the rarer but possible forms *allant chanté*, *venant de chanté*, and *devant chanté*. The series is reminiscent of the infinitive series. The participle, too, can under certain circumstances be accompanied by a personal determinant (noun or pronoun); Latin calls such a participle an absolute participle. A better term would be "personal participle," analogous to the personal infinitive.

French grammar distinguishes participe présent from adjectif verbal. Participe présent is, *Je l'ai trouvé chantant une chanson*. Adjectif verbal is, *soirée chantante*. The verbal has by no means the same series of forms as the active participle. French acknowledges only the form *chantant* as an adjectif verbal. The same is true for the passive participle *chanté*. It too has only the single form. And, finally, the gérondif, *en chantant*, has the same form as well. It, too, has only the single form.

The participle communicates semantic information unconnected to the speaking situation by any further syntactic information. But it does communicate information of a third kind. *Chantant* and *chanté*, for example, form series according to gender, masculine and feminine. The forms *chantant/chantante* (as adjectif verbal), *chanté/chantée*, and *en chantant* are still verb forms. But they mark the boundary of the verbal system. Hence, they have no role in a text that would compare to that of a verb determined by person and tense; instead, they are used like other classes of words, especially like adjectives and adverbs, and must be analyzed like them.

The subjunctive is also semi-finite in modern French—but only in modern French, which has eliminated the old imparfait du subjonctif together with the plus-que-parfait du subjonctif (*que je chantasse, que j'eusse chanté*) from the spoken language and also largely from the written language.[27] These forms have practically become a mode of irony; in Giraudoux, imparfait du subjonctif characterizes the pedant. No one anymore says, "Il voulait que j'écrivisse" (he wanted that I should write), but,

---

27. See in more detail Rothe, *Strukturen*, esp. 406–7.

"Il voulait que j'écrive" (he wanted me to write). Only the present stem of the subjunctive is still in use, thus the subjunctive has also dropped out of the consecutio temporum.

Although some writers still use imparfait du subjonctif under certain circumstances, my analysis will begin with usage restricted to the present stem of the subjunctive. Then the French subjonctif has the following forms: *que je chante, que j'aie chanté, que j'aille chanter, que je vienne de chanter,* and *que je sois en train de chanter.* (The series can again be extended or shortened by a form or two.) In addition to semantic information the subjunctive forms offer syntactic information about person (the series can be transposed into all the other persons), also about perspective (though with a form for the prospection that corresponds to the future of the tense system). The French subjunctive is indifferent with regard to register and to highlighting.

Now let us turn back to subjunctive in classical French and in the occasional writers in whom it still survives under particular stylistic circumstances. For this subjunctive, the series must be extended with the following forms: *que je chantasse, que j'eusse chanté,* and *que j'allasse chanter.* The use of these forms strictly follows the consecutio temporum according to the tense of the main verb or of the entire context. Under these circumstances the subjunctive is a completely different verb form. In particular it respects the structural boundary between discussing and narrating, and thus is more like a finite verb. But it distinguishes itself from the other tenses, to be sure only from the narrative tenses, in that it carries no information about highlighting.

The *imperative* is structurally related to the other forms discussed here. In French it has the forms: *chante, chantez, chantons, qu'il chante,* and *qu'ils chantent.* Apart from the semantic information, it also carries syntactic information about person, except for first-person singular, the person of the speaker. Commands are rarely given to the self, and when they are, then in the second person.

The accompanying table summarizes the characteristics that the various forms do or do not convey.

	Meaning of the Lexeme	Person	Register	Orientation	Profiling
Finite verb (sentence)	+	+	+	+	+
Infinitive	+	-	-	+	-
Personal infinitive	+	+	-	+	-

	Meaning of the Lexeme	Person	Register	Orientation	Profiling
Active participle	+	-	-	+	-
Personal participle	+	+	-	+	-
Verbal adjective	+	-	-	-	-
Passive participle	+	-	-	-	-
Gerundive	+	-	-	-	-
Subjunctive (modern)	+	+	-	+	-
Subjunctive (classical)	+	+	+	+	-
Imperative	+	+	-	-	-

A few remarks on terminology are needed here. I will take the French infinitive as my example, but they are valid by analogy also for the participle and the subjunctive, as well for grammatical terminology in other languages. The traditional names for infinitives as infinitif présent, infinitif passé, etc., is misleading, because they are based on uncritical views of individual tenses or even stages of time. Présent is a tense of discussion. What has the infinitif présent to do with this tense? An infinitive says nothing with regard to register; that is why it is semi-finite. To connect the infinitive to a tense that is on one side or the other of the structural boundary between narrating and discussing is to overlook exactly what makes it infinite. Whatever made anyone think of calling this verb infinitif présent? Simply because the form looked similar. But similarity of form ("present stem" and the like) proves little and cannot replace a functional analysis.

Yet a few more general thoughts about the verb forms I am calling semi-finite. There are various semi-finite forms. They inform listeners and readers in various ways about individual aspects of the speaking situation and ignore others. Register and highlighting are especially often excluded from their grammatical meaning. Why these? And why are there verb forms with restricted information at all? The reason follows from the general principle of economy underlying language and every other purposive communication. If language carries less information in some verb forms than in others, then evidently less information is sufficient for the particular situation. After all, the semi-finite forms do not stand alone. We speak not in series of infinitives or participles or subjunctives; we normally express ourselves in finite verbs, which carry full information about the speaking situation. If the situation is clarified in this manner, then a semi-finite form can follow and skip one or another aspect of the information because it is already obvious. The information from the preceding finite verb either remains valid or is made good by the next one. Semi-finite forms, we might say, promote the efficiency of language. With them, language gives no more information than necessary.

That means, therefore, that the semi-finite forms depend on supplementary information from other sources. Usually, it is information from the linguistic context, especially from another verb with full syntactic information about the situation. The verb is then the "main" verb, the other the dependent one, because it depends on the main verb for its information on the speech situation. Hence semi-finite forms are categorically intended for use in dependence on other linguistic elements that are themselves finite.

The same is true for the imperative, which is considered grammatically a sentence. But why, actually? We receive less information from the plain verb form than from the personal infinitive or participle. If the imperative really has the rank of a sentence, then every verb form should be considered a sentence. Instead of that, I consider the imperative, too, as semi-finite because it communicates incomplete information about the situation. Since it is semi-finite, it can only, like the other semi-finite forms, be used dependently. To be sure, it is not syntactically dependent on a main verb, but it is dependent on the situation. Linguistic context and situational context are interchangeable as a matter of principle. Imperatives are used in concrete speech situations. Hence the narrative world is excluded, hence prospective and retrospective perspectives are excluded, and hence there is no background. The expression is completely clear and unambiguous, but only because the verb forms and the concrete speech situation work together.

In the textual back and forth of finite and semi-finite verbs, language makes a choice. It raises one verb to be a main verb and subordinates another to "secondary verb." That, too, is a kind of highlighting. On the basis of their essential dependence on other information, semi-finite verbs (except for the imperative, which depends only on situation) are as a matter of principle verb forms of the background. This highlighting permeates all language and is not restricted only to narrating. So, it is clear that semi-finite verbs are always restricted within the highlighting information; it is obvious that they are always in the background, behind the main verbs. In the interpretations of Boccaccio's and Hemingway's stories we have already seen the role of the participles in the highlighting. The same could be shown for the other semi-finite verb forms as well.

9 / A Crisis in Narration?

Tense in Old French

Passé simple has disappeared from spoken French. It has occasionally been claimed about this "crisis" that passé composé already competed successfully with passé simple in the Middle Ages.[1] The assertion must be seen in relation to the position sometimes expressed that tense usage in Old French is completely chaotic and lacks any perspective. And yet this latter argument has been contradicted just as often.[2] I do not intend to consider all aspects of the question, but only to examine the tense pair passé simple and passé composé.

Old French tense use deviates the most from both Latin and modern French usage in the epic genres. There are, for example, colorful changes of tense in the *Chanson de Roland* (Song of Roland), with a clear preference for

---

1. Albert Dauzat, *Études de linguistique française* (Paris: d'Artrey, 1946), 63. Emidio De Felice also sees a continuation of Old French tense relations in the modern "crisis of the passé simple," "Problemi di aspetto nei più antichi testi francesi," *Vox Romanica* 16 (1957): 45.

2. Karl Vossler, *Frankreichs Kultur und Sprache* (Heidelberg: Winter, 1929), 59; Walter von Wartburg, *Évolution et structure de la langue française* (Bern: Francke, 1958), 54; Ferdinand Brunot and Charles Bruneau, *Précis de grammaire historique de la langue française* (Paris: Masson, 1949), sect. 525. Bibliography on what Brunot and Bruneau call "Mélange des temps en ancien français" in Hans Helmut Christmann, "Zu den formes surcomposées im Französichen," *Zeitschrift für französische Sprache und Literatur* 68, no. 1/2 (1958): 96.

présent, passé simple, and passé composé, while imparfait is extremely rare.³ Most remarkable is the strong position of présent, which, rather than passé simple, is the dominant tense of the *Song of Roland*. It is hardly possible to identify a system governing the shifts in tense, except perhaps for the vague tendency noted by Emidio De Felice ("Problemi di aspetto," 37) for a laisse (a group of assonating lines) to begin in passé simple and to end in présent. Otherwise, the tenses shift so abruptly that one immediately loses confidence in this observation. Here are two examples: *Franceis escriet, Olivier apelat* (l. 1112; he summons the Franks, he called Olivier); *Trait l'olifant, fieblement lo sonat* (l. 2104; he pulls out his horn, he blew it feebly). Present and past stand right next to each other. The shift cannot be motivated by time relations, since Roland of course raised his horn first, then blew. Nor does the perspective of the epic narration change so quickly. The solution to the riddle evidently lies here in the assonance. The passé simple of the (common) *a*-conjugation ends in the (common) third person singular in *át* (as above *apelát, sonát*). And precisely in the laisses that assonate on *á* there is an accumulation of verbs in the passé simple ending in *át*. It is especially remarkable in laisse 57, in which four lines assonate on *át*. The number may not seem remarkably high, but this laisse narrates a dream, and elsewhere dreams are usually narrated in the otherwise very rare imparfait.

While there is thus a clear affinity between laisses with *á* and passé simple, the laisses that assonate on *é* reveal an equivalent preference for passé composé, and precisely in the assonant position. For in the *a*-conjugation passé composé ends with a stressed *é* (*montez, allez*) and offers the performing bard a large number of convenient assonances.⁴ This is especially easy to see in the *laisses similaires*, the climactic strophes in which an event is told several times with little change in content but with varying assonance. In these cases, the tense often changes with the assonance. Compare these two lines: *Oliviers montet desor un pui halçor* (l. 1017; Olivier ascends a lofty hill) and *Oliviers est desor un pui montez* (l. 1028; Olivier ascended a hill). It is not possible to see a progress in the action or a change in the narrator's position, as becomes clear from the following pairs of lines: *Desoz un pin en est li reis alez* (l. 165; the king went beneath a pine) and three lines later, again referring

---

3. In the roughly 4000 lines of the *Song of Roland* there are only about forty forms of imparfait: Georges and Robert Le Bidois, *Syntaxe du français moderne*, vol. 1 (Paris: Picard, 1935), 436. Exact counts for the Old French texts in De Felice, "Problemi," 21–23.

4. See especially laisses 34 (six forms of passé composé in ten lines), 211 (seven forms of passé composé in eleven lines), 258 (seven forms of passé composé in eleven lines).

to Charlemagne, *Li emperere s'en vait desoz un pin* (l. 168; the emperor goes beneath a pine).

There can be no question that the tenses of the *Song of Roland* and many other medieval French texts are chosen for the sake of the assonance. We have no right to turn up our noses and accuse the poet of incompetence. Old French epic is oral literature and operates under the special demands of oral delivery from memory. Oral poetry does not have the same textual stability as written literature.[5] The performer is permitted to vary the verse and certain formulaic elements in order to fill out the meter and maintain the assonance while improvising. Tenses can be subordinated to what is here the higher law of epic form.

Oral delivery also explains the high frequency of the present tense, as D.R. Sutherland has emphasized.[6] The epic is really *chanson de geste* (a song of action); it is not told or read, but performed by a singer, not much differently from a lyrical song. It is to be considered a kind of recitative supported by lively gestures and mimicry, and, certainly at the climaxes, with dramatic accents. This is how epics are performed today in countries where the epic is still alive, and in contemporary France the *chansons* of the *chansonniers*, which carry the generic signs of oral literature, are still performed this way.[7] The preference for présent, the dominant tense of song (including French *chanson*), can be explained by this quasi-dramatic mode of presentation. The constant shifting between passé simple and présent reflects therefore the middle position of oral epic between narrative and dramatic literature. Spanish epics of the Middle Ages and the Icelandic sagas reveal the same tense relationships.[8]

Several scholars have correctly concluded from this that the Old French tense system should not be based on the epics. Prose tense usage is completely different. Paul Schaechtelin considers only prose texts in his analysis of tenses, while Manfred Sandmann adds to that the dialogue

---

5. Established for French by Jean Rychner's excellent book, *La chanson de geste: Essai sur l'art épique des jongleurs* (Geneva: Droz, 1955).

6. D. R. Sutherland, "On the Use of Tenses in Old and Middle French," in *Studies in French Language and Mediaeval Literature, Presented to Professor Mildred K. Pope* (Manchester: Manchester UP, 1953), 329–37.

7. Further detail in my "Ein Chanson und seine Gattung," in *Literatur für Leser* (Munich: Deutscher Taschenbuch Verlag, 1986), 149–66.

8. See especially Manfred Sandmann, "Narrative Tenses of the Past in the 'Cantar de Mio Cid,'" in *Studies in Romance Philology and French Literature, Presented to John Orr* (Manchester: Manchester UP, 1953), 258–81; also Ulrike Sprenger, *Praesens historicum und Praeteritum in der altisländischen Saga* (Basel: Schwabe, 1951); and Tom A. Rompelman, "Form und Funktion des Präteritums im Germanischen," *Neophilologus* 37, no. 2 (1953): 81.

passages from the epics, because only in these, he says, is the tense usage "realistic" ("Tempora," 292).[9] There is a further step. In order to gain a complete view of Old French tenses it is necessary to go beyond belles lettres and consider texts that definitely contain discursive language. Given the conditions of transmission for the Middle Ages, that means for the French language above all juridical texts. Josef Schoch has examined these texts from a different point of view and made an observation that will sound familiar.[10] Among French documents of the Middle Ages he finds an affinity between passé simple and the third person of the verb, and one between passé composé and the first person. (The second person rarely appears in documents.) Documents are often written such that the juridically relevant information is laid out in the first person, singular and plural, and authenticated by the names of the participants. This is discursive speech in its purest form. Looking backward in these discursive texts is consistently done in passé composé, apart from some formulaic Latinisms. Here is an example of a 1272 CE judicial text from the Ardennes:

> Nous Thiebaus, abbes de Saint Huber en Ardenne, Jaques de Stailes, Baudouins Mores de ce meisme liu, chevalliers, faisons cognoissant a tous ciaus qui ces lettres verront et oiront que com betens a fust et descors entre nous dou patronaige de l'esglise de Stailes nous nous soumes mise sus deus preudoumes, clers sages et discrés, c'est a savoir maistre Gillame, dit de Haienges, et maistre Jehan, dit de Mousai, en maniere que il doient enquerre et rapporter la raison de chascuin de nous, soit par raison de hertaige ou de proprietet, ou de tenour ou d'usaige, et avons promis nous dis abbés audis chevalliers, et nous chevalliers dis audit abbet, sous penne de cent livres de parisis, que nous tenrons et warderons entierement ce que li dit disour raporteront ou par amour ou par droit, et pour ce que ce soit ferme chose et estauble, nous Tiebaus, abbés devant dis, avons mis nostre saiel a ces presentes lettres. Et nous Jaques de Stailes et Baudouins Mores, chevalliers, pour ce que nous n'avons point de propre saiel, avons nous depriet a nostre chier signour Loy, conte de Chisney, qu'il metet son saiel a ces presentes lettres, lesqueles furent

---

9. Paul Schaechtelin, *Das passé defini und imparfait im Altfranzösischen* (Halle: Niemeyer, 1911).

10. Josef Schoch, *Perfectum historicum und perfectum praesens im Französischen: Von seinen Anfängen bis 1700* (Halle: Niemeyer, 1912), 67–68.

faites l'an de graice mil deus cens soixante et douse ans, le lundy devant feste Saint Martin en yver.[11]

We, Thibaud, Abbot of Saint Hubert en Ardennes, Jacques de Stailes, and Baudouins Mores of this same place, knights, make known to all those who shall see and hear these letters that in what concerns the quarrel and discord between us about the patronage of the church of Stailes, we have appealed to two gentlemen, wise and discreet clerics, namely Master Guillaume, of de Haienges, and Master Jehan, of Mousai, so that they shall inform themselves of the explanation from each of us and shall report it, whether for a question of heritage or ownership, or of a condition linked to a fief or a custom, and we have promised, we, the above-named Abbot to the above-named knights, and we, the knights to the Abbot, under pain of 100 pounds in Parisian money, that we will respect and guarantee entirely what Masters Guillaume and Jehan shall report, whether by love or by law, and so that it shall be a firm and stable matter, we, Thibaud, the above-mentioned Abbot, have placed our seal on the present letters. And because we do not have a seal of our own, we, Jacques de Stailes and Baudouins Mores, knights, have requested our dear sire Loy, Count of Chisney, to place his seal on the present letters, which were made in the year of our Lord one thousand two hundred and seventy-two, the Monday before the Feast of Saint Martin, in winter.

The standpoint chosen by the contending parties and the editor of the document is the legal act of accreditation. From this standpoint the parties look back at their announcement of their intentions, which is here officially registered, and they look ahead to the consequences of their agreed settlement. All of this is discussion. It is written in the discursive tenses: présent, passé composé, and futur. The tense usage is just the same as in modern French. (The subjunctive "fust" in the introductory summary of the disagreement and the passé simple "furent" in the date are formulaic Latinisms.)

Thus, we find in Old French passé simple in an unambiguously narrative function and passé composé in the unambiguous function of discussion. Further, we find passé composé routinely in narrative literature only when the specific performance and assonance conditions of oral literature require it. That justifies the assumption that even Old French

---

11. The document is reprinted in Eduard Schwan and Dietrich Behrens, *Grammatik des Altfranzösischen* (Leipzig: O. R. Reisland, 1911), 263. Additional documents are there as well. Our thanks to Denyse Delcourt for the translation.

made a distinction in principle between the discursive and narrative tense groups. Hence it certainly cannot be said that the passé simple was disappearing in medieval French under pressure from the passé composé.

Lucien Foulet, who is of the same opinion, still believes the crisis of the passé simple can be dated back at least into the fifteenth century. He cites a series of texts from various sources from the early fifteenth to the early sixteenth century in which he claims to find the passé composé as a replacement tense for the passé simple. But his texts are not entirely convincing. One is a French conversation book for Englishmen from 1415 CE, which I think intends to show its readers all possible tenses in French. In the immediate neighborhood of the passé composé cited by Foulet as evidence, there also appear passé simple, plus-que-parfait, passé anterieur, imparfait, and présent. Foulet's other texts are political letters. This is important. They are not letters in which information is narrated, but rather in which political and military strategies are discussed. In one of the letters (1412 CE) this sentence appears: "car ils ne font guerre que à ceulx qui, l'année passée, ont tenu le parti du roy" (for they are only fighting those who took the king's part last year).[12] Foulet considers this example to be especially important because it is dated. But the date is irrelevant, especially to the question of whether this letter is narrative or discursive. That can be learned only from the context. In this letter the governor of La Rochelle discusses military strategies that follow from the loyalties of the princes in the last campaign. It is not a matter of narrating what the princes did in the previous year, but of calculating who is now particularly at risk because of the side he took in the last campaign. He will require special protection, and therefore the letter-writer is sending troops. That can only be discussed by looking back at the sides taken in the last campaign. Therefore, passé composé is appropriate. It has not displaced passé simple, because there never was a passé simple verb in that linguistic situation.

Foulet thinks, finally, that passé composé penetrates in its expanded function even into literature with the memoirs of Philippe de Commynes (fifteenth century). Here, too, I can agree only to a limited extent. What changes is not the language, but literature. Memoirs, as invented by Commynes, are a different genre from historiography and certainly from fiction. Memoirs do not simply tell what happened, but they look back through the eyes of a person who considers his experiences significant and worthy of transmission. That does not exclude the possibility that memoirs might include narration. But they always include above and

---

12. Lucien Foulet, "La disparition du prétérit," *Romania* 46, no. 182/183 (1920): 286.

beyond it an element of discussion and judgment that explains the presence of many a passé composé.

Evidence of Language Consciousness in French Classicism

A vigorous fight for priority among the Romance languages began in the sixteenth century. One of the most passionate champions of the "précellence" of French, especially in competition with Italian, was the humanist philologian Henri Estienne (1531–1598). In his *Traicté de la conformité du langage françois avec le grec* (1557, Treatise on the Conformity of the French Language with the Greek), Estienne discusses French tenses and explains the difference between passé simple and passé composé for his readers.[13] If someone says, "je parlay à luy et luy fei response" (passé simple: I spoke to him and answered him), then one is to understand, according to Estienne, that the exchange did not take place on the same day, but earlier. But if someone says "j'ay parlé avec lui et luy ay faict response" (passé composé: I spoke to him and answered him), then it happened on the same day. This is the famous—or notorious—"24-hour rule,"[14] according to which the passé composé expresses recent occurrences; the passé simple distant occurrences; and the night before the speech act is to be understood as the boundary between recent and distant past. The grammarians of the sixteenth century bequeathed the rule to those of the seventeenth. It appears in Maupas (1607), Oudin (1632), and in the eighteenth yet again in Buffier (1709), while Alcide Bonnecase de Saint Maurice and Vaugelas remain skeptical or silent on this rule.

There are linguists who believe that Estienne's rule corresponds to the actual usage of the sixteenth century.[15] But there is no convincing basis for this assumption. Estienne allows exceptions. He observes that the rule is often broken, and he breaks his own rule in the very formulation of it: "mais quand on dit, *je parlay à luy, & luy fei response*, cecy ne s'entend auoir esté faict ce jour mesme auquel on raconte ceci, mais auparauant: sans qu'on puisse juger combien de temps est passé depuis" (but if someone says, I spoke to him [passé simple] and answered him, one does not understand it to have happened on the very day on which it is told, but earlier, without, however, it being possible to judge how much time *has*

---

13. See, on this and the following, Ferdinand Brunot, *Histoire de la langue française des origines à 1900* (Paris: Armand Colin, 1905–38), 3:582–83 and 4.2:977.

14. Cited in Charles Livet, *La grammaire française et les grammairiens du XVIe siècle* (Paris: Didier, 1859), 440.

15. Foulet, "La disparition du prétérit," 293; Wolfgang Pollak, *Studien zum "Verbalaspekt" im Französischen* (Vienna: Rudolf M. Rohrer, 1960), 116.

passed since). "Depuis," that is definitely not just since today, but at least since yesterday. By his own rule Estienne would have had to use the passé simple here, but instead follows his own more authentic sense for the language and uses even in this sentence the passé composé, because he is discussing the tenses. He offers an additional hint that he is generalizing his observations into a false rule. He notices that the passé composé, "j'ai fait," is more commonly used than the passé simple, "je fis" (Livet, *La grammaire française*, 440–41). That is surely true, but it applies not for these two tenses per se, but only for the first person, which Estienne uses as his example. Indeed, there is in general an affinity even in the sixteenth century between passé composé and the first person. If he had focused on the third person instead, he might perhaps have reached a different conclusion, since for the third person a narrative tense is much more common.

All the evidence suggests that even in the sixteenth century passé simple was a narrative tense and passé composé a discursive one. Furthermore, Estienne's 24-hour rule is nothing other than an awkward effort to conceptualize this difference. He had to fail because he began from the unreflected assumption that the difference between the tenses had to be related to time. On this basis he could reach no better result. But he did observe well. We discuss precisely those things that immediately surround us, among which, in the retrospective view, are of course those that happened most recently more than those that happened earlier. What is long past is less likely to be a burning issue than what just happened. Thus, the distant past is more often narrated, the recent past more often discussed. This is the true heart of Estienne's rule. It has to have had a true heart, or it would make no sense that this rule enjoyed such success and formed an obvious part of the general linguistic consciousness among the French classicists of the seventeenth century, as can be illustrated from Madame de Sévigné and Racine.

In November and December of 1664, Madame de Sévigné wrote a series of letters to the Marquis de Pomponne reporting to him on the trial against the former minister of finance and patron of the arts Foucquet, whose fate was the central topic of the day's gossip. Normally, she wrote in the evening about that morning's trial.[16] Thus, for example, in her letter of November 17, 1664:

---

16. Letters cited by date from Mme de Sévigné, *Lettres*, vol. 1, ed. Louis Jean Nicolas Monmerqué (Paris: Hachette, 1862). See especially, "Je vous écrirai tous les soirs" (Nov. 26, 1664; p. 449).

Aujourd'hui lundi 17ᵉ novembre, M. Foucquet a été pour la seconde fois sur la sellette. Il s'est assis sans façon comme l'autre fois. M. le chancelier a recommencé à lui dire de lever la main: il a repondu qu'il avoit déjà dit les raisons qui l'empêchoient de prêter le serment; qu'il n'étoit pas nécessaire de les redire. Là-dessus M. le chancelier s'est jeté dans de grands discours, pour faire voir le pouvoir legitime de la chambre; que le Roi l'avoit etablie, et que les commissions avoient été verifiées par les compagnies souveraines. M. Foucquet a répondu que souvent on faisoit des choses par autorité, que quelquefois on ne trouvoit pas justes quand on y avoit fait réflexion. M. le chancelier a interrompu: "Comment! Vous dites donc que le Roi abuse de sa puissance?" M. Foucquet a répondu: . . . (436)

Today, Monday, November 17, M. Foucquet was in the dock for the second time. He sat down without ceremony like the previous time. My lord chancellor resumed by telling him to raise his hand: he responded that he had already given the reasons that prevented him from taking the oath; that it was unnecessary to repeat them. Then my lord the chancellor launched into long speeches to defend the legitimate power of the court; that the King had established it, and that its commissions had been verified by the ruling authorities. M. Foucquet answered that people often did things by authority that sometimes they didn't find proper when they had reflected on them. My lord the chancellor interrupted: "What! You say then that the King abuses his power?" M. Foucquet answered: . . .

This report has all the characteristics of a narrative. Although Madame de Sévigné is fully in sympathy with the accused, she abstains from all evaluative discussion of the case and reproduces the course of the trial as accurately as possible. Nevertheless, she puts the finite verbs in passé composé.

Sometimes, however, the diligent correspondent does not have time in the evening, or she returns later to an earlier day of the trial. Then she uses passé simple: "Il lui fit excuse l'autre jour de ce que M. Foucquet avoit parlé trop longtemps" (November 28, 1664; he apologized the next day for M. Foucquet having talked too long). On Wednesday, December 18, 1664, she writes: "Je vous mandai samedi comme M. d'Ormesson avoit rapporté l'affaire et opiné . . ." (I sent to you Saturday how M. d'Ormesson had reported the affair and opined . . .). Both times the event lies a few days in the past.

The following passage is especially striking; "Aussitôt que M. Foucquet a été dans la chambre, M. le chancelier lui a dit de s'asseoir. Il a respondu: 'Monsieur, vous prîtes hier avantage de ce que je m'etois assis'" (November 18, 1664; As soon as M. Foucquet was in the chamber, my lord the chancellor told him to be seated. He answered: "Monsieur, yesterday you took advantage of the fact that I was seated"). Did the accused really say that? If so, he would have followed Henri Estienne's 24-hour rule as exactly as Madame de Sévigné—with events on the same day in the passé composé and all earlier ones in the passé simple. Madame de Sévigné follows it without missing a beat.

If any further proof is necessary, it can be found with all desired clarity on December 4. Madame de Sévigné tells what happened on this date twice. First, according to her custom, in her evening letter. The narration falls within the twenty-four hour period and, regardless of the character of the presentation, is told in the passé composé:

> Enfin, les interrogations sont finies. Ce matin M. Foucquet est entré dans la chambre; M. le chancelier a fait lire le projet tout du long. M. Foucquet a repris la parole le premier, et a dit: "Monsieur, je crois que vous ne pouvez tirer autre chose de ce papier, que l'effet qu'il vient de faire, qui est de me donner beaucoup de confusion." M. le chancelier a dit... "Monsieur," a dit M. Foucquet....

> Finally the interrogations ended. This morning M. Foucquet entered the chamber; my lord chancellor had the charge read at full length. M. Foucquet spoke first and said: Monsieur, I think that you can deduce nothing from this paper apart from the effect it has just had, which is to cause me great confusion." My lord chancellor said... "Monsieur," M. Foucquet said,...

A few days later, however, Madame de Sévigné has heard a different version and reports about it in her letter of December 9:

> Cependant je veux rajuster la dernière journée de l'interrogatoire sur le crime d'Etat... Après que M. Foucquet eut dit que le seul effet qu'on pouvoit tirer du projet, c'etoit de lui avoir donné la confusion de l'entendre, M. le chancelier lui dit:... Il repondit...

> Meanwhile, I would like to revise the last day of the interrogation about the crime against the state... After M. Foucquet had said that the only effect one could draw from the charge was to have confused him as he listened, my lord chancellor said:... He responded:...

This time the discussion lies five days in the past and Madame de Sévigné uses the passé simple, even though nothing has changed in the character of the narrative.

It is even possible to identify the temporal boundary between passé composé and passé simple in the letters more precisely. At the time there was a comet visible in the night sky from Paris, at three in the morning. Monsieur d'Artagnan observed it, and so did Madame de Sévigné. She uses different tenses to narrate it: "M. d'Artagnan veilla la nuit passée, et la vit fort à son aise. — J'ai vu cette nuit la comète; sa queue est d'une fort belle longueur" (M. d'Artagnan stayed up last night and saw it comfortably. I saw the comet tonight; it has a nice long tail). Why once passé simple and then passé composé? It depends yet again on Estienne's iron 24-hour rule, which Madame de Sévigné interprets in very amusing fashion. Evidently Monsieur d'Artagnan decided that it would be best for him to stay awake until the comet rose at 3 a.m. Only after that would he have gone to bed. Madame de Sévigné, on the other hand, went to bed and then got up at three in the "morning." For her the occurrence belongs to the following day. Thus, even though both astronomers viewed the comet at exactly the same time, still the occasion belongs for each to different days, because they went to bed at different times. There can be no doubt: For Madame de Sévigné the border between passé simple and passé composé is—bed.

Henri Estienne's iron rule of tense must not be confused with the famous unity of time in French classical drama. This latter derives (ostensibly) from Aristotelian poetics and stood originally in no relation to Estienne's version of the tense rule. Even so the two rules enter into an unexpected relationship in French theater of the seventeenth century. If, after all, the events of a tragedy must be compressed into a single day, as required by the rules of poetics, and if dramatists must also hold to the rule of 24 hours, then passé simple essentially disappears from dramatic literature.

Anyone in seventeenth-century France who had not yet figured that out would have been forcefully reminded of it by the quarrel about the *Cid*. Among the many criticisms made about Corneille's successful play, *Le Cid* (1636), by the newly established Académie Française was one about his use of tense. In act 2, scene 1, Corneille had written: "Je l'avoue entre nous, quand je lui fis l'affront, / J'eus le sang un peu chaud et le bras un peu prompt" (lines 353–54; I admit, between us, when I insulted him / My blood was a bit hot and my arm a bit prompt). The count says that in reference to the quarrel about honor in the play's plot, which has to have occurred within the previous twenty-four hours. Hence Corneille has broken the grammatical rule and has to accept it when the critics in the academy assert: "Il fallait dire: 'quand je lui ai fait,' puisqu'il ne s'etoit point passé de nuit entre deux" (It was necessary to say: when I insulted [in the passé composé], because no night had passed between the two acts [The night follows the third act]).[17] Corneille accepted the criticism and adjusted his text.

Racine took a lesson from Corneille's misfortune. In his personal letters he is not always careful about the iron rule,[18] but he holds strictly to it in his tragedies. In the lively dialogue of the dramatic action it is not difficult for him to obey the rule, since dialogue is always dominated by discursive tenses. He has few difficulties even in the exposition, which often has a narrative character, since the prehistory of the plots lies outside the allotted day. Phèdre begins her famous expository monologue (act 1, scene 3) with the line, "Mon mal vient de plus loin" (My misfortune comes from long ago). After this Racine can proceed with passé simple as appropriate tense for the distant past.

But the ends of tragedies pose serious difficulties. The law of decency (*bienséance*) does not permit a dramatist of the seventeenth century to show on stage the bloody ending demanded by the genre. The heroes die somewhere else, and the death is only narrated on stage. That is the function of the messenger speech, which is the product of two contradictory poetic principles. The tense rule also gets involved in this contradiction. According to the convention of the messenger's speech, the dreadful ending it reports has taken place only minutes earlier. The messenger dashes onto the stage and narrates with the great excitement essential to the pathos of the tragic end. But the 24-hour rule forbids the messenger the use of precisely that tense made for narration, passé simple. And indeed, as far as I can tell, we never find this tense in the messenger's speech of a French classical drama. Instead, we find passé composé, mixed with imparfait as background. This is the mix of tenses in the reports of Éphestion (*Alexandre le Grand* 5.3), Oreste (*Andromaque* 5.3), Osmin (*Bajazet* 5.11), Arbate (*Mithridate* 5.4), Albine (*Britannicus* 5.8), and especially the famous report of Théramène (*Phèdre* 5.6). In fact, Racine heightens the drama by having his messenger modulate into historical present, and then shift toward the end back into the calmer pace of imparfait and passé composé.

Once again, there is an interesting boundary situation, as there was with Madame de Sévigné. In the biblical drama *Athalie* (2.5) the queen reports the terrible dream she has had for three nights in a row. The first two occasions belong to the distant past, the last to the recent past. How

---

17. Cited from Brunot, *Histoire*, 3:583.
18. Foulet, "La disparition du prétérit," 305. Foulet interprets his examples differently.

is it now to be told? Racine decides to follow the model of the messenger's speech, and obediently chooses passé composé in combination with imparfait and climaxing in historical present. His decision makes sense; he could not properly point out that an essential element of his plot exceeded the allowed limit of a single day.

These examples have surely demonstrated sufficiently that the classical French authors of drama and prose submitted to Henri Estienne's 24-hour rule. They belonged to an age that did not experience the laws of poetics as unwelcome compulsion. Furthermore, they would have learned from the Academy's criticism of *Le Cid* that ignoring a poetological rule would bring public criticism. So, they followed it, indeed blindly. Anything from the recent past, that is, since the previous night, is put in passé composé, whether it is to be discussed or narrated. Racine conceals the problem in part by removing much of his narrative from passé composé into historical present. Nevertheless, the fact remains that French classical authors, at the behest of highly respected laws of grammar, adopted the custom of narrating in passé composé. Because it contradicts the normal structure of language, these writers had to constrain themselves to help grammar press language into a form to which it was not suited. That is, as always, the form of time rather than of tense.

Everyone knows that the influence of the classics on the general development of language in France (and on education in general) cannot be overstated. To be a classic is to be a model of language. The French classicists have always been understood in this manner. So, it is obvious that their use of tense continued to influence French literature and schooling. When Voltaire dares to write in a letter, "J'ai receu hier votre lettre" (February 1727; I [have] received your letter yesterday), the editor of the Édition Moland simply crosses it out and replaces it with the "correct" one: "Je reçus hier votre lettre" (I received your letter yesterday).[19] Evidently the editor felt secure in the awareness of crowds of authorities behind him and acted in the best of faith. Even in the twentieth century, where people do not generally think they can measure tense by the clock, it is still possible to find traces of the 24-hour rule. Fritz Strohmeyer believes that passé composé has penetrated into the style of letters and diaries "because of the nearness of the described events to the present." Paul Imbs thinks passé composé in literary language expresses recent events ("des faits d'un passé récent").[20] And Albert Dauzat wants us to believe that he has actually encountered the 24-hour rule "even today" in a dialect of southern

---

19. Reported by Foulet, "La disparition du prétérit," 308.
20. Paul Imbs, *L'emploi des temps verbaux* (Paris: Klincksieck, 1960), 103.

France.[21] Since the observation is not scientifically verified, it is permissible to doubt it, even without traveling there oneself to disprove it.[22]

The Time of Newspapers

The late eighteenth century was remarkable not only for its political changes, but also because a new kind of literary information developed: It brought the newspaper to France. Newspapers began, to be sure, in the seventeenth century, or even, in a sense, with Caesar's *Acta diurna*. But in the second half of the eighteenth century, the newspaper became an institution in France. In 1762 the weekly *Gazette de France* became the official organ of the French government, and the first daily, the *Journal de Paris*, appeared in 1777. During the Revolution, newspapers multiplied beyond counting and from then on dominated public opinion more and more, especially in the large cities. We may also assume that they influenced the public language to an ever-increasing degree.

As the German term "Zeitung" suggests, newspapers have a special relationship to time. "Zeit und Zeitung" (Period and Periodical) is the title of one of Goethe's epigrams. The frequent appearance of the word as the name of a paper points to the relation: *Die Zeit, Il Tempo, The Times*. The newspaper tries, as the French term *journal* implies, to provide the news of the day: the newest and most current, not yesterday's news or what happened long ago. Today's news cannot wait until tomorrow, because tomorrow yet another paper—a daily—will appear. Newspapers must be as quick as Madame de Sévigné, who reports like a good journalist in her evening letters on the day's trial. Of course, the principle that the newspaper offers the news of "the day" is to be taken with a grain of salt. News-reporting technology was not as advanced in the eighteenth and nineteenth centuries as it is today. And that aside, morning papers were always at a disadvantage in that they could offer no more current news than what had happened the day before. So, the principle of offering the day's news is more an ideal than a reality.

Just as Henri Estienne's iron rule of tense was unexpectedly strengthened by its strict observance among the great authors of French classicism,

---

21. See Fritz Strohmeyer, "Das Passé simple und das Passé composé im modernen Französisch," *Die neueren Sprachen* 2 (1953): 483; Albert Dauzat, *Études de linguistique française* (Paris: d'Artrey, 1946), 64. The topic is the Vinzelles dialect.

22. To this day, the Italian tenses that correspond to the French passé simple and passé compose are called passato remoto and passato prossimo. These terms assume the 24-hour rule. Raffaello Fornaciari, *Sintassi italiana dell'uso moderno* (Florence: G. C. Sansoni, 1882), 172, asserts this explicitly.

it was also strengthened from the late eighteenth century on by the newspapers. While the first wave strengthened the status of the rule, the second probably had more influence on linguistic usage. For newspapers do privilege passé composé over the passé simple to a striking degree. I can point here to statistics for French newspapers of August 19, 1959, developed by Robert Martin and reported by Paul Imbs (*L'emploi*, 221). Martin finds the passé composé to be the tense of 21% of all verbs, in contrast to 7.4% for the passé simple. That is an astonishing imbalance for publications that largely narrate what has happened and in which one might expect a much higher percentage of narrative tenses. But in France the high frequency of passé composé in newspapers can be explained by the new tasks that this tense took over from passé simple in the course of the language's history.

Is it possible to project the proportions of tense usage in modern newspapers back into the beginnings of French journalism? I tested it in the earliest French newspapers to which I have access, a collection of issues of the *Journal de Paris* from 1813.[23] (I assume that a projection from the Napoleonic era back to the revolutionary period will not introduce too many errors.) So, when we open the issue for January 1, 1813, our jaundiced eyes are at first disappointed that it begins with a report about a meeting of the imperial ministers that took place on December 30, 1812—two days earlier. Correspondingly, the report of the emperor's New Year's Day reception appears only on January 3. We find in addition in the January 1 issue, depending on when the correspondents' reports have arrived, articles about events all through December, indeed even from November and October. It is striking, however, that the reports from earlier dates are often edited so as to give the impression of currency and novelty. In the January 2, 1813, issue, for example, there appears a report from Frankfurt, dated December 28, 1812, which reads: "Il a été aujourd'hui jusqu'à 12 degrés de Réaumur" (The temperature today was as high as 12 degrees Reaumur). And even if the reports from New York are almost two months old, they are still the latest and the news of the day. They are introduced with the notation: "Les gazettes que nous avons reçues ce matin vont jusqu'au 7 novembre" (January 2; the newspapers we received this morning run until November 7). These are all news of the day in the ideal sense. They concern events that have just taken place and emphasize, to the extent possible, their quality as recent past.

The dominant tense in all these reports is passé composé, even if the report is unambiguously dated the previous day: "S.M. l'Empereur a

---

23. *Journal de Paris*, https://www.retronews.fr/journal/journal-de-paris/01-janvier-1813/2969/4686198/2.

passé hier en revue, dans les cours du palais des Tuileries, divers corps de la garde impériale et d'autres troupes de la garnison de Paris" (February 8, 1813; His Majesty the Emperor reviewed yesterday in the courtyard of the Tuileries various corps of the imperial guard and other troops from the Paris garrison). The same is true for the following report from Warsaw, dated December 19, 1812, published on January 1, 1813: "Le duc de Bassano est parti ce matin d'ici pour se rendre à Berlin; il a passé cinq jours dans cette ville" (The Duke of Bassano left this morning to return to Berlin; he spent five days in this city). All these reports, that could also be read as narratives, stand here as news reports and belong—by convention as journalism—to the sphere of the recent past. This is a temporal expansion of the space of twenty-four hours, but an expansion that is part of the idea of the newspaper.

Passé simple occurs very rarely in the issues of the *Journal de Paris* from 1813, much more rarely, even, than the statistics from the twentieth century would suggest. In the January 1 issue, for example, I find only ten occurrences. Four of them are in a theater review. The other six are in a report from Naples that is so novelistic that imparfait and passé simple, the narrative tenses of the novella, are simply unavoidable:

> Nous apprenons par un bâtiment arrivant de Tripoli, que le pacha ou bey de cette régence est depuis quelque temps en état de guerre avec les arabes bédouins des déserts situés au sud de ce pays. Ses troupes ayant été défaites par ces arabes, ce despote s'avisa de soupçonner que ses courtisans pouvaient avoir trahi ses intérêts en correspondant avec l'ennemi. Voulant donc se venger de leur perfidie réelle ou supposée, il invita quarante d'entr'eux à une fête, au milieu de laquelle ses gardes, à un signal convenu, se précipitèrent sur ses hôtes, les garrottèrent, et en taillèrent en pièces vingt-cinq par ordre de leur maître qui égorgea lui-même les quinze autres.

> We learn from a vessel arriving from Tripoli that the pasha or bey of this regency has been engaged for a while in a war with the Bedouin Arabs of the deserts located in the south of the country. After his troops were defeated by these Arabs, it occurred to the despot to suspect that his courtiers might have betrayed his interests by colluding with the enemy. Desiring to avenge himself for their actual or supposed perfidy, he invited forty of them to a feast, in the middle of which his guards, at a signal agreed upon, threw themselves on the guests, garroted them, and cut twenty-five of them into pieces on the order of their master, who slit the throats of the remaining fifteen himself.

In the January 2 issue there are slightly more passé simple forms. But they also occur only in similar contexts, namely in the review of a Dante translation, in which Dante's life is narrated, and in a letter from an officer in the Spanish army, who recounts an episode from the last campaign. These are evidently without exception those parts of the newspaper that are less the news of the day and do not stand to the same extent under the demands of currency. In these realms passé simple can still hold its own. In all other cases passé composé can be seen as the dominant tense of the (shorter) reports, and indeed also for events beyond the twenty-four-hour limitation. Such events, though actually long since past, are theoretically recent. This surely reflects the linguistic usage of the turn of the nineteenth century. To what extent may it also be assumed that the newspapers have had a decided influence on the general usage in France as we still find it today?

Albert Camus: *L'étranger*

In an interview, the French novelist Alain Robbe-Grillet said about the novel *L'étranger* (1942, The Stranger) that Camus had evidently first had the idea of writing an entire novel in passé composé and only later invented a story to fit his tense structure.[24] Robert Champigny judges that the whole novel would collapse into itself if anyone tried to translate it into passé simple.[25] It would then be just a second *Candide*. So, it might make sense to interpret the novel in terms of tense usage, even though it has already been interpreted from many other points of view.

The novel is set in Algeria during the colonial period. The narrator is also the "hero" of the novel, a young man named Meursault. Camus later called him "the only Christ we deserve."[26] We hear about various events. Meursault's mother has died in a home for the elderly. Meursault takes part in the funeral. Shortly afterwards he encounters a former mistress and takes up with her again. He helps a pimp out of trouble with the police by testifying for him. For Meursault these events are indifferent; he drifts through them as a stranger. His mother's death does not affect him, love does not penetrate his skin, and the company of the pimp neither pleases nor displeases him: "cela n'a aucune importance" (that has

---

24. Arne Klum, *Verbe et adverbe* (Stockholm: Almqvist & Viksell, 1961), 170.
25. Robert Champigny, "Notes sur les temps passés en français," *The French Review* 28, no. 6 (1955): 524.
26. Avant-Propos of the 1955 edition.

no importance).²⁷ On a Sunday excursion to the beach he is harassed and threatened by a group of Arabs. The sun burns in the sky. Meursault shoots one of the men. He is arrested. Approximately a year later he is tried. During the trial, which, ironically, sums up his fate, Meursault's indifference is confronted with the act of murder. All the events that Meursault has shrugged off as insignificant now become significant as moments of guilt. The prosecutor portrays the image of a brute without feelings, whose reprehensibility culminates in murder. Meursault is condemned to death. He awaits his execution in prison. He rejects the prison clergyman with scorn. The novel ends in the approach of death and at the border of tragedy.

Jean-Paul Sartre interpreted Camus's novel as a literary testimony of the absurd and juxtaposed it to the theory of the absurd in Camus's essay *Le mythe de Sisyphe* (1942, The Myth of Sisyphus). He also noticed a particular peculiarity in the language of the novel that he connects, incorrectly, to Hemingway:

> La phrase est nette, sans bavures, fermée sur soi; elle est séparée de la phrase suivante par un néant, comme l'instant de Descartes est séparé de l'instant qui le suit.²⁸ Entre chaque phrase et la suivante le monde s'anéantit et renaît: la parole dès qu'elle s'élève, est une création ex nihilo; une phrase de L'étranger c'est une île. Et nous cascadons de phrase en phrase, de néant en néant. C'est pour accentuer la solitude de chaque unité phrastique que M. Camus a choisi de faire son récit au parfait composé.²⁹

> The sentences are clear, without a blur, closed in on themselves; they are separated from the succeeding sentences by a void, as the instant in Descartes is separated from the instant that follows. Between each sentence and the next the world is destroyed and reborn: as soon as an utterance arises, it is a creation ex nihilo; a sentence in *L'étranger* is an island. And we tumble from sentence to sentence, from void to void. To accentuate the solitude of each phrasal unit, M. Camus has chosen to set his narrative in the parfait [i.e., passé] composé.

Thus Sartre sees even in the use of passé composé a literary sign of the absurd. Just as Meursault passes through the world as a loner and stranger

---

27. Albert Camus, *L'étranger* (Paris: Gallimard, 1957), 98.
28. Discontinuous Cartesian time differs from Bergson's stream of time referred to by Sartre shortly before.
29. Jean-Paul Sartre, "Explication de L'étranger," in *Situations I* (Paris: Gallimard, 1947), 117.

and is unable to connect the events of his life into a meaningful unity, so the sentences of the novel stand isolated from one another.

Did Camus choose passé composé as a symbol of absurdity? We know that Camus thought hard about tense usage for his novel.[30] I think, however, that his reflections took a different course. In his language consciousness passé simple led a strictly literary existence, as was generally the case in the twentieth century. In a novel where the protagonist-narrator is a man who watches his life as if it were a banal film, the literary passé simple could not be used. All the more since passé simple in first person is even less usable than in third person. Camus probably also thought about the sociological alignment of passé simple to the educated bourgeoisie and passé composé to the anonymous masses of the city. Meursault is a man of the masses, and as narrator in the novel he speaks as he speaks every day.

It was evidently not easy for Camus to slip into the reduced social role of the narrator. Maurice-Georges Barrier has noticed that despite his clear intention of avoiding the "literary" passé simple (we have seen that in the history of the language passé composé is just as "literary"), passé simple still sneaks in five times.[31] So do subjunctives of the imparfait, which otherwise count in French language consciousness as at least as literary and pedantic as passé simple. Apparently, it is not so simple in written narrative to do without a tense that exists for the very purpose.

For the modern writer passé composé is thus not the "natural" tense for a story, but passé simple is. In order to maintain passé composé for long stretches of the narrative, Camus had to do violence to his natural use of language. That can be seen in sentence after sentence. The language of the novel contains an unusually large accumulation of various temporal adverbs. Barrier has taken the trouble to count them, at least in the first part of the novel; in some seventy-nine small format pages he found no fewer than 166 adverbs, expressions such as: "alors, puis, ensuite, par la suite, peu à peu, un jour, aussitôt, pour finir, à ce mot, (un) peu après, encore, tout de suite, (assez) longtemps, d'abord, (juste, c'est) à ce moment, un (long) moment, à un moment après, ce moment, depuis un moment," etc. Barrier summarizes: The indications of time are numerous in the extreme. He criticizes Camus for "abusive utilization of temporal expressions." He considers it unnecessary to uninterruptedly emphasize

---

30. Roger Quilliot, *La mer et les prisons: Essais sur Albert Camus* (Paris: Gallimard, 1956), 86, n.1.

31. Maurice-Georges Barrier, *L'art du récit dans L'étranger d'Albert Camus* (Paris: A.G. Nizet, 1962), 10.

the time relationships in the plot and especially their simultaneity (14, 15, 107–8).

Barrier misunderstood. Camus has no interest in the temporal situation. But he does have to deal with a tense not designed for narration; anyone trying to narrate with it must reshape it. Consider this passage:

> La garde est entrée à ce moment. Le soir était tombé brusquement. Très vite, la nuit s'était épaissie au-dessus de la verrière. Le concierge a tourné le commutateur et j'ai été aveuglé par l'éclaboussement soudain de la lumière. Il m'a invité à me rendre au réfectoire pour dîner. Mais je n'avais pas faim. Il m'a offert alors d'apporter une tasse de café au lait. Comme j'aime beaucoup le café au lait, j'ai accepté et il est revenu un moment après avec un plateau. J'ai bu. J'ai eu alors envie de fumer. Mais j'ai hésité parce que je ne savais pas si je pouvais le faire devant maman. J'ai réfléchi, cela n'avait aucune importance. J'ai offert une cigarette au concierge et nous avons fumé.[32]

> Just then the nurse came in. Night had fallen suddenly. Darkness had gathered, quickly, above the skylight. The caretaker turned the switch and I was blinded by the sudden flash of light. He suggested I go to the dining hall for dinner. But I wasn't hungry. Then he offered to bring me a cup of coffee with milk. I like milk in my coffee, so I said yes, and he came back a few minutes later with a tray. I drank the coffee. Then I felt like having a smoke. But I hesitated, because I didn't know if I could do it with Maman right there. I thought about it; it didn't matter. I offered the caretaker a cigarette and we smoked.[33]

It may be observed in this passage that imparfait and passé composé are mixed no differently than imparfait and passé simple are mixed in a literary narrative. This is the structural framework into which passé composé enters, so that it already takes on a narrative character. In addition, this passage, and Camus's novel altogether, contain that unexpectedly large number of adverbs, and that especially in the sentences with the verb in passé composé. They serve not to fix temporal relations, which are here just as indifferent as everything else in the protagonist's thoughts. The adverbs are not adverbs determining time, even if they at first seem to be, but instead are adverbs of narrative succession. They are to be applied to the verbs in passé composé and they give the text a feeling of flowing narrative, which cannot otherwise be achieved with passé composé

---

32. Albert Camus, *L'étranger* (Paris: Gallimard, 1957), 15.
33. Albert Camus, *The Stranger,* trans. Matthew Ward (New York: Vintage, 1988), 8.

as the tense normally used for occasional looking back. We can understand these adverbs of narrative succession, since they recur insistently, as supplementary and not yet fully grammaticalized tense morphemes. That means: If the French language were like the language of this novel, we would have to distinguish between a passé composé as the retrospective tense of discussion and a passé composé enlarged by an "adverb" of narrative succession ("puis, alors" etc.) as a narrative tense. Of course, neither Camus's language nor the French language itself has gone so far as actually to split passé composé into two tenses. But the tendency is visible. It can also be identified in other languages under analogous conditions. Examples will be discussed shortly.

Sartre surely saw the isolating nature of passé composé correctly. Sentences in passé composé are indeed "islands." That is the characteristic of passé composé by its position in the totality of the tense system. But Camus's intention is not so clear as Sartre assumes. It appears rather that the inadequate flow of sentences in passé composé caused Camus substantial difficulties as he wrote. He reacted against that and tried to reestablish the flow not provided by the tenses with other means. Hence the obstinately repeated adverbs of narrative succession. His intention thus opposes the intention Sartre thought he had discovered. One has to admit, Camus's method of combining a discursive tense with adverbs of narrative succession into a new ("synthetic") narrative tense was successful. He was in fact able to write a novel with passé composé as the dominant tense. The stylistic generation of narrative flow is not, however, so effective that passé composé has become a passé simple. The gap between the sentences is not completely filled, and the novel still has the character caused by the tenses, that it tells a story *as if it discussed it*.

It is not right, however, even if only considering tense in *L'étranger*, to be blinded by the unusual use of passé composé and overlook the other tenses. It is not entirely true that the whole novel is written in passé composé. Two forms of narration work in parallel and sometimes interpenetrate. The opening of the novel does not narrate in passé composé, but in présent as the main tense:

> Aujourd'hui, maman est morte. Ou peut-être hier, je ne sais pas. J'ai reçu un télégramme de l'asile: "Mère décédée. Enterrement demain. Sentiments distingués." Cela ne veut rien dire. C'était peut-être hier.
>
> L'asile de vieillards est à Marengo, à quatre-vingts kilomètres d'Alger. Je prendrai l'autobus à deux heures et j'arriverai dans l'après-midi. Ainsi, je pourrai veiller et je rentrerai demain soir. (*L'étranger*, 7)

> Maman died today. Or yesterday maybe, I don't know. I got a telegram from the home: "Mother deceased. Funeral tomorrow. Faithfully yours." That doesn't mean anything. Maybe it was yesterday.
>
> The old people's home is at Marengo, about eighty kilometers from Algiers, I'll take the two o'clock bus and get there in the afternoon. That way I can be there for the vigil and come back tomorrow night. (*The Stranger*, 3)

We must not be deceived by the passé composé here. These are really the tenses of discussion. The narrator has his place in a linguistic situation. We must imagine his speech as talking to himself or as an unwritten diary. (Later Meursault says, "et j'ai compris que pendant tout ce temps j'avais parlé seul" [*L'étranger* 120; and I realized that all that time I had been talking to myself, *The Stranger* 81]). Meursault discusses with himself the situation brought about by the death of his mother. He looks back to the mother's death and the arrival of the telegram, and he looks ahead to his journey to the nursing home and his return from the funeral. At the same time, he reveals that he remains indifferent: "Cela ne veut rien dire" (That doesn't mean anything). In this manner of talking, passé composé corresponds to its normal place in the tense system as a retrospective tense of discussion and occupies its proper place in the tense system beside the dominant tense, présent, and the other discursive tenses. It does not replace any other tense here but stands only for itself. Furthermore, it occurs only occasionally.

Soon after the first sentences of the novel, however, Camus abandons the perspective just sketched and shifts abruptly to the narrative tenses, among which to be sure passé composé has replaced passé simple. This is a completely different tense-perspective. The following sentences come shortly after the ones just cited:

> J'ai pris l'autobus à deux heures. Il faisait très chaud. J'ai mangé au restaurant, chez Céleste, comme d'habitude. Ils avaient tous beaucoup de peine pour moi et Céleste m'a dit: "On n'a qu'une mère." Quand je suis parti, ils m'ont accompagné à la porte. J'étais un peu étourdi parce qu'il a fallu que je monte chez Emmanuel pour lui emprunter une cravate noire et un brassard. (*L'étranger*, 8)

> I caught the two o'clock bus. It was very hot. I ate at the restaurant, at Céleste's, as usual. Everybody felt very sorry for me, and Céleste said, "You only have one mother." When I left, they walked me to the door. I was a little distracted because I still had to go up to Emmanuel's place to borrow a black tie and an arm band. (*The Stranger*, 3–4)

In the first sentences the bus trip is still in the future. In these sentences, barely a page further, the bus trip is in the past. The temporal perspective has jumped forward. It is as if Meursault were beginning a new diary entry at a new time. And the temporal perspective continues to be set so that the events always lie just a little bit in the past. Later the distance from the narrated event becomes longer.[34] The issue is not the temporal distance; I do not assume that Camus chose his shifting temporal perspective at a short distance for the sake of the 24-hour rule. The decisive difference is that Meursault now narrates the events. Verbs in passé composé are no longer accompanied by tenses of discussion (présent, futur), but by narrative tenses (imparfait, plus-que-parfait). It is now a narrative tense and represents passé simple. Correspondingly, it alternates with imparfait, its background tense. In this way the narrative receives its normal highlighting.

This is now the dominant tense structure of the novel. Occasionally Camus falls back into the tenses of discussion. The fifth and final chapter of the novel, where we find Meursault on death-row, begins like the first chapter with présent as dominant tense and shifts after a few sentences into the narrative tenses. It is easy to read over the shift, and perhaps it remained invisible to the author himself. The invisibility of the shift derives from the fact that passé composé belongs to both tense groups in Camus's tense system. This is the switchpoint for the transitions. Here is the beginning of Chapter 5 to show how passé composé functions first as the retrospective discussion tense and then, in the context of a verb of communication, slides over into the other tense group:

> Pour la troisième fois, j'ai refusé de recevoir l'aumônier. Je n'ai rien à lui dire, je n'ai pas envie de parler, je le verrai bien assez tôt. Ce qui m'intéresse en ce moment, c'est d'échapper à la mécanique, de savoir si l'inévitable peut avoir une issue. On m'a changé de cellule. De celle-ci, lorsque je suis allongé, je vois le ciel et je ne vois que lui. Toutes mes journées se passent à regarder sur son visage le déclin des couleurs qui conduit le jour à la nuit. Couché, je passe les mains sous ma tête et j'attends. Je ne sais combien de fois je me suis demandé s'il y avait des exemples de condamnés à mort qui eussent échappé au mécanisme implacable, disparu avant l'exécution, rompu les cordons d'agents. Je me reprochais alors ... (*L'étranger*, 158)

---

34. Carl A. Viggiani, "Camus' *L'étranger*," *PMLA* 71, no. 5 (1956): 865–87, analyzes Camus's novel in terms of time but not of tense.

> For the third time I've refused to see the chaplain. I don't have anything to say to him; I don't feel like talking, and I'll be seeing him soon enough as it is. All I care about right now is escaping the machinery of justice, seeing if there's any way out of the inevitable. They've put me in a different cell. From this one, when I'm stretched out on my bunk, I see the sky and that's all I see. I spend my days watching how the dwindling of color turns day into night. Lying here, I put my hands behind my head and wait. I can't count the times I've wondered if there have ever been any instances of condemned men escaping the relentless machinery, disappearing before the execution or breaking through the cordon of police. Then I blamed myself.... (*The Stranger*, 108)

With the change of tense group at the switch-point of Camus's ambivalent passé composé, the description shifts at "Je ne sais combien de fois je me suis demandé" to a narration of his condition. The perspective of the presentation changes. It is signaled in Camus no longer by tense, but by the combination of tense and temporal adverb, most prominently in the sentence quoted earlier, "La garde est entrée à ce moment" (Just then the nurse came in). The narrative adverb determines the ambivalent tense here. The adverb "alors," too, that we find in the narrative part of this passage serves the same function for Camus. It refers to the narrated world and marks the narrative succession.

Apart from the rare passages written in the tenses of discussion, Camus actually succeeded in writing an entire novel with passé composé as the dominant tense.[35] That was possible not only because of numerous adverbs of narrative succession, but also because it was favored by the subject matter. The novel consists of two parts of approximately the same length. The first part contains the series of events that Meursault considers irrelevant to his existence, including the murder. The second part, located in the courtroom and the prison cell, shows how these things really do concern Meursault's body and life. The arrest of the murderer is the caesura. Everything that came before, not just the murder, becomes the object of the trial and is repeated in narration and discussion before the court. The novel thereby obtains a juridical tinge in all its events.

---

35. Jean Giono's novel *Regain*, identified by Wilbur Merrill Frohock ("Camus: Image, Influence and Sensibility," *Yale French Studies* 2, no. 1 [1949]: 91–99) as the model for Camus's use of tense, reverses the relationship. Usually, présent is the leading tense, and it yields to passé composé as lead tense only relatively infrequently.

I have pointed out now several times with regard to Maupassant and Pirandello that a court situation is essentially a discursive situation, even though it may contain narratives (of the criminal actions). What is narrated never stands, however, for itself and for its own sake, but serves rather to be immediately discussed and judged. Camus's novel is now focused on the trial as the center of the plot, insofar as the court acknowledges Meursault's previous life only as the prehistory of the murder. The meaning that Meursault has not himself given to his life is now replaced by the pseudo-meaning of an existence for crime: "le fil d'événements qui a conduit cet homme à tuer en pleine connaissance de cause" (*L'étranger*, 146; the course of events which led this man to kill with full knowledge of his actions, *The Stranger*, 100). Meursault's entire life is thus interpreted in juridical terms and reduced to a case. His life becomes the object of discussion. A narrative is thereby replaced by a protocol, demonstrated by the bureaucratic style, which Camus underlines in the representation of the trial to the point of caricature. Passé composé fits this mold better than any other tense. It is the penological tense par excellence. The public prosecutor does not narrate the life of the accused in his pleading; he discusses it. And hence he uses, as the passages given in direct speech make clear, passé composé as the tense of retrospective discussion: "Et l'on ne peut pas dire qu'il a agi sans se rendre compte de ce qu'il faisait" (*L'étranger*, 146; And no one can say that he acted without realizing what he was doing, *The Stranger*, 100). That implies no extenuating circumstances and the death sentence.

Meursault does not recognize his life in this distortion into a case: "En quelque sorte, on avait l'air de traiter cette affaire en dehors de moi" (*L'étranger*, 144; In a way, they seemed to be arguing the case as if it had nothing to do with me, *The Stranger*, 98). He experiences this trial also as a stranger. It has nothing to do with him. When the prosecutor begins to talk about his soul, he scarcely even listens:

> Il disait qu'il s'était penché sur elle [mon âme] et qu'il n'avait rien trouvé, messieurs les jurés. Il disait qu'à la vérité, je n'en avais point, d'âme, et que rien d'humain, et pas un des principes moraux qui gardent le coeur des hommes ne m'était accessible. "Sans doute, ajoutait-il, nous ne saurions le lui reprocher." (*L'étranger*, 148)

> He said that he had peered into it [my soul] and that he had found nothing, gentlemen of the jury. He said the truth was that I didn't have a soul and that nothing human, not one of the moral principles that govern men's hearts, was within my reach. "Of course," he added, "we cannot blame him." (*The Stranger*, 101)

In contrast to the prosecutor's passé composé, the accused as narrator uses imparfait as the tense of the narrative background. At the highpoint of the pleading the further talk of the public prosecutor, *qua* idle speculation, moves far away from him.

Oral Narration in French

These days the simple past is essentially dead in spoken French.[36] There are also areas of the written language in which this tense is, if not dead, at least very rare, including letters, diaries, newspapers, and all writing for the stage. It is no longer considered part of the fundamentals of French and no longer taught in beginning courses.[37] In modern plays, when it appears occasionally in dialogue, it serves primarily to establish the pedantry of a character.[38]

At times controversy about passé simple even has political consequences. Marcel Cohen takes a Marxist view of the development and asserts that passé simple is used principally by writers for elite readers. Writers for the masses, according to Cohen, use the same tenses used by the masses. It is inappropriate in the twentieth century to write in the manner of the seventeenth century. Cohen even argues, in a somewhat convoluted manner, that passé simple should be understood as the tense of the bourgeoisie and it should now yield finally to passé composé to open the way to a classless society.[39] Robert-Léon Wagner has stepped forward as a defender of passé simple with the slogan, "Pitié pour le français!" (Take

---

36. The French linguists Meillet and Dauzat confirm that they never use passé simple orally. They consider it "barbaric or pedantic." See Antoine Meillet, *Linguistique historique et linguistique générale* (Paris: E. Champion, 1921), 150, and Albert Dauzat, *Études*, 69.

37. Georges Gougenheim, René Michéa, Paul Rivenc, and Aurélien Sauvageot, *L'élaboration du français fondamental, 1er degré: Étude sur l'établissement d'un vocabulaire et d'une grammaire de base* (Paris: Didier, 1964), 213 ff.. Likewise, the passé antérieur (*j'eus chanté*), which is always covered by the following discussion though not mentioned separately.

38. Many years ago, Stephen Ullmann, "Le passé défini et l'imparfait du subjonctif dans le théâtre contemporain," *Le français moderne* 6, no. 4 (1938): 351–52, counted passé simple forms in modern plays and found no fewer than eleven plays without a single passé simple. Jules Romains's *Knock* as well as Sacha Guitry's plays *Mariette* and *Un sujet de roman* are among them. In other plays the frequency of passé simple is very low.

39. More detail in Marcel Cohen, *Grammaire et style, 1450–1950. Cinq cents ans de phrase française* (Paris: Éditions Sociales, 1954), and "Emploi du passé simple et du passé composé dans la prose contemporaine," *Travaux de l'Institut de Linguistique de Paris* 1 (1956): 43–62.

pity on French!). On the other hand, it is also said that the disappearance of passé simple is not so terrible. It is, after all, being "replaced" by passé composé, according to Gamillscheg, Sten, and Strohmeyer.[40] This view evidently proceeds from the assumption that the French language has several "past tenses," of which now one, but really only one, is disappearing from the spoken language. Many other past tenses are still left, and they ought to suffice.

In the theory of tense expounded in this book the connections necessarily look different. Since the simple past is understood here strictly as a narrative tense, its disappearance from the spoken language requires us to ask how people now narrate orally. Or do they no longer narrate "correctly"? Such claims have been advanced in the framework of cultural and social criticism. Walter Benjamin, for example, expresses the opinion that modern society has forgotten how to narrate.[41] For him the cause is the general flood of information in which we live. Theodor W. Adorno goes even a step further to claim, "it is no longer possible to narrate today."[42] Narration means for him to have something special to tell, and exactly that, for Adorno, is "prevented by the administered world, by standardization and eternal sameness."[43] Such observations are surely true, insofar as oral narration, at least in the structured form of "real" storytelling, has lost much of its earlier importance in modern urban society and its media. The discursive exchange of information from the day's work has taken over the evening as well and displaced the storytelling circle. Storytelling has retreated to the space of belles lettres, where it continues to reign undisputed in the form of the novel and perhaps is stronger than ever. Is that a compensation?

A real oral narrative literature such as existed in the Middle Ages no longer exists, although it would be conceivable given modern news media. To

---

40. Robert-Léon Wagner, "Pitié pour le français!" *Mercure de France*, Sept.–Dec. 1955: 41; Ernst Gamillscheg, "Das sogenannte imparfait historique," in *Im Dienste der Sprache: Festschrift für Victor Klemperer zum 75. Geburtstag am 9. Oktober 1956*, ed. Horst Heintze und Erwin Silzer (Tübingen: Niemeyer, 1958), 272; Holger Sten, *Les temps du verbe fini (indicatif) en français moderne* (Copenhagen: Munksgaard, 1964), 124; and F. Strohmeyer, "Das Passé simple," 481.

41. Walter Benjamin, "The Storyteller: Reflections on the Work of Nikolai Leskov," in *The Storyteller*, ed. Samuel Titan, trans. Tess Lewis (New York: New York Review Books, 2019), 54.

42. Theodor W. Adorno, "The Position of the Narrator in the Contemporary Novel," in *Notes to Literature*, ed. Rolf Tiedemann, trans. Shierry Weber-Nicholsen (New York: Columbia UP, 2019), 30–31.

43. Ibid., and see also Roland Harweg, "Textanfänge in geschriebener und in gesprochener Sprache," *Orbis* 17 (1968): 343–88.

be sure, we still narrate when something special happens to us. But these are usually fragmentary and isolated stories, which have little independent substance as texts and only barely differentiate themselves from discursive speech. On the other hand, the information that Walter Benjamin made responsible for displacing narration is itself of a narrative nature. One look at the newspapers suffices to see to what extent the information presented there is constituted of events, processes, occurrences or chains of occurrences that must be told as such in order even to become the subjects of discussion.[44] Accordingly, German announcers often use Imperfekt in radio and television, English announcers use preterit, and only French announcers avoid passé simple.

So, how do people tell stories in spoken French once passé simple is no longer available as a narrative tense? The question must once again, of course, be asked of texts. I begin with a small text from a radio interview excerpted by Hans-Wilhelm Klein for phonetic purposes. It deals with the theft of a treatise about chess, and the victim describes the course of events:

> Eh bien, j'ai consacré dix années de ma vie à rédiger un traité de dames. Je suis un spécialiste. Ce traité comprenait des centaines et des centaines de problèmes et d'analyses, des dessins, une couverture en couleurs, il était relié par un excellent relieur—il a été premier ouvrier de France—et il pesait environ un kilo. Je le sortais pour la première fois, lundi, et je le proposais à un éditeur. Je l'avais dans une vieille serviette délabrée, et j'empruntais le métro, le métro en direction de la porte d'Orléans. Sur la station de métro débouchent deux escaliers de correspondance, et j'étais adossé contre l'un de ces escaliers, face aux rails, et, tout à coup, je sens qu'on tire, qu'on tâte ma serviette, et d'un seul coup, comme j'avais le dos tourné, on me l'arrache de la main qui tenait la serviette par la poignée. J'ai failli tomber à la renverse. Je suis malade. Un filou m'a arraché donc cette serviette alors que j'allais chez l'éditeur, tout réjoui, satisfait d'avoir enfin terminé ce travail prodigieux.[45]

> Well, I devoted ten years of my life to writing a treatise on chess. I am an expert. This treatise contained hundreds and hundreds of problems and analyses, illustrations, a colored cover, it was bound

---

44. Further thoughts on this topic in my "Tempus-Probleme eines Leitartikels," *Euphorion* 60 (1966): 263–72.

45. Hans-Wilhelm Klein, *Phonetik und Phonologie des heutigen Französisch* (Munich: Max Hueber, 1963), 176.

by an excellent binder—he was the best in France—and it weighed about a kilo. I was taking it out for the first time, on Monday, and I was offering it to a publisher. I had it put in into a worn-out briefcase, and I was taking the Metro, the Metro toward Porte d'Orleans. At the station there are two stairways connecting the lines, and I was leaning against one of them, facing the rails, and all of a sudden, I feel someone pulling, feeling my briefcase, and all at once, while I had my back turned, someone grabs my hand holding the briefcase by the handle. I almost fell backward. I am sick. So a thief grabbed this briefcase while I was going to the publisher, overjoyed, satisfied at finally finishing this enormous work.

This narrative may perhaps be considered representative for oral narration. There is not a single passé simple here. And yet a narrative structure is still present. After a few sentences of exposition, probably responding to the interviewer's question, the real story begins with an imparfait ("comprenait"). That is the narrative background, since the briefcase has not yet been stolen. The foreground action is clearly established by the theme of the story as the act of the theft. Its start is marked by the signal "tout à coup." With this signal the tense also changes. The background imparfait gives way to a foreground tense, présent ("je sens qu'on tire"), but continues to function as background tense in the smaller structure within sentences. At the end of the foreground action the sad event is summarized. That is to be considered a discursive insert ("je suis malade" no longer narrates the theft), and then the last sentence ("alors que j'allais") has the conclusion in imparfait, a pattern familiar from other narratives. To summarize: The sequence of tenses imparfait—passé simple—imparfait as the large-scale structure of written narrative corresponds here to a large-scale structure of oral narrative in the sequence imparfait—présent—imparfait.

This is, however, a relatively organized narrative, such as we do not routinely find in spoken language. I turn instead to another oral text that diverges much more strikingly from the norms of written language. This is an excerpt from the text M 25 of the CREDIF corpus, which was recorded with a twenty-year-old railroad employee.[46] It deals with an adventure while on vacation and reads:

> Alors, c'était un soir de congé. Deux cheftaines étaient en congé, alors on avait décidé d'aller aux Sables-d'Olonne et alors on était parti en

---

46. The text is reprinted and interpreted from a different point of view in Elisabeth Gülich, *Makrosyntax der Gliederungssignale im gesprochenen Französisch* (Munich: Fink, 1970), Appendix A, 23–24.

car. Et même déjà dans le car on s'était amusé parce qu'on préparait une . . . on préparait une espèce de veillée, la fête du directeur était le lendemain, je crois. On avait fait une chanson avec des paroles adaptées, on s'était bien amusé. Alors donc on était allé passer la journée là-bas, puis le soir on avait . . . on avait manqué le car, oui. Le car devait partir vers cinq heures, on s'était pas arrangé pour y être à temps, on avait manqué le car. Alors on se dit: "Il faut absolument rentrer ce soir à la colonie." Evidemment on aurait pu . . . on aurait pu rester à la colonie des garçons qui était aux Sables-d'Olonne, mais enfin il fallait rentrer à la colonie, quoi. Alors on a décidé de faire du stop. On part sur la route qui . . . qui allait vers la Faute, quoi, et puis on essaie d'arrêter des voitures. Mais c'est pas ça: tantôt elles étaient pleines, tantôt c'étaient rien que des messieurs, alors on n'osait pas trop. Ou bien alors . . . ou bien alors . . . ils s'arrêtaient tout de suite, mais ils n'allaient pas à la Faute. On a fait un grand bout à pied, on n'arrivait pas à trouver quelqu'un. Et puis on était en train de se demander si on continuerait ou non, parce qu'on avait déjà fait un bon bout. "Mais si on trouve rien, il vaut autant rester aux Sables-d'Olonne." Enfin, on s'est obstiné quand même. Et puis on avait arrêté une petite fourgonnette. Elle s'arrête, un monsieur descend et nous dit: "Bien! montez derrière." Y avait sa femme et puis un tout petit bébé. Alors il nous a fait monter derrière; il nous a emmenées jusqu'à . . . c'était à peine la moitié du chemin. Mais on s'est dit: "C'est que . . . c'est pas tout! Mais il faut trouver quelque chose pour continuer," parce que c'était en pleine nature. Y avait absolument rien. Alors à la (?), on se met à nouveau au croisement des chemins, parce que là y avait deux . . . deux routes possibles, une qui allait sur la Faute et puis une qui allait . . . Je ne sais plus, sur une autre direction. Alors on s'est mis sur la route de la Faute, et puis on attendait. Puis, c'est que là, alors, c'était un petit chemin, c'était vraiment un petit chemin. La route est à peine . . . elle est . . . mais elle est pas très fréquentée. Alors on commençait à désespérer. On arrête . . ., on a arrêté plusieurs voitures qui s'arrêtaient toutes . . . presque toutes tout de suite, ou qui tournaient, ou alors . . . Enfin y en a une qui s'arrête. Elle était pleine, mais pleine. Et puis on . . . Elle s'arrête. Puis ils nous ont fait monter derrière. On avait juste une toute petite place, et on était deux, oui. Les deux dames avaient déjà trois ou quatre gosses. Y avait . . . ils étaient étendus dans des espèces de lits. C'était une fourgonnette aussi. Et puis . . . y avait trois dames, et puis un . . . un jeune homme; et puis devant y avait deux messieurs: c'étaient les maris des dames, je pense. Alors on s'est mis dans un coin pour ne pas tenir trop de place, parce qu'elles nous faisaient un peu des sales yeux! Et puis au bout d'un moment alors . . . et elles avaient pas l'air contentes du tout . . . on a commencé à lier conversation un peu, parce que c'était pas drôle de se regarder comme ça. Alors on leur a parlé un peu. Alors y en a une qui me dit: "Je ne vois vraiment pas pourquoi mon mari s'est arrêté. Eh bien oui. D'habitude, vous savez . . . Vous avez eu beaucoup de chance qu'il vous prenne." C'était une chance parce qu'autrement! . . . Et ils habitaient juste à côté de la colonie, ils étaient en vacances à la Faute. Alors on est arrivé en même temps que le car, et c'est bien simple, puisque y avait plusieurs équipes qui étaient venues nous attendre au car, on les a retrouvées là-bas en même temps que le car. C'était une chance parce que vraiment, y avait pas beaucoup d'autos qui passaient pour aller à la Faute. Y avait bien dans l'autre direction parce qu'il y a des villes plus importantes dans l'autre côté. Tandis que vers la Faute, y avait pas grand chose.

So, it was a holiday eve. Two troop leaders were on vacation, so we had decided to go to Sables d'Olonne and then we had left in a coach. And even in the coach we were already having a blast because we were preparing a . . . .we were preparing a kind of vigil, the director's birthday was the next day, I think. We had cooked up a song with the lyrics adapted, we were having a great time. Then we had gone to spend the day down there, then in the evening we had . . . we had missed the coach, yes. The coach was supposed to leave around five, we hadn't arranged to be there on time, we missed the coach. So then we said, "we absolutely have to get back to camp this evening." Of course, we could have . . . we could have stayed in the boys' camp which was at Sables d'Olonne, but finally we had to get back to camp. So we decided to hitchhike. We left on the road that . . . that went toward La Faute, and then we tried to stop some cars. But no good: sometimes they were full, sometimes it was only men, and we didn't want to risk it. Or else . . . or else it was . . . or else they stopped right away, but they weren't going to La Faute. We did a big piece on foot, without managing to find anyone. And then we were starting to wonder if we should keep going or not, since we had already done a good bit. "But if we don't find anything, we might as well stay at Sables d'Olonne." Finally, we decided to plug away. And then, we stopped a minivan. It stops, a gentleman gets off and says to us, "Swell! Climb in back." There was his wife and then a tiny baby. So we had to climb in back; he brought us to . . . It was barely halfway. But we said: "It's . . . It's not the whole way! But we have to find something to keep going," because it was in wide open county. There wasn't a thing there. So, at (?) we stood at another intersection, because there there were two . . . two possible roads, one that went to La Faute and then one that went . . . I don't remember any more, in some other direction. So we got on the road to La Faute, and then we waited. Then the thing is that there it was a small road, really small. The road is hardly . . . it is . . . but there's hardly any traffic on it. So we started to get really discouraged, we stop . . . we stopped several cars that all stopped . . . almost all of them right away, or they turned, or else . . . Finally one did stop. It was chock full. And then we . . . It stops. And then they had us climb in back. There was hardly any room, and there were two of us, yes. The two ladies had three or four kids. There was . . . they were stretched out in some kind of beds. It was another van. And then . . . there were three ladies, and then . . . a young man; and then in front there were two gentlemen: they were the ladies' husbands, I think. So we squeezed into a corner so as not to take up too much room, because they were sort of glaring at us! And then in a moment . . . and they seemed to be really happy . . . we started to gab a bit because it wasn't fun to be stared at like that. So we talked to them a little. Then one of the ladies says to me: "I really have no idea why my husband stopped. Really not. Usually, you know . . . You're really in luck that he picked you up." It really was good luck because otherwise! . . . And they lived right next to the camp, they were on holiday in La Faute. So we got there just when the coach did, it was really simple, because several groups were there that had come to wait for us at the coach, we found them down there at the same time as the coach. It was lucky because really there weren't many cars that passed going to La Faute. There were a bunch in the other direction because there are some big towns the other way. But not much towards La Faute.

First some statistics. The text includes the following tenses: imparfait 53, plus-que-parfait 13, second conditionnel 2, présent 26, passé composé 19. There are thus sixty-eight forms of the narrative tenses and forty-five from the discursive register. This result may be considered the first indicator that the text can still be reasonably considered a narrative, even though it corresponds so little to the poetics of literary narrative.

Furthermore, these tenses are all mixed together, not only the individual tenses, but also the discursive and narrative registers. Since passé simple is entirely absent, it seems likely that its functions have been taken over by other French tenses. The previous passage already suggests that the functions of passé simple have not consistently been transferred to passé composé. Instead, passé composé and présent share the old tasks of passé simple, and the question now is whether any specific patterns can be discovered. In general, it can be said that passé composé is more common in fragmentary and isolated passages and présent in longer and more consistent ones. (This is different from *L'étranger*). The usage reflects that passé composé in French is a retrospective tense (information after the fact). A look back is normally taken only occasionally. Thus, by nature of its place in the system of tenses, passé composé is not a good tense for lining things up. In that respect it is different from présent, imparfait, and passé simple, which look neither forward nor back and hence are automatically appropriate for lining things up and, with this quality, can undertake an important role in constituting a text, namely promoting consistency.

Given, now, that even in this text, despite the absence of passé simple, the narrative tenses occur about a third more frequently than the discursive ones, it must be the case that the differences in this text from written narrative texts relate only to the function of the narrative foreground. The background of the narration, expressed in imparfait, remains intact. The structure I have called highlighting—the particular conditions of transition between imparfait and passé simple in written narrative—thus remains as it was, except that it now continues between imparfait and either présent or passé composé. Under these changed conditions, to the extent that présent and passé composé take over the tasks of passé simple, highlighting remains an important signal for recognizing the structure of the narrative.

In this context we should also consider the interaction of adverbial expressions as connectors in the narrative sequence, or as "macro-syntactic organizing signals" in Elisabeth Gülich's sense in relation to tense; she has already analyzed the passage above in this respect. For the current argument it is perhaps sufficient to point to the frequency of the two temporal adverbs "puis" and "alors" (alone and combined) in oral texts. The passage above contains no fewer than thirteen occurrences of "puis" and twenty-one of "alors." These are remarkably high frequencies. The signal "puis" occurs as frequently as the plus-que-parfait, and "alors" more frequently than the passé composé! It is clearly vital to take temporal adverbs into account when analyzing the constitution of texts. That must be true for texts of any sort, oral and written. But it is now evident that connectors of this sort appear with much higher frequency in spoken language. In this passage the frequencies of the adverbs "puis" and "alors," as well as the others that haven't been discussed, are, taken together, almost as high as the total number of tense forms in the text. Under these circumstances it cannot be claimed that macro-syntactic signals can be distinguished as not recurrent from micro-syntactic signals, which are recurrent. Instead, macro-syntactic signals also share the tendency to obstinate repetition discussed in Chapter 1. With this quality they have a significant impact on tense functioning and must always be considered in a linguistic analysis of tense.

A Parallel: Tense in South-German Dialects

The tense-system of the South German dialects makes an ascetic impression. They have significantly fewer tenses than the written language, in that they lack a Präteritum and a Plusquamperfekt. The Präteritum border runs roughly from Trier via Frankfurt and Plauen toward the southeast border of Silesia.[47] Only the Präteritum form *war* (was) can be found widely used in the South-German dialects. Kaj B. Lindgren's excellent monograph on this phenomenon is not only convincing, but is also masterful in its virtuosic control of statistical method. I have adopted his results without restriction, shall describe them briefly, and extend them to show their relationship to the disappearance of the French passé simple.

Lindgren convincingly locates the historical borders of the phenomenon. First, he demonstrates that no weakening of the Präteritum is observable in Middle High German, even in the southern area. It has the same distribution of tenses as is found in North German dialects today and as also in written German. This agreement is complete until around 1450. In the second half of the fifteenth century, South German texts increasingly use Perfekt. Then, around 1535, Präteritum disappears very abruptly from the dialect texts of South Germany. Of course, we are unable to tell whether this tense (and with it Plusquamperfekt) disappeared just as quickly in the spoken language.[48] Lindgren thinks it disappeared in speaking somewhat earlier and somewhat less suddenly, but that can only

---

47. For an exact description of the language boundary see Kurt Jacki, "Das starke Präteritum in den Mundarten des hochdeutschen Sprachgebietes," *Beiträge zur Geschichte der deutschen Sprache und Literatur* 34 (1909): 425–529; Friedrich Maurer, *Untersuchungen über die deutsche Verbstellung in ihrer geschichtlichen Entwicklung* (Heidelberg: Winter, 1926), 22–23; and Kai B. Lindgren, *Über den oberdeutschen Präteritumschwund* (Helsinki: Acta Academiae Scientiarum Fennica, 1957), 44–45.

48. South German dialects partly transfer the function of the Präteritum to a "double perfect" (*ich habe gesungen gehabt*), completely analogous to the French *formes surcomposées*. See Lindgren, *Über den oberdeutschen Präteritumschwund*, 104, and Maurice Cornu, *Les formes surcomposées en français* (Bern: A. Francke, 1953).

be guessed. The remarkable fact remains that the dialect texts in concert around 1535—the time can apparently be determined that precisely—reveal a crisis of the tense system. Lindgren reflects on the reasons and attributes the loss of Präteritum to the phonetic collapse of the third person singular of weak verbs in Präsens (*er sagt*) and in Präteritum (*er sagte*). In effect, the language reacts to a morphological emergency by reorganizing the whole tense system.

Lindgren's results are equally interesting for describing the structure of the language. Although he holds fast to the association of tenses with time, he nevertheless sees that Präteritum in German is a narrative tense and that Perfekt is not. Thus, the often-repeated assertion of Behaghel that another past tense, Perfekt, replaced Präteritum in German dialects can hardly seem convincing (272). A narrative tense cannot be readily exchanged for a different category of tense. So, Lindgren asks himself how people actually narrate in South German dialects, and he has confirmation from dialect speakers "that it somehow feels wrong to tell a continuing narrative entirely in the Perfekt." People mostly narrate not in Perfekt but in Präsens.[49]

I am not prepared, however, to adopt Lindgren's conclusion that Präsens in South German dialects should be considered "an—at least inauthentic—past-tense form" (Lindgren, 98). Lindgren himself points out that most narratives of any length in South German dialects do not remain in Präsens from beginning to end. They open the story, rather, with Perfekt. Then the narrative jumps, with the actual plot, at the latest with the main plot, into Präsens, and often ends with a few sentences in Perfekt to close off. The Präsens narrative is thus framed with forms of Perfekt. A narrative can be identified by the sequence Perfekt—Präsens—Perfekt because the structure of a story can be recognized by the elements of introduction—body of the narrative—conclusion. The tenses, we see here again clearly, have relationships that extend beyond single sentences and relate to the entire text. In specific sequences they thus form textual macro-structures.

This is at bottom the structural model "until further notice" that we saw earlier with letter writing and musical scores. Opening a story with Perfekt invites looking back, then the language jumps, without the intended object changing, into Präsens and thereby changes the orientation. This change in perspective while the object remains the same (thus

---

49. Lindgren, *Über den oberdeutschen Präteritumschwund*, 98 ff., 105. Hans Weber, *Das Tempussystem des Deutschen und des Französischen* (Bern: Francke, 1954), 116, had already pointed this out briefly.

differently from the occasional look-back at something else in a discussion) is interpreted as the signal for the beginning of the real story and is now valid "until further notice," namely until the signal is turned off by a verb in Perfekt that closes the story.

However, one question still remains open in this presentation of the disappearance of Präteritum in the South German dialects. Lindgren locates the ebbing of Präteritum in the early sixteenth century primarily by the increase of Perfekt in dialect texts, yet he shows impressively that people today mostly tell stories in Präsens in South Germany, Austria, and German-speaking Switzerland. Both are true. It must be added, however, analogously to the situation in French, that Perfekt can also function as a narrative tense under certain conditions. These conditions are present in French when the incapacity of passé composé to establish a narrative flow is neutralized. That takes place both through alternation with the background tense, imparfait, and in spoken language, through massive use of adverbs of narrative flow. In the South German dialects, the first condition is not present, because the neutral position of tense group II was occupied from the beginning only by the single tense, Präteritum. When this tense disappears, no other narrative tense remains intact next to it. But the second condition can be met in the South German dialects. And we find in fact in South German narrative texts, analogous to the many *puis* and *alors* of French, a Perfekt combined with adverbs of narrative flow into a new, "synthetic" narrative tense. As far as I can tell, it is mainly the adverbs *da, nun, jetzt* (then, and now, now)—naturally in different wording depending on the dialect.

Already in one of the earliest texts without Präteritum—an Augsburg chronicle from around 1550 reprinted by Lindgren as an example—I notice an unusual accumulation of *und* and *da* (and, then) as sequential signals:[50]

> Item adj. 22 mai hat Anthoni Fugger zuo sant Moritzen am auffart tag ein hergotzbild machen lassen, aim gantzen rath und gemeiner stat zuowider den götzn aufgeführt mitsambt den pfaffen, und haben das loch auf der bin unterm dach, so verschlagen gewesen, on ains raths wissen und willen, auch on die zechmaister Marx Echen un N. wider aufprochen und das pild hinauf zogen. da ist der vogt und Marx Echem und die statknecht kumen und haben das pild mitsambt den engeln zum himel herab geworfen und gestossen, dass den engeln der

---

50. *Die Chronik des Augsburger Malers Georg Preu des Älteren, 1512–37*. Cited from Lindgren, *Über den oberdeutschen Präteritumschwund*, 61. Lindgren dates the manuscript to 1550.

hergot ist zuo schwer worden und seien alle zerfallen. da haben sich die Fugger und die pfaffen hinaus gemacht, dass nit der teufel hernach komme. da ist ein gross gedem worden von der auffart.

Item adj. May 22: Anthony Fugger had an image of Our Lord made for the church of St. Moritz for Ascension Day. In opposition to the entire council and the rest of the town he, together with the priests, had the idol mounted and so damaged the opening under the roof, without the knowledge of the council and against its will, and then without the sextons Marx Echen and N. they broke in again and hauled the image up. The sheriff and Marx Echem and their men came and threw down the image with the angels carrying Him to heaven and smashed it, so that God became too heavy for the angels and they all fell. Then the Fuggers and the priests took off, so that the devil wouldn't catch them. That made a big hullabaloo of Ascension Day.[51]

It is not important, now, to decide exactly which linguistic elements should be understood to be contributing to narrative sequencing. Depending on the text, the most varied elements might contribute to the flow of the narrative.

In more recent dialect narratives, the macro-syntactic organizing signals serving the narrative flow are easier to recognize. Here is an example, a recent Swabian fable, "The Death of the Chicken":

s ischt a'môl a' Hühnle und a' Gockeler gwä, der Gockeler ischts Ma'le gwä' und s Hühnle sei' Weible. Dia beide sind a'môl spaziera ganga und sind an a' Wasser komma und *dô* ischt a Brückle nüber ganga. *Dô* hôt s Ma'le zum Weible gseit: "Gang du zerschta, i komm dann nôcher!" —*Dô* sait s Weible: "Gang du no zerschta, du bischt stärker als i!"—*Dô* sait s Ma'le: "Noi, du muaßt zerschta nüber!"—"Ach, i fürcht miar!" sait s Weible. "O, s geschieht dir nex, gang du no nüber!" sait s Ma'le; und *dô* hôts des Weible gwôgt und hôt wölle nüber gauh', ischt aber ins Wasser gfalla.

Dô ischt des Ma'le hi'gloffa und hôt en Schubkarra gholt und wias da' Karra über d Strôß schiabt, *dô* sind Ratta-n- und Mäus und Hasan- und Reh und älles Vieh zua-n- em komma und hent gsait: "Därf i au mit?"—*Dô* hats Ma'le gsait: "Älles dôher, älls dôher!" und hôt älles aufsitza lau' und hôts mitgnomma, and *dô* hent se mitanander des Weible aus em Wasser zoga; *dô* ischts aber todt gwä'. *Nô* hent ses uf d' Karra glada und send mit fortgfahra und hents uf de nächscht

---

51. Our thanks to Annegret Oehme for help with this translation.

Mischte vergraba. *Dô hôt der Gockeler d Leichared ghalta: "Kikeriki! Kikeriki!" und de andere Tiarle hent derzua gsunga.*[52]

There was once a hen and a rooster, the rooster was the husband and the hen his wife. Once the two went for a walk and came to a stream and there was a bridge going over it. Then the husband said to the wife, "You go first, then I'll come after!" Then the wife says, "You go first now, you are stronger than I am!" Then the husband says, "No, you must cross first!" "Ah, I am afraid!" says the wife. "Oh, nothing will happen to you, go on over now!" says the husband; and then the wife dared to do it and wanted to go over, but she fell into the water.

Then the husband ran and fetched a wheelbarrow, and as he pushes the barrow down the street along came rats and mice and rabbits and deer and all the other animals to him and asked, "May I come along?" Then the husband said, "Everyone come along, everyone come along!" and had them all climb in and took them along, and then all together they pulled the wife out of the water; but she was dead. And then they loaded her onto the barrow and went along further and buried her in the nearest manure heap. Then the rooster delivered the funeral oration, "Kikeriki! Kikeriki!" and the other animals sang along.

This fable, apart from a few Präsens forms in the frame of the short dialogue is narrated in Perfekt. It is possible here because the sequencing adverbs (*dô, und dô, nô*), to which one might add *und*, which links verbs ten times, are used so frequently that one here, even more than in French, is tempted to see Perfekt with the connectors as forming a new narrative tense in the South German dialects.

For comparison, here is a nineteenth-century legend from the Lavant Valley in Austria:

Jo, segn Sö! dos is amol olls Wossa gwesen, do drin hot's unsinnige Fisch geben. Do sein drei Brüader gwesen, recht niederträchtige Herrn: der aani hot z'Hartneidstaan, glei do unten bei der Olm; der indri drentn z'Reisberg; und der dritte z'Rabenstaan, dort in segn oltn Gschlooß, gwohat. No! daß i's recht sog: Do sein s holt werawonn zsammaskemman zan daschgariern. Hiatz is amol der Reisberger ba-n-an z'Hartneidstaan gwesen (i maan, sö ham a Sau-Tag ghabt, wia mein Ahnga verzählt hot); und dawaal is a Wetta keman

---

52. From Gustav Seuffer and Richard Weitrecht, eds., *s Schwobaland in Lied und Wort* (Ulm: Ebner, 1885), 628.

und 's hot scho' o'gehebt z'himmlazn. Der aani hot ober do haam zu seiner Olten wölln und is lei undla in die Zilln gstiegn und in See eini gfohrn. Ober—i waaß nit: hond se so greagerisch grudert, oder hot ihnen s Zoaderle die Zilln umgschmissn—dasoffen seind se amol gwiß. No! daß i sog: Wia sie holt nimmer hinter keman sein, so hebt sei on z'lamatiern, und is schier z'resoniert gwaorden. Z'morgenst is wieer olls blob gwesn, und di Sunn hot aa wider hegeglitzt; do sei o'ghebt z'beten und hot unsern Herrgott a Kiarchn verhoaßn, wann sie die zwean wieder bekennat, daß die Fisch nit fraaßn. Hiatz hamd se noch in See oblossn, obi in die Drog; und wia sie zan Bodn kemman, do leit der Olte zsoommt n Buabm. No! daß i sog! Hiatz ist die Wittib faindla maachti gwesn, hot gleich a Leich und a Gstattung ghaltn, hot die Lotterleut betoalt—siis is se lei hisch kluag gwesn—, und d Kiarchn hot s aa baut. Dos is amal gwiiß: Wann die swoa nit dasoffa waarn, so kinnat mar noh ins Wasser iachi schaugn.[53]

Well, look here. That was once all water. There were lots of fish in it. There were three brothers, pretty nasty gentlemen: one lived near Hartneidstein, right down there by that pasture; the second lived over there near the Reisberg; and the third lived at Rabenstein, in his old castle there. No, so that I tell you right: so they just got together once in a while to chat. So once the one from Reisberger was visiting the one at Hartneitstein (I mean they were having a drinking bout, as my grandsire told it); and then a thunderstorm came up and the lightning started already. The first one wanted to go home to his old woman and went right down into his barge and pushed out into the lake. But—I don't know: it they rowed too wildly or it the water-spirit knocked their barge over—they certainly drowned. Oh yeah, so I tell you: When they didn't come home, she starts to moan and gets very worried. The next day the weather was calm again and the sun came out too; then she started to pray and promised a church to Our Lord if she got the two of them back so that the fish wouldn't eat them. Now they let the water out of the lake, down into the Drog; and when they get to the bottom, there's the old man lying there with the boy. So no! that I tell you! Now the widow was very decisive, held a funeral right away. Paid the poor people—so that was probably very smart—and she built the church too. So one thing is certain: if the two hadn't drowned, you could still see the water.[54]

---

53. Walther Wachinger, ed., *Fleckerlteppich, ein bairisch-österreichisches Mundart-Lesebuch*, (Ebenhausen bei München: Langewiesche-Brandt, 1959), 220.

54. Thanks to Barbara Thiem for this translation.

The story reveals itself clearly as an oral narrative, or at least tries to give this impression. The adverbs of narrative sequencing (especially *do, no, hiatz*) are, if possible, piled up even more strongly than in the Swabian fable. Almost every verb is bound in this way to the next. Perfekt is just as isolated as a looking back tense in German as passé composé in French and here, too, has its perspective neutralized and can serve as a perspective-less narrative tense.

This is not to be thought of as poor style and undisciplined narration. The view is also unjustified when we observe that the language of children also favors connection with *und, und da, und dann* (French *puis, et puis, et puis alors*). In the language of inexperienced narrators, we find this "childlike" style again. But the analogy is only right when we interpret it. So, I offer a few sentences of children's language, transcribed by the already named psychologists, the Sterns, from their just four-year-old daughter:

> De Köchin hat se schaukeln lassen hier de Lampe, *da* ist se paput (=kaputt) gegangen. (Zwischenfrage des Vaters: Hier unsere Lampe?) Nee, sieh mal von den Hühnereßzimmer, *da* is das Brennlicht hier oben paput gegangen, *da* is so die Scheibe von den Brennlicht paput gegangen; der Strumpf auch paput und de Klingel gar nicht paput, *da* haben wir schon wieder so was Neues reingeholen.[55]

> The cook shook the lamp here, then it broke. (Question from the father: Our lamp here?) No, look, from the chicken-dining-room, there the light up here has broken, there the chimney of the light has broken; the mantle is also broken and the bell not broken at all, then we brought in something new.

The family speaks high German. The child is learning narrative tenses at about this time. In this little scene she recounts a household occurrence without narrative tenses and uses Perfekt. But she transforms Perfekt instinctively into a narrative tense with the sequencing adverb *da*. It does for her little speech exactly what the South German dialects do among adults. That is the analogy between the and-then style of children's language and the and-then style of dialect narratives. But one cannot draw from this the conclusion that dialect narratives are more childish than comparable narratives in standard German. They have only in common that they do not (the dialects no longer, the children's language not

---

55. Clara and Wilhelm Stern, *Die Kindersprache* (Leipzig: Barth, 1928), 77.

yet) have at their disposal the narrative tenses and that they therefore "synthesize" a new narrative tense from Perfekt and sequencing adverbs. South German dialect narrators are no more childlike than is Camus's.

When German dialect writers write standard German, they automatically adopt the German tense system. For them also Präteritum is the dominant tense. Lindgren demonstrated that with his statistics. A few German writers do, as exceptions, preserve their South German tense system in some of their high German narratives. Such is the case, for example, in Ludwig Thoma's story "Der Franz und das Mädchen aus Indien" (Franz and the Girl from India).[56] The story is written in Perfekt. Here, too, sequencing adverbs make their appearance: *da, dann, und, und dann, auf einmal*. They are not quite so numerous as in the oral narratives, yet still frequent enough that they are striking. The narrative is a village love story. Read attentively, it reveals a narrative ambience much closer to Camus's *L'étranger* than would be expected from the differences in their styles. In Thoma, too, the sentences are islands. The sequencing adverbs suffice just as little as in Camus to give Perfekt the same narrative fluidity that Präteritum and passé simple "naturally" have from their places in their tense systems. Since the tense constellations are similar, so, too, their narratives are similar, whether they like it or not.

Let me emphasize in closing that the parallel between French and the South German dialects is only partial. In French, passé simple disappears only from the spoken language; in the South German dialects Präteritum is no longer found even in the written language. In French, passé simple is not the only neutral narrative tense; in the South German dialects the only neutral narrative tense, Präteritum, has been lost. The structural conditions vis-à-vis French have been substantially tightened. These dialects must hence combine the remaining tenses more abundantly to achieve the functions of language.

---

56. Wachinger, ed., *Fleckerlteppich*, 48–56.

10 / Other Languages—Other Tenses?

Tense in Ancient Greek

Different languages have different tenses—that is obvious. But do the different tenses in different languages even so have some common ground with the tenses in the languages discussed so far? Are there perhaps structural markers of the tense system that are identical or at least very similar for a larger language group or for all languages? In particular, does the difference between the worlds of discussion and narration occur in all languages? These questions become pressing in light of the previous discussion.

I am not about to answer these questions exhaustively. The limits of my knowledge of languages and literatures prevents it. Yet even with limited capabilities it is still possible to look at other tense systems. It will be necessary to proceed with extreme caution; with the languages already discussed, not everything was to be found in grammars and monographs, and I sometimes had to disagree with previously unquestioned positions. Everything that follows should, therefore, be understood only as remarks and suggestions noted in the margins by an inquisitive reader of the linguistic scholarship. Everywhere one looks, tense seems to be only about time and aspect, often both. But if tense in the Germanic and Romance languages is not simply a matter of time and aspect, it might be possible that these concepts have no firmer basis in other languages as well. After all, modern linguistics derives ultimately from Greek and Latin grammar, in which tense means time and aspect. These would not be the only categories to be subjected to a critical revision long after they were established. It would be especially interesting to examine aspects in the languages from which they were first derived—the Semitic languages. Or in the languages in which they seem to have their best-established home—the Slavic languages. I lack all knowledge of these languages and would be denying my method to depend only on grammars and monographs for information. So, I shall make no judgements about Semitic and Slavic aspects, but reserve the right to be skeptical.

In Greek grammar, half the work has already been done. It was already clear to the Stoics that Greek tenses cannot be considered simply indications of time, and the view has become current again in Greek grammar for the last century or so. In particular the aorist cannot be reduced to a temporal form. Since the *Griechische Schulgrammatik* of Georg Curtius (1852 and many subsequent editions) there have been new efforts to understand Greek tenses in terms of aspect.[1] This attempt still determines the dominant understanding of tense in Greek grammar, even in structural form.[2] The doctrine of aspects convinces me, however, as little in Greek as in other languages; I do not hope for a sensible system of verb forms from aspects.

Does Greek distinguish two tense groups according to register? Its grammar has always distinguished between primary tenses (present, perfect, future I and II) and secondary tenses (imperfect, aorist, pluperfect).[3] The distinction is based on morphology: the secondary tenses have an *e* prefix, the so-called "augment" (examples: *egraphon, egrapsa, egegraphê*). It is also interpreted in terms of temporal stages. The primary tenses are considered the time forms of the present and future, the secondary forms those of the past.[4] But this linkage of tense to time can scarcely be maintained.

---

1. Wolfgang Pollak offers the most extensive disciplinary history: *Studien zum "Verbalaspekt" im Französischen* (Vienna: Rudolf M. Rohrer, 1960), 30.

2. See Eduard Schwyzer, *Griechische Grammatik*, vol. 2: *Syntax und syntaktische Stilistik*, ed. Albert Debrunner (Munich: Beck, 1950), specifically on tense problems; Erwin Koschmieder, *Zeitbezug und Sprache: Ein Beitrag zur Aspekt- und Tempusfrage* (Leipzig: Teubner, 1929); E. Hermann, "Die altgriechischen Tempora: Ein strukturanalytischer Versuch," *Nachrichten von der Akademie der Wissenschaften in Göttingen, philologisch-historische Klasse* (Göttingen: Vandenhoeck & Ruprecht, 1943), 583–648; Martín Sánchez Ruipérez, *Estructura del sistema de aspectos y tiempos del verbo griego antiguo: Análisis funcional sincrónico* (Salamanca: Colegio trilingue de la Universidad, 1954).

3. The division into primary and secondary tenses appears in William Watson Goodwin, *Syntax of the Moods and Tenses of the Greek Verb* (Boston: Ginn and Heath, 1879), 3, and in almost all other grammars.

4. Goodwin, *Syntax*, 3, confuses the two tense groups again with the temporal interpretation. He assigns the historical present to the secondary tenses, the gnomic aorist to the primary ones.

The primary tense perfect can look back to what is past, and the secondary tense aorist can identify not only past events, but also present and future ones. It has often been said that this tense is timeless.[5] I agree, though I would extend the statement to include all tenses. All Greek tenses are timeless.

The category of register with its two groups of discursive and narrating tenses might seem appropriate. The primary tenses would be the discursive tenses, the secondary ones narrative. This explains the oddity that the Greek perfect was not used for narrating before the third century AD.[6] The Greek perfect discusses a situation retrospectively. The concept of discussion automatically implies that what is discussed continues to have effect in the present, for discursive language has as its object only what belongs in some form to the situation of the speakers. One might even consider the reduplicating formation of the perfect *gegrapha* (from *graphô*), "I have written," a hint of its discursive character. Reduplication is a phonic form in the service of emphasis in a great variety of languages, and I have consistently seen discursive speech as the more emphatic form of speech. Since, on principle, the phonic form of a verb gives no information about the place of a form in the system and its function in speech, reduplication can be only a supporting argument. More significant is, for example, Pierre Chantraine's observation that the perfect appears especially frequently in the speeches of Demosthenes and in Menander's comedies.[7] He misunderstands his own observation, however, because he uniformly thinks chronologically ("historically"). The frequency of perfect in Demosthenes and Menander is not, however, a matter of history of the language within or beyond literature, but has rather to do with the fact that these texts are, more than others of their genre, discursive. Hence the perfect, as a discursive tense, is naturally more common in them than in other texts in which there is more narration.[8]

Imperfect, aorist, and pluperfect are unambiguously narrative tenses. All the indications suggest that in Greek the plain narrative tenses, imperfect and aorist, actually distinguish the background and foreground of the narrative. Herbert Weir Smyth's *Greek Grammar* compares imperfect with a line, aorist with a point, a comparison that I know from French grammar.

---

5. Tom A. Rompelman, "Form und Funktion des Präteritums im Germanischen," *Neophilologus* 37, no. 2 (1953): 83: "the old timelessness of the aorist."

6. Jacob Wackernagel, *Vorlesungen über Syntax*, vol. 1 (Basel: Birkhäuser, 1926), 170.

7. Pierre Chantraine, *Histoire du parfait grec* (Paris: H. Champion, 1927), 89.

8. The Greek pluperfect need not be considered here. It is not comparable to the Latin pluperfect. See Wackernagel, *Vorlesungen*, 151 and 185, and Schwyzer, *Griechische Grammatik*, 2:254.

The distinction between the two tenses is commonly illustrated with the example "ebasileue" (imperfect: he was king) and "ebasileuse" (aorist: he became king).⁹ But the example can be misleading: In both cases the verb really means "he ruled as king," but in different contexts. Thus, the form *ebasileue* means "he ruled as king" (but this ruling is in the background of my narrative), while the aorist *ebasileuse* means "he ruled as king" (and this is the main topic of my story because it is new and interesting). Imperfect and aorist then alternate in the narrative according to the same principle analyzed for the Romance languages. Wackernagel (*Vorlesungen*, 183) points out that in Herodotus and Thucydides, "aorist identifies more the climactic moments in a series of actions or events, while the general telling is done in imperfect." This corresponds fairly accurately to the distributions of imparfait and passé simple in French, for which reason the passé simple in French is often called aorist, as for example in Benveniste.

As in every language, metaphoric uses of tense must also be considered in Greek. One example is the so-called gnomic aorist found in proverbs, aphorisms, and similes—a pattern found in many other languages as well. It is best understood from epic similes. The Greek (Homeric) version differs from more modern forms of simile in its relative independence. It is actually narrated, and the wisdom of the simile is gained through narration. In the same way we must think of the wisdom of proverbs and aphorisms not as wisdom conceptualized discursively, but as learned through narration. Aphorisms and proverbs in the gnomic aorist are condensed narrations without background.

So far, I have found a fairly extensive agreement between the tense system in Greek and, particularly, the Romance languages. A great difference becomes immediately obvious, however, when we look at the other verb forms. Subjunctive, optative, imperative, infinitive, and participles, like the corresponding forms in the languages already discussed, fall behind the finite verbs because they provide less information, and thereby end up in syntactic dependence—but in a different way. They are to be sure all indifferent to register and are therefore to be considered semi-finite. But they are not indifferent with regard to highlighting and in their entire paradigm are distinguished according to foreground and background. Hence there is a present infinitive and an aorist infinitive, and the same distinction is drawn for other semi-finite forms. Once again, the analysis is disrupted by unclear terminology. It must be emphasized that none of these semi-forms distinguishes between discussing and narrating. Which

---

9. Herbert Weir Smyth, *Greek Grammar* (Cambridge, MA: Harvard UP, 1956), sect. 1105, 1117.

register they belong to must be discovered from the context or the situation. The so-called present infinitive thus has nothing directly to do with the present tense as a discursive form. It is discursive or narrative, depending on the context, and can stand in equally well for imperfect. In French, where the infinitive contributes no information about highlighting, the present infinitive can also represent passé simple. In Greek, however, the present infinitive cannot stand in for aorist, but only for present and imperfect. Instead, Greek has a second infinitive, inappropriately called the aorist infinitive. While aorist is very clearly a narrative tense, the aorist infinitive, by contrast, just like the present infinitive, can be used for discussion and for narration, depending on the context and the register of the main verb. This infinitive can represent not only aorist, but also its plain discursive analog, present. Both infinitives (and, similarly, the other semi-forms) are indifferent to register, but not to highlighting. The form *luein* (present infinitive) is the background infinitive, and the form *lusai* (aorist infinitive) is the foreground infinitive (Wackernagel, *Vorlesungen*, 174). Since neither infinitive respects the boundary between discussing and narrating, the highlighting of semi-finite verbs (and only of these) is not simply narrative highlighting, but a general grammatical highlighting.

It thus appears that at least some of the ancient Indo-European languages already distinguish significantly between background and foreground in the realm of tense. To review: Latin and the Romance languages distinguish highlighting only in the narrative register; highlighting is therefore a peculiarity of narrative technique. English developed progressive forms and thereby gained the possibility of highlighting according to background and foreground across the entire tense system, in discussing as well as narrating. In this case, background and foreground are degrees of commitment and reliability. Spanish, too, developed new tenses in addition to its narrative profiling (e.g., *está cantando, estaba cantando*) that can distinguish highlighting in both tense groups. The tenses in *-ndo* in Spanish are not, however, as strongly developed as those in *-ing* in English. Greek takes a middle position between the Latin and Romance languages on the one hand and English on the other. Its highlighting is restricted to narrating with regard to tense, but in the case of the semi-forms it extends across the whole language to both narrative and discursive registers.

Tense in Latin

The tense system in Latin seems to be very simple and is held up as a model of logic. In fact, it offers substantial difficulties for analysis. Grammars distinguish between the tenses of the present stem (*dicit, dicebat, dicet*) and of the perfect stem (*dixit, dixerat, dixerit*), and they note the parallelism between the two series. The distinction comes from Varro, who was following the Stoic grammarians. His terms are "infectum" for the present stem and "perfectum" for the perfect stem (*De lingua latina* 9.96-100).[10] The other verb forms also have forms of the present stem (*dicere, dicat, diceret*) and the perfect stem (*dixisse, dixerit, dixisset*). The distinction is based, as one can see, exclusively on the phonic forms and their similarities in the paradigm.

An alternative division of the tenses into principal tenses and historical tenses is suggested by the *consecutio temporum* (sequence of tenses) and also by the analogy to Greek grammar. Charles E. Bennett counts among the principal tenses present indicative, future, future perfect, and present perfect; he considers the historical tenses to be imperfect, historical perfect, pluperfect, and also historical present.[11] Once again we find two sets of tenses that are normally not mixed in a complex sentence ("sequence of tenses") and that are strongly reminiscent of the familiar discursive and narrative tense groups in other languages.

Yet they are also completely different. Indeed, Bennett's arrangement requires doubling some of the tenses. The "perfectum" as a class of forms (*dixi, dixit*) appears in Bennett's system in both registers, once as the perfectum praesens, and a second time as the perfectum historicum. Correspondingly, praesens appears both as plain praesens and again as praesens historicum, but it is always the form class *dico, dicit* that is meant. Surely, we may regard the praesens historicum as a matter of style. Bennett (*Syntax*, 14-15) points out that it is already connected to certain contextual conditions in old Latin. It normally appears framed by perfectum forms.[12] The same is true in the classical language. The linkage to the framing context reveals that praesens historicum is not independent. We may therefore understand the praesens in general as a discursive tense and leave it in tense group I.

The problem of the Latin perfectum cannot, however, be solved in the same fashion. Since the grammarian Priscian, there has been agreement in Latin grammar, especially among historians of the language, that the

---

10. Varro, *De lingua latina* 9.96–100. See also Antoine Meillet, "De l'expression de l'aoriste en latin," *Revue de Philologie* 21 (1897): 81–90, and Jean Perrot, "Autour des passés: Réflexions sur les systèmes verbaux du latin et du français," *Revue des langues romanes* 72 (1956): 137–69.

11. Charles E. Bennett, *Syntax of Early Latin* (Boston: Allyn and Bacon, 1910), 1:338–42.

12. See also Manu Leumann and Johann Baptist Hofmann, *Lateinische Grammatik* (Munich: Beck, 1928), 553.

Latin perfectum is to be understood as a combination of an Indo-European perfect with an Indo-European aorist. The inventory of perfect forms in Latin seems to confirm this understanding: The reduplicated perfectum (of the type *dedi*) points to the Indo-European and the Greek perfect, the *s*-"perfectum" (of the type *mansi*) points rather to the Indo-European aorist and the Greek aorist, while the perfectum in -*vi* (of the type *amavi*) represents a new Latin formation (Leumann and Hofmann, *Lateinische Grammatik*, 302). As shown for Greek in the preceding section, the Indo-European perfect and the Indo-European aorist are now probably to be aligned with the discursive and narrative registers respectively. If, therefore, the Latin perfectum combines these two tenses in itself, then it combines a discursive and a narrative tense and contradicts the possibility of a sharp structural boundary between the two registers. This is the real problem with the Latin tense system. If there is a single tense that cannot be unambiguously assigned to the one or the other of the registers, then either the tense system is organized according to entirely different principles, or the perfectum does not fit into the system. After all, we had defined the tenses as verb forms that could be labeled unambiguously as discursive or narrative, while semi-finite verbs cannot be so identified.

André Burger offers a historical explanation for this problem. He agrees with the general consensus that the Latin perfectum combines the markers of the Indo-European perfect and aorist. The tense thus has two functions (*valeurs*); in his terminology it is présent achevé (present realized) and passé narratif (narrative past). Burger emphasizes that these two functions are very different and even speaks of them as, in effect, homonyms of one another. To be sure, he sees it from the point of view of a modified theory of aspects, but it corresponds accurately to the considerations prompted by a background of two registers. Burger concludes from it, "Il est probable que le système latin [i.e., of tense] n'a jamais été parfaitement cohérent" (the Latin tense system was probably never perfectly coherent).[13]

This incoherence (how far we have come from the admirable logic of the Latin language!) explains a further linguistic development in Burger's view. Late or vulgar Latin develops a new perfect constructed from the perfect participle and the forms of *habere* or *tenere* (*habeo dictum, teneo dictum*), which are now unambiguously perfect in the Indo-European sense. Traces of this new perfect can be found in Old Latin (Plautus:

---

13. André Burger, "Sur le passage du système des temps et des aspects de l'indicatif du latin au roman commun," *Cahiers Ferdinand de Saussure* 8 (1949): 22.

omnes res relictas habeo) and in classical Latin (Caesar: *aciem instructam habuit*). The tense is fully developed in the Romance languages as passé composé, perfecto compuesto, passato prossimo, etc., and it belongs unambiguously to the discursive register (with the reservations already discussed for the passé composé in modern French). The original Latin perfectum is thus relieved of its double function and returned to the status of a narrative tense. And, in fact, the successors of the Latin perfectum in the Romance languages (passé simple, perfecto simple, passato remoto, etc.) are all narrative tenses. The path of linguistic history thus would lead from a coherent tense system in Indo-European to an incoherent one in Latin back to a coherent one in the Romance languages that basically once again agrees with Indo-European.

Burger's historical explanation is impressive. It very cleverly replaces one problem with another. In fact, the peculiar middle position of the Latin perfectum is not the only crux in the Latin tense system; the other is the formation of a new Romance-synthesized perfect. Earlier explanations found the expression of a "robust sense of existence" or "human longing to hold time fast" in the new perfect with "habere" or "tenere."[14] These days, we have lost our taste for such rapid global interpretations. The formation of a new tense is an occurrence that affects the entire tense system. The new tense does not simply join existing tenses but rearranges the whole system. Other tenses are also affected. In this case, especially (but not only) the existing perfectum, that now is unambiguously assigned its place as a narrative tense. It is actually amazing how similarly the tense systems are structured in Greek and French, and how greatly the Latin system deviates. It gives the impression of a system that got out of balance and then found it again. Yet there are significant difficulties connected with this historical interpretation. It shows little respect for classical Latin to treat its grammar as only a somewhat problematic transitional phase between the Indo-European and the Romance languages. It would not only distress the ears of humanists but would also not do justice to the status of Latin in the world. The tense system of classical Latin is natural and correct, as is the tense system of every other language; otherwise, the language would not have been able to meet the varied needs

---

14. Eugen Lerch, "Das Imperfektum als Ausdruck der lebhaften Vorstellung," *Zeitschrift für romanische Philologie* 42, no. 3 and 4 (1922): 312–13; Leo Spitzer, "Über den Schwund des einfachen Praeteritums," in *Donum natalicium Schrijnen: Verzameling van opstellen door oud-leerlingen en bevriende vakgenooten opgedragen aan Josef Schrijnen*, ed. St. W. J. Teeuwen (Nijmegen: Dekker and Van de Vegt, 1929), 87. The later Spitzer would never have written thus.

of a sophisticated culture. There must be a reason why Latin diverged so strikingly from the structural norms of Indo-European.

Let us look once more at French for comparison. In spoken French there has been for two centuries now a tense on both sides of the tense system: the passé composé. Nevertheless, the strict division between discursive and narrative tenses has remained intact. The passé composé belongs unambiguously to the discursive tenses; only under specific conditions can it fulfill narrative tasks and even then does not completely lose the tense markers that belong to it as a discursive tense. I have described in detail how tenses work together with macro-syntactic sequencing signals in different kinds of oral and written texts (Chapter 9). It might well be that there was something similar to French in Latin, but in reverse. The perfectum would then be a narrative tense and might take on discursive tasks only under certain conditions, namely in conjunction with certain adverbs. This is for now a strictly hypothetical idea that cannot be verified or falsified without further investigation. There does not yet exist a text-linguistic survey of Latin macro-syntactic forms, and it cannot be established within the framework of this investigation. So, the question must remain open.[15]

However, it seems possible, if not to solve, then at least to narrow the question of the function of the Latin perfectum from another point of view. Let us begin with the assumption that we have in the Latin perfectum a syncretism of the discursive and the narrative tense groups. In the Romance languages (with the exception perhaps of Portuguese), this syncretism has disappeared, and a discursive perfectum (passé composé, etc.) exists next to a narrative perfectum (passé simple, etc.). Somewhere in the course of history the two functions must have split. Did that happen in the dark centuries of late antiquity or the early Middle Ages? If so, then the chances of proving our argument are poor. It is much better for the argument if at least traces of such a development can be found already in the classical period, where there is generous documentation.

For this investigation I turn again to the way tense forms combine in texts, in particular the combination of the perfectum with the syntactic signals called "diathesis" (active, deponent, passive). It appears that perfectum serves different functions depending on whether it is combined with the signals for active, on the one hand, or with those for deponent or passive, on the other. In the active voice, the perfectum (*laudavit*) seems to fulfill the task of narration to a greater degree than the deponent (*mentitus est*) and the passive (*laudatus est*), both of which are more directed toward

---

15. Very different results would be expected here for the pre-classical, classical, and post-classical periods.

discursive tasks. The difference may be related to the present form of the verb *est* (is), which is used to form the deponent and passive verb. Let us accept this as fact. That would explain why the perfectum of deponent and passive verbs has a higher frequency in discursive than in narrative texts.

In Caesar's *Bellum Gallicum* (first century BCE, Gallic War), for example, there is a clear tendency to use the perfectum of active verbs together with the praesens historicum as transition.[16] Caesar does not entirely avoid deponent and passive verbs. They appear in forms from the present stem and a few other forms quite often, but in the perfectum they are surprisingly rare. In their place, Caesar uses satellite forms such as the participium perfecti (*profectus, laudatus*), which is then subordinated to an active verb, usually in perfectum. With deponents he occasionally uses the participium presentis (*proficiscens*) or the participium futuri (*profecturus*).

Here are two examples to illustrate the accumulation of participial forms:

> Legionis VIIII. et X. milites ... transire *conantes insecuti* gladiis magnam partem eorum *impeditam* interfecerunt (2.23.1; The soldiers of the ninth and tenth legion ... slew with their swords a great part of [the enemy], who were blocked while trying to cross [the river]).

> His de rebus Caesar certior *factus* et infirmitatem Gallorum *veritus*, ... nihil his *committendum* existimavit (4.5.1; Caesar, informed of these matters and afraid that the Gauls were untrustworthy, decided not to confide anything to them.

Thus, Caesar does not write, "insecuti sunt et interfecerunt" and "veritus est et existimavit," but he replaces the perfectum of the deponent with the corresponding participium perfecti, *insecuti, veritus*. This is not simply a matter of style, but a syntactic phenomenon related to the structure of the tense system. For participles in Latin are semi-finite forms. That means above all that they are indifferent to the structural boundary between discussion and narration. If the perfectum of an active verb is a narrative tense, as it clearly is in Caesar's writing about the war, then all the semi-forms made to depend on it have narrative character. Hence Caesar does not reach for these deponent and passive forms only occasionally, as one would expect from a stylistic trait, but he does it constantly, in almost every sentence.

---

16. Julius Caesar, *Gallic War*. Trans.by W. A. McDevitte and W. S. Bohn (New York. Harper & Brothers, 1869). Perseus. http://www.perseus.tufts.edu/hopper/text?doc =Perseus:text:1999.02.0001.

Caesar's participles are not supposed to express "having happened earlier" or some such thing. In both the sentences quoted it is not the case that Caesar's soldiers first chase the enemy and then kill them and that Caesar first is afraid and then has an opinion, but these events are simultaneous. Or, if they are not simultaneous, then they stand in the normal narrative sequence. But just this normal sequence seems not to be offered by deponent and passive verbs in perfectum. I made a similar observation, although with regard to the tense of all classes of forms, about passé composé in French and about Perfekt in the South German dialects.

Of course, perfect forms of deponent and passive verbs do occur in the *Bellum Gallicum*. But they are generally rare and, what is more important, they come in characteristic locations. They are less common in the flow of the narrative, but appear fairly dependably at the beginnings and ends of sections—just as with the German Perfekt. Of Caesar's seven books on the Gallic wars, no fewer than four end with a deponent or passive verb in the perfectum. That is an unusually high proportion:

> ipse in citeriorem Galliam ad conventus agendos *profectus est* (1.54; [He] set out for Cisalpine Gaul to hold the assizes).
>
> Ipse ... in Italiam *profectus est*. Ob easque res ex litteris Caesaris dierum XV supplicatio decreta est, quod ante id tempus accidit nulli (2.35; He went down to Italy. A thanksgiving of fifteen days was decreed for the achievements reported in Caesar's letter, which before that time had never happened for anyone).
>
> His rebus gestis ex litteris Caesaris dierum XX supplicatio a senatu *decreta est* (4.38; For these successes, a thanksgiving of twenty days was decreed by the senate upon receiving Caesar's letter).
>
> In Italiam ad conventus agendos *profectus est* (6.44; he set out for Italy, as he had determined, to hold the assizes).

They also occur much more frequently at the ends of chapters than in the main narrative.

It can also be noted from the cited sentences that they are formulaic. This observation can also be cautiously generalized: There is a certain attraction between formulaic language and the perfect tense of deponent and passive verbs. Thus, one often finds in narrative passages sentences like these:

> Acriter in eo loco *pugnatum est* (2.10.2; There was a severe struggle in that place).
>
> Acriter utrimque usque ad vesperum *pugnatum est* (1.50.3; The battle was vigorously maintained on both sides till the evening).

Aegre eo die *sustentatum est* (2.6.1; [The assault] was with difficulty sustained for that day).

On the basis of their content these sentences are already removed from the narrative flow. They summarize—even evaluate—a day of battle. They can be considered as titles in a detailed narrative. In such sentences we again find deponent or passive verbs in perfectum more often than might be expected from their frequency in the whole of the *Commentarii*.

In Cicero's letters, by comparison, the perfectum of deponent and passive verbs occurs more frequently than in Caesar's narrative.[17] No statistics are necessary; any page opened at random makes it evident. The perfect forms of passive verbs stand freely among the other discursive tenses and obviously belong: "Ita sunt res nostrae, 'ut in secundis, fluxae, ut in adversis, bonae.' In re familiari valde *sumus*, ut scis, *perturbati*. Praeterea sunt quaedam domestica, quae litteris non committo" (*Letters to Atticus*, 4.1.8; So stand my affairs: 'Unsettled,' when our luck is in; / When out, we call it 'fair.' My financial position, as you know, is in very far from good order. Moreover, there are certain private matters which I don't trust to a letter.). The same is true for the deponents: "Qua re velim ita *statutum habeas*, me tui memoriam cum summa benevolentia tenere tuasque omnes res non minori mihi curae quam meas esse. Quod maiore in varietate *versata est* adhuc tua causa, quam homines aut volebant aut opinabantur, mihi crede, non est pro malis temporum quod moleste feras" (*Epistulae ad familiares*, 6.2; So I want you to be sure once for all that I keep you in mind with the most friendly feelings and pay as much attention to all your affairs as to my own. Considering the bad times we live in, you ought not, believe me, to take it hard that your case has hitherto gone through more ups and downs than was generally hoped or expected). Among the discursive tenses of this text is the form "statutum habeas" (consider certain), which already points toward the structure of the discursive Romance perfect (passé composé, etc.).

The different status of the Latin perfectum according to the specific active or passive diathesis is also confirmed by the history of the Romance languages. While perfectum forms of active verbs routinely turn into the narrative passé simple (perfecto simple, passato remoto etc.), the perfectum forms of the deponents (which last in Latin until very late antiquity and even increase in number) feed into the discursive perfect tenses

---

17. Marcus Tullius Cicero, *Letters to Atticus* (Cambridge: Harvard UP, 1999), doi: 10.4159/DLCL.marcus_tullius_cicero-letters_atticus.1999; *Letters to Friends* (Cambridge: Harvard UP, 2001), doi: 10.4159/DLCL.marcus_tullius_cicero-letters_friends.2001.

(passé composé).¹⁸ They do so either without morphological change ("mortuus est" → "il est mort") or with a change of morpheme ("mentitus est" → "il a menti"), but the difference is irrelevant, since both occupy the same position in the tense system and the entire tense now unambiguously qualifies as a discursive tense.

It thus seems to me possible to describe the formation of a new tense in more nuanced terms than has already been done. Even in the Latin perfectum of the classical period the structural boundary between discourse and narration is present grammatically. It separates the perfectum of deponent and passive verbs, used primarily discursively, from the perfectum of active verbs, which are used mostly for narration. The further development of the languages clearly elaborates this structure. Both categories are filled out: the discursive perfectum with the helping verb *habet*, the narrative perfectum with the helping verb *fuit*. Both elaborations remain morphologically within the structural framework already prepared by classical Latin.

Whorf, Spengler, and the Hopi Indians

How should we describe the tense systems of languages very different from ours? It seems simple if we just impose the categories we know, or believe we know, from our own language. Of course, it is possible in most languages to identify, somehow, past events and future events, incomplete events and those completed. This question is only whether the verb forms of this language are really organized in terms of time and aspect. It could well be that they are organized by quite different categories and into quite different structures. It is difficult to tell. Most of the linguists who have addressed the task of describing a language very distant from the family of Indo-European languages have scarcely bothered with this question. They have applied the categories of time and aspect to them with tiresome uniformity, certain that they were in possession of a philologically reliable and philosophically verified assumption. The result is a list of aspects and tenses whose length depends on the language; the labels vary in part even though certain terms like perfective/imperfective, progressive, and iterative constantly recur. Do these tense descriptions really do those languages justice? Of course, no one can judge that definitively without knowing the language at least as well as the linguist or missionary who

---

18. Leumann and Hofmann, *Lateinische Grammatik*, 545–46. See also the interesting discussion by Jerzy Kuryłowicz, "Les temps composés du roman," in *Esquisses linguistiques* (Warsaw: Polskiej Akademii Nauk, 1960), 104–8.

described it. Even so, it is possible to draw certain inferences as to its plausibility just from the arrangement of the description.

Consider the description of Shambala, an African Bantu language described by Karl Roehl in 1911. Roehl worked in Africa for many years and seems to have known the language well. Yet the description makes a strange impression. Roehl distinguishes and catalogues no fewer than some thousand different verb forms just for the indicative first-person active. And despite this extraordinary number of forms, he still asserts that Shambala has no tenses for expressing the past, present, and future. Some identical verb forms identify the most distant past as well as the most remote future. In the face of his observation, Roehl quickly decides that the Shambala have only "the most primordial, most naive possible view of things" and no logical concept of "the essence of time." No wonder the Shambala "live thoughtlessly and mindlessly for the moment."[19] He then listlessly describes the verb forms, and we find the old familiar aspects in undreamt-of variations. Shouldn't we automatically mistrust a description driven by the conceptual arrogance of the white man?

Similar preconceived opinions, but not the same arrogance, might have been held by the American linguist Benjamin Lee Whorf (1897-1941) when he moved to Arizona in 1935 to study the language of the Hopi Indians. Hopi belongs to the Aztec language family, is divided into four dialects, and was spoken by some two thousand people, mostly on the Hopi reservation in northwest Arizona. In his first description, Whorf dispenses with the idea of time, which is of no help to his mind, but still treats the Hopi verbs in traditional fashion under the heading of "aspects." He identifies nine aspects in the language, to which he gives the following names: prime aspect (zero form), punctual, durative (corresponding to English "progressive forms"), segmentative, ingressive, progressional, projective, spatial, and continuative.[20] Whorf was unsatisfied with this description, however, and spent the rest of his life trying to understand and describe Hopi more adequately. It became clear to him that his description was driven by preconceptions derived from Indo-European, which made the Indo-American language seem full of irregularities. Only when the preconceptions are removed could the regularity of the non–Indo-European language become visible. In a 1938 essay, "Some Verbal

19. Karl Roehl, *Versuch einer systematischen Grammatik der Schambalasprache* (Hamburg: L. Friedrichsen, 1911), 108–9.
20. Benjamin Lee Whorf, "The Hopi Language, Toreva Dialect," in *Linguistic Structures of Native America*, ed. Harry Hoijer and Cornelius Osgood (New York: Viking Fund, 1946), 158–83. The essay was published posthumously and draws on studies going back to 1935.

Categories of Hopi," Whorf confessed, "Later I found it was quite regular, in terms of its own patterns."[21]

Whorf proceeds by isolating particular categories from the different versions of his lists of aspects in order to organize a system of tenses and verb forms around them. His first attempt, "The Punctual and Segmentative Aspect of Verbs in Hopi" (*Language*, 65-71), takes the notion of aspect to extremes and claims to see with these two Hopi aspects precise verb categories for motion in nature. The punctual aspect identifies the *point-locus* in the physical sense, while the segmentative aspect, also in the physical sense of the word, identifies "the type of force known in physics as torque = tendency to produce rotation" (68). Both aspects are independent of time and space. In them, Hopi organizes nature according to the principles of a simple, yet scientifically respectable physics (70: "with very thorough consistency and not a little true scientific precision"). These two aspects do basically correspond to the modern principles of particle and force field. And these concepts, according to modern physics and Whorf's own convictions, are more significant in our epoch than the outmoded concepts of space and time, or even past, present, and future.

In the same essay, Whorf refers to three tenses in Hopi, without saying anything about them but their names: factual (present-past), future, and generalized (usitative). Subsequently, "Some Verbal Categories of Hopi" (*Language*, 143–58) returns to these tenses, now with the names reportive, expective, and nomic. He now emphasizes explicitly that none of these has anything to do with time. The reportive tense, for example, stands for things past and present and is neutral with regard to time. Whether it refers to the past or the present is only determined by the situation. If the sentence contains additional determination from the situation, then it refers to the present—if not, then to the past. The expective tense is similarly indifferent to time. Whorf translates it with: *is going to*, *begins to*, *was going to*, and *began to*. The nomic tense is used, finally, for general observations and acknowledged truths. It is clear that Whorf is now trying to understand the mysteries of Hopi verbs not from the point of view of physics, but from logic and cognitive theory. The three tenses are distinguished according to Whorf's summary as three different kinds of cognition under the heading of assertion.

This is still not Whorf's last word on the Hopi language. In the posthumous essay, "An American Indian Model of the Universe," Whorf repeats

---

21. Benjamin Lee Whorf. *Language, Thought, and Reality: Selected Writings of Benjamin Lee Whorf*, ed. John B. Carroll (Cambridge: MIT Press, 2012), 143.

yet again that Hopi has no tenses, by which he means, no verb forms for expressing time.[22] Indeed, Hopi does not even have a word to identify time in the mathematical-physical sense, much less any to identify past, present, or future. It also has no words for identifying space.

Arguing more philosophically, Whorf compares the "metaphysics" that underlies Hopi to the underlying metaphysics of the Indo-European languages (he calls them Standard Average European or SAE languages). SAE languages impose the forms of intuition of space and time upon nature. Whorf has read his Kant; his "cosmic forms" are a linguistic parallel to Kant's "pure forms of sensible intuition." With these linguistic forms of perception as the grammatical categories of our native languages, we Westerners order and interpret the world. The SAE culture thus has built into its foundations an indestructible element of understanding the world in terms of space and time. For, as Whorf says in his earlier essay, "language first of all is a classification and arrangement of the stream of sensory experience which results in a certain world-order, a certain segment of the world that is easily expressible by the type of symbolical means that language employs" (*Language*, 70). It is easy to recognize the grammatical equivalent in Whorf's view of the more semantically oriented doctrine of world view of one's native language in German linguistics from Humboldt to Weisgerber.

According to Whorf, then, the Hopi language interprets the world completely differently. It does not impose space and time on it, but two other "cosmic forms," which Whorf calls manifested form (objective form) and manifesting (also unmanifest, subjective) form. That is the metaphysics of Hopi as it is expressed in its verb forms. Whorf tries to grasp the metaphysical sense of the linguistic dichotomy in ever new approximations. The category manifest is relatively evident. It includes everything accessible to the senses: the world as nature and history, present and past. The category manifesting is more difficult to grasp. Whorf calls it the category of the subjective, but warns against misunderstanding it as what is "only" subjective. Manifesting represents perhaps a higher form of reality for the Hopi mind than what is accessible to the senses. It includes everything that we call mental, which the Hopis, however, imagine as located in the heart. But not just in the hearts of people, but also in those of animals, plants, things, indeed of the entire cosmos. It is a magical and religious category. The future belongs to it also, because it is already present to our

---

22. *Language*, 73–82, and tentatively dated by John B. Carroll to 1936 (*Language*, 379). The title is a replique to P.D. Ouspensky's *A New Model of the Universe*, 1931. Whorf was not entirely uninfluenced by the mystical theses of this book.

feeling and thinking. No concept of time or aspect can do justice to this category. It demands entirely different concepts. Whorf attempts it with the word "hope." This is the idea that identifies the totality of this category the best. But in principle even this concept is an unsuitable label for a worldview that is "an American-Indian model," not one of the standard European sort.

Is it possible to compare the two worldviews with one another? Whorf defends himself passionately against the simplistic judgment about the "mysticism" of the indigenous peoples. That way of judging means that the standard European views of dynamic time and static space also constitute a "mysticism." These prejudices must be overcome. The language of the Hopi Indians involves just as good a metaphysics as the European languages. Perhaps even a better one, Whorf implies. Here his linguistic analysis becomes cultural criticism.[23] Western culture is built on the assumptions of the Standard European languages. Especially the commanding role of time in modern European and American industrial society (the omnipresence of clocks, the pressure of deadlines, "lack of time," etc.) is in his opinion a consequence of that linguistic worldview that plunges all action into the stream of time with the aid of tenses understood as temporal forms. Without our languages oriented toward tense our civilization would be less obsessed with time and would likely be a completely different civilization. The proof is to be found among the Hopi. Their language is so constructed that time plays no role; instead, it is dominated by completely different categories that we can scarcely comprehend and only paraphrase with difficulty. Hence, they have not produced a civilization of chronometers and machines, but a different form of life that may to be sure offer less economic success, but perhaps reflects the world more authentically than a civilization that in the end only turns time into money.

Whorf's cultural criticism must be seen in relation to Oswald Spengler's interpretation of Western culture in *Der Untergang des Abendlandes* (The Decline of the West). In Spengler's suggestive interpretation the declining West is a culture distinguished from almost all other cultures in the world by its pronounced sense of time.[24] But time is more than a form of perception for Spengler. Time is fate, and time is history. Only for

---

23. See especially the essay "The Relation of Thought and Behavior to Language" (1939) in *Language*, 173–204.

24. According to Spengler, Egyptian and Chinese culture also developed the sense for time: Otto Spengler, *Der Untergang des Abendlandes: Umrisse einer Morphologie der Weltgeschichte* (Munich: Beck, 1921–22), 1:188.

the West does the world even exist as History or is there such a thing as World History. Spengler's evidence for the towering importance of time in western culture are the great symbols of time: clocks, museums, historiography, tragedies, astrology, funerary rites, etc. "Without the most careful measurement of time," he says, "western man is inconceivable" (1:18–19). Spengler dates the beginning of the culture of time in Western Europe to around 1000 CE, that is, from about the time that Abbot Gerbert, later Pope Sylvester II, invented the mechanical clock.

Spengler also draws the tenses of the European languages into his reflections on the morphology of culture. He does not, however, count them among the great temporal symbols in Western culture, but sees in them rather examples of how an originally more authentic and lively sense of time has gradually degenerated. The spatialization and materialization of time in modern philosophy, psychology, and physics has already begun to manifest itself in language, according to Spengler; "thinking in verbs" subjects life and its real time to reason and reduces "historical time" to a "spatially shaped, surrogate phantom" (1:174; 2:171–72). Here Henri Bergson stands behind Spengler. Thus, tense is more closely linked to "decline" than to "the West," yet, if only in respect to degeneration, it also belongs to this historical, specifically Western culture. As he says, "For the savage the word 'time' can have no meaning. He lives without needing it to be in contrast to anything else. He has time, but knows nothing of it" (1:173).

It is well known how much excitement Spengler's interpretation of history caused in its day. The book was translated into English in 1926 by C. F. Atkinson and immediately aroused a lively echo. Wyndham Lewis published a book called *Time and Western Man* and criticized particularly Spengler's thesis about exclusively Western time: "Alas, the poor Indian! and his untutored ahistoric mind! Spengler treats the poor Indian, or Greek, that he visits in the course of his time-travel, with the same lofty pity and disdain that the conquering White showed for the 'poor Indian' of the English verse."[25] The energy of his reaction is doubtless also to be explained by Spengler's additional argument (2:140) that the immigrants to America increasingly resembled the original inhabitants with each passing generation.

I do not know whether or when Whorf read Spengler. To the best of my knowledge, he never mentions his name. But the section "Some Impresses

---

25. Wyndham Lewis, *Time and Western Man* (Boston: Beacon, 1957), 220–1. Alexander Pope's lines, "Lo! the poor Indian, whose untutored mind / Sees God in clouds, or hears him in the wind," come from *Essay on Man* 1.99–100.

of Linguistic Habit in Western Civilization," in an essay revised in 1939 (*Language*, 195–200), can be understood as a brief summary of Spengler on time. Whether he read Spengler himself or knew about him from the general discussion is less important than the fact that Whorf's philosophizing description of the Hopi language responds to Spengler from the non-Western point of view. Whorf accepts Spengler's interpretation and simultaneously offers complementary evidence. He establishes that Hopi indeed has no tenses, and that means for him precisely that Hopi culture has no temporal consciousness.

We can even find Spengler's focus on decline in Whorf, although in different form. As far as the West is concerned, Whorf is convinced that modern science is making all possible efforts to escape the tense-time spiral derived from cultural morphology: "It is trying to frame a NEW LANGUAGE by which to adjust itself to a wider universe" (197). Its bond to time is thus associated with a cultural phase that is ending. As for Hopi culture as a specimen of non-Western culture, Whorf rejects all cultural snobbery. He now finds something completely different from time to be the central category of this language, namely hope. Based on this insight he transforms himself into the advocate for Hopi culture and reclaims for it the same cultural-morphological status claimed for itself by European-American culture.

Viewing the dialogue between Spengler and Whorf from a certain distance, I would now happily believe Whorf that he found new tense forms in the Hopi language. That only confirms my position that tense and time are separate categories. But I am not so convinced about Spengler's great symbols of time and in any case certainly refuse to consider the Indo-European tenses to be expressions of time. As a result, Whorf's cultural critique of the bondage of "SAE culture" to time applies more to Spengler's reading of history than to the reality of the Indo-European languages in Europe and in the modern world. Our Western tenses have no more to do with time than the tenses of the Hopi Indians and are perhaps much more closely related to them than Whorf dared to think.

Toward a New Method of Description

If the concepts of time and aspect do not seem adequate to describe non-Indo-European languages, should we not try to dispose of all preconceived concepts and allow foreign languages to act on their own, without prejudgment? That is easier said than done. It takes more than an act of will to free ourselves from all the notions trained into us by years of familiarity with Indo-European languages. The more we believe in our own lack of prejudices, the more slyly do they sneak into all our investigations and descriptions. Positivism in linguistics failed in just this respect. As a result, it could not create a syntax and tried, by systematically veering off into historical analysis, to pretend that it had not gone a single step further than ancient and late-ancient grammar.

It is not possible to describe any language outside our own system without preconceptions. If we don't ask an intelligent question of the language, we won't receive an intelligent answer. So, it is not a matter of eliminating all preconceptions, but of replacing bad preconceptions by better ones. The best preconceptions are those that are prepared to take account of formed texts in the new language from the start. A language reveals its form and structure only when it is examined in the life situations to which it is native. The description of a language can, hence, hope to be adequate only in conjunction with a description of the pragmatics. If, then, a particular correspondence emerges between typical speech situations of a culture and grammatical categories, then the describer can see certain preconceptions justified and validated. The linguist trying to describe an unfamiliar language should also not begin with the preconception that tenses and verb forms in all languages must be organized in terms of a dichotomy between discursive and narrative registers. It is equally important, however, not to paint all sentences in the language with the same grammatical gray. Instead, it is necessary to try to sketch out a typology of speech situations characteristic of this culture. The best way to avoid the danger of arbitrary typologies is to be led by real texts in the language. The literary genres, whether written or oral, should be seen on principle as typified speech situations and used as the first, safest framework for grammatical investigation. The texts of a language do not stand at the end, far beyond the grammar, but at the beginning. It is the great contribution of text-linguistics to have uncovered the error that a grammar can be built from the tiniest elements to ever larger unities. The largest units must come first with the smaller ones to be understood from the structure of the whole thing. The largest units, now, are not sentences or phrases, but speech situations and text with the conventions of their literary genre. They are the beginning of grammar.

It cannot hurt to begin the description of a language with the question, "How are stories told in this language?" Storytelling seems to be a universal form of linguistic expression. In the process the linguist may find certain verb forms (tenses) that recur with obstinate repetition and are typical for narrative situations and genres. In many descriptions of languages, half hidden by terminology of time and aspect, such narrative tenses can be recognized. In describing Shambala, Roehl (*Versuch*, 111-12) identifies a special tense for narrative and proverbs, and he particularly comments that it is not tied to time. If a past event is told, then it is a past tense, but if current or future events are being told about, this same tense is used. I have the impression that this tense could well be the neutral narrative tense, and perhaps even the only narrative tense. The African Pala language also has a special tense for folk tales and fairytales.[26] And Whorf, in his description of Hopi, has the amazing formulation about the "cosmic form of hope"; "the Hopi realize and even express in their grammar that the things told in myths and stories do not have the same kind of reality or validity as things of the present day, the things of practical concern" (*Language*, 81). Could that be the categories of narrating and discussing that we have also found in the Indo-European languages? Perhaps also, if Whorf's interpretation is correct, in the opposite direction, so that what is narrated is real, what is (only) experienced unreal. Should this conjecture be correct, then the two "cosmic forms"—the manifest and the manifesting—in Whorf's description are perhaps nothing other than the registers of discussing and narrating, and it would then be a good idea to seek them in other languages of the world.

The methods developed thus far in language atlases and monographs are not suited even to ask such questions. They hardly address units larger than the sentence, and rarely proceed beyond morphology to syntax, to text-syntax. But there are promising beginnings. I find them above all in the school of the American linguist, Kenneth L. Pike, author of *Language in Relation to a Unified Theory of the Structure of Human Behavior* (The Hague: Mouton, 1967). The book begins from the position that language cannot be dissected out of life situations and that the structures of language are embedded in surrounding structures of behavior and in concrete situations. On this basis, Pike's school developed a model of structural description to take account of the hierarchy of levels of language. It proceeds, from lowest to highest, by (grammatical) levels: word level, phrase level, clause level, sentence level, utterance level, and finally discourse level.[27] The text (discourse level) is thus the highest level of the grammatical hierarchy, embedded only in unarticulated behaviors.

26. Hans Jensen, "Der sprachliche Ausdruck für Zeitauffassungen, insbesondere am Verbum," *Archiv für die gesamte Psychologie* 101 (1938): 333.

27. Velma Pickett offers a simplified presentation of the tagmemic theory appropriate for a practical description of a language in *The Grammatical Hierarchy of Isthmus Zapotec* (Baltimore: Linguistic Society of America, 1960). See also Pickett, "Isthmus Zapotec Verb Analysis I/II," *International Journal of American Linguistics* 19 (1953): 292–96, and 21 (1955): 217–32.

The practical descriptions of language based on Pike's "tagmemic theory" model, differ from older descriptive techniques, in addition to the essential consideration of situation, above all by their use of the higher levels in the hierarchy in describing syntax. We learn not only how a sentence is constructed, but also how a conversation begins and ends, how a speech is framed by conversations, and which behavioral situations form the bases for narrations. The process looks different in different descriptions, and the model is used sometimes more creatively and with different kinds of consistency. Velma Pickett (87 ff.) distinguishes monologue from conversation on the highest level, and considers monologue to include exclamations, conversations with oneself, instructions, narratives, and episodes of narrating. Yet no connection to tenses is established. The distinction is evidently determined purely superficially on whether one person or many people speak.

Eugene E. Loos depends on Pike and Pickett in his description of the Capanahua language, spoken by 400 speakers in the eastern part of central Peru.[28] Loos, too, does not connect tenses to the stance of the speaker (register). He identifies tense with time and treats the problem only in passing. He is mainly interested in the topmost level of Capanahua, which he also calls the discourse level. Differently from Pickett, he distinguishes the two basic forms as conversation and narration. A clear border runs between them: "There are two classes of sentence structures in Capanahua: narrative sentences and conversational sentences. Narrative sentences compose the paragraphs of the narration; conversational sentences compose the non-narration part of the discourse but also occur within a paragraph as quotations" (703).

Although he doesn't refer to tense in this context, Loos still makes several observations that fit perfectly with what we have found in the tenses of completely different languages. He pays close attention to the paragraph as a narrative unit. It can consist of one or several narrative sentences—one-sentence paragraphs being more common in formless narratives, longer paragraphs in more artistic narratives (legends). A simple story can consist of a single paragraph but can also be composed of an indefinite number of connected paragraphs. In a longer narrative of this sort the beginning of a new paragraph is always marked by a grammatical sign, which Loos calls the "paragraph marker." This marker connects the paragraph with the preceding one in terms of person and tense, or, in Loos's formulation, "in terms of time and subject referent" (701). The

---

28. Eugene E. Loos, "Capanahua Narration Structure," *Texas Studies in Literature and Language* 4, suppl. (1963): 697–742.

signal remains in force for the entire length of the paragraph. A signal for person and tense stands at the beginning of a sentence only if these change. If there is no signal, person and tense continue in force from the preceding sentence.

Capanahua has apparently—at least in its narratives—developed a structural pattern of tense indication like the ones we saw in the introduction with dating letters and indicating tempo in musical scores, which we described as "until further notice." Most languages do not use this pattern in their use of tenses; they require a tense marker in every sentence, almost with every verb. Yet some languages, as we saw with South German dialect narrative, are, under certain conditions, familiar with an "until-further-notice" pattern where the signal for opening the narrative then continues in effect for the length of the story. It indicates exactly just what the tenses of a language are supposed to indicate.

If I have understood Loos's (very terse) description correctly, then there is generally a connection between the structure of language and the distribution of tenses in Capanahua. The nature of this connection is, however, not so precisely defined as one would like. It may be that the two registers—discussing and narrating—that determine the tense systems of so many languages, are visible in the two types, conversational sentence and narrative sentence. But that cannot yet be determined from the material presented thus far. More important is to develop a method and technique for description that attends to possible correspondences between the tense system and the basic forms of communication. This applies not only to the indigenous languages of the Americas and Africa, but also to the languages of the large cultures of the world, which we often describe so poorly because we think we know them so well.

Index

absolute participle, 207
absurdity, 49, 193, 228–229
Académie Française, 221, 223
accusative, 206–207
accusative-with-infinitive, 206
Adelbert von Chamisso Prize, 1
Adorno, Theodor W., 237
adverbs, 190–198; free indirect discourse and, 161, 203, 205; in French, 191–192, 195–196, 198–199, 229–231, 234, 243–244; in German, 69–70, 202, 204, 246, 248, 250–251; imparfait de rupture and, 123; imperfect and, 195; indefiniteness and, 77; in Italian, 145, 161; in Latin, 260; narrative continuity and, 201; narrative sequencing and, 250; narrative succession and, 231; obstinacy of, 231; passé composé and, 229–230, 234; perfect and, 70, 77, 202, 246, 248, 251, 260; pluperfect and, 204; questioning and, 198–199; transitions and, 200–201
Alarcos Llorach, Emilio, 92, 187n3
À la recherche du temps perdu (In Search of Lost Time) (Proust), 180–184
Andromaque (Racine), 178–179
L'Année derniére à Marienbad (Last Year at Marienbad) (Robbe-Grillet), 47, 100
anticipation, 12, 22, 62–68, 174, 193–194
aorist infinitive, 256
aorist tense, 189, 253–256, 258
Apollonios Dyskolos, 35

Aristotle, 9n1, 221
articles: morphemes as, 16; as supplementary signals, 34–36; syntactic function of, 35; textual time and, 62
aspect, 103, 122–123, 131, 139, 142; argument against, 2–3, 252–253; background and, 132, 136; in Burger, 258; death and, 117–119; in Diver, 77; foreground and, 132, 136; in Greek, 253; in Hopi, 264–266; imparfait de rupture and, 121
Athalie (Racine), 222–223
Atkinson, C. F., 269
Auerbach, Erich, 6–8
Augustine, 27, 60–61
"À une passante" (Baudelaire), 5–6
autobiography, 189. *See also* memoirs

background, 3, 105, 116, 130, 140, 148–152, 177–178; adverbs and, 200; aorist and, 254–255; conclusion and, 137, 152; death and, 119–120; discussion and, 142, 162; in English, 136; imparfait de rupture and, 122; imperfect and, 103–104, 106, 110, 119–120, 129, 133, 143, 196, 222, 233, 236, 239, 243, 246, 254; infinitive, 256; -ing and, 139; participles and, 141, 144; preterit and, 137; simple past and, 108; summarization and, 125
Bainville, Jacques, 172–173
Balzac, Honoré de, 110, 115, 150–152
"Banal Story" (Hemingway), 135

276 / INDEX

Barrier, Maurice-Georges, 229–230
Barthes, Roland, 4
Baudelaire, Charles, 5–6, 111–117
"Bécasses, Les" (The Snipes) (Maupassant), 201–202
"Bedeutung der Zeit in der Erzählkunst, Die" (The Significance of Time in Narrative Art) (Müller), 29
Behaghel, Otto, 69, 245
Bellum Gallicum (Caesar), 261–263
Benjamin, Walter, 5, 116, 237–238
Bennett, Charles E., 78, 257
Benveniste, Émile, 188–190, 255
Bergson, Henri, 97, 269
Bernard, Claude, 42–43, 173–174
biographies, 29, 44, 93, 189
Blumenberg, Hans, 8
Boccaccio, Giovanni, 142–148, 150, 210
Bonnard, Henri, 118
Bon usage, Le (Grevisse), 45–46
Brave New World (Huxley), 51n25
Brower, Reuben Arthur, 5
Bruneau, Charles, 121, 165, 211n2
Brunetière, Ferdinand, 109
Brunot, Ferdinand, 164–165, 211n2
Bühler, Karl, 35–36
Bull, William E., 43–44, 92–93
Burger, André, 258
Butor, Michel, 29, 187
Buzzati, Dino, 89–90

Caesar, Julius, 261–263
Camus, Albert, 42–43, 48–49, 102–103, 102n2, 150, 154–160, 201, 227–236, 251
Candide (Voltaire), 99n35, 106–108
Canterbury Tales (Chaucer), 149–150
Capanahua, 273–274
"Casa del Granella, La" (The Haunted House) (Pirandello), 126
Cervantes, Miguel de. *See Don Quixote* (Cervantes)
Champigny, Robert, 84, 106, 227
Chanson de Roland, 211–213
Chantraine, Pierre, 254
"Chapter XII" (Hemingway), 140–141
Chaucer, Geoffrey, 149–150
children: fairy tales, 52–57; imperfect tense and, 56; perfect tense and, 56–58, 250–251; tense in language of, 55–59; writings of, 57–59
Cicero, Marcus Tullius, 47, 144, 263
Cid, Le (Corneille), 221–223
classicism, French, 217–224

Claudel, Paul, 98, 175
code, linguistic, 12, 33
Cohen, Marcel, 236
Collège de France, 1
communication: breaks in, 13; concentration and, 41; exposition and, 198; genres as, 37; non-linguistic, 105; objects of, 25; present tense and, 41; simple past and, 116; syntax and, 32–36, 62, 155, 157; tense forms in process of, 12, 63. *See also* oral communication
Commynes, Philippe de, 216
concentration, 41
conclusion: background and, 137, 152; in fairy tales, 54, 57; imperfect and, 103, 122, 129, 143, 239; in narrative, 75, 104, 119
conditional tense, 10; consequences and, 180–182; counterfactuals and, 182–184; discussion and, 184; future and, 64–65; in historical narrative, 173; hypothetical information and, 176–177; imperfect and, 183, 185; journalistic style and, 176–177; narration and, 63–64, 184–185; politeness and, 177; tense metaphor and, 173–174
conditionals, tense metaphors and, 180–183
Confessions (Augustine), 60–61
consequences: tense metaphors and, 180–183
context: of conditional sentences, 183; exposition and, 115; fiction and, 49n22; in German, 3; linguistic signs and, 34–35; meaning and, 5; sign validity and, 16; situation and, 105; tense distribution and, 115
Corneille, Pierre, 221–222
"¡Cosas de Franceses!" (The Ways of the French!) (Unamuno), 132–133
counterfactual conditionals, 182–184
Course in General Linguistics (Saussure), 12
culture: Latin and, 260; narrative and, 147; Western, 267–270
Curtius, Ernst Robert, 6–8
Curtius, Georg, 253

Dahlhaus, Carl, 8
Darío, Rubén, 133–134
Dauzat, Albert, 223–224, 236n36
death, 117–120
"Death of the Chicken, The" (fable), 247–248
Decroly, Jean-Ovide, 55–56
de Felice, Emidio, 149, 211n1, 212

Degand, Julia, 55–56
de Gaulle, Charles, 64–66
deixis, 35–36, 196
Descartes, René, 97, 165–168, 170, 228
"Deux aventuriers et le talisman, Les" (The Two Adventurers and the Talisman) (La Fontaine), 66–68
dialogue, 38, 40, 43–45, 92–93, 153–164, 222. *See also* oral communication; speech
diathesis, 260, 263
Dictionnaire philosophique (Voltaire), 61–62
"Difesa del Mèola" (In Defense of Meola) (Pirandello), 87–89
Dionysius Thrax, 60
Discours de la méthode (Descartes), 165–168
Discours sur l'origine et les fondements de l'inégalité parmi les hommes (A Discourse upon the Origin and the Foundation of the Inequality Among Mankind) (Rousseau), 168–170
discursive tense(s), 24–25, 42, 44, 63, 84, 102n2, 157, 191; adverbs and, 191–192, 203–205; audience and, 36; in complex signals, 201; context in, 179; counterfactuals and, 182; in dialogue, 222; dialogue and, 92; empathy and, 254; fairy tales and, 54, 56; free indirect discourse and, 161–162, 166; in French, 85, 104; future as, 38, 64; in Greek, 254–255; historical criticism and, 99; in historical writing, 71–73; Indo-European and, 258; infinitive and, 256; in Latin, 260; narrative vs., 32, 36, 97, 216; Old French and, 214–215; passato prossimo as, 87; passé composé as, 42–43, 83–84, 218, 232, 260; passive verbs and, 263–264; perfect as, 69–70, 75, 78, 80, 238–259, 263; perfecto compuesto as, 93–94; present tense as, 63; preterit as, 58; representative genres of, 40, 45; tension and, 38; as term, 4n1; time and, 63–64, 97–98; truth and, 100, 202
discussing tenses. *See* discursive tense(s)
discussion, 45–59; adverbs and, 191–193, 201–202; conditional and, 184; in memoirs, 216–217; narration and, 147; narration vs., 104–105, 145–146; passato prossimo in, 87–91; passé composé and, 83–84; syntax and, 42; truth and, 100
distribution, tense, 17–22, 45, 60, 108, 115
Diver, William, 76–77
Don Quixote (Cervantes), 48, 55, 132
drama, French classical, 221–223
dreams, 212

Echegaray, José, 134–135
economy of language, 40–41
L'Éducation sentimentale (A Sentimental Education) (Flaubert), 108–110, 125–126
Éluard, Paul, 84–85
"L'Enfant" (Maupassant), 151
English: accusative-with-infinitive and, 176; free indirect discourse and, 158; highlighting in, 256; imperfect tense in, 135–136; infinitive in, 206; -ing in, 152; narrative frame and, 149–150; perfect tense in, 75–83; progressive tense in, 135–142; tense metaphors and, 176; tenses in, 10; time in, 9
epic poetry, 25–27, 30, 46, 100, 141, 211–214, 255
Estienne, Henri, 217–218, 221, 223
L'Étranger (Camus), 48–49, 227–236, 251
L'Être et le néant (Being and Nothingness) (Sartre), 84
Europäische Literatur und lateinisches Mittelalter (Curtius), 7
event time, 62–64
L' Exil et le royaume (Exile and the Kingdom) (Camus), 150
expective tense, in Hopi, 266
L'Expiation (Atonement) (Hugo), 119–120
exposition, 6, 103–104, 115, 143, 149–150, 152, 198–201

fairy tales, 52–57
"Femme adultère, La" (The Adulterous Wife) (Camus), 154–159, 201
"Ficelle, La" (Maupassant), 122–123
fiction: direct quotation in, 153; in Pascal, 49n22; past and, 202; preterit and, 30; third person and, 187; time in, 66–67; truth and, 98–99
Fields of Light, The (Brower), 5
Fifty British Novels (Lass), 50
film scenarios, 47–48
first person, 33, 64, 89, 139, 157, 187–189, 214, 218, 229, 265
Flaubert, Gustave, 108–110, 125–126, 194–195
folk narrative, 5
foreground, 136, 139–143, 162, 166; adverbs and, 196, 200; aorist and, 256; death and, 119; in Greek, 254; imperfect and, 129; narrative, 103–105, 110, 116, 119, 124–126, 243; narrative tempo and, 106; narrative tenses and, 3; present tense and, 239; preterit and, 138; simple past and, 104, 110, 116, 198; simple perfect and, 133

278 / INDEX

Foulet, Lucien, 188, 216–217
frame narrative, 142–147
Frau mit dem Dolche, Die (The Woman with a Dagger) (Arthur Schnitzler), 97n34
free indirect discourse, 104n3, 111, 157–164, 203, 205
French, 9–10; Académie Française, 221, 223; adverbs in, 191–192, 195–196, 198–199, 229–231, 234, 243–244; in children, 55–56; classicism, 217–224; discursive tenses in, 85, 104; drama, 221–223; free indirect discourse in, 158–160; future tense in, 64–69; highlighting in, 101–109, 111–112; imparfait de rupture in, 121–126; imperative in, 208; imperfect in, 3, 43, 46, 66, 101–102, 105–106, 108–111, 117–120, 135–136, 157, 167, 183–184, 195, 199, 201, 212, 239; imperfect subjunctive in, 208, 229; infinitive in, 209; narrative tenses in, 85, 104; Old French, 211–217; oral narration in, 236–244; past tense in, 188–189; present participle in, 207; present tense in, 45–46, 231–232; sequence of tenses in, 164–165; simple past in, 3, 66, 83, 86, 102–103, 104n3, 105–110, 116–117, 119, 123–125, 135, 149, 157, 159, 187–188, 196; subjunctive in, 207–208, 215, 229. See also passé composé tense
Friedrich, Hugo, 6–8
future (time): aorist tense and, 254; expressed by preterit, 51–52; historiographic, 173; imperfect and, 130; present tense and, 46
future tense, 10, 21–23, 52, 64–69; as discursive tense, 38, 64; in Greek, 253; in historical narrative, 173; time and, 64–69. See also conditional tense

Garey, Howard B., 118
Gelhaus, Hermann, 68nn7–8
gender (grammar), 34, 207
genres: as communicative situations, 37, 39–40; representative, for discursive and narrative tenses, 40; tense in different, 42–59
German: adverbs in, 69–70, 202, 204, 246, 248, 250–251; context in, 3; free indirect discourse in, 162–164; future in, 68–69, 68n8; imperfect tense in, 29, 238; perfect tense in, 21–22, 56, 69–75, 78, 83–84, 202, 244–246, 248, 250–251, 262; present tense in, 69; preterit in, 30, 244–245, 244n48, 246–247, 251; restricted validity in, 177; South-German dialects, 244–251; tense combinations in, 202–203; time in, 9
Gide, André, 46–47, 175–176
Gili y Gaya, Samuel, 92, 118, 129, 129n5
Giono, Jean, 234n35
Glasperlenspiel, Das (The Glass Bead Game) (Hesse), 52
gnomic aorist, 255
Goethe, Johann Wolfgang, 14–15, 25–27, 73–74, 104, 132, 203–204
"Goethes Laufbahn als Schriftsteller" (Goethe's Career as Writer) (Mann), 17–24
Goodwin, William Watson, 253n4
Greek, ancient, 9, 117, 171–172, 217, 252–256
Grevisse, Maurice, 45–46, 182–183
Griechische Schulgrammatik (Curtius), 253
Gülich, Elisabeth, 200, 200n17, 243

Hamburger, Käte, 5–6, 30–31, 46, 99, 99n34, 202–203
Heidegger, Martin, 97
Hemingway, Ernest, 135–142, 144, 150, 210, 228
Heptaméron (Marguerite de Navarre), 150
Herodotus, 255
Hesse, Hermann, 52
highlighting, 3, 256; adverbs and, 194–195; in ancient Greek, 256; aspect vs., 121–152; death and, 120; frame and, 150–153; imperfect tense and, 105–106, 143–144, 168, 243; narrative, 101–106, 127, 132–133; repeated descriptions and, 127; in Romance languages, 3, 126; semi-finite verbs and, 209–210; simple past tense and, 105–106, 168
Hill, Archibald, 76
Hilty, Gerold, 87n25
Histoire de France (History of France) (Bainville), 172–173
Historia septem sapientium (Story of the Seven Wise Men), 147–149
historical criticism, 99
historical narrative, 170–173, 189
historical writing, 70–73
historiographic future, 173
Hitler, Adolf, 8
Homer, 26–27, 60, 92, 255
Hopi, 265–268, 270
"L' Horrible" (Maupassant), 39
Hugo, Victor, 117, 119–120

Husserl, Edmund, 97
Huxley, Aldous, 51n25
hypothetical information, 176

Ides of March, The (Wilder), 78–83
I-here-now, 35–36, 196
Iliad (Homer), 60
Imbs, Paul, 164–165, 176, 223, 225
imparfait. *See* imperfect tense
imparfait de rupture, 121–126, 129, 152
imperative, 208–210
imperfecto. *See* imperfect tense
imperfect subjunctive tense, 207–208, 229
imperfect tense, 10–11; adverbs and, 195; in ancient Greek, 254–255; background and, 103–104, 110, 236; children and, 56; conditional and, 183, 185; death and, 117–118, 120; description and, 105–106; dreams and, 212; first person and, 188; free indirect discourse and, 157; in French, 3, 43, 46, 66, 101–102, 105–106, 108–111, 117–120, 135–136, 157, 167, 183–184, 194–195, 199, 201, 212, 239; future and, 130; in German, 29, 238; highlighting and, 105–106, 143–144, 168, 243; in historical writing, 189; in Italian, 126–129, 143–144; in Latin, 117; as narrative tense, 3, 29, 43, 46, 104n3, 135–136, 148–149; perspective and, 101; progressive vs., 135–136; Proust on, 111; in realism and naturalism, 109; second person and, 188; simple past and, 101–103, 105, 108, 196, 201; in Spanish, 129, 131–133; tense metaphors and, 177–179; in Voltaire, 106–107
Imperfekt. *See* imperfect tense
imperfetto. *See* imperfect tense
"Indian Camp" (Hemingway), 136–139
Indo-European, 78, 256, 258–260, 265, 267, 270
infinitive, 178, 206–207, 209, 256
"In Memoriam" (Tennyson), 5
interrogation, 85–86
interviews, 238–239
Introduction à l'étude de la médecine expérimentale (Introduction to the Study of Experimental Medicine) (Bernard), 42–43, 173–174
irony, 207–208
Italian, 9, 51–52, 87–91, 126–129, 142–147; 24-hour rule and, 224n22; adverbs in, 145, 161; free indirect discourse in, 160–162; passato prossimo in, 87–91, 146, 224n22, 259; passato remoto in, 52, 88, 104, 104n3, 126–128, 142–145, 147, 186, 224n22, 259, 263

James, Henry, 47
Jauss, Hans-Robert, 6–7, 29
Jespersen, Otto, 75–76
Jeux sont faits, Les (Sartre), 47
Journal de Paris (newspaper), 224–226
journalistic style, 176–177. *See also* newspapers; reports
Joyce, James, 8, 29
Justes, Les (Camus), 102–103, 102n2

Kafka, Franz, 74–75
Kant, Immanuel, 267
Kayser, Wolfgang, 27
Keller, Gottfried, 150
Klein, Hans-Wilhelm, 238
Klum, Arne, 191–194

La Fontaine, Jean de, 66–68, 149
Lämmert, Eberhard, 29
Language in Relation to a Unified Theory of the Structure of Human Behavior (Pike), 272
Lass, Abraham, 50
Latin, 256–264; absolute participle in, 207; accusative-with-infinitive in, 206; imperfect in, 117; infinitive in, 206; narration in, 147–149; present tense in, 47; tenses in, 10; time in, 9
Lausberg, Heinrich, 171–172, 172n4
law of retardation, 25–26
Le Bidois, Georges, 119, 176
Le Bidois, Robert, 119, 176
Lerch, Eugen, 109
Lessing, Gotthold Ephraim, 4
letters (correspondence), 14–15, 78–83, 216, 223
Lévi-Strauss, Claude, 4
Lewis, Wyndham, 269
lexemes, 10, 13, 33–34, 155, 208–209
Lied von Bernadette, Das (The Song of Bernadette) (Werfel), 99–100, 163–164
Lindgren, Kaj B., 43–45, 70, 244–245, 251
linguistic code, 12, 33
linguistics: structural, 11–12; text, 11–13, 34, 121, 155, 165, 168, 171, 186, 190, 198, 260, 271
linguistic sign. *See* sign, linguistic
"Lit 29, Le" (Bed 29) (Maupassant), 123–124
Loos, Eugene E., 273–274

280 / INDEX

Lotte in Weimar (Mann), 202–205
Lyon, John, 11

Madame Bovary (Flaubert), 194–195
Magic Mountain, The (Mann), 27–29
"Main d'écorché, La" (The Flayed Hand) (Maupassant), 122–123
Malaparte, Curzio, 51–52
Malraux, André, 195–197
Mann, Golo, 71–72, 98
Mann, Thomas, 17–24, 27–29, 48, 51, 162–163, 202–205
Marguerite de Navarre, 150
Marie Tudor (Hugo), 117
Martin, Robert, 225
Martinet, André, 40–41
Martinon, Philippe, 178
Maupassant, Guy de, 39, 85–87, 121–126, 151, 199–202, 235
Maurer, Karl, 150
Meerfahrt mit Don Quixote (At Sea with Don Quixote) (Mann), 48
Meillet, Antoine, 109, 236n36
memoirs, 65, 216–217. *See also* autobiography
messenger speech, in drama, 222–223
metaphors: free indirect discourse and, 160; grammatical, 171; lexical, 171–172; morphemic, 172
metaphors, tense: conditional and, 173–174, 180–182; conditions and, 180–183; consequences and, 180–183; imperfect and, 87n25, 177–179; invalid opinions and, 179–180; politeness and, 177; preterit and, 177–178; rhetoric and, 172–173; sentence structure and, 175–176; in texts, 171–180
Middle Ages, 147–150
Mimesis (Auerbach), 8
Modification, La (Second Thoughts) (Butor), 29, 187
Montaigne, Michel de, 4
mood, 205–206
morpheme(s): as articles, 16, 62; obstinacy of, 32; person and, 36, 187–188; syntax and, 155, 197; tense and, in French, 10; tense combinations and, 186–187; tense groups and, 32; time and, 202
morphemic metaphor, 172
Müller, Günther, 29
Mythe de Sisyphe, Le (The Myth of Sisyphus) (Camus), 228

narrating tenses. *See* narrative tense(s)
narration: adverbs and, 191–192, 198; children and, 56–57; conditional tense and, 63–64, 184–185; of conditions and consequences, 181–182; death and, 119; description in, 105–106, 110; discussion and, 147; discussion vs., 104–105, 145–146; as fundamentally human, 40; imperfect tense and, 29, 104n3, 135–136, 148–149; in Middle Ages, 147–150; in novels, 44; oral, 236–244, 250; passé composé and, 230–231; perfecto simple tense and, 93–94; perfect tense and, 148–149; pluperfect tense and, 64; preterit tense in, 30–31, 46, 64; self and, 30–31; as speech, 29; suspense in, 41; tension in, 41–42, 148; time and, 28–29; truth and, 96–100; wisdom and, 147; world of, 50–55
narrative, 3; background in, 103–105, 110, 116, 119, 130, 137, 140; conclusion in, 75, 104, 119; culture and, 147; exposition in, 115, 152; folk, 5; foreground in, 103–105, 110, 116, 119, 124–126, 140, 243; frame, 142–147; highlighting, 101–106, 120, 132–133; historical, 172–173; introduction in, 104; speech, 40, 239–244
narrative tempo, in novels, 106–111
narrative tense(s), 24–25, 32, 40, 43, 63–64; adverbs and, 191–192, 231; audience in, 36; children and, 59; conditional and, 177, 181, 184; dialogue and, 45; discursive vs., 36, 97; discussing tenses vs., 216; free direct discourse and, 162; free indirect discourse and, 205; in French, 85, 104; imperfect as, 3, 29, 43, 46, 149; infinitive and, 256; passato remoto as, 147; passé composé and, 233; passé composé as, 189; perfect as, 246; preterit as, 46, 70n10, 96, 139, 245; restricted validity and, 178; simple past as, 43, 86, 87n25, 149, 187, 237–238; as term, 4n1; third person and, 218; time and, 63–64, 97–98; truth and, 98–99
naturalism, 109–110, 125
New Criticism, 5
newspapers, 224–227. *See also* journalistic style
Nietzsche, Friedrich, 4
Nineteen Eighty-Four (Orwell), 50–51
nomic tense, in Hopi, 266
non-linguistic communication, 105

noun(s): in Aristotle, 9n1; articles and, 34. *See also* pronouns
nouveau roman, 29
novellas, 3, 86, 88–89, 93, 104, 142–143
Novelle per un anno (Stories for a Year), 150
novels, 29, 48, 50; epistolary, 78–79; first person in, 187–188; free indirect discourse in, 104n3; narration in, 44; narrative tempo in, 106–111; naturalistic, 125; sketches for, 47; in third person, 187–188; truth and, 99–100. *See also specific novels*
"Nuits partagées" (Shared Nights) (Éluard), 84–85

obstinacy: 14–17; of adverbs, 231; of macrosyntactic symbols, 243–244; of morphemes, 32, 36; of person, 32–33; of tense, 17, 21–22, 40–41, 271
Old French, 211–217
"Old Man at the Bridge, The" (Hemingway), 138–139
oral communication: frame narrative and, 73; pauses in, 13; written narration as, 10. *See also* dialogue; speech
oral narration, 236–244, 250
Ortega y Gasset, José, 94–96
Orwell, George, 50–51
Ovid, 4

"Pacto, El" (Echegaray), 134–135
"Padrino Antonio, El" (Godfather Antonio) (Unamuno), 131
Paiva Boléo, Manuel, 91–92, 92n29, 187
Pala, 272
paradigmatic structure, 12–13
"Parapluie, Le" (The Umbrella) (Maupassant), 124–125
"Parricide, Un" (A Parricide) (Maupassant), 85–87
participles, 4n1, 56, 76, 136–137, 141, 149, 207, 209–210, 258
"Parure, La" (The Necklace) (Maupassant), 199–200
Pascal, Roy, 5, 47, 49n22, 80
passato prossimo tense, 87–91, 146, 224n22, 259
passato remoto, 52, 88, 104, 104n3, 126–128, 142–145, 147, 186, 224n22, 259, 263
passé composé tense, 83–87, 87n25, 211–215; 24-hour rule and, 217–218, 221–223; absurdity and, 228–229; in Camus's *L'Étranger*, 229–236; children and, 55–56;

as discursive tense, 42–43, 83–84, 218, 232, 260; in historical narrative, 170; isolating nature of, 231; Latin perfectum and, 260; narration and, 230–231; in narrative speech, 243; as narrative tense, 189; in newspapers, 225–226; sociological class and, 229, 236
passé simple. *See* simple past tense
passive participle, 209
past (time): fiction and, 202; future in, 130; narration and, 80, 96–100; perfect tense and, 69–71; present tense and, 46; preterit and, 30, 51, 76; truth and, 202. *See also* retrospection
past anterior tense, 102
past tense. *See* aorist tense; imperfect tense; passato prossimo tense; passé composé tense; preterit tense; simple past tense
Père Goriot (Balzac), 110
perfecto compuesto tense, 91–96, 179, 187, 259
perfect participle, 56, 258
perfect tense: in ancient Greek, 254; children and, 56–58, 250–251; as discursive tense, 69–70, 75, 78, 80, 238–259, 263; in English, 75–83; in German, 21–22, 56, 69–75, 78, 83–84, 202, 244–246, 248, 250–251, 262; in Latin, 257–263; narration and, 148–149; as narrative tense, 246; preterit tense and, 70–71; preterit tense vs., 75–76; as term, 69–70. *See also* passé composé tense
person (grammatical), 32–34, 153, 186–190, 214. *See also* first person; third person
personal infinitive, 206–208, 210
personal participle, 209–210
Peste, La (The Plague) (Camus), 201
Petsch, Robert, 54, 99n35
Phèdre (Racine), 105–106, 222
Pickett, Velma, 272n27, 273
Pike, Kenneth L., 272–273
Pirandello, Luigi, 87–89, 126–129, 150, 160–162, 235
Plato, 4, 60
plot summaries, 192–193
pluperfect tense, 10, 21–23, 45, 56, 64, 102, 104, 157, 179, 182, 189, 194, 198, 204, 207, 233, 242–244
Plusquamperfekt. *See* pluperfect tense
plus-que-parfait. *See* pluperfect tense
Poe, Edgar Allan, 50–51
Poétique (journal), 4

poetry, 44; epic, 25–27, 30, 46, 213; lyric, 45; metaphor in, 111–112; truth and, 100
pointing, 35–36. *See also* highlighting
politeness, 6, 177
Portuguese, 206–207, 260
Präteritum. *See* imperfect tense; preterit tense
Pregel, Dietrich, 57, 59
present (time), 8, 46, 48, 76, 80–81, 223, 254, 266
present infinitive, 256
present participle, 4n1, 136, 207
present tense, 10; as discursive tense, 63; examples of use of, 47–48; in French, 45–46, 231–232; future events and, 46; in German, 69; in Grevisse, 45–46; historical present and, 99n35; past events and, 46; as register of communication, 46; in sketches for future writings, 47; in summaries, 48–50; tension and, 38; uses of, 46
preterit tense, 10; children and, 56; epic, 30, 46; fiction and, 30; foreground and, 138; future expressed by, 51–52; in German, 30, 244–245, 244n48, 246–247, 251; in narration, 30–31, 46; narration and, 29–31, 64; as narrative tense, 46, 70n10, 96, 139, 245; perfect tense and, 70–71; perfect tense vs., 75–76; tense metaphors and, 177–178; as term, 11; time and, 51. *See also* simple past tense
progressive tense, 135–142
pronouns: demonstrative, 16, 161; in free indirect discourse, 159; personal, 15, 32; possessive, 16; present participle and, 207; renominalization of, 156
prospection, 27, 63–64, 193–194, 208
Protagoras the Abderite, 60
Proust, Marcel, 8, 109–111, 180–185
Prozeß, Der (The Trial) (Kafka), 74–75
Puits de Babel, Les (The Wells of Babylon) (Zumthor), 187

Quintilian, 60, 171–172, 205
quoted dialogue, 153–157

Racine, Jean, 105–106, 178–179, 222–223
realism, 98, 109–110, 125
recurrence values, 16–17
"Redondo, el contertulio" (Redondo and His Coffeehouse Circle) (Unamuno), 130–131
Regain (Giono), 234n35

register, 3, 36–42, 46, 209, 253, 256. *See also* discursive tense(s); narrative tense(s)
Reis, Hans, 70
reportive tense, in Hopi, 266
reports, in drama, 218–223. *See also* journalistic style
Resnais, Alain, 100
restricted validity, 174–180
retrospection, 27, 63–64, 73, 75–76, 83, 87, 96, 101, 119, 138, 193–194, 198, 210, 218, 231–232, 235, 243, 254
rhetoric, 41–42, 75, 99n35, 153, 172–173
Robbe-Grillet, Alain, 47, 100, 227
Roehl, Karl, 265, 271–272
Romance languages, 259; accusative with infinitive in, 206–207; background in, 136, 162, 177–178; foreground in, 136, 162; highlighting in, 3, 126; tense groups in, 105. *See also specific languages*
Rousseau, Jean-Jacques, 168–170

Sandmann, Manfred, 213–214
"Sangre de Aitor, La" (Aitor's Blood) (Unamuno), 130
Sartre, Jean Paul, 47–49, 84, 97, 228–229, 231
Saussure, Ferdinand de, 12
Schaechtelin, Paul, 213
Schiller, Friedrich, 14–15, 25–27, 61, 162
Schlegel, August Wilhelm, 26–27
Schnitzler, Arthur, 97n34
Schoch, Josef, 214
"Schwere Stunde" (Painful Hour) (Mann), 162–163
second person, 15, 33, 154, 187–189, 208, 214
"Semejante, El" (Another Fool) (Unamuno), 132–133
Semitic languages, 253
Shambala, 265, 271–272
sign, linguistic, 13; application of, over time, 15–16; context and, 34; continuing validity of, 15–17; metaphor as, 171; obstinate, 17; in paradigmatic structure, 12; supplementary, 34–35; in text linguistics, 12; in texts, 13, 16, 24–25; textual time and, 62
simple past tense, 10; 24-hour rule and, 217, 221; adverbs and, 198; children and, 55–56; communication and, 116; death and, 117, 119; disappearance of, in spoken French, 83, 187–188, 236–237; foreground in, 103–104, 110, 116, 198; free indirect discourse and, 157, 159; in French, 3, 66, 83, 86, 102–103, 104n3, 105–110, 116–117, 119, 123–125, 135, 149, 157, 159, 187, 196;

highlighting and, 105–106, 168; historical narrative and, 173; imperfect and, 101–103, 105, 108, 196, 201; in memoirs, 216–217; as narrative tense, 43, 86, 87n25, 149, 187; in newspapers, 226–227; in novels, 109; in Old French, 211–216; passé composé vs., 217–218; person and, 187–189; perspective and, 101; reporting and, 221; sociological class and, 229, 236; in Spanish, 129–135; third person and, 187–188. *See also* aorist tense; preterit tense
"Sinngedicht" (Epigram) (Keller), 150
Smith, Herbert Weir, 254
Soirée avec Monsieur Teste, La (Evening with Monsieur Teste) (Valéry), 84
Sorrows of Young Werther, The (Goethe), 73–74, 203
Spanish, 9, 43–44, 91–96, 118, 120; highlighting in, 256; imperfect and simple past in, 129–135; imperfect in, 129, 131; perfecto compuesto tense in, 91–96, 179, 187, 259; tense metaphors in, 179
speech: appellative, 189; messenger, in drama, 222–223; narrative, 40, 239–244; register and, 36–42; tension and, 38. *See also* dialogue; oral communication
Spengler, Oswald, 268–270
Spitzer, Leo, 6–7, 259n14
Sprachtheorie (Theory of Language) (Bühler), 35–36
"Sprüche des Konfuzius" (Sayings of Confucius) (Schiller), 61
"Staat und Heer" (State and Army) (Mann), 71–72
Stammerjohann, Harro, 104n3, 186–187, 200n17
Stanzel, Franz, 203
Sten, Holger, 47, 105, 118
Stern, Clara, 56
Stern, Wilhelm, 56
Stern der Ungeborenen (Star of the Unborn) (Werfel), 52
Storia di domani (A History of Tomorrow) (Malaparte), 51–52
"Storyteller, The" (Benjamin), 5
storytelling, 39, 41, 71, 146, 149, 237–239, 271
Strohmeyer, Fritz, 223, 237
structuralism, 4
structural linguistics, 11–12
Structure of Modern Poetry (Friedrich), 8
subjunctive, 21, 42, 45, 180, 205, 207–209, 215, 229, 255

Sutherland, D. R., 213
syntax, 11, 13; articles and, 35; communication and, 32–36, 62, 155, 157; defined, 155; morphemes and, 155, 197; person and, 33–34; quoted dialogue and, 155–157; tension and, 38

"Ten Indians" (Hemingway), 135
Tennyson, Alfred Lord, 5
tense(s), 2–3; discussing, 24–25; distribution, 17–22, 45, 60, 108, 115; genre and, 42–59; groups, 22–25, 32, 45; names of, 9–10; obstinacy of, 17, 21–22, 40–41, 271; recurrence values of, 16–17; sequence of, 21–22, 164–170; syntax and, 11; time and, 9–11. *See also* discursive tense(s); narrative tense(s)
tension, 38–39, 41–42, 148
testimony, 85–86
text(s): as category, 13; linguistic signs in, 13, 16, 24–25; tense metaphors in, 171–180; time, 60–64
text linguistics, 11–13, 34, 121, 155, 165, 168, 171, 186, 190, 197–198, 260, 271
third person, 33–34, 153–154, 187–188, 214, 218, 229, 245
Thucydides, 255
"Tierras de Castilla" (The Lands of Castile) (Ortega y Gasset), 96
Timaeus (Plato), 60
time, 2–3, 8; adverbs and, 196–197, 199, 230; apart from language, 9; application of linguistic signs over, 15–16; in Augustine, 60–61; in Descartes, 167, 228n28; in Dionysius Thrax, 60; direction, 62–63; in epic poetry, 26–27; event-, 62–64; in fairy tales, 52–54; in fiction, 66–68; future tense and, 64–69; in Hopi, 266–268; in Mann, 27–28; narration, 28–29; newspapers and, 224; in novels, 29; "once upon a time," 52–53; preterit tense and, 51; in Quintilian, 60; in Shambala, 265; stages of, 60–62; stages of, in Greek, 253–254; tense and, 9–11; in texts, 60–64; unity of, in French classical drama, 221; Western culture and, 268–270
Time and Western Man (Lewis), 269
Togeby, Knud, 118, 129
Traicté de la conformité du langage françois avec le grec (Treatise on the Conformity of the French Language with the Greek) (Estienne), 217–218
transitions, 197–205

translation, vii–viii
"Tres Reinas Magas, Las" (The Three Wise Queens) (Darío), 133–134
truth: discursive tenses and, 100; discussing tenses and, 202; narration and, 96–100; narrative tenses and, 98–99; past and, 202; poetry and, 100. *See also* validity
Twaddell, William Freeman, 76
24-hour rule, 217–218, 220–224, 224n22

Ulysses (Joyce), 29
Unamuno, Miguel de, 129–133
"Unparalleled Adventure of One Hans Pfaall, The" (Poe), 50–51
Untergang des Abendlandes, Der (The Decline of the West) (Spengler), 268–270
"L'Uomo solo," (The Lonely Man) (Pirandello), 127–129

"Va bene" (Things are fine) (Pirandello), 160–162, 161n3
Valéry, Paul, 84
validity, restricted, 174–180
Varro, Marcus Terentius, 257
verbs: in ancient Greek, 9; in Aristotle, 9n1; of communication, 115–116, 155–159, 167–168, 170, 172n4, 203; death and, 119; in Dionysius Thrax, 60; helping, 174; in Latin, 256–257; modal, 174; passive, 261–264; person and, 33–34; semi-finite, 205–210, 256; telic, 118; of thinking, 167; time stages and, 60
Verne, Jules, 52
"Vieux saltimbanque, Le" (The Old Mountebank) (Baudelaire), 111–117
Voie royale, La (The Royal Way) (Malraux), 195–196
Voltaire, 61–62, 99n35, 106–108, 135, 223

Wackernagel, Jacob, 205, 255
Wagner, Robert Léon, 236–237
Weber, Hans, 70
Weinrich, Harald, 1, 6–8
Werfel, Franz, 52, 99–100, 163–164
Western culture, 267–270
Whorf, Benjamin Lee, 265–270
Wilder, Thornton, 78–83
Winckelmann, Johann, 4
Wordsworth, William, 5
Wunderlich, Dieter, 202
Wunderlich, Hermann, 70

Zauberberg, Der (The Magic Mountain) (Mann), 27–29
Zumthor, Paul, 187

VERBAL ARTS: STUDIES IN POETICS

Lazar Fleishman and Haun Saussy, series editors

Kiene Brillenburg Wurth, *Between Page and Screen: Remaking Literature Through Cinema and Cyberspace*
Jacob Edmond, *A Common Strangeness: Contemporary Poetry, Cross-Cultural Encounter, Comparative Literature*
Christophe Wall-Romana, *Cinepoetry: Imaginary Cinemas in French Poetry*
Marc Shell, *Talking the Walk and Walking the Talk: A Rhetoric of Rhythm*
Ryan Netzley, *Lyric Apocalypse: Milton, Marvell, and the Nature of Events*
Ilya Kliger and Boris Maslov (eds.), *Persistent Forms: Explorations in Historical Poetics*. Foreword by Eric Hayot
Ross Chambers, *An Atmospherics of the City: Baudelaire and the Poetics of Noise*
Haun Saussy, *The Ethnography of Rhythm: Orality and Its Technologies*
Andrew Hui, *The Poetics of Ruins in Renaissance Literature*
Peter Szendy, *Of Stigmatology: Punctuation as Experience*. Translated by Jan Plug
Ben Glaser and Jonathan Culler (eds.), *Critical Rhythm: The Poetics of a Literary Life Form*
Craig Dworkin, *Dictionary Poetics: Toward a Radical Lexicography*
Harald Weinrich, *Tempus: The World of Discussion and the World of Narration*. Translated by Jane K. Brown and Marshall Brown

Harald Weinrich (1927–2022), after holding professorships in Romance philology and in linguistics at several universities, was founding chair of the Department of German as a Foreign Language at the Ludwig Maximilian University of Munich, and, following his retirement in 1992, for six years held the Chair of Romance Languages and Literatures at the Collège de France. Among his many books on literature, linguistics, French and German grammar, language pedagogy, and the sociology of cultures, three have previously been translated into English: *The Linguistics of Lying and Other Essays* (Washington, 2012), *On Borrowed Time: The Art and Economy of Living with Deadlines* (Chicago, 2008), and *Lethe: The Art and Critique of Forgetting* (Cornell, 2004).

www.ingramcontent.com/pod-product-compliance
Lightning Source LLC
Chambersburg PA
CBHW020357080526
44584CB00014B/1059